'A magnificent book that reads at some places like a thriller but which is solid, academic history about one of the most important, but also least known, parts of the war. I recommend it thoroughly.'

– **Christopher Catherwood, Archives By-Fellow of Churchill College, University of Cambridge and author of *A Brief History of the Middle East***

'This book is a deeply-researched account of an important but neglected episode in World War II. It combines a fast-paced narrative with judgements that are judicious, nuanced and humane.'

– **Richard Toye, Professor of History, University of Exeter and author of *Churchill's Empire: The World That Made Him and the World He Made*'**

Henri de Wailly teaches at the Saint-Cyr Special Military School. A specialist in military history, he has written several books in French including *1945. L'empire rompu: Syrie, Algérie, Indochine* and *Liban, Syrie: le mandat: 1919–1940*.

William Land holds a PhD from the University of Sydney. A retired reserve group captain of the Royal Australian Air Force, he was awarded *Officier* of the *Légion d'honneur* in 2015.

INVASION
SYRIA
1941

CHURCHILL AND DE GAULLE'S
FORGOTTEN WAR

16/50
02/07/16

HENRI
DE WAILLY

TRANSLATED BY WILLIAM LAND

I.B. TAURIS
LONDON · NEW YORK

Published in 2016 by
I.B.Tauris & Co. Ltd
London • New York
www.ibtauris.com

First published in French as
Syrie 1941: La guerre occultée, Vichyistes contre gaullistes

Copyright © 2006 Éditions Perrin
English translation copyright © 2016 William Land

The right of Henri de Wailly
to be identified as the author of this work has been asserted by the author in
accordance with the Copyright, Designs and Patents Act 1988.

Every attempt has been made to gain permission for the use of the images in this
book. Any omissions will be rectified in future editions.

References to websites were correct at the time of writing.

ISBN: 978 1 78453 449 3

A full CIP record for this book is available from the British Library
A full CIP record is available from the Library of Congress

Library of Congress Catalog Card Number: available

Typeset by Free Range Book Design & Production Limited
Printed and bound in Sweden by ScandBook AB

MIX
Paper from
responsible sources
FSC
www.fsc.org   FSC® C007584

Contents

List of Maps and Illustrations

Maps

Plate Section

Plate 1. General Lavarack inspecting the troops in Beirut, 1941. (Reproduced courtesy of the State Library of Queensland.)

Plate 2. Commemorative tablet with inscription. (Photo taken by Frank Hurley.)

Plate 3. General Catroux and Field Marshal Wilson, Cairo, May 1941. Wilson in foreground, Catroux in background, partially obscured. (From the author's personal collection.)

Plate 4. Generals Spears and Catroux, Beirut 1943. Spears in civilian dress, Catroux in uniform. (From the author's personal collection.)

Plate 5. Photo with dedication from General Dentz to General Keime, April 1942. (From the author's personal collection.)

Plate 6. An Australian Vickers Light Tank Mk VI and crew at rest during the advance into Syria, 11 June 1941. (© Imperial War Museum (E 3148E).)

Plate 7. A 15-cwt truck passes a sentry as it leaves Fort Weygand at Palmyra, Syria, 12 July 1941. (© Imperial War Museum (E 4079).)

Acknowledgements

The author wishes to thank all those who have helped him in his research by allowing him access to the resources of their culture, their relations, or their documentation, and by facilitating his visits to private archives and those of military establishments and theatres of operations, notably His Excellency Monsieur Henri Servant, former Ambassador of France in Damascus, Generals Ghassan Farès and Ibrahim Salloun of the Syrian Army, Monsieur Abdallah Attrache, Member of Parliament for Soueida, General Elias Farhat and Lieutenant-Colonel Joseph Badawi of the Lebanese Army, Colonel Louis Christian Michelet (a graduate of the US Command and General Staff College and holder of a doctorate in history), Monsieur Roger Keime and Mademoiselle de Verdilhac. The author thanks Messieurs Jacques Sicard and Bernard Geffray for their invaluable assistance. He thanks the actors and witnesses of these events who agreed to be interviewed and who are quoted in the following pages, as well as to the families who have opened their archives for him. Without their help, this story would have remained theoretical.

Preface

France in the Middle East

Following the destruction of its fleet at Navarino in 1827, the collapse of the Ottoman Empire accelerated. In Istanbul, the Sultan exercised no more than a shaky authority over his immense territories that were increasingly threatened by European appetites. France, England, Austria and Russia prevented him from carrying out savage massacres of his Greek subjects. And, encouraged by France, Egypt escaped from his authority; Algeria was already French and the Dey of Tunis was ruined. In Libya, as in Arabia, nothing had changed for ten centuries, and poverty was endemic. In the whole of the Empire, the administration was simply focused on financial exploitation. Idle, greedy and cruel the ruling pashas kept the population in a state of poverty. The army was outdated. The contrast with the dynamism of Europe became increasingly obvious. Sheltered by the Dardanelles, the Sublime Porte, as it was called, tried to retain the trappings of a powerful nation, but it was only a sham. This empire only endured due to the diplomatic scheming of other nations, who supported it but simultaneously watched each other and awaited its end – ready to seize its territories as soon as they collapsed.

The imprecise area that in Europe is called the 'Middle East' was at that time a province with hazy boundaries that potentates, either local or Egyptian, fought over, but on which Istanbul maintained its hold, which was both weak and cruel. In Tripoli, Damascus, Sidon, Jerusalem and Jaffa wealth was relative; income was more important. Assisted by the beys, the pashas exercised their ruinous financial pressures. This area was inhabited by numerous minorities which were very varied and strongly rooted in competing religions. Of the 17 religions present, four dominated: the Maronite Christians, the Muslims, the Druse and the Alawites. Outbursts of violence, generally against the large Christian minority, had shaken the relative peace from time immemorial. Heirs of the first Christians and ancient allies of the Western Crusaders, the Maronites had been pushed back into the central Lebanese mountain range, along with the Druse, whom Islamic orthodoxy considers heretics. Supported by an active clergy, this Christian population had a strong sense of identity. This was thanks to its links with Rome and the relative protection that, since François 1st, had been afforded by the treaties between France and the Sublime Porte – the *Capitulations* – which favoured its culture and dynamism. Moreover, silkworm farming had permitted commercial links with France, via the *Echelles* – commercial centres on the coast. Finally, staffed by Italian and French religious figures, very old Roman Catholic missions maintained links with the West. The Druse were jealous of their much more dynamic, more sophisticated and relatively richer neighbours, the Maronites. In 1860, the prevailing tension became unbearable, and the Christians of the central Lebanese mountain range were subjected to appalling massacres. Villages were destroyed and their inhabitants killed. The survivors fled towards the coast, towards Beirut, Tyre and Sidon. To jealousy was added the lure of pillage. The Muslims soon joined the Druse, and it is estimated that 28,000 Christians were murdered, including 10,000 in Damascus.

Horrified by this bloodbath, five European nations gathered in Paris and charged France with sending an expeditionary corps, a delegated intervention mission, in their name. General d'Hautpoul[1] commanded it. When it arrived, the killing had stopped, but its presence was reassuring. Order was restored, but England, hostile to this demonstration of French influence, supported the Druse behind the scenes. The Sublime Porte, which showed the greatest reluctance to punish the guilty had, however, to accept that a special political regime was installed in the Lebanese mountains. Peace, then, returned.

At the beginning of the twentieth century, the religious crisis (*laïcité*) which convulsed France – the separation of Church (religion) from State (political power) which was formalised in law in 1905 – caused the exile of a large number of religious people, teachers and others. Many of them left for Lebanon, where France was appreciated and where the political regime had become tolerant. As a result the political and social influence of France continued to grow.

In 1914, the Sublime Porte allied itself with Germany. Provoking the uprising of Arabs to whom it promised thrones, England in 1917 launched, from Egypt, General Sir Edmund Allenby's army in the assault on the Middle East, this rather unsettled zone which comprised Palestine and Syria, to which Lebanon belonged. A small French force accompanied the British Army, in which there was a large contingent of Australians. The French fleet, which watched over the coastlines, contributed greatly to the success of the mission. Jerusalem, Beirut and Damascus then fell one after the other, and Cilicia, in Turkey, was conquered. Allenby's forces occupied all these areas.

In Cairo, in parallel with the military operations, much thought was given about how to carve up the territory that the Ottoman collapse was soon going to make available. On a large map open before them, Sir Mark Sykes, an Englishman, and Monsieur François Georges-Picot, a Frenchman, decided upon zones of influence and drew, with red and blue pencils, the approximate limits of what would become Palestine and Syria.

At Damascus, where T.E. Lawrence (Lawrence of Arabia) had led the Arabs, the conquerors were getting ready to receive the thrones that England had promised them. Faisal, future King of Syria, had to go to Damascus to reign.

The famine, that the Turkish authorities had let happen in 1918, caused, it is estimated, 700,000 deaths in Lebanon; but the war was over and negotiations were taking place in Versailles. England and France received confirmation of the carve-up concluded in Cairo by the Sykes-Picot accords. The new League of Nations entrusted them with the task of guiding these new nations along the road to independence: England and France received a mandate to administer them; to train managers, an army and public servants; and to establish a land register, a constitution and democracy.

In Lebanon, in 1919, France was greeted enthusiastically. The powerful English army was withdrawn very quickly, handing over immense empty regions to the weak French contingent. Damascus, where Faisal settled, at once called into question the French presence. How could Christian France, protector of the Maronites, occupy this very holy Muslim city, the ancient capital of the Umayyad princes, where Saladin is buried – the legendary oasis from which every year the pilgrim caravan leaves for Mecca? Even during the Crusades, from which the French liked to draw so much inspiration, Damascus was never conquered.

For the moment, General Gouraud,[2] the first French High Commissioner, had cares other than Damascus. The young Turkish general, Mustafa Kemal, who had decided to prevent foreigners settling anywhere on the national territory, started to fiercely attack French garrisons in Cilicia, in the south-east of Turkey. The campaign, pursued during extremely cold weather, was marked by sieges and counter-attacks, destruction of convoys, and markedly heroic deeds; but the French were forced to negotiate, then to withdraw, abandoning the Syrian port of Alexandretta. The episode passed unnoticed in a France that had been bled white, exhausted by World War I; but it alarmed the Syrians.

With Cilicia lost, Gouraud had his hands free. He gathered his troops together, and, forcing his way through, conquered Damascus, causing Faisal to flee. There in Damascus, France would establish the foundation of a modern nation. A bicameral legislature was set up, political parties were formed, and the challenges which occurred were within a republican framework.

In Beirut, where the High Commissioner was installed, things were easier; France's authority was accepted. The Republic was founded, and commercial activity developed with surprising speed. General Maxime Weygand[3] succeeded Gouraud. Weygand, a Catholic, stood out by his prestige and he was loved. For strictly political reasons, Paris replaced him with General Sarrail,[4] a militant anticlerical who did not understand that, in the Middle East, religion is much more than a conviction; it is the very source of one's identity. In 1925, this High Commissioner, through ignorance, provoked the Druse revolt – a real war lasting several months. Artillery, aircraft and tanks were used. And in a shock to the whole world, Sarrail shelled Damascus, which had revolted, and bloodily crushed the revolt. There were hangings. France's prestige collapsed, and Sarrail was recalled. Henri de Jouvenel, a liberal, replaced him and succeeded, by his courtesy and good manners with people, his culture and his intelligence, in restoring peace. He offered the Syrians a liberal constitution, which they accepted, but which Paris refused.

Parliament, like the French Army, seemed in effect to forget its mission as the mandatory power. The vast majority of Members of Parliament considered that the Levant was a colony like the others. For the French, Damascus or Beirut belonged, like Abidjan, to the colonial empire. The English presence in the Middle East caused them to assert their opposition to it. Since 1860, a muted struggle had occupied the two powers.

Force had been a failure, liberalism had been refused, and a period of indecision remained. The high commissioners, who succeeded one another, no longer had any role. Paris governed without being involved. Nevertheless, Damascus was restless and progress had to be made. In 1936, the *Front populaire*[5] finally granted independence to Damascus. The text was signed with great pomp in the salons of the Quai d'Orsay, but the treaty was not submitted for acceptance by the parliament (*Assemblée Nationale*) in Paris. In Damascus, the disappointment was very great: the Syrians understood that France would do nothing for them, and that it was indeed an occupying power whose word was worthless.

In 1939 war started. This book tells the drama of what took place.

Part I

The Noose Tightens

1

1939: Weygand

On 25 August 1939, Édouard Daladier, France's Prime Minister, accepted the nomination of General Weygand. Gamelin[1] handed him his letter of appointment:[2]

> General Weygand is designated to fill, in case of mobilization, the post of Commander-in-Chief of French forces in the eastern Mediterranean. The territories of the Levant under French mandate will be placed under military control [...] In addition, General Weygand will be charged with coordinating the action of our military missions to the Turkish, Greek, Yugoslav and Romanian forces [...] He will communicate directly with the [British] Commander-in-Chief in Egypt who will address to him any requests concerning potential cooperation of the forces in the Levant with the British forces.

Personal and secret instructions accompanied him: General Weygand will 'coordinate, as far as possible, the actions of the various Allied armies throughout the Balkans and the Eastern Mediterranean [...] Command of naval forces will be entrusted to British authorities [...] Being based in Egypt, the theatre of operations includes Egypt, Djibouti, Aden and the Levant. The commander-in-chief will be English [...] General Weygand will, as far as he judges possible, respond to the demands of the British Commander-in-Chief in Egypt regarding the cooperation of French forces and the use of the territories of the Levant for British needs.' Weygand considered that the text did not spell things out sufficiently clearly. 'Potential cooperation [...] As far as is possible', but in an Allied grouping dominated by England, the French leader was broadly autonomous. He had authority over the High Commissioner in the Levant, Gabriel Puaux.

On 29 August he set out and, via Marseilles, Tunis, Malta and Alexandria, reached Beirut on 30 August.

Weygand was a thin, small and wrinkled man, and did his uniform up tightly. He had piercing eyes, dressed to the nines and everyone who approached him was struck by his energy and his youth. He was Foch's former chief of staff, defender of Warsaw when it was threatened by the Bolsheviks in 1920, former Army Chief of Staff, Vice-President of the Supreme War Council, Inspector-General of the army, and designated generalissimo (1931–5) – in summary, quite an aura surrounded the Commander-in-Chief of the theatre of operations in the Eastern Mediterranean (*Théâtre des opérations en Méditerranée orientale)*, the TOMO.

Beirut welcomed him, he shook hands, consulted, and then left again immediately. On 31 August, he was in Cairo where he met General Sir Archibald Wavell,[3] Commander-in-Chief of British forces in the Middle East, Admiral Sir Andrew Cunningham,[4] commanding the Allied fleet in the eastern Mediterranean, and Air Marshal Sir William Mitchell,[5] commanding the RAF. The atmosphere was excellent. Weygand liked and understood the English, with whom he had worked a great deal previously. Appointed on 29 July – only a month previously – Wavell was the former chief of staff of General Allenby during the 1917 campaign, and had occupied the post of commander of British forces in Palestine. 'Right from the first day', Weygand wrote, 'he appeared to me straightforward, direct, loyal, full of intelligence and experience, an impression which he always maintained [...] This interview left me with a feeling of confidence in the English leaders [...] and the impression that links, forged in the previous war, were still as strong'. Mutual confidence was strong and these men got along well together.[6]

Even if Italy was still neutral, it was a threat. Its navy and air force were powerful, and a large army was stationed in Libya. In addition, Eritrea borders the Red Sea through which passed oil supplies from Iraq and troops from India, Singapore, Australia, Indochina and Madagascar *en route* to France. This passageway was vital.

On 1 September 1939 the Germans attacked Poland. It was war; a general mobilisation of troops was ordered.

In April 1940, the country seemed to be asleep: the armaments industry was half-asleep, the army was in peacetime mode, and parliament was simply talking. For eight months, nothing had happened. In the Levant, the people were quiet. 'One can say that, at the time, and without risk of error, all the Lebanese Christians 'thought' French', wrote Major Brochet. 'The Lebanese Arabs were divided; as for the Syrians, they were very susceptible to the anti-French propaganda generated by the Fascist Italian colony and by Muslim scholars in Damascus.'

On 10 May, all hell broke loose when Hitler launched his forces in the *Blitzkrieg* (lightning war). The explosion was unbelievably violent. Behind the units that were sacrificed in Belgium, there was panic: Belgium imploded and the Belgians took flight. On 13 May, in the south, General Paul Ewald von Kleist (later Field Marshal) broke through from Sedan. General Heinz Guderian sped towards the Channel Coast – it was an irresistible, scythe-like thrust. The Army of the North, the British Expeditionary Force and the Belgian Army were caught in a net. Gamelin had no reserves. The campaign was lost in four days. On 15 May, Paul Reynaud[7] alerted Churchill, on 16 May he called Pétain and Weygand, and, on 19 May, he went to Notre-Dame de Paris to pray. Under the scourge of *stuka* dive-bombers, the roads were clogged by crowds of people fleeing; eight to 12 million refugees were without bread, without help, without shelter, and exposed to air attacks. Cities were burning, bridges blown up, dead were piling up, and the trains were packed. High officials fled, policemen ran away and hospitals collapsed under the vast numbers of patients. France was emptying, terrified, and the world was witnessing, dumbfounded, the spectacle of a world power which had abruptly collapsed – like a big monument, swept away by terror and abandoned by its politicians.

On 17 May, at 8:05 a.m., at the Grand Serail[8] in Beirut, an orderly handed to General Weygand a message marked 'Decipher personally'. It was from Paul Reynaud: 'Given the gravity of the situation on the Western Front, I would be grateful if you would come to Paris with the greatest urgency, after having taken the necessary measures to transfer command to someone on the spot in whom you have confidence. As far as possible, please keep your departure secret.'

Weygand complied immediately. He entrusted command to General Massiet and, at daybreak on 18 May, his Glenn Martin aircraft took off from Beirut. Roger Gasser accompanied him, as did Pierre de Leusse, a diplomat attached to Monsieur Puaux. On

19 May, after a stop at Tunis, his aircraft had a belly landing at
Étampes, close to Paris. The rebuilding of the army that he left in
the Levant was scarcely finished, but it was better than nothing
and had been considerably reinforced.

2

1940: Time of Choice

On 20 May 1940, following a totally unexpected and irresistible German push which took them to the Channel, General Weygand accepted the command with the hope of being able to redress a situation which had become catastrophic. In France, everything around him was collapsing. On 4 June 1940, Dunkirk fell and, on 7 June 1940, the front that he had set up on the Somme fell apart. On 12 June, by his orders declaring Paris an open city, Weygand saved Paris from disaster. General Dentz was charged with the heart-rending duty of receiving the enemy and handing over the capital.

In the Levant, at the beginning of June, General Mittelhauser[1] replaced the aged Massiet who had succeeded Weygand. Recalled from retirement on the outbreak of the war, Mittelhauser had miraculously escaped from Holland under enemy fire.

On 20 June, on Mittelhauser's invitation, General Wavell came to Beirut to dfraw up a plan of military cooperation. To contribute to the defence of the Suez Canal, which was threatened by the Italians, Mittelhauser agreed to send French troops to Egypt. The very next day, a symbolic flight of three Dewoitine D.520 fighters set out for Cairo. Ten thousand men and two squadrons of light bombers were supposed to follow. A battalion of the 29th French Colonial Infantry Regiment embarked for Cyprus. In return, an English squadron of heavy bombers was supposed to come to Syria to attack the Italians on the island of Rhodes. Also on 21 June, Mittelhauser informed the government in Bordeaux, to which it had withdrawn, of these arrangements, but France was embroiled in a debacle. Paul Reynaud had resigned during the catastrophe and, on 17 June, Marshal Pétain asked for an armistice.

On 18 June, General de Gaulle, known to only a few people, launched his appeal to the French forces, asking them to join him and carry on the war. In the Levant, no one heard him; life continued there as before. No one could imagine the extent of the drama. 'We are rather poorly informed about what is happening in France,' wrote Captain Jourdier. 'Everyone sees that the situation is alarming without being able to believe that defeat is imminent [...] In the officers' club in Damascus, there is only one topic of conversation [...] Some people have seriously entertained the idea of taking possession of the first sailing boat they come to and landing at Marseilles, even if only with a light machine gun, solely for the glory of getting themselves killed.'

Houzel reasoned: 'Each day our inaction became more and more burdensome. We did not have the heart to exercise while our comrades in France were fighting courageously, in spite of the defeat of our forces that the newspapers made increasingly clear.'

By July 1940, the drama was over. France was abandoned and facing the monster alone: America had not stirred, Poland had disappeared, the USSR had deserted, and England was entrenched behind the ditch of the Channel. Confirming the general collapse, France signed an armistice at Rethondes on 22 June. Although severe, it was not, rather surprisingly, excessively unfavourable. In the conqueror's mind, it had only to last six to eight weeks, the time needed to defeat England. If France gave up its arms and Germany kept the prisoners,[2] France kept its fleet and its empire with its garrisons and its rump of an army. Being now pointless, the killing stopped and the refugees were saved. Although half-occupied, France kept its flag, its diplomatic representatives and its merchant navy. Dominated, humiliated, exhausted but still in existence, she was out of a conflict that carried on without her. The Marshal declared: 'At least honour is saved. No one will use our fleet or our aircraft. We will keep the land and naval forces necessary for the maintenance of order in metropolitan France and in our colonies. The government remains free, and France will be administered by Frenchmen.'

On the BBC, de Gaulle rebelled and spoke of capitulation. He stood up both against authority and unanimous French public opinion which, relieved by the cessation of hostilities and the possibility of a return to normal life, wildly cheered Marshal Pétain. De Gaulle condemned the state that France applauded. In his appeal, that almost no one heard but which became historic, he lumped together 'armistice' and 'capitulation'[3] and, in very violent terms, accused Pétain, Weygand and Darlan of cowardice – and even treason. In the text of the famous small poster which today passes for the historic appeal,[4] he condemned them even before attacking the Germans. 'Members of a makeshift government have managed to capitulate, giving way to panic, forgetting honour, delivering the country into servitude. However, nothing is lost [...] This is a world war.'

Raymond Aron,[5] in England at the time, wrote: 'the Manichean interpretation of the Armistice, asserted right from the beginning [by General de Gaulle] and upheld against all the odds, has all the ingredients of a legend or a *"chanson de geste*.[6]" Neither those holding high public office nor the mass of Frenchmen and women subscribed to this epic vision. The "Appeal of 18th June" has kept its moral and political significance, but the speeches which followed immediately after it already came from a party chief and not from the spokesman of a muzzled country.'[7] And Roger Rouy said: 'Only a wilful mistake, maintained by hostility, can confuse this armistice with a capitulation.'[8]

Henri Lamouroux:[9] 'Gaullism has put forth the idea that we did not have to sign the Armistice and that Vichy was illegitimate. That's a myth! But it is not taken seriously.'[10] Guy Raïssac: 'The systematic confusion between "armistice" and "capitulation", deliberately committed by its adversaries, is an improper comparison [...] which has all the characteristics of a hoax.'[11] Moreover, General de Gaulle knew this very well himself. On 12 December 1941, confiding his plans to General Odic, who had come from North Africa with the intention of joining him,[12] de Gaulle said to him: 'Never admit that the Armistice could not have been avoided.'

In the Levant there was immense fright. 'The news of the disaster strikes people with astonishment. Consternation can be read on every face', noted Major Brochet in his diary. 'The churches toll the knell. The Lebanese people pray for the safety of France. Many Beirutis refuse payment which is due for requisitioned goods, and women decide not to wear jewels any more. Even in Damascus, the feeling of mourning is evident. The native population preserves a dignified attitude. No nationalist or anti-French demonstrations take place, and the political and religious leaders expressed to the High Commissioner, as well as to the General Commanding-in-Chief, the sympathy of the Lebanese and Syrian peoples for France in mourning.'

If General Mittelhauser 'showed himself to be rather favourable to the Armistice, it was not the same with the officers of his staff who, as a majority, did not accept the defeat', wrote Major Brochet, who met them that day. He continued:

> They openly urged an unconditional establishment of cordial relations with the British. For them, the French Army, beaten in metropolitan France, had not been defeated overseas; it remained powerful. For the whole of the Army of the Levant to go over to the English seemed to them the best solution [...] My direct superior, Colonel Coudrain, Director of Transport and Services of the TOMO, as well as his chief of staff, were won over to this will to resist. Their first reaction was to give me the responsibility of a mission to Iraq to study, with the English there, the conditions in which a French base could be sited at Basra. Cut off completely from metropolitan France, our expeditionary corps could only survive by relying on the support of the British Army.

Thus, under the command of Major Brochet, an official mission of three officers, who had been provided with a letter from General Mittelhauser to the French Minister in Baghdad and a diplomatic passport dated 22 June issued by the secretary-general of the High Commission, left Beirut for Iraq on 23 June. Taking the train as far as Damascus, then travelling by coach, the mission reached Baghdad on 24 June. The British warmly and confidently greeted these Frenchmen who had refused to submit to the Armistice. Travelling by plane and escorted into military installations, they visited the military bases of Habbaniya and Basra, and returned, very optimistic, on 2 July. Alas, when they returned, everything had changed in Beirut, where they had been forgotten: 'My poor Brochet,' exclaimed Colonel Coudrain, 'we are not thinking about you any more [...] There is no longer a question of joining the English. The Army must remain in the Levant, remain neutral and wait to see what is going to happen.'[13]

As it happened, on 24 June a major event took place in the Empire which was not noticed in metropolitan France. Sent to all the governors and residents-general[14] in the Empire – Catroux in Indochina, Noguès in Morocco, Boisson in Dakar – General Mittelhauser and High Commissioner Puaux received a telegram from London signed by General de Gaulle, saying: 'Completely in agreement with you in the wish to continue the war. [We] are setting up a French National Committee [*Comité national français*] to forge the elements of resistance in France. [We] ask you personally to join this committee. With our respect and hope, for the French National Committee, General de Gaulle.'

The offer generated enthusiasm in Beirut. Both Puaux and Mittelhauser immediately declared themselves in favour of continuing the war alongside the English. Without responding directly to the message from London, Mittelhauser gathered together the officers of the garrison and, in a sensational declaration, affirmed that he 'dissociated himself from a government of defeatists'. 'Whatever happens', he declared, 'the Army of the Levant, with the support of the Franco-British fleet, will remain alongside the British and will pursue its mission with unquenchable energy'. These remarks sparked a storm of acclamation; all approved it, no one thought about the government. Only Colonel Tony Albord[15] considered that it was a 'sentimental' position which was without a solid foundation.

On 26 June – a day after the Armistice had come into force – Bordeaux in turn got in touch. Minister Paul Baudouin[16] sent three telegrams in succession to Beirut. There was a call for unity, along with three orders: (1) Send the British liaison mission back to Cairo without delay; (2) Recall immediately the three fighter aircraft sent to Egypt – which seemed very like a disciplinary measure; and (3) The theatre of operations in the Middle East [the TOMO] is abolished; hand over command of the troops to General Massiet. The last telegram announced that an Italian military mission would come to supervise the implementation of the Armistice.

Behind closed doors, Mittelhauser and Puaux immediately analysed these messages and, after much discussion, decided to obey the minister. In a private conversation, Massiet confided to Houzel that Mittelhauser had made up his mind to obey only after receiving a telegram from General Noguès stating that [French] North Africa could not continue to fight. The orders from Bordeaux were therefore carried out: the fighters were recalled and the English mission left Beirut. The British, in response, drastically reduced the output of the oil pipeline from Iraq to Tripoli. Was this a hostile act? It does not seem to have been regarded as such; two days later, on 28 June, General Mittelhauser signed a 'good neighbour' agreement with the British.

Also on 26 June, a long telegram from Weygand informed the TOMO that a resolution of the Council of Ministers had concluded that it was impossible for the Empire to resist. Then, on 27 June, a telephone message, from the staff of TOMO to all troops in the Levant, clarified the situation: 'The clauses of the Armistice with Italy brought about the cessation of hostilities in the Levant. They did not include the foreign occupation of the states under mandate. French troops would continue their mission to maintain order without change. Commanders at all levels must maintain firm discipline.' The message was signed by order of the chief of staff, Colonel de Larminat. A note specified: 'Send in clear to all addressees urgently.'

Larminat, who had just signed this message, had however decided to rebel and to put into execution a plan that he devised several days previously: to take the best units, with a minimum of equipment, over to the English.

During the night of the 26 June, taking advantage of his post as chief of staff, Larminat composed a note calling for revolt which ended: 'The aim [...] is to organise [...] a group of volunteers to go to Palestine [...] Each detachment must have a full load of ammunition [...] The decision is full of consequences: separation from one's family, exile from one's country of birth, loss of nationality, execution in case of capture, service in a foreign army [...] Under no circumstances involve the civilians in this business.' One hundred copies were printed and its text was sent by the fastest means – couriers and aircraft – to the four corners of the country where it had a dramatic effect.

'On the morning of 27 June', said Larminat, 'General Mittelhauser came into my office where General Massiet and Colonel Keime[17] were already. He asked me to recover the message, [but] it was too late. He was extremely angry, unable to make up his mind to change his position. "It is impossible! I can't accept that! I can't return to France to be under an oppressive regime!" I then said to him: "General, you can no longer do anything from an official point of view, but if you personally do not want to submit, there is a way. I am currently organising departures for Palestine; you have only to do the same as those who prefer to serve with the English rather than accept slavery." I then presented him with my circular which had just been printed and of which General Massiet and Colonel Keime had a copy. He read the first page and said, his face beaming: "It is very good! I am with you! I will take the lead! Not for long, naturally. A symbolic gesture. But I don't want to return to France without having done something." He then left my office carrying the circular.'

In the evening, having thought about things and weighing up the extent of the disorder that the two contradictory messages had caused, Mittelhauser changed his attitude completely. At 6:00 p.m., he dashed down to Larminat's office; Mittelhauser was beside himself. Larminat said 'I found a man in a frenzied panic', wrote the latter. 'He shouted curses and threats at me, conjuring up the court martial that would have me shot.' While waiting to be shot, Larminat was arrested and was sentenced to 30 days' prison in Damascus.

As a result, there was considerable turmoil; in the garrisons, everyone was discussing the situation. Should people leave or stay? People challenged one another; sometimes voices were raised. The most violent incidents occurred at Baalbek where the 11th Battalion of Foreign Volunteers was quartered. On the evening of 27 June, at the officers' club, the battalion commander announced that he had come from Homs where he had conferred with Colonel Barré, the regimental commander, on the subject of a message that he was now going to read. In total silence, he took Larminat's paper from his pocket and read. 'A moment of profound silence followed this reading', remembered Houzel, 'then the major spoke again. He explained that upon receiving this circular, the colonel commanding the 6th Foreign Legion Infantry Regiment had decided to leave for Palestine with his regiment so that it could continue the struggle under his orders [...] Our commander, he announced, had taken the same decision [...] Before informing the troops, he left us to think about it overnight. He would ask for our answer the next morning. He added that, on returning from Homs, he had made a detour to warn the 1st Battalion, which was busy on road maintenance. Its commander had also decided to leave.' Was the whole of the 6th Foreign Legion Infantry Regiment[18] going to rebel?

Roger Houzel:

In spite of its grave consequences, I had made my decision [...] I did not consider my job finished since the enemy was still master in France. There were only two or three of us to have such a clear opinion [...] All the others were very hesitant. Some even showed themselves to be hostile [...] No one slept much that night. In the morning, at about 6 o'clock, we gathered around our commander [...] He called out our names, asking us to answer only with a 'yes' or 'no'. There were far more 'no's [...] Out of the 22 officers, only nine wanted to leave.

The commander then asked us to go and announce to the troops the formation of a group of volunteers [...] He appointed, among the officers staying behind, the person who was to succeed him in Baalbek and nominated to various positions those who were following him into rebellion [...] First of all, I assembled my NCOs [...] All their answers, except for three, were negative. I then assembled my company and had my intentions translated into Spanish. They became visibly excited and about three-quarters wanted to go to Palestine. I was going to realise that the respect of the men for their officers played an important part in their choice – the results varied a great deal from one company to the other.

Departure was planned for 4:00 p.m. One of the two motor transport parks in the Levant had come and set up next door to us, so that 800 different vehicles were at hand, and the commander of the vehicle park, who had decided to leave with the legionnaires, provided them with all the transport they needed. At lunch, however, it was learned that a certain number of Spaniards had taken possession of some trucks and were already making their way towards Turkey. Houzel left straightaway in a car, with a man accompanying him. At the exit from the town, it was reported that trucks filled with soldiers had just passed, going towards Homs. Then started a chase, but after about 30 km he saw two trucks stopped on a bend in the road. Around them were a number of soldiers, weapons in their hands, who seemed to be waiting. 'I stopped my car,' he began.

In front of me, the men remained still, holding their carbines. I approached and reproached them vehemently for having left without orders [...] Revolver in hand, I went towards the lead truck and noticed a man who was aiming at me [...] I raised my weapon [...] our two shots rang out together. I was unhurt but the man had disappeared: I had killed him. I heard shots [...] Some men were firing at me from the hip [...] I could see small flames jumping from the muzzles. Continuing to curse in a mixture of French and Spanish, I jumped into a ditch [...] I could see some men aiming a light machine gun [...] I laid down [...] I had only three bullets left [...] Someone shouted to me not to fire, no one would do me any harm. I stood up and, throwing down my weapon, moved forward [...] Some men from my company ran up and surrounded me, saying not to worry. However, a big redheaded fellow, pale with anger, came towards me with his arms outstretched and his hands open to strangle me [...] I had killed his mate. Another ran towards me, with a bayonet in his hand.

I moved forward, nevertheless, shouting [...] Some men came up
to me and shook my hand, assuring me that I could rely on them,
that they would follow me.

The revolt thus seemed quelled. Everyone turned around. At
Baalbek, the rebels stacked their weapons and, in column of
threes, made their way back to the barracks. When Houzel asked
why they had departed, he learned that there was a rumour that
the Italians were arriving in Beirut and therefore they had to leave
immediately. The Spanish Republicans did not want to fall into
the hands of the fascists, who would hand them over to Franco.

Houzel then understood. Announcing that he had shot a
man, he heard someone else say: 'Ah, you too!' In fact, another
Spaniard had been killed by a NCO. The revolt did not, however,
stop there. A group of the Spanish volunteers that Houzel
had picked up went to Sheik Abdullah, a small fort which
overlooked the town, and barricaded themselves in with 12 light
machine guns. Order was finally restored but, on the morning
of 28 June, it was noted that 120 men had disappeared, taking
with them the signal equipment. Fifty of them were arrested in
Homs, Damascus, Tripoli and Hama, but 70, it was learned, had
managed to reach Palestine.

The unruliness had to be stopped. Taking things in hand, Colonel
Barré, who commanded the 6th Foreign Legion Infantry Regiment,
arrived in person during the afternoon. Some old Legion NCOs
accompanied him. He had the men form up in ranks, separated out
the Spaniards, disarmed them, and had them taken to a barracks
where, under the direct orders of the Foreign Legion, they were
going to find out the strictness of its discipline. Everything was
thus settled without spilling any blood, but it was too late to leave.
Moreover, the commander of the 6th Foreign Legion Infantry
Regiment announced that he himself had changed his mind – he
would not leave, and he pressured the officers to stay.

The unrest had been such that the next day General
Mittelhauser himself came to Baalbek. 'Early in the morning,'
Houzel said, 'officers and NCOs received the order to gather
round to listen to him'.

He arrived, I may add, late, followed by General Massiet, Colonel
Barré and several officers. He walked forward slowly, looking
down. He was wearing an old patched canvas jacket, with a
stand-up collar. His neck was thick and reddened by the sun. He

stopped in a scrap of shade, made a circular gesture with his arms, and invited us to come closer. After a moment of heavy silence, he started to speak to us in a deep voice, in a sad tone, without interruption or big words. The very simplicity of his speech made it moving and the emotion, which was visibly affecting him, quickly became general.

First of all he told us of his sadness at the defeat of France, of which no detail had yet reached the Levant, except that it was complete. He did not hide from us how much he would have liked to carry on the struggle in our company, with [French] North Africa and all the colonies intact, but the fleet had decided not to pursue the struggle and North Africa had copied it. Under these conditions, it had become impossible for the Army of the Levant to carry on the fight alone. In addition, Marshal Pétain and General Weygand considered it completely hopeless to pursue any hostilities, and had asked him to order the laying down of arms in the best interests of France and the French population. Under these conditions, the only duty of the military was to obey their leaders [...] He alluded to the 'criminal' initiative taken by his chief of staff whom he had had arrested and placed under close arrest in the citadel in Damascus. He acknowledged the noble spirit which had inspired it, but begged us not to answer an appeal whose consequences could be as disastrous for us as for our country. He had, moreover, given orders so that elements still trying to make their way to Palestine would not reach the frontier. He did not reproach us for starting to put into execution our departure and passed over rapidly 'the regrettable incidents of the day before'. The theme of his windy discourse was again the duty to obey one's leaders and to follow the flag.

This failed departure and the incidents accompanying it had caused a feeling of deep uneasiness among the officers. Those of our comrades who had opted against leaving for Palestine then assumed an air of superiority. Following the failure of our enterprise, they almost openly rejoiced and laid the responsibility for it at the door of the higher command.'[19]

The disorder in the Legion was not limited to the volunteer unit attached to it, but spread to the Legion itself. In it, the turmoil was deep, close to disorder.

All the units were nervous. No one knew what was happening. During all this time, unit commanders were telephoning and asking for explanations. Some units had already taken to the road. The tanks from Homs had started off. 'We saw the tank battalion from the garrison at Homs arrive at Baalbek on its way to Palestine, without its commander, Prince Murat[20]', observed Houzel. 'The tanks and trucks parked in good order to spend the night. They had left at dawn.'

At Tripoli, Captain Folliot of the 24th Colonial Infantry Regiment invited his company – 340 men already repatriated from Cyprus – to follow him into rebellion. On the night of 27 June, the troops set off, with weapons and kit, in trucks which had been spirited away thanks to false orders. A part of the battalion of Colonial troops that had been sent to Cyprus in June 1940 at the request of the English[21] refused to return to Lebanon. On 12 July, Colonel Fonferrier, commanding the 24th Colonial Infantry Regiment, came from Tripoli to urge a return to good order and military discipline, but without success.[22]

Following the example of their leaders, Captain Jourdier, Lieutenant de Villoutreys and a squadron of the 1st Moroccan Spahis, on manoeuvres near Rachaya – about 100 men – crossed the frontier into Palestine on 30 June. On 6 July, this squadron bivouacked in Amevra camp in Palestine, near Saint-Jean-d'Acre. Jourdier:[23] 'I found old Folliot[24] there with his Colonials [...] I heard there for the first time talk of General de Gaulle. When I saw him [de Gaulle] eight months later, he asked me why I had not sent him a telegram after I had crossed the frontier. I felt stupid: I still did not know that 18 June was a historic day!' As for Folliot, he was as ignorant as Jourdier.

A pilot of the French Fleet Air Arm (*Aéronavale*) took off for Cairo in his seaplane, and two Air Force pilots fled on board an ambulance aircraft. In total, about 11 aircraft landed on English airfields.[25] On the ground, officers, NCOs and men crossed the frontier daily. Captain Morel-Deville, who found the atmosphere in Beirut 'detestable', escaped alone, in uniform, by train! Répiton-Préneuf, an artillery lieutenant, a graduate of the *Polytechnique*[26] and an engineer with the Iraq Petroleum Company, also decided to leave.

This haemorrhaging of people had to be stopped. Everything – aircraft, patrols, and couriers – was put in motion to halt those leaving. General Mittelhauser himself left for the south to search along the coast road. He met up with the tanks at Chtaura[27] in the Bekaa Valley, following which they turned around.

Was it only the rebels who wanted to leave? The Polish General Kopanski, who commanded the Polish Brigade at Homs, was haunted by the thought of seeing his unit handed over to Germany. He went to the Grand Serail every day to ask, increasingly furiously, for permission to leave Lebanon. Unwillingly and after much discussion, General Mittelhauser finally agreed. Before leaving, Kopanski's unit was equipped as completely as possible. The Poles set off fully armed, with vehicles, automatic weapons, 25mm anti-tank guns and supplies of ammunition.[28]

Larminat remained in prison. Shut up in an isolated part of the Service Corps prison in Damascus, he awaited his fate. But he was not forgotten. Considering him not guilty, young Legion officers from the 1st Battalion, 6th Regiment thought it their duty to rescue Larminat from the disastrous fate awaiting him. Major Taguet, Lieutenants Joly d'Haussy, Aïdubat and others organised his escape. A sham drunken fight was organised opposite the guard room in such a manner as to compel attention. At the same time, Joly d'Haussy and Aïdubat climbed the wall and dashed towards the prison. However, they found Larminat completely demoralised. Surprised by the intrusion of two officers whom he did not know, Larminat feared a plot and did not want to follow them. Refusing to have run such a risk for nothing, they forced him to get dressed and follow them. They climbed back across the wall and, on the other side, Major Taguet was waiting with a taxi. However, its engine would not start so they had to get out and push! Finally, the taxi took them as far as Kuneitra where Captain Fougères and his squadron of Circassians got Larminat across the frontier. The next day, he launched a call to rebellion over Radio Jerusalem.

Wavell, whom Larminat contacted after arriving in Cairo, refused him access to a microphone. The Commander-in-Chief of the British forces did not favour confusion – he considered the French were more useful in Lebanon. 'The English had hoped', wrote Répiton-Préneuf, 'to see us come over to them with our leaders and our weapons. They were much less keen on these irregular arrivals of deserters, naked and exhausted.' For obvious reasons, the French Consuls in Palestine, at Jerusalem and Haifa, were also hostile to French rebels.

On 1 July, Beirut had broadcast this warning: 'General Weygand, Minister of National Defence, wants it made known to everyone that crossing into Palestine, or any other British territory, by French soldiers, isolated or in groups, armed or not, constitutes desertion in the face of the enemy in time of war. The high command [...] has the strict duty of preventing it. No initiative in this direction will be tolerated any longer [...] All those who undertake propaganda against the government's orders will be subject to very severe penalties.' The same day, General Massiet signed this note: 'In the circumstances that we have just experienced, a certain number of officers have wondered where their duty lay. The question must be settled in this way: for a soldier, duty always and everywhere consists in obeying the orders of his leaders.'

As for Massiet, he never hesitated. His conduct had been sounder than that of his unfortunate superior officer, 'old, indecisive, overwhelmed by events'. Weygand therefore decided to change the leadership group. On 1 July, Massiet replaced Mittelhauser at the head of the troops, and Colonel Keime became his chief of staff. The period of disturbances came to an end. On 20 September, departures having ceased, it was noted that 35 officers, 117 NCOs and 747 men had disappeared, i.e. at least 900 men of the 40,000 in the Army of the Levant, which was enough to form a battalion. By a large majority, the army remained loyal to its government. 'The capitulation caught up almost all our officers', noted Répiton-Préneuf bitterly.

Wavell, British Commander-in-Chief in the Middle East, maintained as close a contact as possible with Beirut, and the Armistice did not cause any apparent clash. If London gave the order to reduce the supply from the Tripoli oil pipeline from 25 June onwards and to no longer refuel French ships calling at Haifa, nothing changed on the spot. The trains from Palestine to Iraq crossed the French mandate and the British consulates in Damascus and Beirut, like the French consulate in Jerusalem, remained open. Captive in Alexandria but refuelled by the British Admiralty, Admiral Godfroy's fleet maintained daily radio contact with the staff in Beirut.[29]

On 3 July, a week after the Armistice, England's attitude suddenly hardened. To the west, the attack on Mers el-Kebir took place: 1,500 were killed, the *Bretagne* was sunk, and considerable damage was caused to the *Provence* and the *Dunkerque*. 'If there is a stain on a flag, it is not on ours', declared Admiral Gensoul, standing in front of his men's coffins. In the Commons, however, Churchill received an ovation. As for French public opinion, it was shocked. No one understood the reasons for this tragic attack. Speaking on the BBC, however, General de Gaulle approved of it, which caused immediate damage to his cause. Many of those who were getting ready to join London suddenly drew back. How many airmen, prepared to go to Gibraltar, stayed in North Africa? Already, opinions were crystallising.

In Egypt, at Alexandria, Admiral Godfroy's Force X escaped the same tragedy. Simon, who was there, tells:[30] 'At daybreak, the French ships at anchor in the harbour suddenly found themselves surrounded by British units with guns trained, at point-blank range. They were surprised like a rabbit in his burrow surrounded by hunters with gun in hand. If they moved, they were dead. The French admiral had his torpedo tubes loaded, but left his gun turrets trained fore-and-aft in order not to provoke the British aggressor. Moreover, he continued shipboard routine as if nothing was happening. Sailors in working dress resumed painting the hulls again under the nose of the English who were still at battle stations. It was a ridiculous situation. On an order, they secured their weapons. Aware of the stupidity of mutual destruction, Admiral Cunningham took it upon himself, in spite of Churchill's orders, to negotiate a peaceful solution which was acceptable to both parties. Responsible for their ships and crews, Godfroy and Cunningham saved a large amount of shipping. Munitions were taken ashore, fuel tanks were emptied, but, still flying their flag, the French ships remained untouched under the command of their officers. Thus, later, the two fleets could fight together again. A daily radio link continued to keep Force X in touch with Beirut and, thanks to it, contacts between the Levant and Cairo never ceased completely.

Everywhere the Royal Navy could reach them, French ships were seized. At Port Said, it was two liners of Messageries Maritimes, the *Félix-Roussel* and the *Paul-Doumer*, and at Suez, two tankers. In response the French Navy seized three English colliers, and their crews were interned. The frontier was sealed and exchanges ceased. The naval blockade was complete and a slow suffocation commenced.

Reaching Beirut from Piraeus, where it had taken shelter at the time of the Armistice, the liner *Théophile-Gautier* was challenged by a British aircraft which ordered it to go first of all to Haifa for an inspection of its cargo. The ship's captain refused and reached Beirut where 2,000 demobilised soldiers as well as about 30 active-duty officers on a black list waited to return to France. The ship berthed, the passengers embarked and it was then that the English warned that, as soon as it reached the open sea, it would be stopped and inspected. Its departure was therefore put back, and was finally cancelled. The *Théophile-Gautier* remained holed up in Beirut for the duration of the war. The Levant was now isolated.[31]

Following the attack on Mers el-Kebir, the attack on Dakar in September destroyed all hope of dialogue. Undertaken by England and Free France in concert, the operation had proved a fiasco. The English were annoyed by the cost, Free France felt it demonstrated its weakness, and Vichy considered it fratricide. Learning of the indiscretions committed by the Gaullists in London before the operation, Roosevelt was scandalised;[32] he would never forget. Churchill, who was seriously attacked in the Commons, undertook to never again pass on strategic secrets to the French. Darlan found it easy to stress the collusion of the Free French with the British. De Gaulle was distraught to such a degree that, according to Pleven, he contemplated suicide.

On 20 October 1940, off Libreville, a second Franco–French duel took place: the sloop *Savorgnan de Brazza* of the Free French Naval Forces destroyed its sister ship, the *Bougainville*, which had remained loyal to its government. The *Bougainville* was set on fire and run ashore. It was a total loss. On 14 October, in the same waters, the English sank the submarine *Poncelet*.[33] There were about 20 dead taken ashore, and the governor hanged himself. Four hundred people were interned.[34] The French were distraught at seeing their country dismembered. All around France, her neighbours went in for the kill: the Germans seized Alsace, the English wanted the fleet, America the Caribbean, de Gaulle Sub-Saharan Africa, the Italians Tunisia, and the Japanese Indochina. On 21 July 1941, Darlan wrote to Marshal Pétain: 'London and Washington are in competition to lay their hands on the colonies in Africa [...] the best platform for military operations [...] The longer the war lasts, the more trouble we will have in preventing [our colonies] from becoming dependencies of the Anglo-Saxons. They declare that they will hand back our Empire but I don't believe a word of it. Such generosity on their part would be new.'

The attacks against Oran, Dakar and Libreville saved the French Air Force. Having realised that in disarming France they risked delivering its empire to the British, the Germans admitted that, in order to defend herself, France needed armaments. At Wiesbaden, the French and German representatives agreed that France could keep its forces on condition that she agreed to defend her territories against all aggression, no matter where it came from. Armed with this agreement, she could keep her Air Force and her tanks in North Africa, Senegal and the Levant. Breaking this accord would be considered as a breach of the Armistice with its consequences: invasion of the Unoccupied Zone and seizure of the fleet; free access to [French] North Africa and the plight of the prisoners would be used as a basis for blackmail. Moreover, Major Paillole's secret service had warned Vichy that as early as December 1940, the German High Command had studied a response to a possible revolt of the French colonial empire. *Operation Attila*, occupation of the Unoccupied Zone had already been anticipated.[35]

Henceforth, two Frances opposed each other in a fight to the death. There was no link between Vichy, which wanted to respect the Armistice in order to protect what could still be saved, and the one in London which wanted to continue to fight, no matter what the price. And from this division a drama was born: with each accusing the other of treason, the French killed one another.

3

From One War to the Next

Henceforth, the positions were clear. There was no longer a question of choice about what position to take; the Allies and Free France were on one side and Vichy was on the other.

On 15 November 1940, at the Grand Serail in Beirut, General Fougère, who on 23 September had replaced General Massiet, addressed some 30 officers who had arrived from France:

> Our relations with the British are excellent. On 28 June last, we signed a 'good neighbour agreement' with General Wavell, Commander-in-Chief in the Middle East, which brought some relief to the blockade. We understand their concerns: they fear that the Germans will invade the Levant or occupy some of our airfields to attack the Suez Canal from behind. But we are here precisely to prevent such a thing happening. We are thus able to allay British fears. However, I must nonetheless put you on guard against the lies from their radio which believes it is obliged to be a propaganda vehicle for the so-called Free French, who seek by every means to cause the military, the civilians and the natives to revolt and to put us on bad terms with the British. The danger is all the greater as, in the whole of the Middle East, 90 per cent of the population is nationalist and favourable to the Germans [...] I must also tell you that the strike by the Gaullists against Gabon has caused 20 deaths. They sank a sloop, while the English sank a submarine.[1]

Colonel Amédée Keime who replaced Larminat in the post of chief of staff on 1 July 1940, was also aware that the Levant could be the object of an attack. They had to prepare for one: 'The Germans have for the moment achieved good results and France has undergone a defeat, but it is not final. Consider yourselves still at war,' he declared to his officers.

Keime was tall, calm, confident and smiling. A Saint-Cyrien from the class of 1906, this Lorrainer fought with the cavalry in the Woëvre region of Lorraine and in the trenches at Ypres during World War I. In the Somme he was in contact with the British Army, whose style he admired – an opinion which he maintained. He studied for entrance to the *École de guerre* (Staff College) and, passing out amongst the top students, spent his command time with the armoured car group in Mainz. This cavalryman was interested in machines. As a young man he had become passionate about cars: at the age of 18, armed with his driver's licence and taking part in rallies, he participated in motor racing. He wielded the spanner, repairing his Peugeot himself. A lieutenant in the 11th Cuirassiers, his practical knowledge was most useful and exceptional in his arm of the service.

Unfortunately, the painful job of welcoming the Italian Control Commission[2] to the Levant fell to the chief of staff. This Commission was tasked with overseeing the application of the Armistice agreement, the demobilisation of the army, and the stockpiling of surplus armaments. Presided over by General de Giorgis, it included three officers, three NCOs, five secretaries, but no German.[3] It would be learned later, reading the memoirs of Jamil Mardam Bey, a Syrian Member of Parliament, that it had to fulfill a secret mission of establishing contacts with the Syrians to win them over to the Axis cause. The Italians will have 'little success because of the Italian occupation in Libya, a disastrous experiment.' The Muslims, moreover, despised the Italians.

Arriving by train from Istanbul, the Commission had to present itself on the evening of 28 August 1940 at Meidan-Ekbes, a tiny town on the Turkish frontier. By the end of the afternoon, everything was ready to receive it. Colonel Keime awaited with a detachment of troops which, according to protocol, had to present arms; but night came and nobody arrived. Time passed and darkness fell on the deserted station. It was rather humiliating. Finally the train arrived and the head of the delegation, General de Giorgis, alighted. He was in mufti and asked that no honours be rendered to him. Keime smelled a trap. It is necessary, he said, to carry out the ceremonial, as is the rule. After a long exchange, the Italian finally gave way; and in the dark, in front of a herder and his goats, the French presented arms. Thus no ceremony took place the next day in front of the inhabitants of Tripoli.

The following day, the Italians put on their magnificent uniforms. Their heel-clicking and Fascist salutes initially caused astonishment and, later, ridicule; but soon they appeared only in mufti.[4] Opinions about them varied – some found them finicky, others were more tolerant. On 31 August, as soon as the Italians settled in, they asked for a report on the state of French forces as at 1 June 1939, 25 June 1940 and 1 September 1940. Colonel Keime answered ten days later, and Giorgis, on 10 September, facing a delegation of the three services, Army, Navy and Air Force, discovered the truth. He was astonished. Demobilisation not being finished, the figures were still large,[5] but he had thought that the Army of the Levant was much larger. The gloating campaign of Weygand before the war had triumphed.

The Control Commission had to oversee the stockpiling of weaponry not included in the regulation table of equipment of authorised units. The French complied by getting rid of the outdated weapons which had equipped the army in 1939 before the arrival of Weygand: venerable 1874 Gras rifles; Gauchat submachine guns from 1915, which were often unusable; civilian vehicles that had been requisitioned from various sources; outdated artillery, etc. Using his brains, Keime obtained more. If Article VI of the Armistice Convention forbade 'the manufacture of new war material in non-occupied territory', Article IV on the other hand stated that 'excepted from this obligation [are] troops necessary for the maintenance of order. Their number and their armaments are determined by Germany and Italy respectively.' Thus Keime convinced Giorgis of the necessity of manufacturing new materiel on the spot if the defence of the mandate was to be assured.

The Army of the Levant, after the Armistice, was not in a good state. If army and air force equipment had been considerably improved by Weygand, its personnel had remained the same – narrow-minded, hidebound and addicted to routine. Colonel Tony Albord: 'This army was in all ways identical to the one watching along the Rhine or on the Belgian frontier [...] With hidebound culture and limited ambition, mainly made up of those who had fought in 1914–18, with no other training than the practical aspects of soldiering learned in the trenches, the officer corps was sticking to schemes of "active defence", and the "dash" among the NCOs was blocked by strict conformity in the minor tasks that were entrusted to them [...] The reserve officers, more open-minded, saw themselves stuck in their lower ranks.'

Houzel, a member of the Foreign Legion: 'Life had become completely devoid of interest. We no longer had the prospect of one day being involved in operations, and manoeuvres had no other object than to keep us occupied. We had lost faith. The enthusiasm which animated all the officers and men of our unit gave way to a sort of disgust. The NCOs, and many of the officers, had come to criticising, almost as a matter of principle, all the orders emanating from the commander. Everyone ended up suffering from the atmosphere but no one made the effort to ease the tension.'

Those who had been called up were increasingly impatient and had to be repatriated, but the return route home was blocked – England was watching it. It was not until August that permission to travel was secured. The first departure took place on 20 August, but it was not until the middle of October that the flood of returnees picked up. From 17 October onwards, a convoy of ships left Lebanon each week.[6] Because of the lack of ships, clearing the backlog was relatively slow, but it was finished on 15 December. Not a single one of those called up went over to de Gaulle. 'Passing from 80,000 to 35,000 men, without counting the locals – 12,000 men – the Army of the Levant underwent a sharp drop in the number of effectives, and a number of units had to be disbanded. In the army, there remained[7] the Foreign Legion, the Algerian, Tunisian and Senegalese *tirailleurs*,[8] and the *spahis*.'[9]

Starting on 1 July 1940, six days after the Armistice, a study of the re-organisation of the troops had been undertaken because, after the departure of the reserves, the remaining troops would have to carry out their duties, especially the maintenance of order and the defence of the frontiers. This army had not been in action. It did not take much encouragement for a part of it to cross over to the British side. To give each person a conscience vote became an urgent task. The old soldiers were too old; they were going to be replaced by new ones who had taken part in the war in France. These latter had experience of modern war; they understood the importance of mechanised units and the vital role of signals; and they talked about revenge. There was 'new blood' in the Levant.

As soon as the demobilisation was finished, things started to be put in order. In February 1941, the liner *Providence* repatriated to France those suspected of Gaullist sympathies and brought to the Levant 200 officers, often tank and artillery specialists, as well as several hundred volunteers from the Armistice Army. From August 1940, the Army High Command had called for volunteers to serve overseas in Indochina, French North Africa and the Levant. Within a few months, the Army of the Levant found a new cohesion and a new effectiveness. Because it was a colonial army and its sympathies were with Marshal Pétain, one sometimes thinks that this army was on its last legs. This is wrong. Its conscientiousness and its discipline made it an inventive, tough and hard-fighting force. Massiet and his staff – Dentz, Verdilhac, Arlabosse, Keime and others – were going to reform and restore the army. To standardise it, the first decision taken was to place it under a single command, that of the staff of the Army of the Levant. The regional staffs were thus disbanded. The departure of the reservists having left big gaps, some units were changed, some were disbanded, locals were promoted, troop numbers and armaments were redistributed. Meanwhile, the teaching of NCOs and junior officers, and the training of the troops, were all intensified. In February 1941, the Army of the Levant had the equivalent of two small divisions. 'The Levant then lived through difficult times', wrote Major Brochet. 'Heartbroken, but still imbued with an ardent patriotism, the instructors began the task of reforming an army that the repatriation of the reservists had reduced by more than half.'[10]

The sailors, airmen, and the junior officers and NCOs of the colonial troops and of the Foreign Legion were all Europeans. The other ranks had come from the whole Empire – Moroccans, Algerians, Tunisians, and blacks.[11] All were volunteers attached to their officers. It was their officers whom they obeyed, not popular opinion. They did not make any political choice, and propaganda did not affect them. They went where they were ordered, without qualms. Fighting was their job and the army their family. Often crude and unpolished, but faithful and devoted, they formed strong units. For them France had a prestige that we can no longer imagine.[12]

The Syrian and Lebanese troops were less hardy. According to General Albord who commanded them, 'the Alawite soldier is capable, the Syrian simple and disciplined, but anti-authority, easily upset and uncultured. His martial spirit is reduced. The Lebanese are conscientious mercenaries, civilians dressed in military uniform. The Lebanese and Syrian middle classes have no esteem for the army; their sons must be lawyers.'[13]

Everywhere, discipline was tightened and the atmosphere improved.

Abandoning the presidency of the Military Tribunal and promoted to command the cavalry, a very relieved Colonel

Keime left the staff on 15 September 1941. At a time when mechanised forces represented modernity, it was a job of primary importance and Keime, who raised the 1st RDP,[14] felt right at home. His predecessor, Massiet, a traditional cavalryman, 'did not perhaps have all the knowledge necessary for a commander to carry out an action in modern warfare', according to General Prudhomme.[15] Keime then found a true command in his arm of the service, matched with an independence which was going to allow him to put his ideas into practice. In spite of the Italian Control Commission that he had neutralised, he was going to give his best effort.

In this mountainous country, often lacking roads, the horse remained an irreplaceable means of fighting, as described by Sub-Lieutenant Oddo:[16]

> Horsed cavalry in very open order are but slightly vulnerable in open country, without barbed-wire entanglements, where they can wheel about at top speed. Where infantrymen would get themselves caught up and could not withdraw without loss, and where armoured patrols would have vehicles destroyed, a horsed formation will succeed in gathering intelligence with insignificant losses, because a horse can receive several bullets and can still continue carrying his rider and even galloping [...] In addition, the endurance of a horsed squadron, its ability to cover 50 to 80 kilometres a day for several days, are precious attributes in all circumstances.

Two regiments of horsed cavalry, the 1st Moroccan Spahis and a mixed regiment[17] of Algerian and Tunisian *spahis*, were thus retained, and the number of local squadrons was trebled: the Circassians increased from six to 19 squadrons. The 13 new ones were placed under the orders of Colonel Collet, who remained autonomous.

Taking advantage of lessons learned in Europe, from November 1940 onward the staff had already decided to group its mechanised forces together. It was now a matter of training a mobile armoured force capable of powerful movements. To blend together all the armoured assets into a single force was without precedent in the French Army. This decision came two years before the setting up of an armoured cavalry arm in 1943.

Are horsemen and tanks capable of functioning together? Not normally. They are not people from the same world. The horsemen are heirs of Lassalle and Murat, the others of Estienne

and Renault. One lot wears blue *képis*, gloves and shining boots;
the others wear black *képis* and wipe their hands on greasy rags.
The first have trumpets and the second bugles. The differences are
fundamental. If in 1940 they had fought together, it was always in
parallel. Even their armoured vehicles were different models. All
European armies had had the same experiences.

Upon taking up his command, Keime found the armoured
vehicles divided into two groups: one was made up of the tanks of
the 63rd Tank Battalion (*63ᵉ Bataillon de chars de combat*),[18] the
other by the vehicles of the 8th Armoured Car Group (*8ᵉ Groupe
d'automitrailleuses*).[19] In November he announced the creation,
on 1 December, of a single motorised brigade which would
include two regiments, the 6th and 7th African Light Cavalry
Regiments (*6ᵉ* and *7ᵉ Régiments de chasseurs d'Afrique*),[20] each
comprising an additional squadron, an armoured car group and
a tank group. Thus, he announced, the cavalry would be able
to provide 'a rapid, powerful and flexible tool, indispensable in
carrying out operations in modern warfare'.

The leaders of these two regiments knew their job. Both had
fought in France. Lieutenant-Colonel Le Couteulx de Caumont
commanded the 3rd Armoured Car Regiment attached to Colonel
de Gaulle's 4th Armoured Division (*4ᵉ Division cuirassée*) at
Montcornet where he was seriously wounded. Captain de
Gastines, his deputy, had fought at Stonne with the B1-*bis* tanks
of the 3rd Armoured Division. Appointed to the head of the
7th African Light Cavalry Regiment (*7ᵉ Régiment de chasseurs
d'Afrique*), Le Couteulx de Caumont assembled his officers and
declared: 'Gentlemen, whether we belong to the tanks or to the
armoured cars, here we represent the armoured corps, and we are
going to work together.' He described the general organisation
and the role of each group. 'Given the scanty number of troops,
we will be authorised to recruit local auxiliaries.' The plan was
well accepted. Everyone knew the importance of large mechanised
units, and the feeling of being part of one raised everyone's morale.
At last, action in sight! All ranks set to work. People got to know
each other. In the mess, armoured officers and horsemen sat at the
same table. With visits to the various units by the leaders, plus
lectures, exercises and personal contacts, and meetings of unit
commanders, the amalgamation was quickly accomplished. Alas,
equipment was lacking.

Although the 90 Renault R-35 tanks were new and strong,
they were designed for working with infantry. Slow, lightly armed

and without a radio, they also lacked range. Their task was not hit-and-run attacks, nor rapid action, but they were irreplaceable. Completely at the end of their life, the 50 old Renault FT tanks in service in the Levant since 1919 were only suitable for use as mobile bunkers for defending airfields, and the 135 armoured cars in service were barely usable: 39 White armoured cars, with solid rubber tyres, which dated from World War I. Refurbished a hundred times, they could not easily move forward and, on rollers distorted by the jolting on the roads, their turrets rotated only with great difficulty. During an inspection on 12 March 1941, General Dentz remarked when passing in front of one: 'Heavens, this one was with us in 1926 when we recaptured the Djebel Druse.' Only 27 of the vehicles were capable of reaching a speed of 60 km/hr: 16 Panhard TOE (*théâtre d'opérations extérieures:* overseas theatre of operations) and 11 White-Laffly armoured cars whose axles were starting to give way. The most important resource was the strong technical infrastructure, the workshops managed by Captain Bich.[21] They were well equipped and staffed by competent mechanics. Nonetheless, it was a situation filled with drama.

To solve the various problems, the two partners were going to have to invent new machines capable of facing vehicles of the same tonnage. Immediately on studying the problems, Keime devised a makeshift plan. He thought deeply about possible solutions, and devised a programme to convert the material that he had available. Plans were drawn up, wooden models produced, and prototypes were soon trialled. Finally, the vehicle park and a few civilian workshops started to produce new equipment, somewhat odd-looking but fast and reasonably armoured. Bich got to work enthusiastically. The staff and artillerymen did all in their power to support him. A large amount of steel was necessary, and a hunt for it soon started.[22] The Commander-in-Chief requisitioned 140 tonnes of steel which had been stockpiled for future work in the port of Beirut, and old boilers from silkworm-breeding establishments were brought down from the mountains. Shipwrecks were inspected, and an unused water pipeline was cut up. The owner protested to the Italian Control Commission but, thanks to Keime's know-how, the matter was closed.

The aim was to have, within ten months, in October 1941, 250 vehicles.[23] The manufacturing programme was forecast to have several stages going from 27 armoured cars to 161, then to 235, all capable of a consistent speed of 70–75 km/hr. For that,

200 new American Dodge five-tonne trucks, capable of reaching 80 km/hr and which had been bought by Weygand, were retained for the workshops. Beirut was thus going to produce, in record time, two new types of armoured cars, the Dodge-White and the AM (*automitrailleuse* = armoured car) Dodge.

The Dodge-White armoured car was old equipment revitalised. Reinforcing the chassis of new Dodges, Bich installed on top of them the armour plates taken from outdated White and White-Laffly armoured cars, thus obtaining a perfectly acceptable machine. Fast, but with pneumatic tyres, it proved to be rather fragile on rocky ground. Several spare wheels were therefore placed in the large boot of these vehicles, giving them a characteristic elongated silhouette. The armament was improved; the cannon and machine gun, which were on opposite sides in the old turret, were replaced by a 37mm cannon and a Reibel machine gun placed in parallel but operated independently. The Dodge-White had a separate rear driving position. The rear driver, called the 'reverser' (*inverseur*), could drive, accelerate and brake; but to start off, after having declutched, he had to call to the front driver to first engage the gear. From his position, only once the front driver had engaged the gear and shouted 'Ready!', could the vehicle be driven off. The only gear available was the reverse of the original Dodge, which functioned perfectly. 'With two trained drivers, one scarcely needed to double-declutch', remembered Lieutenant Michelet.[24] Thirty-nine Dodge-White armoured cars were thus produced.

The fastest vehicle, not the best armoured but no doubt the most original, was the AM Dodge with shield. It had a cube-shaped armoured body mounted on a truck chassis. The cabin and engine were also protected. It had a four-man crew, and a passage allowed a crew member to move to the rear platform. In the middle of the vehicle, a vertical shaft supported a 37mm cannon and there was a light machine gun in a twin mounting, protected by a shield. A second light machine gun could be used for anti-aircraft defence or for close combat through slits. Christened the 'Tanaké', the local name for petrol cans, and with a good turn of speed, the AM Dodge did not always live up to expectations.

Another strange machine to have come out of the Beirut workshops was the 'cavalry cannon truck' (*camion-canon de cavalerie*). It was an armoured Dodge, carrying a 75mm cannon whose wooden-spoked wheels had been replaced by smaller metal wheels. The cannon could be aimed and fired from the truck tray or lowered to the ground where it could be towed. Capable of destroying modern armoured vehicles at a range of more than 2,000 metres, and of being moved as soon as it had fired, it was an excellent weapon.[25] The production of these cannon trucks was severely delayed by there being too much work, and they did not appear on the battlefield until ten days after the beginning of hostilities. Finally, the workshops produced armoured trucks for motorised infantry from which, in order to disembark rapidly, the soldiers were seated back to back. Each vehicle was equipped with a turret taken from a Potez aircraft, but only one squadron of Moroccan *spahis* was equipped with them.

In six months, with makeshift means, Keime and Bich succeeded in equipping two regiments of African Light Cavalry (*chasseurs d'Afrique*). In June 1941, they had 90 tanks and 70 armoured cars capable of a consistent speed of 70 km/hr, all armed with a 37mm cannon and an automatic weapon. All the squadrons with four platoons of five vehicles received their entitlement; the squadron commanders and the captains had command vehicles. Only the cannon trucks could not be delivered.[26] As for fuel, the crude oil stored at Tripoli had until then been refined in Marseilles. As supplies now depended on British goodwill, an improvised refinery was built in four months with the resources of the army, navy and the railways. On 20 December, the day the refinery was inaugurated, the installation was capable of refining three cubic metres (3,000 litres) per day, and of producing petrol, diesel fuel and fuel oil.

The achievement of this project – vehicles and infrastructure – was truly remarkable. The Army of the Levant had proved its dynamism and enthusiasm but, for political reasons, this success remained unnoticed.

If machines were scarce, personnel were equally lacking. It had been hoped to receive volunteers from France, but the English did not authorise their transit. As a result, General Keime ended by obtaining, from a reluctant command, permission to recruit local auxiliaries – who ended up representing 60 per cent of the total force. Well trained and strictly disciplined, the Syrians and Lebanese produced, after only four or five months of instruction, effective troops. Overall, these ill-assorted troops, 'willing, easy to instruct, but relatively unmotivated', fought properly, said their officers.

While the scaling down of the Army of the Levant continued, a detailed study of possible operations was undertaken by the staff.

The conclusion reached was as follows: after having crossed an extremely arid zone, an aggressor coming from Iraq would run up against the major obstacle of the Euphrates river. This possibility could be disregarded if one had sufficient warning and in the north Turkey was neutral. The only serious threat therefore was from across the frontiers of Palestine, and it was on this hypothesis that work would proceed.

The overall assessment? In April 1941, the Levant had a large force: 35,000 professional soldiers – including 8,000 from metropolitan France – structured in 27 infantry battalions, and an armoured brigade. It also had 14 artillery batteries, 90 modern combat aircraft and two destroyers. Its reserves in fuel and ammunition, it was estimated, could provide for six weeks of fighting.[27]

4

1941: Dentz

Regarded as 'very defeatist [...] but full of good intentions', Monsieur Puaux, the High Commissioner, felt quite overwhelmed by events. The former Ambassador to Austria at the time of the *Anschluss*, Gabriel Puaux could assess the magnitude of the German threat perfectly. His sympathy was with the Allies but he refused to become a rebel. In November, on Radio Levant, he answered attacks by Catroux, but too feebly according to Pierre Laval, then Vichy's Vice-President of the Council and Minister of Foreign Affairs. Laval decided to replace Puaux. 'I am going to send Chiappe to Syria,' he announced to Otto Abetz, the Ambassador of the Reich, 'I have full confidence in him to oppose the English vigorously.'

On 20 October 1940, although no threat seemed to weigh on the Levant, Puaux asked the military high command to return the whole of his powers to him, powers which had been reduced since the declaration of war, but General Huntziger considered 'that because of special conditions' nothing should be changed. Annoyed, Puaux complained to his Minister, who did not reply. His weakness against Catroux and his blundering at the time of the Chahbandar affair, an important local event, were strongly criticized[1] and he was recalled on 27 November.[2]

The same day, Jean Chiappe[3] boarded a new four-engine Farman aircraft, *Le Verrier*, piloted by Henri Guillaumet, the hero of *Terre des hommes*.[4] His co-pilot was Marcel Reine. Both were veterans of the *Aéropostale* service, friends of Daurat, Saint-Exupéry and Mermoz. The big aircraft had to follow a course laid down by order of the Control Commission. It was impossible to deviate from it. The aircraft therefore had to enter a dangerous zone where an Italian–British naval engagement (the Battle of Taranto) was taking place. At 12:05 p.m. the aircraft's

radio operator, Le Duff, sent: 'Being machine gunned – on fire
– SOS.' It was his last message. The Farman disappeared; there
were no survivors. On the ground, a French radio operator, Jules
Routin, declared later that at 12:10 p.m. he had heard an Italian
fighter transmit: 'Have shot down an unknown large aircraft.'
Vichy then published this communiqué: 'Monsieur Jean Chiappe,
Ambassador and High Commissioner for Syria and Lebanon,
has just been killed in dramatic circumstances. He left France
last Wednesday by plane to reach his post in Beirut, the stop
beforehand being Tunis. When flying over the Mediterranean, the
aircraft carrying him was machine-gunned in flight by an English
fighter, on Wednesday at 12:06 p.m., halfway between the coast
of Sardinia and Africa.'[5]

There was a rumour, naturally, that being unwanted in the
Levant, Chiappe had been murdered by the British Intelligence
Service. Some people accused *France Libre,* and Catroux said
later that this rumour increased his standing in Egypt. Lacking
a replacement, Puaux remained in the job temporarily, but after
only ten days his successor was named. It was a soldier, General
Henri-Fernand Dentz. Dentz had already been designated as
the replacement of General Massiet, Commander-in-Chief of
the troops. Vichy, caught short, had also appointed him High
Commissioner, as Weygand had been previously. However, Jean
Chiappe's aircraft having been shot down, Dentz had to reach
Beirut after a roundabout, exhausting and chaotic voyage.

'A very conformist general officer who was disposed to apply
literally the orders given to him by Darlan', was the portrait of
him given by General de Gaulle, and that is the image of him
that remains. Yves Gras, a Free Frenchman: 'An Alsatian patriot,
he saw himself placed in a dramatic situation. Unfortunately he
had neither the stature nor the character necessary to deal with
it.' He was an honest soldier, animated by a heightened sense of
duty, an 'intelligent and gentle' officer according to his former
chief of staff, Colonel Groussard, 'capable of being a brilliant and
invaluable deputy' but 'lacking the energy, boldness and initiative
needed to be a commander-in-chief'. This intelligent and gentle
officer, lacking energy, boldness and initiative, held his own so
effectively against his British opponents that they had to treble the
number of their troops after they attacked him. The Free French
later criticised him for having shown too much determination in
fighting them. The gravest accusation made against him was not,
however, military but political. Yves Gras: 'Not conceiving of a

higher quality than discipline, he simply obeyed Darlan's orders blindly and allowed himself to be persuaded that, acting in this way, he would save the Unoccupied Zone and [French] North Africa from a German invasion.'

Tall but thickset, some labelled him a 'gentle giant'. Lucien Romier, a minister, said: 'He is a policeman', but if Dentz did not really seem to be 'a character' and if he wasn't a Guderian, he nevertheless chose his subordinates well and supported their decisions.

For Weygand, Dentz was 'a loyal soldier who did not consider discipline a matter of sophistry.'[6] Robert Aron has painted him as 'an irreproachable soldier, a convinced patriot, profoundly anti-German, victim of an extraordinary situation that few chiefs could have overcome at the price of gifts he did not have.' The Australians, his adversaries, said of him: 'Dentz was a professional soldier and an honourable man who did his duty obeying the orders of his government.'[7]

His father had left Alsace in 1871 in order to avoid becoming Prussian, and his son had inherited his patriotism. The intellectual and moral qualities of Henri-Fernand Dentz became apparent at Saint-Cyr. He graduated first in his class and was one of the youngest to enter the *École de guerre* (Staff College). During the 1914 war, he commanded a battalion at the front before being appointed chief of staff of an infantry division. In 1940, he commanded an army corps in Alsace. Alas, this was the end of a faultless career. Weygand, who held him in high esteem, replaced him on 2 June with General Hering, the elderly Military Governor of Paris, and then gave him the dreadful task of receiving the Germans in Paris which had been declared an open city. On 14 June, at the Hôtel Crillon, he had handed over the city. Propaganda accused him of 'having signed, in June 1940, the capitulation of Paris', but that was contentious. There was no capitulation, no signature and Dentz had to obey orders. His reaction to the collapse was identical to that of Marshal Pétain. 'It is not only the army that was beaten on the battlefield' he wrote. 'It is the whole nation that collapsed. The cause is that it had no soul and did not have a solid framework. It lived for 20 years without ideals and seeking only material pleasures, leisure and enjoyment. It renounced the guiding principles of effort and work...All that will have to be corrected.'

It was in December 1940, during an official visit to Marseilles, where Dentz commanded the military district, that the Marshal announced Dentz's appointment to the Levant. He was given no written directives, but it was said that when he took his leave of Vichy, raising the possibility of an English attack, Pétain had advised him: 'A gallant last stand, nothing more, nothing less'. At the end of a particularly trying overland journey, he reached Beirut, where it was raining, on 28 December 1940.

Dentz was an officer who had a mission which he cared about. Responsible for a region, it was inconceivable that he would treat it as he pleased. His sense of duty left him with no choice. 'To disobey', he wrote, 'would be to breach the Armistice, to remove all restraint from the Germans, and to expose the country to demands and invasion: occupation of the free zone, disbandment of the army and air force, loss of the whole fleet and, especially, a takeover of French North Africa.' Dentz, seeing the big picture, could not adopt any attitude other than obedience to his government. He would therefore defend the Levant 'against anyone who wanted to invade it'.

When he arrived, his appointment received lacklustre support.[8] He was 'not greeted enthusiastically in military and civil circles in Beirut' noted Major Brochet. 'Everyone felt that he symbolised the defeat of France, and the rumour quickly spread that his choice had been imposed on Vichy by the Germans in order to serve their policies in the Middle East.' That was an unfounded accusation. Was he a Gaullist? Probably not, on the evidence, but he was not a politician. He was going to counter the propaganda, seize the leaflets, scramble the radio broadcasts coming from Palestine and expel supporters of de Gaulle, but he urged unity. Was he unworthy? 'I do not belong to any clan, to any clique', he affirmed, and he preached moderation. The only important measure he took as soon as he arrived was military in nature: General de Verdilhac replaced General Fougère in command of the troops.

When Dentz arrived, he assembled his troops, first in Beirut and then in Damascus, which he visited without waiting, and declared to his officers: 'Get it into your head that what we are defending here is not Syria, it is French North Africa, because if we fail in our defensive mission, the Germans will take advantage of it to say: You are incapable of using the weapons that we left you, we are going to look after French North Africa ourselves.'

5

De Gaulle

On 24 June 1940, on the eve of the Armistice, all the representatives of France throughout its Empire received an individual call to resistance from General de Gaulle. Even before leaving for London, where he had been for only six days, the leader of Free France (*France Libre*) had already devised his plan.[1] From 18 June onward, he promoted his worldwide vision, illustrated by the poster that all France laughed at: 'We will win because we are the strongest.' To finally defeat Germany, France had to be separated from her colonies. On 30 July, on the BBC, the General renewed his appeal and directed it to the governor-generals:

> Since it is proven that those men who are looking after themselves at Vichy are instruments subservient to the will of the enemy, I assert, in the name of France, that the Empire must not submit itself to their disastrous orders. I affirm that, in the name of France, the French Empire must remain, in spite of them, a French possession! High Commissioners! Administrators! Residents of our colonies and protectorates! Your duty to France, your duty to our colonies, your duty to those whose interests, honour, and life are dependent upon you, lies in refusing to carry out conditions of a terrible armistice. You are responsible for French sovereignty which has currently lapsed!

Vichy, on the other hand, was required, following the Wiesbaden accords, to protect its territories against all aggression, no matter whence it came. Otherwise, the Armistice would be breached and, hence, no longer apply. From this perspective, alas, a Franco–German war implied Franco–French clashes, since the Armistice would no longer exist, and, unfortunately for the country, there was no underground link between the two parties, Vichy and

Free France. De Gaulle accused Vichy of betrayal. On 4 July, Vichy condemned him to four years in prison, and also declared him guilty of treason, of an attack on the safety of the state, of desertion, and of incitement to disobedience. It then condemned him to death and the seizure of his property. What did it matter! His vision went beyond the current situation.

Vichy, on the other hand, carried the crushing burden of the present, with heavy war reparations, loss of rolling stock, raw materials, etc. – France in distress, exhausted, bled dry, with millions of refugees. If London worried about France, Vichy cared about the French. For de Gaulle the prophet, this distress was only incidental and inherent in war. It demanded a soldier's moral standards. For him, 'armistice' and 'capitulation' were the same thing. He stuck to his views. All those who did not agree with him were nothing better than traitors. Nothing was too strong to condemn them. His rebukes were extraordinary: 'The men who are taking care of themselves at Vichy' must appear to be 'instruments subservient to the will of the enemy'. 'Giving way to an inexcusable panic, this clique is in the pay of Germany.' This 'very old marshal and those old beaten generals', 'the team made up of defeatism and treason' form a 'clique of corrupt politicians, racketeers without honour, go-getting public servants and bad generals who rush to take power at the same time as slavery.' They 'sacrificed France to better serve Hitler [...], they 'boast of their servitude' and 'are in the process of handing over to the enemy France's Empire intact'. Beside himself with rage, de Gaulle accused 'Pétain and Weygand whose selfishness, treason and moral decay are so widely known that no one can ignore them.' He continued: 'Surrounded by old men who look after themselves' the Marshal is a 'man from another time', an 'old man 84 years of age, a sad exterior with a past glory [...] carried shoulder high by defeat to take responsibility for the capitulation and to deceive a stunned population.' Weygand? Darlan? 'These despicable or senile leaders, colluding with the invader'; 'these soldiers who are no longer soldiers, who are no longer men and who, because of panic, old age or despair, have abandoned their duty'.

One could give many more examples. On whom was de Gaulle declaring war? Hitler himself was not the object of such diatribes. In London, Raymond Aron had, at times, the impression that General de Gaulle 'seemed to want to wage war more on Vichy than Berlin, on the French, who were prisoners, than the enemy.'

There were plenty of Frenchmen in London who denounced this tone of voice, saying that it did a disservice to Gaullism and that, by insulting the Marshal, it was France that was being humiliated. 'I was certainly not the only one to find, from time to time, that the General's methods were too brusque,' affirmed Maurice Dejean.[2]

Only he represented France, de Gaulle claimed: 'The organisation located at Vichy which claims to carry this name is unconstitutional and submissive to the invader [...] The Free French henceforth constitute the only opportunity for the motherland [...] We are France!' 'I am France,' he declared to Monclar,[3] reiterating the phrase of the young Louis XIV.

The English did not care for this very much. The highest British military authority, Field Marshal Sir Alan Brooke,[4] Chief of the Imperial General Staff, did not think much of de Gaulle. He noted, after their first meeting on 19 August 1940: 'Lunched with Anthony Eden to meet de Gaulle. Was not much impressed by him.' And a little later he added: 'Whatever his qualities were, they were spoiled by his authoritarian manner, his megalomania, and his lack of the spirit of cooperation [...] In all the discussions, he let it be understood that the problem of the liberation of France was mine, while he would concentrate on the way in which he would govern it, as its dictator, as soon as it was liberated.'[5] Lady Spears who, during Christmas 1940, received the General and Madame de Gaulle at her residence, spoke of 'this mysterious giant whose face is never enlivened by any expression, except a grimace of contempt when he speaks about the French people.' The Frenchman's pride fascinated her, 'He was', she wrote, 'like a tormented soul who, at the slightest contact, wants to bite [...] His only relief, in reality his only pleasure, was to hate. He hated everyone, especially those who tried to be his friends.'

Maurice Dejean also shared this impression: 'I was brought along to explain to the English that they had to consider General de Gaulle as a man with the sensitivity of a tormented soul [...] The simple appearance of wanting to encroach upon French sovereignty made him really jump and caused extremely violent reactions, like those of a very sensitive person touched with the tip of a match.' According to General Diégo Brosset,[6] who admired de Gaulle, he always 'had that extreme something which came from his being a visionary and made him go beyond the reality of the moment with a curious mixture of realism and acting like a prophet'.[7] His haughty attitude, like that of an exiled sovereign, caused concern. Spears deplored his propensity for playing at being a monarch, which drew sarcastic remarks. André Labarthe, head of the armaments service in London, labeled him 'Képi 1ᵉʳ' (*Képi the First*).[8] More seriously, Raymond Aron in London, Kérillis in Canada, Roosevelt in Washington and others all feared that he was a new Boulanger, or even another Franco. It was doubted that he was a Republican – he never uttered the word 'republic.'[9]

On 7 April 1941, in Jerusalem, François Coulet, a Free Frenchman, described de Gaulle differently: 'He was already 51 years of age, but he appeared much younger. He had a sturdy body and an unusual face that I could compare to some of Clouet's sketches in the sixteenth century, which show people who are embarrassing because of their eyes which bore into you, or fifteenth century sculptures from Champagne of saints or prophets that are seen in churches.' Saint and prophet: a cult was born.

De Gaulle was born in the nineteenth century. The evidence suggests he mistrusted the English, and from childhood harboured the idea of revenge. The mind of this infantryman was turned towards the continent. He spoke German and his thought was impregnated with German culture. 'This man was thoroughly familiar with Schiller, Hölderlein and Nietzsche, and regarded Bismarck as a model statesman, and considered Clausewitz as one of his masters. His intellectual leanings and his historical fascination were, above all else, turned to this great people solidly ensconced in the centre of Europe' observed Jean-Luc Barré.[10] 'There remained much for him to learn about the homeland of Lloyd George and Chamberlain, whom he considered egocentric and malevolent.' De Gaulle had already become indignant about its diplomatic double-game which, between the wars, had left France alone to 'restrain the Reich'. For him, England remained peripheral: an ally, but of a different kind, basically a competitor; both maritime, pragmatic and commercial, England was in opposition to that sublime France, that Virgin in the stained-glass window, that had he had revered since childhood.

But the General was not alone at the microphone; in London, Brazzaville and Haifa, the radio stations of Free France broadcast his thoughts. According to Guy de Charbonnières, Radio Brazzaville was 'the temple of the Gaullist hard line'.[11]

More than a soldier, Catroux was a diplomat. Appointed by Mandel in July 1939 as Governor-General of Indochina, he was one of the very few who, via his son who acted as an intermediary, lent his moral support to General de Gaulle in response to his appeal to the colonial governors. On 20 June 1940, isolated at the end of the earth, the Governor accepted, on his own authority, the ultimatum made by an enemy considerably more powerful than him. Saving his flag, his administration, his garrisons and his people from the abominable fate of the Dutch in Indonesia and the British in Malaya, he accepted the installation of a Japanese-controlled commission to prevent the passage of all supplies to China – did he have the ability to do otherwise? Criticised by the French government in Bordeaux, he answered on 23 June with a telegram: 'When one is beaten, when one has no aircraft, no anti-aircraft artillery, and no submarines, one tries to keep what one has without having to fight, and one negotiates. That is what I have done. I accept full responsibility and will continue to do so. You say to me that I ought to have consulted you, but I am 4,000 leagues from you and you cannot do anything for me.' In response, Catroux was relieved of his command, and recalled.[12] General de Gaulle never reproached Catroux for his attitude in Indochina, which was, however, similar to that of Pétain in France.

Leaving for France by aircraft with his wife, Catroux slipped away when it stopped in Singapore, and continued his journey to London by flying boat. When he reached London on 17 September, the Battle of Britain was in progress. The English were holding out but nothing was yet decided. When he presented himself at the headquarters of Free France, General de Gaulle was in the middle of attacking Dakar, and René Cassin received him. Catroux: 'I ask you to tell me the whole truth about the Free French movement founded by de Gaulle.'[13] Cassin: 'I gave him a truthful outline of events and our complete lack of all sorts of supplies, especially men, as well as our moral and legal position.'[14] Cassin, giving the reasons for his confidence, indicated the place that France will have among the victors 'if she succeeds in taking part in the battle for reconquest', and he then gave Catroux the text of 7 August concerning the make-up of the Free French forces (*Forces françaises libres*). Finally he stopped talking. 'My silent wait lasted a rather long moment' he remembered 'General Catroux finally broke the silence, saying "All that is a much more serious matter than I dared hope."'

The same day, Catroux went to visit Churchill who knew who he was dealing with; he knew the Frenchman's career. He could measure the influence of this officer, known to the whole of the French Army, accepted in the political sphere and who spoke English – rather than that of an energetic brigadier-general, without connections, who was practically unknown. The two men examined the current situation, and Churchill concluded: 'At this time, I definitely think that you would be more useful in London. The Free French movement needs to be led and I think you ought to take charge of it.'

'The suggestion', wrote Catroux, 'was unexpected and worrying. I could only decline, and I answered the Prime Minister that I had put myself at the service of General de Gaulle, without conditions.' Churchill did not insist, but the idea spread to other British leaders, since Lord Lloyd, Minister for the Colonies, made the same proposal the next day to General Catroux, who declined it in the same fashion. Asked to explain, the Englishman answered: 'Winston Churchill's gratitude and affection for General de Gaulle is unquestioned, but the future of the Free French movement worries him. He [General de Gaulle] had made it his thing.' Churchill:

> had reckoned on Free France rapidly becoming a force and a reality, now his hopes had been dashed. Not only were the members of Free France few in number, but there is no widely known political or military figure or one from intellectual circles able to give depth, weight or dynamism to the movement. In addition, a significant amount of the Frenchmen living in Great Britain are standing apart from Free France, although their commitment to the alliance is clear. It can be concluded that the General's personality is not strong enough and his influence is not sufficiently powerful to elicit the attraction that was expected. Someone else other than him, better known to the general public and more familiar in international circles, would doubtless be successful. The Prime Minister [...] is sensitive to the criticisms that inadequate results attract. Some parliamentary circles were against the principle of the expedition to Dakar.

Older and much higher in rank, Catroux gave his allegiance to de Gaulle. The two men, moreover, knew each other. Prisoners of war together in 1917 in Ingolstadt Castle (Bavaria), they found themselves together again in the Levant in 1930 and de Gaulle was struck by the depth of knowledge of the Muslim world that Catroux displayed.[15]

Unobtrusive, moderate, organized, Catroux had talents that de Gaulle did not. He was adaptable, some said 'Levantine'.

Michel-Christian Davet quotes this cruel portrait drawn up by an adversary: 'Machiavelli had the beauty that is said to be like Don Juan's, tall, thin, conscious of his appearance [...] An old man delighted with himself but charming, attractive and always ready to charm, a long face with regular features, with a hint of the exotic and somewhat Levantine, a perfect nose, dim tired eyes but with an autocratic chin and a quavering voice.'[16]

Spears didn't give a much more favourable opinion of him: 'He can give sensible advice in a pontificating tone of voice which gives it even more weight. The fact that he never declares himself to be in disagreement with the British civil and military authorities has made him very popular with our compatriots. On the other hand, he is incapable of organising anything. His staff is completely laughable. It is composed of public servants who have found refuge in sleepy offices from which no plan or any concrete measures emerge. I am convinced that de Gaulle is correct in considering that, if the name Catroux is an important asset for the Free French movement, it is impossible on the other hand to give him important or difficult tasks.'[17]

At midnight on 27 September 1940, only ten days after arriving in London, Catroux, having been appointed Commander-in-Chief and High Commissioner for Free France in the Middle East, left England. With his plan to stir Syria into revolt having failed straight away, he went on to Fort-Lamy[18] on 18 October to meet the Chief of Free France. When he left the aircraft, while de Gaulle moved forward, this five-star general (*général d'armée;* British four-star), 63 years of age, heels together, saluted de Gaulle, 50 years old, a temporary brigadier-general (French two-star; British one-star). By this regulation gesture, Catroux expressed his allegiance. On 14 November, back in Cairo where he unashamedly set up quarters, he launched a call to rebellion in the Levant. 'In November 1940, he had written to M. Puaux, High Commissioner in the Levant, General Fougère, military supreme commander, and to General Arlabosse, his deputy, in order to outline ways to get in touch with them. But these multiple attempts had produced no result [...] From Beirut, Arlabosse sent Catroux a correct but frosty answer.'[19] From Beirut, General Dentz did not answer his letters, nor did Admiral Godfroy in Alexandria.

Among the people who have major roles in the gathering drama is Major-General Sir Edward Spears KBE CB MC.[20] Little known among the French, he worked ceaselessly to progress the action and to prepare for the final result. Head of the British Military

Mission to General de Gaulle in 1940, General Spears supported him initially, before changing his attitude completely. Having become hostile to French interests in 1941, he became more and more openly opposed to the Free French. Doing a U-turn in 1942, he encouraged the Syrians and Lebanese to get rid of the French.

Nurtured on French culture, very much at home in Parisian high society, this man knew France intimately. In 1917, he carried out liaison duties between the commanders of the two Allied armies, the future Marshal Pétain and Field Marshal Sir Douglas Haig. Fabre-Luce in 1940: 'General Sir Edward Spears had many friends in France. He spoke French extremely well and, in a snobbish way, called himself Francophile. He was a Member of Parliament and President of the Franco-English Club in the British Parliament. In fact, he pursued British policy, which was Churchill's, and that of the English since General Bonaparte had landed one day in Cairo, that is to say that he wanted the Middle East to be an exclusive preserve of the English and that all the Arab and Muslim countries on the way to India would remain obedient to the English.'

Georges Buis, a Free Frenchman: 'General Spears was an attractive man in spite of a square-shouldered and thickset physique. He knew French marvellously well and was capable of singing Burgundian songs and doing Provençal imitations. Everyone said: "What a great friend of France!" Apparently when he said "I adore France" he meant that he loved living in France, that he adored French cooking, and that he adored the French countryside, the Côte d'Azur and the rest, but he detested France itself. All his actions had obviously been to oust us from the Levant.'

It was on 11 June 1940, during the dramatic Briare conference,[21] that he met General de Gaulle for the first time. On 17 June in Bordeaux, when everything was collapsing, he accompanied de Gaulle to London in the aircraft Churchill had put at his disposal. Spears considered himself to be the 'inventor' of de Gaulle and tried to guide and protect the General in London society, but the General extricated himself brusquely. As the incarnation of France, he could not be a 'Society' attraction. Spears did not insist, but the atmosphere between the two men immediately deteriorated. Spears admired de Gaulle nonetheless, and Churchill asked him to resume his role as intermediary between Free France and the British chiefs: himself, Sir Alan Brooke and General Dill. Spears thus became an essential linchpin in Allied relations. As such, in September, he accompanied de Gaulle in the planning of the disastrous affair at Dakar – a fiasco that, according to Catroux, caused a gulf between the two men. General de Gaulle, however, went to spend Christmas with General and Lady Spears at their country home, but their relations, already difficult, rapidly deteriorated. De Gaulle noted in his *Mémoires* that already in March 1941, during a weekend at 'Chequers', Churchill remarked to him: 'I know you have grievances against Spears as chief of our liaison with you. However, I ask you earnestly to keep him on and to take him to the East. That is a personal service you can do for me.'

On 26 March, seated next to Colonel Diégo Brosset during his flight to Khartoum, Mrs Brittain-Jones, the more or less covert envoy of London to King George of Greece, informed him, speaking to a Gaullist: 'Spears hates you!'

Commander-in-Chief of the British forces in the Middle East, Sir Archibald Wavell had lost an eye in France during World War I. He was, all agreed, a great soldier. He had always had excellent relations with the French, first of all with Weygand, and then with Mittelhauser. He knew that Weygand, who had become the Minister for National Defence at Vichy, was keen to observe the Armistice, but that he was in no way hostile to England. Had not Weygand personally congratulated him on his successes in Cyrenaica? Via the High Commissioner in the Levant, Vichy had also signified its sympathy for England. Puaux had declared to the British Consul in Beirut: 'The Army of the Levant will re-enter the battle, but let me set the time of this decision.'

The likelihood of collusion between Vichy and the Axis powers thus seemed, in Cairo, much less probable than an Arab uprising. However, upsetting France in Syria would risk causing problems which could spread. Faced with German victories in Europe, France and England could both see their prestige wane. Seized by the hope of independence, the Arab world seemed gripped by unrest. Being anxious for stability, General Wavell, like the British High Commissioner in Cairo, therefore wished that the exchanges between the two mandates were not upset. 'The problem of winning over of the Levant must not be raised', he affirmed to Catroux when he arrived in Egypt.

In spite of Italian protests, the collaboration between the former allies continued on without upset after the Armistice in France. The mood of Franco–British relations in the Middle East remained excellent. Supplies coming from metropolitan France arrived without difficulty, and exports – wool, cotton, silk – left in the opposite direction for France. Convoys of British weapons for Turkey continued to transit French territory via the Syrian railways, and British troops still used the track which, crossing Lebanon for over 60 km, linked Transjordan to Palestine. In exchange, the English only partially applied an economic blockade.

Naturally, de Gaulle learned very quickly that the supposed blockade, which he had been demanding for many months, did not exist. He even learned that commercial negotiations were taking place between Cairo, Beirut and Djibouti. Supported by Spears, he protested but without success, and at the end of April 1941, a commercial treaty, assuring the regular resupply of the Levant, was concluded between Cairo and Beirut. The English double game was evident. Even Spears denounced it: 'If we support General Weygand [...] we can only do it to the detriment of General de Gaulle. It seems to me that we must choose once and for all between the two men. But if we choose General de Gaulle, we have to give him unwavering support. If he feels that we remain faithful to the ideal of Free France, we will be able to count on his loyalty [...] He will make a loyal ally, on condition that we ourselves remain faithful to the ideal that we were defending when he came and linked his fate with ours.'[22]

Thus Gaullist sternness for the first time came up against English pragmatism. Outraged, the General was very soon convinced that England was pursuing its aims of hegemony over the French Mandate.

On 8 December 1940, Catroux wrote to General de Gaulle: 'Syria is a bitter fruit which continues to not want to ripen. I fear that we can have it only by force.'[23] Soon, he wrote a confidential note, dated 31 March 1941, that Jean-Luc Barré found in his archives:[24]

It would be futile to dispute the failure of the French Mandate in the Levant in the years before the war. Accepted in Lebanon as a means of defence against absorption by Syria, it has always encountered subdued hostility, declared or armed, from inside Syria which has not buckled under, because we have armed forces and we remain, in spite of our faults, the victors of the Great War. They have submitted to us, they fear us, they do not like us in Damascus or Aleppo and, more generally, in the Muslim world. The Armistice and especially our decline, the result of our acceptance of defeat, have destroyed the respect that people still had for us [...] A large degree of aversion for all things French has developed, which has been aggravated by the clumsiness and incompetence of the Mandate authorities and the prevarication of too many public servants. The wishes of the Syrians have, since then, been finally freed from French supervision, whether it be that of Vichy or that of Free France [...] The minimum that the nationalists are asking for is total independence, the removal of all forms of control and the removal of all French public servants, in exchange for which they would agree to conclude a treaty of alliance, the conditions of which are still unclear.

Great Britain does not have political and territorial aims in the Levant. She is loyal with regards to Vichy France; she is the faithful ally of Free France [...] the current policy of Great Britain, imposed by necessity, aims to help General Dentz, to reassure him, to obtain advantages from him and, if possible, to win him over. This policy, as can be seen, foresees the occupation of Syria by force only in case of absolute necessity [...] Free France must obviously abide by this policy [...] The retaking of the Levant by Free France strikes obstacles which for the moment cannot be overcome. We do not have the hope of being called upon by the army [...] A recourse to force is momentarily prohibited and a policy of stalling must prevail.

If the analysis was clear and was a warning, the Chief of Free France – 'too uncompromising in everything' according to Barré, and haunted by his latent hostility towards the British – did not draw inspiration from it. The looming drama came from this attitude.

6

The Noose Tightens

Secret contacts took place between Vichy and London. For example, conversations occurred between the embassies in Madrid; the British Consul in Tangiers was given the responsibility of contacting General Weygand in Algiers[1] by Churchill and, on 23 October 1940, coming from Vichy, Professor Rougier was received by Lord Halifax, head of the Foreign Office in London. On 25 October, King George VI had a 'message of good will'[2] sent to Marshal Pétain. Moreover, via the intermediary of M. Pierre Dupuy, Ambassador of Canada in France, a correspondence was started between Lord Halifax and his personal friend Jacques Chevalier, Secretary of State in Vichy. Negotiations also involved Admiral Auphan.[3, 4] These contacts, ended on 9 December 1940 with a secret accord ratified by the British government.

'De Gaulle', remembered Churchill, 'naturally saw with a very bad eye all the dealings we had with Vichy. He felt that we had a duty of loyalty to him alone. To maintain his image with the French people, it seemed to him equally necessary to adopt a proud and haughty attitude towards "perfidious Albion", at a time when he was only an exile living among us and receiving our protection. He had to show himself inflexible with the English in order to demonstrate to the French that he wasn't in the pay of England.' Churchill added mischievously, knowing what came next: 'It can be truly stated the he pursued this policy persistently!'

These secret contacts, although exceptional, did not stop, since on Tuesday 31 December 1940, Mr Matthews, United States Chargé d'Affaires, forwarded two notes from the British government to Marshal Pétain, who dictated a reply. On 24 October 1940, a serious turning point occurred. At the station at Montoire (Loir-et-Cher), Marshal Pétain met the *Führer* of the *Reich*. The interview was fairly limited to personal contact and light topics, but, posted in all the newspaper shops in France, was a photo on the front page of *L'Illustration*, the only large illustrated paper of the time, showing the Marshal shaking Hitler's hand. It caused a great deal of disapproval. Worse still, in his speech on 25 October, the Marshal announced to the nation that he would embark on a process of collaboration. The photo would not be forgotten, and the word 'collaboration' had been uttered. As a result, there was widespread astonishment. The first crack had appeared in the image of the Marshal of France who, until then, had been unanimously revered; the state of grace had lasted four months. However, on the same day that the Montoire meeting took place, the leader of Vichy had made it known to Churchill, via Louis Rougier, his chargé de mission in London, that he would not try to retake the colonies that had revolted, but also that he would resist all attempts to conquer any part whatsoever of the Empire. This message confirmed the assurances given by Weygand.

Only Laval seemed convinced that Germany would maintain, long term, its predominance over Europe. For him, the only future for France was an alliance with Germany. Persuaded that he could overcome his adversaries by talking, Laval multiplied his contacts with the occupying forces in Paris. At the same time, the Germans expelled the French from Lorraine. Laval, who carried out this policy alone, never gave the Head of State anything but notes. His attitude pushed the Marshal to carry out a brutal act: on 13 December, at a meeting of the Council of Ministers (*Conseil des ministres*), on the pretext of a reshuffle, he asked for a written resignation from each member, which he then gave back to each person, with the exception of Messieurs Laval and Ripert. Put under house arrest, Laval left Vichy under escort. In Autumn 1940, Vichy suddenly interrupted all efforts at collaboration.[5] The Germans were furious. 'The *Reich* cannot be confident in a government that does not include M. Laval,' declared Otto Abetz, the German Ambassador. Hitler was very annoyed; for him it was an affront. On his orders, all relations with France ceased immediately, except the Control Commission. On 14 December, the line of demarcation between the Occupied and the Unoccupied Zones, already strictly policed, became watertight, even for French ministers.

At Vichy, Darlan soon replaced Pierre-Étienne Flandin, the temporary Vice-President. Would Darlan's arrival change anything? In a spectacular gesture of symbolic reconciliation, the enemy tried to bring the two parties together: the German *Reich* was going to give back to France the ashes of the King of Rome,[6] who had died in exile in Vienna in 1832. The Marshal refused the invitation to attend the ceremony for fear, it was said, of being arrested. Darlan was the only prominent French person present. In the dull December light, with a cavalry escort, the gun-carriage, on which the coffin was placed, moved up the esplanade of the Invalides, which was absolutely deserted under driving snow, before going under the porch. There was no band and it was a really mournful atmosphere. The gesture fell flat. Hitler shouted, 'It was a trick!' Franco–German relations became even worse. Nevertheless, to sound out Darlan, Hitler summoned him, on 24 December, to his train at the Ferrières-sur-Epte station near Beauvais. During the interview the *Führer* spoke a lot, even excessively. He got carried away, declaring: 'I hate Weygand, the most notorious of your anti-German people!' Finally, however, and against all odds, he settled down and became more formal; speaking 'as a soldier', and 'for the last time', he agreed to implement the policy of collaboration spoken of at Montoire.

Pleasant, reserved and self-controlled, Darlan gave Hitler a letter from the Marshal detailing his good faith: 'I intend moving forward in the very spirit of Montoire', it asserted. The result? Words and more words, words that committed but still just words. No agreement was reached.[7] The French lack of will was evident.

From then on, Germany blackmailed by hunger. With the demarcation line unable to be crossed, a shutter was closed across France. Trains could no longer enter. In the free zone, there was a severe lack of coal and food: France was strangled.

Saint-Exupéry:[8]

> Let us be calm. We really need a trustee to negotiate with the victor for the provision to France of a little grease for our railway wagons [...] France is undergoing a permanent and heinous blackmail [...] A quarter of a turn of the key on deliveries of these goods and 100,000 children will die in six months. When an executed hostage dies, his sacrifice becomes widely known. His death serves to strengthen French unity. But when the Germans murder, by a simple delay in reaching an agreement on grease, 100,000 five-year old hostages die; nothing makes up for this slow and silent bloodletting [...] We all condemn any spirit of collaboration between France and Germany, but while some

people accuse France of treason, others read into its behaviour only the result of uncompromising blackmail.[9]

Jean Ferniot: 'There has been much talk about food restrictions during the Occupation. Deadlier among old people was the lack of coal. The majority of dwellings before the war did not have central heating. There was heat only in one room, rarely in the bedrooms unless there was someone sick.'[10]

Tightening the screws, Germany increased its demands everywhere. The government received an 'order' from Wiesbaden for military equipment, aircraft, aircraft engines, munitions, explosives, and trucks. The occupiers demanded almost the whole of France's production of aluminium, and its stocks of Moroccan copper and cobalt. In the Ardennes, Meuse, Meurthe-et-Moselle, Aisne and the Vosges regions, German colonists took possession of 170,000 hectares and evicted 20,000 French agricultural workers. An obligatory work-service was imposed in Alsace and Lorraine. Vichy, powerless, stood by the pillage of France. This situation lasted four months.

This crisis should be clarified in order to understand what happened later; it explains the negotiations which followed and the war in Syria. When, four months later, Germany, at the beginning of May, suddenly came and asked for France's help, Admiral Darlan, happy to see Germany renewing the dialogue, tried to take advantage of it and to argue over his reply. If one has to remain dignified, one also has to eat. London failed to take into consideration the effects of the loss of French raw materials, its greatly reduced food supplies and the loss of French farmland to German interlopers.

Dentz, 3,000 km away in the Levant, found himself confronted with delicate tasks. Invested with the highest civil powers, this soldier had to resolve diplomatic, economic and political problems for which he had not been prepared and for which he had received no directive. 'When I arrived on 29 December 1940,' he stated, 'I received members of the French colony, the public servants and all the diplomatic corps. There were the consuls of Turkey, Brazil, Argentina, Sweden, even Greece and Poland. There was a representative of the British Consuls-General in Damascus and Aleppo, the American Consul-General, as well as M. von Hentig, the German who was then in Damascus.'

'I found M. Havard, the British Consul-General, rather embarrassed. I received him straight away, welcomed him warmly, and said to him a sentence that I remember verbatim: "I am keen to have appropriate relations with the representative of Great Britain, between the representatives of two great countries which, as allies, have fought two great wars against Germany." The Consul left immediately, completely reassured about my attitude and the welcome that he expected from me.' Dentz, in effect, was going to strive to maintain as friendly relations as possible with his neighbours, Turkey to the north and Palestine to the south. 'On the frontier of southern Lebanon', he said, 'very frequent contacts took place between the representatives of the High Commissioner and the English mandate. They were always marked by the greatest courtesy, and they always settled frontier questions and business questions favourably. The head of foreign business services went to Jerusalem frequently to negotiate deals.'[11] 'At the same time I closed my eyes to the trafficking that happened at our frontiers [...] The deliveries of weapons to Turkey, which were carried out as much by England as by the United States, went via Basra [before crossing Syria by train] I knew what was happening: wagons supposedly carrying bags of wheat clanked slightly from the noise of weapons when they were trodden on [...] I never tried to eliminate this business. The Turks, however, admitted it later.'

Although relations between General Dentz and the British representative remained good, they weren't with the German representative, Otto von Hentig. Dentz had only just arrived, so the French could not oppose the arrival, on 11 January 1941, of this specialist in Arab matters, who was also a high-ranking public servant from the Wilhelmstrasse.[12] Saying he was put in charge of an information mission, this diplomat was mainly a propaganda agent for the Germans who, naturally, wanted to take advantage of the latent disorder in Syria to stir up the malcontents against France. Interned on 3 September 1939, then liberated by the Armistice, the German residents in the Levant were again free. Businessmen, shopkeepers or archeologists; many were probably enemy agents.

'I knew perfectly well what he was doing' said General Dentz of Hentig during his trial. He began to run around the country and caused an enormous amount of turmoil. The majority of political and nationalist leaders contacted him, if not directly at least via intermediaries. It is known that he contacted Riad el-Solh,[13] as well as very active Palestinians. He also made a great impression on the nationalist student youth, in particular members of Pierre

Gemayel's *Phalange*, a movement dissolved in 1937 because of its pro-Nazi stand. In Syria, the *Najjadehs*[14] demonstrated, shouting: 'Arab countries for the Arabs.'

Were the Germans the only problem? In the short term there was another important problem: supplies. The situation that Dentz found when he arrived was dangerous: no wheat, no sugar, no petrol, and no electricity in the evening; taxis not working, prices climbing, and empty cash-drawers. Having no business, the shopkeepers were worried and, having no work, the workers were dying of hunger. Extreme poverty was increasing. There was a threat of demonstrations breaking out. Soon after his arrival, on 10 January, the new High Commissioner wrote to his government: 'I must win the wheat battle and I have everyone against me [...] the population [...] the businessmen [...] the English' and, naturally, the Germans.

Dentz immediately took steps: sugar and rice were rationed, stocks of cereals greater than 200 kg had to be declared, and a bonus payment was instituted for informers about hidden stocks. Prices, however, continued to climb. If the Syrian population still seemed well disposed towards France, nothing resisted hunger. In March 1941, the price of bread quadrupled. Everywhere there was agitation. A revolt threatened. In Damascus 40 agitators were arrested.

Before he met people in political circles, the Directory which governed Damascus, and the nationalist groups, Vichy suggested to the High Commissioner that he adopt a hard line. Noting that the leaders still remained as inflexible as before, the General recommended to Vichy that a charter be set up defining the remit of the mandatory power and the Syrian government. Alas, whether it was under Blum or Pétain, old-time French inertia blocked all hope of reform. In spite of Dentz's advice to urgently adopt a liberal attitude, nothing changed. The tension continued to mount. Swastikas appeared in Damascus; that had to be stopped and Dentz took action. Armoured vehicles left the barracks, and the police were reinforced by the army. Gunfire was soon heard. Matters escalated. The demonstrations degenerated into violence: on 5 March there were six wounded in Damascus; on 14 March, three dead and two wounded at Homs; and on 23 March nine dead and eight wounded in Aleppo. In solidarity with the struggle for independence, Lebanon declared a general strike and, in Beirut on 1 April, a demonstration by Muslim women and children got out of hand. A volley of rifle fire resulted in two dead and six wounded. The Directory resigned. A major crisis loomed. Were the events of 1925 going to recur?

The unrest assumed alarming proportions on 7 March. At the Grand Mosque in Aleppo, an imam denounced 'oppression by the colonisers'. At Homs, Hamma, and Deir-ez-Zor, the markets closed following the call of the *Najjadehs*, and a brutal repression caused deaths and injuries. The High Commissioner had the *Najjadehs* dissolved in Damascus and the *Phalange* in Beirut. Pierre Gemayel was arrested, questioned and locked up. In a letter of 12 March to Jamil Mardam Bey, Choukri Kouatli, leader of the Syrian nationalists, described the situation: 'There were hundreds of arrests. Some prisoners like Sobhi Komanu – an old man – and our friends in different areas were condemned to forced labour. There was a great deal of oppression and limitless injustice [...] The Senegalese were everywhere [...] there was a general strike [...] the army and its tanks occupied the streets. There were victims. All the Syrian towns took part in the strike.'

To prevent communications, the military blocked telephone traffic that they controlled, vehicular movement was prohibited and, on 2 April, police powers were transferred to the army. To travel by car, a permit was required. All public places closed at 8:00 p.m. Dentz informed Vichy that, the situation having worsened after the death of 48 people, he proposed to promulgate three decrees: the first concerned designating a head of government assisted by a Council of Ministers; the second dealt with how to choose its members; the third created a Council of State with judicial and legislative powers. A French adviser would fulfill the duties of a commissioner of the government. Finally, Dentz insisted on having an agreement with the nationalists in order to find a *modus vivendi*.

General Dentz contacted the Syrian government once more in an endeavour to calm the persisting unrest, but the strike continued. Now realising that he could not reach an agreement with the nationalists, he circulated a solemn declaration in which he confirmed France's wish to grant independence 'when the world situation had stabilized' and announced that an economic and social programme would be immediately implemented to reduce unemployment and improve food supplies. Giving guarantees to the rebels, the High Commissioner announced the creation of a consultative assembly, 'composed of the principal representatives of the political, economic and cultural life of the country and of the younger generations.' To do this, he sought the collaboration of the Syrian authorities, and although his declaration fell short of meeting their claims, the members of the independence movement, given the gravity of the situation, agreed to respect a truce. Thus, on 2 April, the president of the Damascus Chamber of Industry and Commerce, M. Khaled Bey el-Azem, agreed to form a government. In Lebanon, Émile Eddé, who had resigned as president of the Directory, was replaced by Alfred Naccache. The nationalists did not take part in either of the two new governments, but the general strike was lifted. The bloodshed was stopped. Nevertheless, a platoon of armoured cars was stationed at the citadel in Damascus, ready to intervene in the central suburbs.

The High Commissioner's suggestion no doubt was agreed to by Vichy, since it was published. France proposed that the High Commissioner would appoint the head of government who would himself designate the ministers. The nationalists indignantly refused such a solution, and sent a memorandum to the High Commissioner demanding the return of the constitutional regime. The crisis was thus not resolved. On Thursday 3 April, rioting resumed in the provinces. French officers were attacked, there were three dead and 85 wounded on 18 April at Hama, and one dead on 22 April at Aleppo. In spite of this, the government began its functions on 5 April. Twenty-six of the 34 political prisoners were released, and eight suspects were brought before a military court. Students demonstrated to obtain the release of their comrades, but Damascus calmed down. The strike was over.

In April, at a time when the Levant was in turmoil, France withdrew from the League of Nations which had, in 1919, mandated it to guide Ottoman Syria towards independence. By leaving the League of Nations, France called into question its right of trusteeship. The nationalists sent a note to General Dentz to once again demand an immediate return to the constitutional regime.

From Cairo, the English watched this turbulence anxiously. Half-reassured by his confirmation to the British Consul, General Dentz had said: 'I have no intention of having an anti-British policy' – the British felt that the ground, undermined by German propaganda, was crumbling under their feet. The Arab world was in turmoil, German forces were advancing everywhere, and British rule seemed close to its end. In Egypt, King Farouk refused to declare war on the Axis, whose forces were close to his territory; Iran became a German den; and Iraq, through which reinforcements travelled from India, was affected by hostile activity. The disturbances which beset the French mandate threatened to engulf the whole of the Middle East. A British military document confirmed that, in Syria, the majority of the political parties and men of influence were pro-German. An Arab success would therefore be a German success. Henceforth, in the face of a grave threat, what policy should be adopted? England, it seemed, hesitated.

Glubb Pasha, head of the Transjordanian forces: 'For 11 years, I worked in Transjordan and made a tremendous effort in the middle of problems and clashes along the Syrian frontier. During this whole period [...] we were constantly accused by the French of plotting against them [...] We had, however, always abstained from interfering in any way in Syrian affairs [...] And suddenly, in February 1941, we received secret instructions from England turning the situation around. We were ordered to contact the people in Syria with a view to preparing a possible resistance against German-Italian-Vichy governments. With this aim, we had at our disposal all the money needed. We then agreed that Kirkbride would deal with the Druse and I would look after the bedouin tribes.'[15] Glubb Pasha contacted the Syrian bedouin and Druse, confirmed Davet. Moreover, contact was made with Dentz. What did it matter about the Gaullists? A dialogue had to be maintained with the French in the Levant in order to avoid increasing their problems to the point that they would join the opposite camp. In March, secret conversations were held between Cairo and Beirut. At the end of April, an agreement was concluded and the British blockade was partly lifted, business with the United States could resume and the French, relieved, suddenly felt less isolated.[16] Catroux, who was disturbed by it, wrote to Anthony Eden, Secretary of State at the Foreign Office: 'The duplicity of Dentz, his lack of character and his obedience to Vichy can only help our enemies.'

It was now seven months since the Battle of Britain had been won. However, in the Mediterranean, Germany continued its conquests. General Sir Alan Brooke, Chief of the Imperial General Staff, the highest British military authority, wrote this appreciation:

> England is not only threatened by invasion, her maritime links are at the mercy of the enemy. This overpopulated island, heavily industrialised, depends on sea transport for two-thirds of its food and the bulk of its raw materials [...] Her vital lines of

communications are threatened [...] The crucial route to Egypt, the Persian Gulf and oil from Iraq, India, Malaya and Australasia must pass along hostile coasts for over nearly 4,000 miles in the Red Sea, the Mediterranean and the Bay of Biscay. [...] The French Fleet and French North Africa being neutral in the most favourable of circumstances and hostile in the worst, with Italy controlling the two shores of the central Mediterranean and hence a geographical situation cutting it in two, this ambitious nation, with an air force and six battleships, 23 cruisers and more than 200 destroyers and submarines [...], the historical naval domination by the Royal Navy seemed as threatened in the Mediterranean as in the Atlantic.

In the Nile Valley, a British Army of 55,000 men, equipped with about 200 old aircraft, found itself alone, after the defection of the French Armies in Syria and French North Africa, to counter an attack by 415,000 Italians, based in Libya to the west, and in Ethiopia and Eritrea to the south, supported by 1,700 modern aircraft of which 500 were already in Africa. The Mediterranean Fleet – reduced by the French flotilla neutralized in Alexandria – having fallen back to Alexandria, hence Malta found itself in the position of an isolated outpost only 60 miles from the coast of Sicily, but 800 from the closest British air base. Even Franco's artillery was in a commanding position over Gibraltar. It was thus not very surprising that the majority of American officials considered that the British position was extremely dangerous. Aware of the rapidity with which its army collapsed, the French high command considered that in three months Britain would have had its 'neck wrung like a chicken'.[17]

What disturbed General Wavell, Commander-in-Chief of British Forces in the Middle East, was obviously not only the French in the Levant to the north, but the Italians in Eritrea to the south and, to the west, those in Cyrenaica. To face the 250,000 Italians, he had only 55,000, under-equipped and poorly trained men.

On 11 November 1940, Swordfish torpedo aircraft from the aircraft carrier HMS *Illustrious* had surprised the Italian fleet at anchor in Taranto, and immobilised three of its six battleships; and on 28 March 1941, Cunningham's fleet had inflicted a severe defeat on the Italian fleet off Cape Matapan.[18] From now on, being out of contention, the Italian Navy no longer put to sea. The Royal Navy had regained the mastery of the Eastern Mediterranean which was an immense relief, even if the *Regia Aeronautica* (the

Italian Air Force) still maintained air superiority in the Central Mediterranean area. However, major threats remained. Not only did Italy occupy a dominant strategic position in its African strongholds but, France being occupied, the *Wehrmacht* was now available to reach Gibraltar through Spain, and so block access to the Mediterranean, and invade French North Africa. Franco now reinforced his friendship with the Axis, and Hitler met him at Hendaye in October, to ask him to join Germany in the war. If the Spanish dictator showed himself to be friendly on the surface, nothing was agreed to. For the moment, he remained neutral.

In November 1940, prodded by an extremely impatient Mussolini, and a month after having received the order, Graziani set off towards Alexandria with 150,000 of his colonial army. O'Connor crushed its vanguard at Sidi Barrani on 9 December, then pushed the bulk of the Italians back beyond Benghazi which he himself entered on 6 February 1941. It was a splendid success. In eliminating six Italian divisions, and capturing 130,000 men, 400 tanks and 850 guns, O'Connor, for the loss of less than 2,000 men, restored British control of the Central Mediterranean.

What triumphs did the *Duce* dream about, this new Caesar? Having concentrated his national army in Albania, he launched himself on Greece on the night of 27 November 1940. He wanted to dazzle the Germans. Thwarted in his plans, Hitler rushed to Florence where a radiant Mussolini announced that his troops were advancing. They were moving forward on the Epirus plain that the Greeks, withdrawing 35 km, had abandoned. The Italian advance soon slowed, then ground to a halt. The Greeks waited for the invaders in the mountain gorges of the Pindus range. Counter-attacking, the Greek General Alexandros Papagos pushed the Italians back 48 km and took 5,000 prisoners. Only the bad weather and snow saved the Italians from disaster. Dismayed, Mussolini called for help from the Germans. His situation was becoming grave: facing him, British forces were coming to support the Greeks.[19] For three months, the *Duce* will suffer failures if the *Reich* does not help him. In March, the Germans intervened: on 27 March 1941, the *Luftwaffe* bombed Belgrade for two days – there were 17,000 dead – and on 10 April General Wilhelm List's XIIth Army crossed the Yugoslav frontier. Belgrade fell on 12 April 1941, Yugoslavia capitulated on 17 April, and Anglo–Greek resistance collapsed, so that panzers camped on the Acropolis on 27 April. On 28 April, the British Expeditionary Force re-embarked, being bombed as it did so, and leaving behind 21,000 men and a large amount of equipment.[20]

To try to save what remained of the Italians in Tripolitania, Rommel landed in Africa on 12 February 1941. On 17 February, the DAK – *Deutsche Afrika Korps* (German Africa Corps) – was set up administratively. But maritime transport had been seriously affected by the Royal Navy and Royal Air Force[21] and Rommel had to wait until 24 March 1941 before he could attack. Overrunning the forward post at El-Agheila, he reached Tobruk on 11 April. The British continued to withdraw. Tobruk was now encircled. Faced with such rapid progress, the Cairenes took fright and an exodus commenced. It was expected that the Germans would soon appear. King Farouk, delighted, telegraphed to the *Führer*: '90 per cent of Egyptians are clearly sympathetic to Germany on which I have refused to declare war [...] The people will receive the Germans and Italians as liberators.'

In this conflict, which was played out on an enormous scale, the Germans regained what the Italians had lost, but Abyssinia was too far for them. On 19 January, under Wavell's orders, two small Commonwealth armies[22] and the Orient Brigade (*Brigade d'Orient*) of the Free French Forces (*Forces françaises libres*) attacked Italian forces in Eritrea, which were four or five times larger. On 6 April, having lost 185,000 prisoners, the Italian Army capitulated. For their part, Colonel Ralph Monclar's French Foreign Legionnaires conquered Massawa on 8 February and took 10,000 prisoners. At the beginning of summer the Negus was restored to his throne. However, the situation was increasingly critical. Germany now dominated all of Europe, except Spain; in Africa, she had reached the Turkish frontier and the edges of Egypt. Her shadow also lay over the Near East. Crete, Cyprus and Syria were threatened. Her objective was the Canal.

'Towards the end of April, General Dill [Chief of the Imperial General Staff] informed Wavell [in Cairo] that, given the threat of a German invasion in Syria, the Foreign Office envisaged drawing Dentz's attention to the danger of an airborne attack and asking him to make preparations for its defence. He [General Dill] asked Wavell what troops he could spare to help Dentz counter this invasion, adding that he advised against using the Free French unless he was asked for them. Dentz replied that he would resist any encroachment, but he had to obey his government's instructions. Wavell replied to Dill on 28 April, at the time when Britain was evacuating Greece, that he had only some spare cavalry.[23] London answered that if Dentz resisted, all available means ought to be devoted to helping him. If he didn't, Wavell would undertake 'all action that was, in his opinion, possible'. The Air Force should strike immediately. De Gaulle was going to be informed, but it would be up to Wavell to decide if it was necessary to use Free French troops.'[24]

In London, on 7 August 1940, a basic agreement was concluded between Churchill and de Gaulle. It was agreed that General de Gaulle would start to form a French volunteer force. Organised against 'common enemies', this force 'could never bear arms against France'.

In England at this time, General de Gaulle had won over some of the legionnaires (*Légion étrangère*) and mountain infantry (*Chasseurs alpins*) of the expeditionary force sent to Norway, as well as some sailors from ships seized by Great Britain. Free French land forces then numbered fewer than 2,000 men, and Free French naval forces (*Forces Navales Françaises Libres*) less than 500 men. With nearly 50,000 men, the Poles were much more numerous.

In England, on 30 June, General Béthouart, who commanded the troops repatriated from Norway – 14,000 mountain infantry, cavalry, sappers and legionnaires – had authorised de Gaulle, a classmate from Saint-Cyr, to come and recruit from his men. In an hour, he had won over 1,300 volunteers, as well as 900 of the 1,619 legionnaires of the *13ᵉ Demi-Brigade de la Légion Étrangère* (13 DBLE; 13th Demi-Brigade of the Foreign Legion), especially Spanish Republicans who were anxious not be handed over to Franco. Until victory was achieved, these forces remained the spearhead of Free France. Among the officers who rallied to de Gaulle were Monclar and Koenig.[25] Thanks to these men joining him, the Free French forces had about 3,000 men on 14 July 1940: 2,000 in Great Britain, 600 in Egypt and 300 in Gold Coast (now Ghana). In April 1941, with the addition of four battalions coming from French Equatorial Africa and escapees from Syria, the Gaullists had about 5,400 in their ranks. Therefore, by grouping together all available troops, after the success in Eritrea, General de Gaulle decided, on 11 April 1941, to create the 1st Free French Division (*1ʳᵉDivision française libre*) and to appoint General Legentilhomme as its commander.[26]

The operational aims of Wavell and de Gaulle did not completely coincide. Wavell had only one care – the Canal. De Gaulle's was quite different. Without a territorial base, almost without an audience, he was still a cause without a base. Only the possession of a capital and a large territory would give credibility to his cause. It alone would show that he was not a pawn in the British game but an independent reality. Since the failure at Dakar in September, he wished, he said, 'to extend Free France's authority to Damascus and Beirut', as well as, if possible, to win over to his cause the large army there. The addition of the force of 37,000 men in the Levant would enormously inflate his meagre 5,400 men.

Churchill, in spite of Dakar, now pushed de Gaulle all the way. He showed total confidence in him – support without reservation. On 4 April, he sent him a telegram in Brazzaville: 'We are very grateful for the support the Free French forces gave us in the victorious campaign [in Eritrea] [...] You have never hesitated nor failed in the service of our common cause, you have the full confidence of His Majesty's Government and you embody the hopes of millions of French men and women who do not despair for the future of France and the French empire.'

Now that Syria found itself threatened by the enemy, she presented a strategic stake. De Gaulle:

> It seemed evident to me that the enemy was soon going to send some aerial squadrons to Syria from Greece. Their presence in the middle of Arab countries would cause disturbances which could be a prelude to the arrival of the *Wehrmacht*. On the other hand, from airfields in Damascus, Rayak, and Beirut – 500 km from Suez and Port Said – German aircraft could easily bomb the Canal and its approaches [...] But these plans would not meet with British approval. General Wavell, occupied by three battlefronts, did not want to open a fourth one at any price [...] He told himself that, on the strength of reports from the British Consul-General in Beirut, Dentz would resist the Germans, if it became necessary.

René Cassin: 'De Gaulle let me know that he wanted the advice of the members of the Defence Council regarding the attitude to be taken in case England and Turkey should be induced to occupy by force all or part of the Levant [...] Do we have to stand by and witness this occupation as a matter of form along with supporting protests or would we not be better advised to join forces in the occupation?'[27]

On 3 March 1941, for the first time, the members of the Defence Council of the Empire were consulted – by cable if they were far from London – on the possibility of entering Syria by force. The military men – Muselier, Leclerc, Sicé and Larminat – were against. They showed that, for reasons of troop strength, the operation would not be possible without the British, and Leclerc was against the idea of a fratricidal conflict. The politicians – Cassin, Éboué and Pleven – were in favour of intervention. The character of the conflict was becoming clearer.

Shortly afterwards, on 14 March, the Chief of Free France left London for the Near East. He was accompanied by Spears whom he didn't like but had to put up with on Churchill's insistence. This trip inspired the famous phrase, in the best de Gaulle style: 'Towards the complicated Orient, I flew with simple ideas.' The formula became a slogan for some and an admission for others who speak of simplistic ideas.

On 1 April 1941, de Gaulle arrived in Cairo. Wavell received him 'in a small overheated office', and confirmed to him that no operation was envisaged against the French Levant. Only a threat by Germany could alter this attitude. Wavell would support Dentz if he resisted them, but he would invade the Levant if Dentz did not fight the Germans – but this hypothesis seemed unlikely to him.

General de Gaulle felt sincere esteem for General Wavell, certainly one of the greatest leaders of the period. He praised his 'coolness and noble equanimity', for he measured the weight of the constraints he experienced from the politicians and the tensions caused by military events.

To the difficulties gathering around Wavell was added the interference. There were telegrams from London. For Mr Churchill, impatient and capable, did not fail to ask for explanations and give directives. Independently of the visits by Mr Eden, at first as Secretary of State for War then, in April 1941 – when I met him in Cairo – as Secretary of State at the Foreign Office, there were the moves of the Ambassador, Mr Lampson [...] There was the fact that the army in the Middle East was composed mainly of Dominion contingents from Australia, New Zealand and South Africa, whose governments closely watched the use that was made of their forces, as well as troops from India who had to be used carefully to avoid appearing to abuse them. In short, Wavell exercised his military command only with all sorts of political constraints. I must say that he suffered them with a noble calmness [...] and here I have arrived, awkward and insistent, having made up my mind to resolve, on behalf of France, problems that implicated the British and, first of all, the Commander-in-Chief. [...] With General Catroux, I outlined our future prospects. The essential question for us was what would become of Syria and Lebanon. Sooner or later we would have to go there [...] The authority of Free France must to extend to Damascus and Beirut as soon as events permitted it.[28]

For his part, Marshal Pétain wanted to keep France out of the global conflict. At Vichy on 7 April he gave a speech obviously directed at London, and especially at de Gaulle. 'Honour demands [France] do nothing against former allies', he declared. He continued:

The first law of patriotism is the maintenance of unity in the homeland. If each person defines their own ideas about what constitutes patriotic duty, there will no longer be a country or a nation. There will be only factions pursuing their own ambitions. Civil war, dismemberment of the country and fratricidal disputes would be the natural sequel of this discord. In reminding you of the sacred law of the unity of the motherland and of this duty of discipline, I am only following the example of all the leaders who have led France in difficult times. Under no regime, since France has been in existence, no government has accepted that the principle of national unity be brought into question [...] France's pride is not only the integrity of its territory, but also the cohesion of its Empire. The links which so tightly bind its most diverse elements together are the struggles and the sacrifices of its best sons which have built it. But here we have a subtle and insidious propaganda, inspired by Frenchmen, which is working hard to shatter it. French blood has already flowed in fratricidal struggles. Enough is enough [...] For a Frenchman, there is no other cause to defend than that of France: it is she who has entrusted to me her safety and her hope. Serve her with me with all your heart. That way, and only that way, will we secure her future.

The next day, 9 April, in a speech in the House of Commons, Churchill answered him:

Two million Frenchmen are prisoners. Germany is helping itself to a large part of France's supplies. Germany will be able to release in dribs and drabs, from month to month, prisoners and supplies by way of payment rewarding anti-British propaganda or acts hostile to Great Britain. On the other hand, the Germans will be free to choose to increase further the occupation indemnity they are extorting and which is already a cruel and exorbitant tribute [...] Admiral Darlan has told us that the Germans have shown themselves generous in the way they treat France. All the information that we receive from Occupied France and from Non-Occupied France forces me to seriously doubt that the bulk of the French population is disposed to associate itself with this odd and somewhat sinister homage that he is rendering to the enemy. However, it is up to the French to judge German generosity [...] Some time ago we were disposed to open economic negotiations with the French, but the 'generous' Germans nipped in the bud all possibility of having economic negotiations, as Wiesbaden has imperiously given the government in Vichy the order to break off all contact with us.

In other terms, Churchill declared himself as distrustful towards Darlan as Darlan was towards him. The two men detested each other. Gripped by the throat by a *Reich* which was silent, and now condemned by London, France was dreadfully alone.

7

Rachid Ali

Following the social and, particularly, the economic collapse of Germany at the end of the 1914–18 war, the Germans had kept hardly any ties with the Near East. Only 1,800 Germans lived there. In 1934, just after the election of Hitler, there was a 'Levant' section in the NSDAP[1] in Hamburg, but the party then had only six members in Palestine.[2] In the *Arab Clubs* in the Middle East, German–Arab cultural clubs, Germans and Muslims shared their common values: the confirmation of their own excellence, an aggressive anti-Semitism, jealousy mixed with hatred for the cosmopolitan plutocrats and contempt for moral degenerates. Because it had been very much in evidence at the time of the 1936 disturbances in Palestine, the English had banned the Nazi Party, which had then gone underground. Nonetheless, in that year, subversive actions by the Germans had taken on a new dimension. Berlin had set in motion a concerted political action directed at the Near East. The *Führer* had asked the *Abwehr*[3] secret service, as well as the colonial office of the NSDAP, to cooperate closely on anything to do with Islam, and Admiral Canaris, head of the *Abwehr*, had started to establish a network of agents. To avoid being seized, newspapers, books and propaganda films were sent to the Levant by diplomatic pouch. On archeological 'digs' and through other contacts, German archeologists played a major role in their distribution.

In 1937, Baldur von Schirach, head of the Hitler Youth, travelled to the Middle East to encourage the formation of structured movements but, closely watched by the mandatory powers, the latter could not do anything. Presided over by Amin Effendi el-Husseini, the Grand Mufti of Jerusalem, a 'Permanent Committee for Palestine' was founded in Berlin in 1938, to support the Palestinian Arabs. A flamboyant personality, an

orator with a wide audience, and a well-known activist with great
energy, the Grand Mufti caused constant trouble for the British.
When he was finally threatened with arrest, he took refuge in
Syria and was placed under house arrest by the French. He then
escaped to Iraq where he was greeted with respect. In Baghdad
he was able to speak out. Overall, the German actions in the
Near East had only a qualified success. Profiting from Arab anti-
semitism and hostility to the mandatory powers, the Nazis gave
the impression of having simply wanted to take advantage of a
permanent agitation in the Middle East without however taking
a resolute part alongside the Arabs in a struggle against the West.
Hitler, who was racist, admired England deeply.

At the 'invitation' of London, Egypt and Iraq broke off
diplomatic relations with Berlin when war broke out, but they
were forced to do so by the British. Although arrests took place,
Farouk and his government remained favourable to the *Reich*. On
6 July 1940, when France had just collapsed, the Iraqi Minister
of Justice had gone to Ankara to seek an audience with von
Papen, the German Ambassador. 'Like you' he reminded him,
'we are opposed to Franco–British imperialism [...] We hope that
Germany will prevent Italy from taking its place in the Near East
and that it will help the re-establishment of a free Arab national
government in Syria.' Already outlined by Ciano and submitted
to Mussolini, Italian plans for the French Levant were ready, and
discussions with the future Arab states had already taken place.
Independence in principle was there and then granted to Syria,
Lebanon, Palestine and Transjordan.

As soon as the French had asked for an armistice, the Grand
Mufti of Jerusalem sent a personal letter of congratulations to
Hitler, written in French: 'The Arab people, mistreated by our
common enemies, confidently await the result of your final
victory. They know that it will mean independence for them [...]
their unity and a treaty of friendship and collaboration.' Could
direct relations have been instituted between the Third Reich
and the Arab nations? On 27 August 1940, after a complicated
voyage, a representative of the Grand Mufti reached Berlin to
announce that a 'Committee for Collaboration with Germany'
had been set up in Iraq, of which he was the president. Choukri
Kouatli was also a member. As soon as the Axis had confirmed the
independence of all the Arab states and their right to unity, these
countries would rise up and, he confirmed, Iraq would oppose
the passage of Indian troops to Egypt. The Jewish problem could

then be settled 'following the solutions adopted in Germany and in Italy'. The 'Committee for Collaboration with Germany' suggested that arms be provided by Italy. For that, it would be sufficient to take them from the French weapons stockpiled by the Italian Control Commission in Syria. The Iraqi was ready to welcome the necessary German and Italian agents. On 23 October 1940, a common declaration in favour of independence was made by the Axis powers, and Radio Berlin started transmitting in Arabic. However, in spite of all this commotion, the Middle East did not occupy an important place in Berlin's strategy. Although hundreds of thousands of pamphlets were distributed in French North Africa and a few desertions were reported from British and French Muslim units, simple police measures sufficed to control the German pressure.[4]

Pro-Hitler agitation developed in Baghdad, encouraged by certain political and religious figures. The Grand Mufti was a formidable orator, and calls for an Arab revolt were a recurrent theme in the mosques. The British demands – in effect, free passage for their troops and weapons across the territory, control of the railways, retention of their air bases at Habbaniya and Shaibah, as well as use of the port of Basra – irritated hostile opinion more and more, hostile opinion that understood that the so-called independence offered by London was a sham. The last demand of the British was for the dismissal of the 'Golden Square', a group of Iraqi senior officers hostile to Britain – which appeared unsupportable interference. While Nouri el-Saïd's government showed itself to be cooperative, the opposition, headed by Rachid Ali al-Ghaïlani, a well-known pro-Nazi, caused a lot of unrest and, on 3 April 1941, a *coup d'état* occurred in Baghdad. Rachid Ali overthrew Nouri el-Saïd, taking control and dissolving Parliament. He took possession of the radio station and telephone exchanges, and forced the Regent from the kingdom. This latter, informed that he was going to be arrested, rushed to Basra, embarked on a British ship and fled.

Supported by the 'Golden Square', the new leader formed a new cabinet which, before any other initiative, opened diplomatic relations with Berlin, which had been broken off since the declaration of war. Backed by the Grand Mufti, he called for *jihad* against the British in 13 languages. Among Muslims of the British Indian Army, desertions started to increase.[5] Meanwhile, Syria threatened to boil over again. Much more serious for Britain, the oil fields of Iraq – notably at Kirkuk – passed into the control of the insurgents.[6] By closing the oil pipeline from Iraq to Haifa, Rachid Ali interrupted the supply of fuel to Palestine, i.e. to the British forces. However, he restored the pipeline to Tripoli cut off by England since the Armistice. Given the ambiguity of Vichy's policies, Rachid Ali could potentially place the supplies of precious fuel at the disposal of the Axis.

General Sir Alan Brooke, Chief of the Imperial General Staff: 'All the engines at sea, on land and in the air, across the Middle East, the Indian Ocean and India, depend entirely on oil from Kirkuk and Abadan (Iran). If we were to lose this source of supplies, it would be impossible to compensate for it from American sources, given the scarcity of tankers and the continual losses caused by submarine attacks. If we were to lose oil from the Middle East, we would inevitably lose Egypt, the mistress of the Indian Ocean and imperil the whole of India-Burma.'

In France, *Le Temps* wrote: 'If Iraq were to succeed in escaping from [the control of] Great Britain, the whole of the Imperial system of communications would be compromised.' Thus it was a very grave crisis that had erupted. The revolt of Rachid Ali cast the whole of the conflict in a new light, as was understood by everyone: Hitler, Churchill, Wavell, de Gaulle, Catroux, Darlan and Dentz, as well as the governments in Damascus, Ankara and Cairo. The threat to the British was exceedingly grave.

'In all the Arab countries' one reads in a note from the French High Commission in the Levant, 'the Iraqi revolt was followed with obvious sympathy [...] Each success was magnified in the general enthusiasm. Red Crescent support committees were set up across the whole country, collecting funds from the smallest localities. Pamphlets and demonstrations extolled Arab unity [...] Underground recruitment offices for Iraqi troops opened throughout the country [...] A wave of Anglophobia broke out. The British Consulate in Damascus was attacked by demonstrators and its windows were smashed.'

The Iraqi revolt generated much enthusiasm. After religious leaders called the Middle East to holy war, demonstrations broke out in the Levant. Damascus was in turmoil. Dentz telegraphed Vichy: 'Events in Iraq have caused much agitation in Syria and Lebanon. The Iraqi cause is presented as that of all the Arab states, and that the struggle in Baghdad is the prelude to their liberation.'

Beirut was so disturbed that General Dentz sent Air Force Colonel Montrelay, chief of staff to General Jeannekyn, commanding the Air Force in the Levant, to Vichy to explain the fear that was being caused by the threat of a possible German landing, and to obtain instructions as to what attitude to adopt. As for the government in Damascus, it sent Mr Naji Shawkat to Ankara to have discussions with the Germans and Turks. He was then astonished to discover that Rachid Ali had received no aid and no assurances from the Turks, nor had he obtained any commitment from Germany.

The *coup d'état* had, in fact, surprised everyone, especially the Germans themselves. They did not have a mission in Baghdad, where the Axis was represented by only the Italian Legation. The German secret services had not detected any of the preparations for the *coup d'état*. Tony Albord even states that they were not in favour of any intervention in Iraq, Hentig not having found 'a cause for intervention by the *Wehrmacht*.' Although it could have been of decisive importance, this overthrow of the government took place much too early. However, be that as it may, it did happen and did succeed, and Hitler understood that it had to be supported. Although he was thinking only of *Operation Barbarossa* – the invasion of Russia planned for the coming weeks – he could not remain passive in the face of this revolt, and he started by immediately recognising Rachid Ali as 'Governor of Iraq'. Furthermore, he had to make a gesture. He demanded that those in charge act immediately. 'It was Hitler' confirmed Hentig, 'who decided that Iraq had to be supported in its struggle'.

In Vienna (Austria), German diplomats and soldiers got together to consider the situation and the *OKW*[7] produced Directive N°30 entitled *Mittlere Orient*[8] in which were spelled out the general intentions of the *Führer*:

> The Arab liberation movement is our natural ally in the Middle East against England. From this perspective, the uprising in Iraq takes on a special meaning [...] It interferes with communications [...] it settles the position of the British troops and Navy [...] I have thus made up my mind to pursue the development of the struggle in the Middle East by supporting Iraq [...] I have decided to send help by means of the *Luftwaffe* and arms shipments [...] Members of the mission will wear tropical uniforms with Iraqi insignia [...] These insignia will also be worn on all aircraft[9] [...] the limited presence of the *Luftwaffe* will serve, alongside military action, to reinforce Iraqi confidence and the will to resist [...] The arms deliveries will be carried out either by Germany or following conversations with the French.

The themes of the propaganda, he continued, will be: 'Friends of liberty must unite against England. On the other hand, propaganda against French ownership must stop.'

On the ground, the situation deteriorated when, on 19 April, the British Ambassador in Baghdad warned the Iraqi government that British troops coming from India would disembark at Basra. Rachid Ali declared his opposition, stating it was a hostile act that could not be tolerated, and in the streets, anti-British disturbances became general. Judging the situation to be dangerous, the British Ambassador decided to urgently assemble, at the Habbaniya air base near Baghdad, with their families, all the British personnel from the oil installations. On 29 April, a part of the Iraqi Army left Baghdad and encircled the base.[10] In the early morning, an ultimatum called upon the English not to make any movement by land or by air.

Habbaniya was a large base. 'I still remember this camp which seemed like a veritable oasis in the middle of the desert', wrote Major Brochet, who visited it in July 1940. 'It was a real town, with schools, church, tennis courts, swimming pools, golf course and a race track, with kilometres of green lawns and hundreds of bungalows, sheltering in the shade of all sorts of trees. I was truly dumbfounded.' This large base was, however, defended only by a battalion of the King's Own Royal Regiment, some companies of locally raised troops of uncertain loyalty, 96 old aircraft and 18 old armoured cars of the RAF Regiment. The encircled British felt threatened, but refused to give in, and offered negotiations which took place the next day, but failed. Aerial reconnaissance flights allowed the besieged British to size up their opposition. With 11 battalions and 50 guns, 16 tanks, 14 armoured cars and 63 aircraft, the Iraqis were not without strength.[11] To pre-empt a certain attack, the British decided to attack in a surprise move the next morning. On 30 April, the old British biplanes quickly eliminated the Iraqi Air Force which was supported by a few Italian fighters. Confronted by this energetic defence, Rachid Ali's army was incapable of capturing the base and as a result the siege lasted only four days. The British aircraft machine-gunned the attackers and then, flying over Baghdad, dampened down the warrior-like excitement of the population by the sight of a number of wounded ending up in hospital. In spite of the inflammatory calls by religious leaders, general enthusiasm flagged. The radio however celebrated successes invented by Rachid Ali who, overestimating his forces, announced the impending arrival of powerful German aid. On 4 May, British patrols discovered that the enemy, abandoning large amounts of weapons, had lifted the siege and, on 6 May, helped by Blenheim light bombers from Egypt, it needed only a single battalion to remove the enemy's grip around the base. Had the situation turned around? Not quite. The revolt could not be stopped without external help. In London, Churchill took up the affair, whose gravity he well understood. Ignoring all objections, imposing his own ideas, and brushing obstacles aside, the 'Bulldog' awoke. He ordered General Auchinleck,[12] commanding in India, to send an extra brigade as reinforcements,[13] and Wavell to get together a mobile column to attack the rebels.

A column, wailed Wavell – with what? Where would he find troops, weapons and vehicles? After the losses in Greece, the Abyssinian campaign, the Battle for Egypt, and the defence of Malta, Wavell, harassed on all sides, was desperately lacking supplies and men. He was in need of everything. He therefore protested strongly against Churchill's request, which seemed to him unrealistic. He recommended negotiating rather than fighting, and telegraphed London to say so: 'I feel compelled to warn you, in the strongest terms, that in my opinion, prolonging the war in Iraq will gravely compromise the defence of Palestine and Egypt. The political repercussions would be incalculable and could well provoke what I have been trying to avoid over the past two years – serious internal disturbances in countries where we have bases. In consequence, I stress once more with the greatest possible force that an arrangement be negotiated as soon as possible with [Rachid Ali].'[14]

Taking no heed of any advice, the Prime Minister ordered Wavell to carry out his orders. As a result, Wavell jumped to attention and, assembling everything that he could find in Palestine, Egypt and Transjordan, put together *Habforce*,[15] a column of 2,000 men and 500 vehicles,[16] under the command of Major-General Clark.[17] It took five days to be formed.

In Iraq, meanwhile, fighting continued.

From 26 April onwards, Hitler and Ribbentrop studied the type of aid that Germany could provide the insurgents. They envisaged sending a fighter and bomber wing, but the range of the German aircraft was insufficient to fly direct from Rhodes to Mosul, the nearest Iraqi aerodrome. It would have to make a refuelling stop, and this was only possible in French Syria. With this in mind, they had to speak to the French – that is to say, break the outraged silence they had adopted towards Vichy following the dismissal of Laval on 13 December 1940. Didn't the Wiesbaden accords impose upon the French the duty to defend their territory against anyone who wished to enter it? The treatment meted out to France now turned to its advantage.

It was annoying, but rapid action was needed. On 2 May, Rachid Ali made a desperate appeal to Germany. His situation was desperate: Habbaniya had held out, two Indian brigades landed at Basra, and British columns were converging on him. He urgently needed weapons and political support. He would have to wait to obtain aerial support, until authoritisation was obtained from the French allowing a stop-over on their territory; as for weapons, Germany was going to send him excellent British ones seized in Greece. In Ankara, von Papen immediately contacted the Turks to send the weapons by rail, but the Turks, who had adopted a wait-and-see policy and were keen to remain neutral, refused transit across their territory. Therefore the only solution was to send French arms, already seized and stockpiled in Syria by the Italian Control Commission. They were also going to have to discuss the weapons with Vichy.

The renewed dialogue between Germany and France was important. In the European context, it was not just a matter of settling a simple question of air traffic. The French, as Berlin knew, were preoccupied by grave economic questions. It would be necessary therefore to negotiate. The same day, Ribbentrop decided to act and, on 3 May in Paris, Otto Abetz, Ambassador of Germany, received from the Wilhelmstrasse the order to contact Darlan, head of the French government. Moreover, Colonel Jung, commanding *Luftflotte 3* based in France, was summoned to Germany on that very day to form a special mixed unit, *Sonderkommando Jung*, composed of bombers, twin-engine fighters and transport aircraft, to go to Mosul to aid the Iraqis. On the same day, Hitler signed this directive: 'The Arab liberation movement in the Middle East is our natural ally against Great Britain. It is particularly important that we stir up a rebellion in Iraq. That rebellion will spread.'

On 29 April, the British Consul-General in Beirut, Mr Havard, asked for an audience with General Dentz to report to him that a concentration of German and Italian aircraft had been spotted on the Greek island of Leros by British reconnaissance aircraft. A German attack on Cyprus was feared, as was one on the Levant.

What would be his attitude if there was attack, he enquired? Dentz:[18]

> When the Consul-General of Great Britain visited me, the situation was extremely grave and British worries that he echoed were justified. I fully shared these concerns [...] The hold of the Axis extended from Crete to Rhodes, Egypt was threatened, Iraq was in revolt. One could expect a German attack on Cyprus whose occupation would complete the encirclement of the central Mediterranean and, in completing the link with Iraq, that of the British possessions and bases in the Near East. The Germans were now at work on plans for an attack on Cyprus. They could thus, explained Mr Havard, be tempted to obtain a foothold by a strike on the Syrian airfields with a view to using them to attack Cyprus from the rear. I reassured him immediately. I said to him that I would not tolerate the use of force against the Syrian aerodromes by anyone whatsoever and that I would have them guarded against any surprise attack [...] I would defend Syria against any aggression.

And the French general added: 'I will obey my government's orders.'

The next day, to demonstrate his good faith, General Dentz communicated to Mr Havard the text of a telegram he sent to Vichy:[19] '30 April, 7:15 p.m. [...] Article 10 of the Armistice convention forbids all hostile action against German forces. The instructions given [...] to the Navy and Air Force nonetheless anticipate opposing by force any landing or any hostile act by a foreign air force, even ex-enemy [...] I would therefore be grateful if you let me know urgently if this point of view is in accordance with the intentions of the French government and send me all relevant instructions in this matter.' And to prevent any attack, the Commander-in-Chief had the airfields watched by armoured units of the Air Force. The British Consul-General declared that he was satisfied and sent to the High Commissioner London's satisfaction.

During his trial, Dentz explained his position: 'I did not know what instructions I would be given by Vichy. At that time, I was probably forced to defer to it, at least to a certain extent.'[20] Dentz thus intended to maintain the neutrality that the Armistice convention imposed on him but, in his answer of 4 May, Huntziger gave him these instructions: 'In case of an aircraft landing, you will take note that the Armistice convention does not give any right to the Axis powers to be stationed on the territory nor to overfly it, and you will take measures to isolate the crews on the airfields by asking them to resume their flight as soon as possible. You will not provide any material help except to facilitate their departure. You will oppose, naturally by force, any intervention by British forces which, faced by a similar situation, would like to intervene in any way.' This answer was a choice, Vichy's. It was the fundamental act on which the Syrian affair was based.

At a conference in Egypt on 15 April, even before the siege of Habbaniya began, de Gaulle announced his plan to invade Syria with the sole Free French Division.[21] 'From 17 April, Catroux had defined the general lines of the campaign', wrote Jacques Soustelle,[22] who added 'this note was the basis for the plan General de Gaulle sent, from Brazzaville, to Catroux on 25 April, via General Spears.'[23] This was *Operation Georges*: 'To send to Damascus and then to Beirut a military force able to ensure the authority of the High Commissioner of Free France.'[24] According to the General, the sudden appearance of the 1st Free French Division (*1re Division française libre*) in Damascus and then in Beirut would cause a psychological shock which would bring about, in the face of the German threat, the rallying of the Army of the Levant to de Gaulle. The hypothesis is debatable, as the General himself admitted later: 'I fooled myself with the hope that many of them would refuse to tolerate the [German] presence and would keep them covered with their weapons.' Still, he took the risk and, considering rapid execution to be essential, he asked Catroux to submit the plan to the British without delay.

Catroux therefore asked for an urgent meeting at the highest possible level and, on 5 May, Sir Miles Lampson, British Ambassador in Egypt, Air Marshal Longmore, commanding the RAF in the Middle East, Admiral Cunningham, commanding the Royal Navy, and General Wavell, Commander-in-Chief in the Middle East, met to hear him. Catroux said that the concentration of German troops and aircraft on the Greek island of Leros represented a grave threat which demanded immediate preventive action. With or without the support of the French Army of the Levant, it was of major importance to prevent the Germans from occupying the Syrian airfields, he said. He therefore put forward General de Gaulle's plan for *Operation Georges*: send the 1st Free French Division, assembling in Palestine, to Damascus immediately. It would be enough to succeed. The Vichy forces

were, in their hearts, with England, he stated. Moreover, they
have already withdrawn northward and would offer only token
resistance. To succeed, the Free French Division needed only 300
trucks and air cover. Therefore they have to be provided to 'help
Dentz if he fights or to fight him if he doesn't'.

At first the British made no objections, but Wavell answered
the next day about the trucks, 'that because of his responsibilities
in Iraq and the Libyan Desert, he is prevented from providing
them during the current month'. Moreover, according to him,
Operation Georges 'would be of no help and would only aggravate
the situation.' Wavell therefore refused. It was on his shoulders
that the immense battle, on which depended England's very fate,
rested. Compared to this, what importance did Catroux's theories
have? On 18 May, the Frenchman returned to the charge. It
was time to attack, he stated, informing Wavell that 'according
to his intelligence' the French were withdrawing their troops in
the direction of Lebanon in order to abandon Syria to Germany.
Now, via his own intelligence services, Wavell knew that, far from
withdrawing, Dentz was reinforcing his military presence along
the Palestinian border. 'My intelligence doesn't confirm yours',
he retorted to Catroux, and he politely but firmly refused to send
the troops that were assembling in Palestine. On 19 May, the
Frenchman returned once more and met the same refusal: 'In that
case,' he said, 'my decision is taken: I will march on Damascus
alone. I ask you only to furnish me with the means of transport.'

From Brazzaville, de Gaulle supported him against Wavell, to
whom he sent several messages: 'The success of the advance on
Damascus is a question of hours. We must push on to Damascus,
even if it is only with a battalion in trucks. The psychological
effect will do the rest.' And: 'Why aren't the Free French forces
advancing towards Damascus yet?'[25]

From London, the British Defence Committee telegraphed
Catroux: 'The decision of the Free French forces to enter Syria or
not is left entirely to the judgement of the general commanding
the French troops. It is not possible for British troops to reinforce
the French troops, those who were available having been sent to
Iraq.'

In his *Memoirs*, Wavell remembered this insistence. 'On 18
May, General Catroux [...] had affirmed that he was in possession
of intelligence indicating that the [Vichy] French would transfer
all their troops from Syria to Lebanon and intended to hand
Syria over to the Germans. General Catroux declared that the

road to Damascus was open [...] He insisted vigorously that, in consequence, I issue orders, but experience had taught me to accept, with a certain degree of reserve, intelligence from the Free French [...] I insisted on the intelligence being verified [...] General Catroux, who [later] went to Palestine, admitted that his information was completely erroneous [...] meanwhile I received several telegrams from General de Gaulle, who was then in West Africa, who asked in imperious language, why the Free French were not on their way to Damascus.' The Free French, one feels, exasperated him. In the restrained style of a British officer, he alerted Churchill.[26] 'This incident illustrates the difficulties that sometimes occur in our relations with the Free French.'

For Wavell, the Free French Division was not of great interest. Understrength, ill-equipped and not homogeneous, almost without artillery, without engineers, without a medical corps and without trucks, these troops did not form a force that was easily usable in in the British order of battle. Unlike the Poles, the French refused to enlist in the British forces.[27] They claimed a total independence that they could not maintain. Their language, organisation, weapons and procedures were quite different. 'Wavell was absolutely convinced that the Gaullists would never be any help,' wrote Churchill in his *Memoirs*. 'He hoped that he would not be saddled with this new burden unless absolutely necessary.'

Wavell, on whose shoulders rested all the responsibility, finally warned Churchill that if he was ordered to attack Syria, he would send in his resignation. Churchill did not condemn him. In his *Memoirs*, Churchill wrote, with a hint of malice: 'General de Gaulle insisted immediately on undertaking a campaign with the Free French forces, if needs be without British support. But remembering Dakar [...] we thought that it was not prudent to employ Gaullist troops alone, even to oppose a German advance in Syria.'

The great unknown was Dentz. He obeyed Vichy and said that he was pro-English. Would be switch sides? The Imperial General Staff in London asked Cairo to be ready to help him, if he opposed the Germans, with immediate aerial and naval operations, and then to conclude an agreement with him. Wavell answered: 'I consider that any contact made with Dentz risks having as its only result the enemy knowing our strength, or rather our weakness.' He asserted to Dill, on 22 May, that he did not envisage invading Syria 'before being capable of it' and that he did not care for 'political adventures'. After the Iraqi revolt and the riots in Syria, his political advisors feared that a Franco–British conflict could set the whole of the Middle East ablaze. For all these reasons – lack of troops, frittering away his troop strength, political risks and the threat of opening a new front – he brushed aside *Operation Georges* that was proposed by the Free French.

Faced with this refusal, de Gaulle and Spears appealed to Eden, in London, to intervene, but Wavell remained inflexible. Such an action is 'absolutely out of the question' answered Cairo to the Minister, for, at the present time, Wavell had neither the necessary tanks nor aircraft, and even if he did have them, he would post them to other fronts where they were needed even more. The British chiefs of military operations in the Middle East no longer wanted to hear about an invasion of Syria.

De Gaulle, in Brazzaville, was greatly annoyed. He explained his plans and telegraphed to the British Ambassador in Egypt, as well as to General Wavell, to protest against 'the delays caused to the concentration of the Legentilhomme division within striking distance of Syria, while the arrival of the Germans there is more likely with each passing day.' 'I noted that under these conditions,' he wrote 'I did not intend to go to Cairo soon [...] and it was in Chad that I would henceforth carry on the effort of the Free French. I then let it be known in London that I would recall General Catroux from Cairo as his presence was becoming useless.'

He wrote to Catroux in fact: 'Given the negative policies that our British friends thought that they had to adopt in the Middle East towards matters involving us, I think that the presence in Cairo of a High Commissioner representing Free France and a personality as important as you is no longer justified [...] Please leave Cairo as soon as possible [...] Kindly advise the British in Cairo of this decision. There is no need for you to hide from them the reason for your departure [...] Naturally you will not be replaced in your current position.'

And before leaving Brazzaville for London, General de Gaulle warned Mr Parr, the British representative, of the disgraceful consequences that all sorts of concessions made to Vichy were bound to have on the morale of the French people.

It does not seem that, at that date, the General had learned of the landing of German aircraft at Aleppo four days earlier. He made no allusion to it. Did the English keep Free France up to date? Spears did not mention it in the cable he sent to General de

Gaulle to confirm the impossibility of transporting his troops in under a month, which therefore brought about the cancellation of *Operation Georges*. He added: 'No operation is currently envisaged for the Free French.' And he ended with these unpleasant words: 'The Commander-in-Chief [General Wavell] has asked me to tell you that, although he is always happy to meet you, he does not see the necessity for you to come to Cairo now or in the near future. There would even be some disadvantage for you in doing so. The Ambassador shares this view.'[28]

There was now a running battle. De Gaulle refused to set foot in Cairo where Wavell, on the contrary, had seen enough of it.

8

Darlan/*Die Pariser Protokolle*

Paris, Hôtel Matignon, 3 May 1941, 10:00 a.m. The telephone rang on the desk of Jacques Benoist-Méchin,[1] the assistant secretary to the Vice-Presidency of the Council. It was a call from the Ambassador of Germany in France, Otto Abetz. Otto Abetz? With contacts with the *Reich* being interrupted – except at Wiesbaden – since mid-December, this was a surprise. It was Abetz in person. He seemed very agitated and wished to meet the high-ranking public servant as soon as possible at the German Embassy in the rue de Lille. The two men knew each other, but not wanting to show too much willingness, Benoist-Méchin offered to go to the Embassy in the late afternoon. 'That is too late', answered Abetz who insisted and, finally, came himself.

'I have just received an urgent message from M. von Ribbentrop,' he said straight off. 'The Minister of Foreign Affairs of the *Reich* has asked me to ask you the following question: would the French government be prepared, in return for certain favours, to allow 50-odd aircraft to land in Syria on their way to Iraq. It is simply a technical stopover; the aircraft will have Iraqi colours, the pilots and crew will be wearing civilian clothes, and will remain confined to the base during their stay. However, Germany wishes to buy the weapons stockpiled at the disposal of the Italian Armistice Commission."

Vice-President of the Council since 23 February 1941,[2] Admiral Darlan was, even more importantly, the '*dauphin*' (the heir apparent) of the Marshal: he would succeed him in case of death or incapacity. Did he want to collaborate with Germany? It was the question that everyone asked themselves, especially the Anglo-Saxons. Was he a '*collabo*'?, as people would say in France. Surely not, he wanted only to defend France's interests but, in the Spring of 1941, he believed in the victory of Germany and was fixed on that belief. History reviews the Admiral negatively. The picture of him drawn up in London, and broadcast by newspapers around the world, was indelibly engraved in people's memories. He was not a pleasant man, and public opinion that divides men into the good and the bad, traitors and heroes, damned him. However, for all that, was he a bad Frenchman? The Admiral did not like England, that is certain, and there were several reasons for this attitude. But, until the end, he respected the oath he made to Churchill in June 1940 to never hand over a single ship to Germany; but he was pilloried and unable to defend himself. Coming from the parliamentary world – Georges Leygues was his backer – the builder of the world's fourth largest fleet did not doubt his own political capabilities. He believed himself to be a very good diplomat. In a Europe that, in the Spring of 1941, he still thought, but without wishing it, was inevitably going to be under German domination, he wanted to look after the future. Even though his wife was English, he did not like the English, for serious reasons.[3] Moreover, they disliked him intensely. When in February 1941 he became Vice-President of the Council, Churchill, who knew him, wrote to the Foreign Office: 'I look upon this event with apprehension and mistrust [...] It would have been preferable to have had Laval rather than Darlan, a dangerous man, embittered, ambitious but without the odious label attached to the name [...]' And six days later, to Sir Alexander Cadogan:[4] 'I am convinced that Darlan is an ambitious crook.'

Today Darlan appears like a man who thought about things, observed what was going on and played it by ear. Informed by a competent staff, he was, above all else, pragmatic. His enemies accused him therefore of being an opportunist. Darlan, in fact, did not have a defined strategy, unlike de Gaulle and Weygand – but he believed himself to be a sufficiently good diplomat to negotiate with the Germans. A negotiator by necessity rather than a collaborator by politics, he detested the *Reich* and held Italy in contempt. Defending what France had left, he distrusted the instincts of others. The Gaullists? He considered them to be playthings of the British, but he protected their families. In Occupied France, pensions were, with few exceptions, paid to those who were entitled to them but had joined Free France, and the wives of these rebels continued to receive a special pension after the Armistice. Darlan may have detested, but he didn't hate.

On the evening of 3 May 1941, Darlan was sleeping at the Hôtel Bristol in Paris.[5] Since 13 December, the future had looked increasingly gloomy. The Occupation war indemnities were crushing – 400 million francs per day; the Germans were exploiting French industry – aircraft, engines, trucks, munitions, explosives; and they were also taking over agricultural production, raw materials and an enormous amount of war booty, for example, 2,500 locomotives out of 5,200, and 200,000 carriages out of 450,000.[6] Subjected to systematic looting, France had to pay to be pillaged. All trade having ceased between the two zones, Occupied and Unoccupied, she was being strangled. Quite obviously, there had to be discussions with the occupying power. To deny it would be irresponsible. The negotiations which commenced on 4 May at the German Embassy were an opportunity. The Germans were in a hurry and Darlan wanted to take advantage of this. He hoped to obtain much in exchange for a facility that he considered, it seemed, insignificant. If he was aware that agreeing to the right of a stopover represented a military involvement, it was a fleeting, indirect and secondary consideration. Sensing Abetz's impatience, the Admiral thought he had the upper hand. That very evening, he left for Vichy to report to the Marshal, then returned to Paris. Who were the people he was dealing with? Alongside Abetz were only small fry: Vogl, Warlimont, Hemmen, and the members of the Wiesbaden commission. The Marshal considered that there were insufficient people to deal with such wide-ranging business. He therefore wrote to Hitler to ask him to receive the Admiral who, he thought, would obtain much more at the at the top than in detailed discussions.

To assess the possible consequences of German aircraft landing in Syria, Huntziger sent a telegram to Dentz:[7] 'I ask you to let me know personally by telegram if such a measure runs the risk of causing disturbances in the Army of the Levant. Telegraph your suggestions. Nothing will be done before your answer has been communicated to the Armistice Commission.' Dentz replied stressing the turmoil that such a measure would cause. He let it be known that, while awaiting new orders, he would apply the order to fire on all foreign aircraft overflying the Levant. Huntziger answered: 'If German or Italian aircraft overfly the Levant, avoid any retaliation. If some of these aircraft land on your airfields, welcome them and ask for instructions. On the other hand, English aircraft must be attacked by all means.' No doubt Huntziger feared that Dentz would be incensed by this choice, as he then he warned him: 'If you do not obey, you will break the Armistice and you will be responsible for the consequences which will be grave: occupation of the Unoccupied Zone, dismissal of the personnel of the army, and, no doubt, invasion of French North Africa.'

This telegram from the Minister for War was crucial: in choosing between the aircraft that he had to welcome and those that he had to shoot down, he was committing a political act of extreme importance but, to preserve the unexpected advantages of the Armistice, Vichy had to choose sides.

On 5 May in Paris, the discussions restarted. The French repeated their requests to Abetz who, on reading them, gave a start. Darlan was asking for:

- immediate release of the 350,000 military prisoners;
- delivery of weapons to the Armistice Army;
- facilitation of passage across the demarcation line;
- restoration of the Nord and Pas-de-Calais regions to French administration (they were then under the control of the military government of Brussels);
- reduction of the Occupation war indemnities from 400 million francs per day to 100 million;
- recognition in the peace treaty of French sovereignty over the Levant and even guarantees on all the other territories of the Empire.

Abetz disputed such demands, but Darlan put forward the risk of seeing French colonies join in the revolt. Abetz argued, Darlan remained firm. There was no progress and, on 6 May, after difficult negotiations, the Ambassador finally agreed to transmit these demands to Berlin for a decision. To general surprise, the answer arrived very swiftly: the *Führer* accepted all the demands except the guarantee 'on all the other territories'. Darlan thought he had won.

Everything was going to be decided now, very quickly, and by mischance. Benoist-Méchin described the scene, which was crucial: as the conference was finishing and people were getting ready to leave, an orderly brought a despatch. Abetz opened it, read it and frowned. Transmitted by Berlin was a dramatic appeal from Rachid Ali. The Iraqi was in desperate straits and asking for urgent help. Then, Abetz: 'The first group of fighter aircraft is ready to leave Salonika at any moment; couldn't you send instructions to Beirut?' he asked Darlan. 'We must ensure that our pilots are not machine-gunned as they land.'

'The technical details have not yet been settled', exclaimed the Admiral.

'They will be tomorrow!' answered the Ambassador. 'Since we are agreed overall, it remains only to settle a few practical details. These cannot cause any serious problems. By giving orders immediately to the High Commissioner, we will gain 48 hours. All the remainder of the operations can be modified.'

Darlan, 'whose first negotiation of this kind this was' stressed Benoist-Méchin, then committed the fatal error. Suddenly allowing himself to be distracted from his objective, abandoning all his trump cards and consulting no one, he gave the Germans written authorisation to land in Syria. Abetz passed on the authoritisation and the aircraft, which were waiting, took off. The Ambassador was triumphant. He telephoned Berlin: 'The concessions by the French go beyond all that could have been expected.' It was not understood until later: the fate of Syria was sealed. Going beyond the Marshal's orders, Darlan, who had decided things alone, had been outwitted.

On the morning of 7 May, Dentz received, via Navy channels, a top secret personal telegram from the Ministry of Foreign Affairs: '1. General discussions are being undertaken between the French and German governments. 2. It is important, in the highest degree, for their success that, if German aircraft on their way to Syria, were to land on an airfield in the mandated territory, that you give them all facilities to resume their journey. 3. Acknowledge receipt via the Navy [...]'. It was signed Darlan. Dentz answered: 'Received, understood, I will issue instructions accordingly.'

In Paris, negotiations continued. On 7 May, at 11:00 a.m., the two delegations found themselves at the German Embassy in the rue de Lille. According to Benoist-Méchin, agreement was speedily reached on the military questions, including the arms sale. There was talk about a German presence in Dakar, but no conclusion was reached because of the lack of real German compensation. The Germans agreed to release the 1914–18 veterans from their camps and granted 'minimal facilities for travellers and postal traffic across the line of demarcation'. The negotiations on economic matters turned out badly: no agreement on the Occupation costs was reached, and the delegate from the financial administration refused to sign anything whatsoever.

On that day, Darlan found himself opposite a formidable, hard, brusque and unyielding man, Minister Hemmen, President of the Economic Commission for France. The elements of the compensation that he had thought he had obtained disappeared one after the other. The number of prisoners to be liberated fell from 350,000 to 83,000; restrictions around the demarcation lines were reduced; and the reduction in the Occupation costs was granted only until 15 July. Instead of reinforcing the Armistice Army and the forces in the Empire, Darlan obtained only the refitting of a few ships. This compensation could, moreover, only be obtained in exchange for outrageous French concessions: refuelling of submarines and other ships at Dakar, replacement of French public servants who 'did not inspire confidence', deliveries of bauxite, recognition of the exchange rate of the mark at 20 francs, placement of German controllers at the Bank of France and exchange control, and payment of part of the Occupation costs in gold and foreign exchange. Germany tightened the screws and Darlan had got himself trapped. On 8 May, he realised it. 'Henceforth, we will give nothing to the Germans without them paying for it in advance,' wrote Benoist-Méchin. It was true but it was too late.

A meeting with Hitler was arranged.

On 10 May, accompanied by three colleagues, Darlan, dressed in civilian clothing, boarded a special train at the Gare du Nord (Paris). The train arrived on the morning of 11 May in Salzburg (Austria) where '*Zwei Grosse Mercedes mit Kompressor*' (two big supercharged Mercedes), those enormous black limousines that were favoured by the Nazis, awaited them. Everyone rested for a short while, followed by a two-hour interview between Ribbentrop and Darlan. The Admiral put on his full-dress uniform – sword and decorations – and the cars set off for the *Berghof*, the 'Eagle's Nest', where Hitler was waiting for them. They entered at 2:30 p.m. Perhaps overcome by the idea of meeting face to face the man who made the world tremble, the Admiral, noted Benoist-Méchin, 'was visibly nervous, his emotion making his Gascon heredity become obvious, giving him a sort of exuberant good humour.' The impeccable honour guard – black helmet, high boots, black breeches with silver braid – presented arms by turning their heads. Hitler was waiting for his visitors in an immense room lacking in style. There were tree trunks burning in the fireplace. Through the immense bay windows, the view stretched towards the Alps. Introductions having been made, Hitler, Darlan, Abetz, Ribbentrop and the interpreter went into an adjoining room. The door was closed behind them. The meeting lasted two hours. Schmidt served as interpreter. Speaking straight away, and to soothe Hitler of whose absolute cynicism he was ignorant, Darlan started by using this 'incredibly naïve phrase' by thanking him 'for the great honour done to him by being received on the birthday of Joan of Arc, the national heroine who drove the English out of France'! What did the *Führer* think of this rather odd reference? He didn't answer, seeming faraway, almost on edge. He listened to the Admiral somewhat impatiently, then, starting to speak, he launched into a long, rather jumbled monologue in which threats and promises followed one another, interspersed with social pleasantries. He recalled bitterly how he had learned of the palace revolution of 13 December at Vichy. He spoke of collaboration which, since this had been started, had not progressed. He went through the French requests and challenged all of them under various pretexts. He feared, for example, that liberated soldiers would 'join an anti-German movement', commit acts of sabotage, and even leave France 'working their way to join de Gaulle.' Coming to an end of his long speech – feverish, irritable, strained and speaking increasingly loudly – he added: 'Germany is waging a war against England, a war of life or death.'[8] All in all, nothing had changed in his attitude towards France.

Coming finally to the question of the Levant, Hitler offered a trade: 'If France supports the German war effort as it already does in Syria', he said 'the government of the *Reich* is prepared, in a case-by-case scenario, to follow up the requests of the French government to obtain facilities or concessions.' Without interrupting himself, he went on speaking about future prospects, talking about communications and the future of Europe. The Admiral understood that he was in the process of falling into a very dangerous trap. Caught by the throat politically, dominated psychologically, he unwisely declared: 'I promise faithfully to direct French policies towards integration into the new European order, to no longer tolerate a swinging policy between the warring powers, and to ensure continuity of this political direction.' Did he really believe it? One would say so. Two days later, he explained in a note to Vichy that 'if we collaborate with Germany, without lining up with her to deliberately make war on England, that is to say to work with her in our factories, we can save the French nation, reduce our territorial, metropolitan and colonial losses to a minimum, and act in an honourable, if not important, fashion in a future Europe.'

After having agreed to a resumption of negotiations in Paris on 20 May, Darlan and Hitler parted. There was no feeling of confidence between the two men, and Darlan did not hide his bitter disappointment: 'Beware of microphones', he whispered into Benoist-Méchin's ear, before adding: 'This fellow seems mad! There is nothing to be gained. And then something seemed to annoy him. He wasn't really listening to the conversation. Obviously, at times, he was thinking of other things.'

Conversations with the others continued in the big room: 'In front of the bay window stood a table more than six metres long whose top was made of a single slab of porphyry', remembered Benoist-Méchin. 'I laid out my maps and documents. Hitler stood on my right. The Admiral, M. von Ribbentrop, Ambassador Abetz and Schmidt were grouped behind us. A slim and distinguished man, whom I had not noticed before, came and joined us. It was Otto Werner von Hentig,[9] a diplomat at the Wilhelmstrasse, who specialised in questions about the East. At 5:00 p.m., tea was served, then they parted.' Otto von Hentig wrote:[10] 'On the return journey, Benoist-Méchin, like Darlan, told me of their bitter disappointment. I left them at Karlsruhe, and it was in a newspaper bought at the railway station that I learned that on 11 May Rudolf Hess [...] had flown to Scotland. Hitler's thoughts followed him in this flight and I could understand his inability to concentrate that day.' A personal friend of Hitler's and a member of the Reich Defence Council, Rudolf Hess knew many strategic secrets, and they were five weeks away from the invasion of Russia.

By coming to the *Berghof*, the Admiral had become involved in a dangerous chain of events. While it was true that discussions about Bizerta and Dakar never reached a conclusion, he was involved in Syria. It was he who signed the treaties and he who was seen climbing the staircase at the *Berghof* to shake Hitler's hand. These devastating photos changed a diplomatic manœuvre into treason. That is all that is remembered. Spread around the world, that picture was henceforth indelibly associated with him. Overwhelmed by his bad reputation, he was demonised and the Marshal found himself dragged by Darlan onto a downward slope. He soon declared, however: 'I was never consulted about the business of the aircraft. Do you hear me? Never! But now the first step is taken, there is no going back. I don't want a new Armistice. I want to boot the English out.'

At Vichy on 14 May 1941 a meeting of the Council of Ministers was held, presided over by the Marshal.

Darlan described the contents of the accords concluded with Germany, which he had signed, and then told of his interview with Hitler. 'With the approval of the Marshal, I went, at the invitation of the Chancellor of the *Reich*, to Berchtesgaden' he began – before enumerating, at length and in detail, the points covered during the interview, which he then summarised in order to justify himself. 'It is the last chance for France to have a reconciliation with Germany. French help to England would bring about the disappearance of France as a nation, a wavering policy would prompt the annexation of the north of France and other regions, Tunisia, and Morocco.' He went on: 'without deliberately waging war on England, a policy of collaboration with Germany would permit us, as he has already said, to play an active role in the future Europe' [...] 'For me', he concluded:

> my choice is made: it is collaboration and I will not allow myself to be deflected [...] Admitting that external help could get England out of abyss into which she is currently falling, all French people would be dead or in slavery before this intervention produces results. The only possible intervention is by the United States [but] the lack of military preparation of that country is such that many years would pass before a single one of their soldiers sets foot in Europe. Moreover, the state of American society would not allow them to maintain the war. They are in a state of decay, perhaps more advanced than that in which we found ourselves in 1939 [...] In the current state of the world, and taking into account our defeat, I do not see any other solution than collaboration to safeguard [our interests].

The passage of the German aircraft having been accepted, a telegram was sent to General Dentz: 'The government [...] has adopted the principle of collaboration with Germany. This does not imply hostility towards England. The orders are still for you to oppose by force any British attack.'

Aware of the shocking aspect of this decision, especially for a soldier, the Head of State sent General Dentz a telegram confirming these decisions: 'I am keen to stress personally the great impact of these negotiations and the wish that I have to pursue, without reservation, the policy which flows from them. The reference to Syria must stress your need to defend, by all possible means, the territory placed under your authority, to ensure, as at Dakar, the freedom of its skies, and to carry out, in conditions that I know are politically and materially delicate, the extent of our wishes to collaborate with the new order. I trust you.'[11]

Dentz thus saw himself forced to carry out orders of which he disapproved. He hoped that his sacrifice would find justification in the superior interests of the country. Moreover, no one, at this stage, imagined that the crisis could become so acrimonious to the point of becoming an open and bloody conflict.

Staggering news started to leak out in Europe. On the evening of Friday 18 May 1941, the attack that Germany was preparing against Soviet Russia, *Operation Barbarossa*, would take place in a month, on 20 June.[12] After a moment's silence, the Marshal said calmly: 'They are buggered!' There is no doubt that those who mattered were also aware. Churchill had already warned Stalin. The day before, on 17 May, Darlan wrote to Weygand: 'I think we are at a turning point and that we can perhaps see some of the links that bind us together becoming undone.'

The negotiations, decided upon at Berchtesgaden, opened on 21 May in Paris. The German General Warlimont presented new requests. He asked to establish a technical base at Aleppo, the transfer by France of the weapons stockpiled by the Italian Control Commission in the Levant, and the use of Tunisian ports. Darlan authorised 'the use of Aleppo airport, and of the ports and communications in the Levant by the *Reich*, and the transfer to the Iraqi rebels of three-quarters of the munitions and arms stockpiled in Syria.' Although these things answered Berlin's wishes, clashes were however ongoing and the discussions constantly came up against points of detail. The Admiral was annoyed. All this seemed to him to be pathetic pettiness. He asked Abetz that an additional protocol, taking into account French requests, be added to the agreement that he had signed. He understood that the German appetite had no limits. He asked therefore that these accords, with conditions that he knew were extortionate, be subordinated – which was inadmissible for his adversaries. 'The additional protocol was a way to ensure that undertakings in principle are never executed.'

The Germans hit back; only Abetz signed the additional protocol. Darlan returned to Vichy, leaving Huntziger, Admiral Platon and Benoist-Méchin to pursue discussions in an increasingly tense atmosphere.

Darlan, who was at Vichy, asked Benoist-Méchin to telephone him with the final text of the protocols that he would sign upon his return on 27 May.

First protocol: <u>Iraq</u>: Three-quarters of the supplies stockpiled in Syria by the Italian Armistice Commission will be delivered to Iraq. Germany will pay for a part in cash and Iraq the balance in the form of agricultural supplies. The remaining quarter will be left for France, but will be stockpiled once more and placed under the supervision of the Italian Commission.

Second protocol: <u>Bizerta</u>: Germany obtains the use of the port for the unloading and reinforcement in supplies of German troops in Africa, with a reduced number of support staff (wearing civilian clothes) as well as the right of transit by railway to the south. France will ensure the protection of Axis convoys between Toulon and Bizerta. In exchange, she will receive modern armaments and will be able to transfer 11,000 men to French North Africa.

Third protocol: <u>Dakar</u>: In principle, from 15 July onward, German submarines will be able to put in at this port on the Atlantic coast in order to refuel from German merchant vessels. Later, warships and an airfield could be based there. The French requests for compensation were rejected as being extortionate. This third protocol was the most disturbing for the Allies by far. The submarine war could take a dramatic turning if the French accepted it.

Having listened to the reading of the three protocols, the Admiral accepted them and asked Benoist-Méchin to initial them. He would come to sign them himself on 2 June. It was a very grave error. The Paris accords (*Die Pariser Protokolle*) exposed Vichy to the risk of a rupture with the Americans, for whom Dakar was of strategic importance. Hadn't Vichy stated on several occasions that no German would enter? With Governor-General Boisson inflexible on this point, the agreement risked provoking the rebellion of French West Africa. To sign was, quite obviously, to betray. The impact would be catastrophic. Vichy gambled with its credit. Darlan assessed the risk, but committed himself. On 27 May German aircraft continued to land in Syria, and the stockpiled arms had been delivered. What had he received in exchange? Almost nothing. Moreover, at the end of the month, the Germans would go back on the deal that they had made. The Admiral only obtained some administrative advantages, including an easing of the conditions for crossing the line of demarcation, a temporary reduction in the Occupation costs, and the return of ex-servicemen, as well as a few officers, including General Juin.[13] On the other hand, he would become a Nazi agent in the eyes of the world. Denounced by the London press as 'the man

of military cooperation with Germany' or 'the Frenchman who
went to Berchtesgaden', he continued to receive scores of insults.
Mocked, denounced and sometimes even demonised, but without
being able to explain himself, he never got over it. What he did
so far only involved him. The State had to ratify it, but the news,
which started to filter out, caused indignation.

While Darlan proceeded to Paris, Weygand flew to Vichy
where he had been summoned the day before. Informed when
he arrived of the negotiations in train, he was scandalised and
showed the greatest disapproval when he met Pétain. He refused
to be compromised in this policy and threatened immediately
to resign. The Marshal listened to him with great attention and
called for on the next day, 3 June, a reduced Council of Ministers
meeting which Weygand was asked to attend. M. Boisson,
Governor-General of French West Africa was also asked to
attend: brought up to date about the Franco-German contacts,
he agreed completely with Weygand. Admiral Estéva was coming
from Tunis.

Having returned from Paris during the night, Darlan brought
the texts that he had signed the day before. At 11:00 a.m. the
Council of Ministers opened, in a particularly solemn mood. The
atmosphere was icy. Everyone knew that Darlan and Weygand did
not like each other and all expected a commotion. In total silence,
the Admiral spoke and described the nature of his contacts in
Paris, and everyone then realised the seriousness of the accords
that he had signed. The ministers were appalled. 'Weygand was
to the left of the Marshal. I could feel him champing at the bit like
a thoroughbred wanting to jump. Darlan had no sooner finished
than General Weygand took the offensive. He literally pulverised
Darlan's agreements and the planned agreements, so that nothing
remained of them.'

Weygand was categorically opposed to any sort of compromise.
'His policy to safeguard the Empire', according to Georges Hirtz,[14]
a member of his staff, 'would be irretrievably compromised if
the government continued to give the impression of not sticking
firmly to conditions fixed by the Armistice. In giving way on any
point whatsoever, we would immediately open the door to doubt,
rebellion, chaos,' he said. 'The members of the army and the
political leaders in the African territories would never agree to
the slightest collaboration with Germany or Italy [...] We must
not allow ourselves to be dragged on to the slippery slope of
collaboration, even if camouflaged, at any price.'[15]

The General expressed his categorical opposition to the protocols and he read a note that he had prepared:

> I am obliged to remind the government of the promise that has been made to Africans that their territories would be defended against any invader [...] It is important to remain faithful to this policy. I cannot say it too strongly! [...] Any policy of negotiation with Germany can only end in a military collaboration and war against our former ally, England [...] We are still at war with Germany and cannot make war on our allies [...] If the alliance agreements with England have been suspended, they have not been broken by the Armistice, which is only provisional.

The General then recalled the agreement with Murphy, Roosevelt's personal representative, and finished by losing his temper: 'I will fire on the Germans rather than carry out your orders,' he said loudly to Darlan. 'That's a different policy than the one I have been ordered to carry out in Africa.'

Darlan: 'It is not a new policy. There is no military collaboration. We have to live or even survive.'

Weygand: 'No! The two policies have no connection. The Armistice did not say "military collaboration with the enemy".'

Darlan: 'It is not military collaboration!'

Weygand: 'There is equivocation which means that no one can have confidence in this government any longer! Moreover, my place is not in your deliberations. I have said what I had to say. I would only repeat myself. I have been entrusted to carry out a different policy in Africa.' And Weygand, having threatened to resign, rose and withdrew.

There was total silence in the room. Everyone was overwhelmed. Ministers and governor-generals were silent [...] Finally the Marshal asked the ministers to give their opinion. Huntziger: 'I do not have the army for a war against England.' Bergeret:[16] 'My air force is only a shell. I have nothing to defend the Unoccupied Zone, Africa, Syria.' Finally, the Marshal: 'For the moment, nothing will be ratified.'

On 6 June, a new meeting of the Council of Ministers took place. The debate resumed, and suddenly Darlan, surprisingly, reversed course. Suddenly, he no longer defended the accords that he was the only one to sign. 'The die is cast', he declared, somewhat relieved. 'In refusing the advantages that we hoped to obtain in exchange for our concessions, we no longer have

any undertakings [...] We are going to restart the negotiations.'
Darlan seemed happy to have been dragged back from the edge
of the precipice. Faced with this new development, Weygand did
not renew his offer to resign, but a sharp, incisive and aggressive
dialogue resumed between these two adversaries.

Weygand: 'Nothing has changed in my mission to defend
Africa against any invasion? No base will be handed over to
anyone at all?'

The Admiral: 'Yes'

Weygand: 'Afterwards I won't see any equipment or personnel
arrive, nor any sort of advance party?'

The Admiral agreed with a nod.

Weygand insisted: 'If someone wants to come to Bizerta, I will
sink them?'

Darlan: 'You do not have the right to do so: we have signed an
armistice which forbids any hostile act against Germany.'

Weygand: 'But in that case they will have violated the
Armistice! I would have the right and duty.'

No one commented upon this proposal and the Council
meeting ended. Firmness thus carried the day: the Paris protocols
were never ratified.

Two days later, Darlan sent an answer stalling for time. Abetz
spoke about a swindle, but Darlan stood firm and never heard
talk about the protocols again.[17] Alas, for Syria, it was too late.
Germany had its way.

9

Stirring Up a Hornet's Nest

While discussions were being held in Paris, Berlin and Vichy, in Baghdad, Rachid Ali's cause was in its death throes: every day he was losing his effectives, his army was less and less combat-ready, and public opinion was less and less enthusiastic. He was waiting for the Germans, his only possible last resort. Every day, he announced their imminent arrival. Every day, he called Ribbentrop. This latter had done everything in his power to support him as quickly as possible, since the very day when Abetz contacted the French, even before they had been sounded out. Air Force Colonel Jung, of *Fliegerkorps 3*, based in France, had received the order to go to Berlin to become commander of a special mixed unit, *Sonderkommando Jung*, made up of 79 aircraft – bombers, fighters and transports – and to get ready to go to the Middle East to take aid to the Iraqis.[1] On 6 May, he received the order to send to Mosul a *Fliegerführer Irak,* a German officer tasked with coordinating aircraft movements from the ground.

General Huntziger immediately informed Dentz that the right to stopover in Syria – landing, refuelling and taking off – could be granted to the Germans. Obeying his government, but being careful to protect the peace, Dentz warned the English. His communiqué, whose tone was as moderate as possible, was broadcast on Beirut Radio, but it confirmed that he would respond to any attack. On 7 May, a top-secret telegram informed him of the imminent passage of German aircraft on their way to Iraq and ordered him to 'give them all facilities necessary to resume their flight.' Upon its receipt, Dentz sent a reluctant order to the bases at Rayak, Damascus, Aleppo and Palmyra: 'In case of a landing by German or Italian aircraft, do not treat them as enemies. Inform them that the terms of the Armistice agreement do not give them the right of overflight or of staying. Isolate the crews and ask them to resume their flight as quickly as possible. Give them only the help required to get them on their way.' And General Jean Jeannekyn, the Air Force commander, added on the same day: 'Take all necessary measures to avoid any incidents. Demand correct behavior and attitude from the [French] staff dealing with the [German] aircraft and passengers.' The General counted on the discipline of all ranks to carry out this order strictly and properly. 'The consequences of non-observance would have not only local importance but also national implications.'

For Dentz, careful to maintain the strict neutrality of the mandate, these landings were a catastrophe. Transmitted by the Navy, a telegram from the Foreign Affairs Ministry reached him on 8 May: '1. Major von Blomberg of the German Air Force will arrive in Damascus on 9 May on a mission. 2. Put at his disposal an officer to show him around and to provide help and protection during his mission. 3. The aircraft will be of German manufacture and will probably carry German markings. 4. The German aircraft that will overfly Syria at night will use as a recognition signal a red flare with three white stars. 5. Indicate to Major von Blomberg the importance, for reasons of discretion, of him wearing civilian clothes. 6. Take all necessary precautions to keep the matter secret. Acknowledge receipt.' Dentz went to Damascus to welcome Blomberg, but the German did not arrive.

The next day, at 7:00 p.m., a Heinkel 111 bomber in French colours – F-ADBX – and two other Heinkels in German colours landed at Aleppo-Nérab. They arrived unannounced. When, on 10 May, Colonel Montrelay, who had returned from Vichy with written instructions for the High Commissioner, learned of their arrival, he was dumbstruck. In keeping with the air of mystery – everything was top-secret – all the passengers had false names. 'Monsieur G', whose false papers said that he was a journalist attached to the High Commission, was in fact Guérard. He was delegated by Darlan, he said, although his hand-written accreditation bore no signature. 'M. Renouard', who accompanied him, spoke French but was a German diplomat. It was Rudolf Rahn, a counsellor at the Embassy and a former assistant to Abetz in Paris. For communications with Berlin, a radio operator accompanied them. The fourth passenger, 'Martin', was also German, but with a French mother. It was rather complicated: his name was Mulhausen but he signed his name as Malaucène to the articles he published in *La Gerbe*, a collaborationist newspaper that he founded in Paris with Alphonse de Châteaubriant. The last passenger, Grobba, was the German

Ambassador to Iraq before the war. He was taking advantage of the aircraft to rejoin his former post, and continued on to Iraq. This mission, of which Rudolf Rahn was in charge, had snatched him from the office life that he detested. In his *Mémoires*,[2] he recounted the story of his trip:

> The revolt that we had fomented in Iraq broke out too soon, and it was decided that I would go to Beirut accompanied by a French collaborator from the *La Gerbe* newspaper, named Guérard.[3] We therefore caught a Junkers aircraft and stopped off at Rhodes. Was it prudent to land in Lebanon in an aircraft with German colours? It seems not, and an Italian painter covered the black swastikas with French roundels. He did his best, but one shouldn't look too closely. Overflying Cyprus, we were suddenly surrounded by British aircraft, and we did not feel very full of ourselves. They soon left, and Guérard handed me a flask of excellent whisky which we really needed.[4]

Passes not signed, assumed names, parallel missions, fake Frenchmen, fake professions, fake French roundels, all these forgeries speak volumes about the predicament of Vichy. Darlan, who was behind this mess, wanted to avoid people learning of his part in it.

Later, at 3:30 a.m. on 9 May, Major von Blomberg, *Fliegerführer Irak*, accompanied by five or six officers, landed at Mezzé-Damascus airbase. Captain Veyssière, the base Officer of the Day, received him so badly that his attitude brought him a stern warning and threats of punishment. At 8:30 a.m., Lieutenant-Commander Voisard, Navy deputy chief of staff, arrived from Beirut by aircraft to greet him officially. This mission, which settled in for the night at the Orient Palace Hotel in Damascus, left the next day for Baghdad.[5]

Beirut, Résidence des Pins. 10 May, 11:00 a.m. Received alone and coolly by General Dentz, 'Monsieur G' introduced himself. An Inspector of Finances who had left the public service to join the private sector, then becoming chief of staff to Paul Baudouin, Guérard was a friend of Laval's.

'Well then, you have come for the aircraft?' Dentz asked him.

'The aircraft? What aircraft? I have come for the armaments!' answered Guérard, surprised.

'What armaments?' exclaimed the General. 'No one has been warned of your arrival.'

The mysterious 'Monsieur G' then explained to the General that three-quarters of the weapons placed under the control of the Italian Armistice Control Commission had been sold to the Germans. They had to be sent to Iraq as quickly as possible. Rahn had come to supervise the operation on behalf of the Germans, while he was to do the same for the French. Dentz was flabbergasted. He wasn't aware – he had never heard about the weapons. However, Guérard was aware of the passage of the aircraft.

Rahn was then introduced. Dentz welcomed him without ceremony. In his *Mémoires*, the German relates:[6] 'General Dentz greeted me with the words 'My father left Alsace in 1870 so that his son did not become German. You can guess how happy I am to receive you!' I thanked him for his frankness and reminded him of Talleyrand's phrase: 'A diplomat who needs to lie is not a good diplomat."

'What do you want from me?' Dentz asked.

'Weapons for the Iraqi Army: 21,000 rifles, 200 heavy artillery pieces, 400 light artillery pieces, 5 million rounds of ammunition, 100,000 hand grenades, enough to arm two Iraqi divisions. The whole lot delivered to the Turkish frontier.' General Dentz raised his arms to the skies: 'You wish to arm all the British [*sic*] regiments. I will need three weeks to collect all that.'

'I began to laugh: General, our army beat yours by its speed. I give you 10 hours.'

'Kindly explain to an old career officer what you would do in his place?'

'It is very simple: I would summon a junior officer in whom I had full confidence, I would swear him to secrecy, I would then give him the order in question.'

Seventeen hours later, the equipment had arrived at the Turkish frontier, accompanied by a guard of 200 French soldiers of the 16th RTT (*Régiment de Tirailleurs Tunisiens*; Tunisian Tirailleur Regiment) who were armed for the unavoidable crossing of a stretch of Turkish territory. The official reason given was the fear of seeing disturbances break out at the Syrian frontier. General Dentz was concerned about the reactions of the Italian Control Commission to such a move. 'I will take care of it,' I replied. 'The Italians are extremely reasonable people.'

'And the aircraft,' enquired Dentz, 'what is that all about?' Rahn explained: 'It is a simple matter of German aircraft, flying with Iraqi colours, transiting en route to Mosul and Baghdad. The exact number is not known, but they have to be refuelled.' 'We will never have enough fuel!' exclaimed Dentz. 'Where am I going to find some? Nothing has been prepared.' The General expressed his doubts about the chances of success of such an expedition. Nevertheless, he obeyed. At his request, Rahn received papers in the name of Renouard, and two vehicles were placed at his disposal.[7]

When the German and his team left for Damascus, Dentz reported to Vichy: 'We have the impression that, on the German side, there are improvised solutions without a definite plan. The choice does not seem to be made between a far-reaching military intervention and a simple demonstration without a real impact on the fate of Syria. We hope that the British reaction will be moderate, if it is simply a case of aircraft transiting; but if there is installation of bases, we can expect a strong reaction.'[8] Weapons or aircraft, this aid was really more symbolic than effective, according to the technical people. The landing of aircraft, lost far from their base and deprived of proper logistics, can lead only to a useless confrontation with the British. The *Luftwaffe* pilots who, for their part, never believed in the expedition, called it the 'Wilhelmstrasse[9] campaign'. As for the weapons, they were mainly outdated and in bad condition, but what did the *OKW*, which was preparing for the invasion of Russia, care about the fate of Rachid Ali?

Rahn, who had a radio transmitter and operator, communicated with the Wilhelmstrasse: 'After meetings that lasted hours and during which Guérard supported me in excellent fashion, the High Commissioner let himself be convinced, and promised to support Darlan's policies loyally.' Nevertheless, not everything was settled. The French did not have enough petrol. Some had to be found from elsewhere. Go to Turkey, answered Berlin: we will release some Romanian oil. Rahn therefore flew to Ankara. 'It was in Turkey that I had the most problems', he remembered. 'Our Ambassador, Mr von Papen, was given the task of finding petrol for us [...] In Ankara I asked to see him immediately. He had a message sent to me that, being tied up in a tennis tournament, he could not receive me that very day. When I saw him arrive, elegant and distinguished, putting on the airs of an English gentleman, I was not surprised to hear him say that three or four tankers of petrol would perhaps be delivered, but not in under three weeks. Which was, in fact, what happened.' Back in Damascus, Rahn contacted the Syrian nationalists and got them to agree to be quiet until the end of the war, then made his way towards the Iraqi border where Arab tribal chiefs, paid by England, threatened the Iraqi rebels from behind. He calmed them down by announcing a completely unexpected piece of news: a German army was crossing the Caucasus and would soon be at the Euphrates. He had the plans, he said, but they were false. Rahn made such gross errors of geography that he did not convince the bedouin.

How could one take a position alongside Germany without being against England? This essential ambiguity ended up undermining everything, including confidence in the Marshal and the international credit of France.

None of that remained secret. The British learned of the arrival of the German aircraft on the very same day. On 12 May, cables from British consuls in Syria confirmed to Cairo the landing of three 'presumed German' aircraft at Aleppo. The British high command learned equally quickly of the forthcoming weapons delivery. Tension increased sharply. A conflict in Syria now became possible. Faced with possible British reprisals, Dentz took precautions and, on 9 May, he ordered his troops to leave their camps and occupy their so-called 'dispersal' positions – five to ten kilometres from the garrison positions. The armour went to shelter under the trees in the Ghouta – the oasis of Damascus – and the infantry bivouacked in the gardens.

In an endeavour to make the German presence less visible, Dentz tried to minimise it. He asked the Germans to land at Palmyra where their presence would be less obvious and, to deny their increasingly pressing demands, he sheltered behind his orders refusing, as much as he was able, all forms of cooperation which could drag him towards military collaboration. When the *Luftwaffe* people wanted to unload a spare engine, he forbade it and alerted Vichy: 'I ask you to intervene so that they remain within the framework of your previous instructions.'[10] German pressure was being felt everywhere. Dentz had to oppose Rahn's request to open a German consulate in Beirut that he would manage. 'To set up this consulate' he said at his trial, 'was to oust the High Commissioner of France in favour of a High Commissioner of the Reich. This abdication had to be avoided.' Dentz caused the plan to be aborted. But how to mask the German presence? By denying it? He tried. Getting himself deeper and deeper in a lie, which each day became more obvious, the General for several days officially denied all the rumours which were circulating. A professor came from Aleppo to question him on the subject, to whom he shouted:

'It seems that you claim that you have seen German aircraft?
There is not a single German aircraft in Syria.'

'But General, I have seen them and I see them every day. I
could even point out to you the hotel where some pilots in civilian
clothing are staying.'

'You are dreaming [...] There are no German aircraft in Syria.
Take it from me and stop spreading this rumour.'[11]

No one was taken in by it. Rumours were circulating in the
city, and the hostile reactions of French airmen were reported. In
Palestine, naturally, the Free French were soon up to date. Vichy
was caught 'with its hand in the till' and Radio Haifa found it an
extraordinary subject for indignation. Several days later, a Free
French airman, Sub-Lieutenant Labat, back from a reconnaissance
mission, informed General Catroux that he had just seen German
aircraft in Aleppo. He did not want to machine-gun them as he
refused to fire on French Syria.[12]

Faced with this confirmed news, the British Consul in Beirut
was asked by Cairo to demand explanations from the French
High Commissioner. This latter did not deny anything: 'It is true,'
he answered, 'We have had to give into German demands but we
have done everything possible to make the weapons unusable or
to delay their delivery.' Havard then asked the question: 'What
would be your attitude if the instructions from your government
ordered you to allow the Germans to occupy Syria?' Dentz did
not hide his revulsion nor the fact that he would obey orders:
'I can tell you straight away that if such orders reached me, I
would carry them out.' A very grave statement. Could the British
run such a risk? On 9 May, when the Germans were landing
in Syria, the British Intelligence Service reported an abnormal
concentration of enemy aircraft in Greece. The threat became
clear: after the transport aircraft came combat aircraft. On 11
May, about 5:00 p.m., French fighters intercepted three twin-
engine Messerschmitt 110 fighters approaching the coast and
forced them to land at Rayak. Their destination, they explained,
was Damascus. They were authorised to proceed there, but the
airmen, shocked by the presence of aircraft bearing the swastika,
obeyed with very bad grace.[13] In a telegram dated 13 May, Dentz
reported the landing at Mezzé-Damascus of about 15 aircraft.
The German fighters went into action in Iraq on 13 May and
the bombers on 15 May. The BBC broadcast the news, which
caused strong feelings. Many could not believe it. In Alexandria,
Sub-Lieutenant Simon of Force X:[14] 'London radio confirmed

that the government of Vichy had authorised German aircraft to use Syrian airfields to help the Iraqi insurgents. We had trouble believing it, all the more so as Vichy denied it.'

Aircraft in Syria? A concentration of planes in Greece? Talks in Vichy? The convergence of these three events was extremely alarming. Churchill telegraphed to Wavell: 'You certainly realise the danger that there would be if these thousands of Germans, transported by air, were to take over Syria.'

Even faced with these threats, and even pressured by Churchill, Wavell remained inflexible and refused to open a new front. However, he reacted and authorised the RAF to enter Syrian air space. On 14 May, for the first time, British fighters entered the Levant and attacked Luftwaffe aircraft on French airfields. While some fighters were machine-gunning the airfield at Damascus, others were bombing Rayak – eight to ten bombs. On 15 May, they attacked the aerodrome at Palmyra. 'At siesta time, three aircraft arrived at treetop height and machine-gunned the airfield at Mezzé-Damascus from end to end,' noted Lieutenant Michelet. 'No one turned a hair. Other aircraft, flying higher, distributed leaflets signed by Catroux.' Probably piloted by Frenchmen of the French Squadron,[15] some aircraft dropped leaflets over Damascus, Baalbek, Homs, Tripoli and Beirut,[16] calling on the population to revolt. This very long document, written in a literary style, evoked no response. Faced with repeated attacks on Palmyra, where enemy aircraft passing through were most numerous, the Germans decided to use other bases. According to various accounts the following were bombed in turn: On 16 May, Damascus; 17 May, Aleppo and Palmyra; 18 May, Aleppo and Rayak; 19 May, Damascus and Palmyra; 20 May, Damascus; and on 24 May, Aleppo. The British were careful not to bomb French installations that they knew about.[17] Although several aircraft of the French Air Force (*Armée de l'Air*) were damaged, no Frenchman was hit. On 18 May, in conformity with the orders of General Huntziger to oppose the British 'by all possible means', French fighters received the order to intervene, but even though they took off, they allowed the British to operate freely. Not retaliating in any way, they did not cross the border. When the Hurricanes saw the Dewoitines, they broke off. Everyone refused combat. Wavell and Dentz both tried to avoid the confrontation that was imposed upon them. Until 24 May, British air attacks were only aimed at German aircraft.

Between the phoney war and the declaration of hostilities, there was a strange mood for several days. The French approved of the British actions and did not feel threatened. Wavell, in fact, still envisaged only air and naval retaliation. Until 16 May, French ships continued to pass by Gibraltar freely. Then the blockade resumed: on that day, the Royal Navy seized the French tanker *Shéhérazade* and the cargo vessel *Winnipeg*, and on 22 May, the phosphate carrier *Rabelais* was sunk in the port of Sfax by an aerial attack.

Dentz, faced with this sharp rise in tension, strove to limit the number of airfields used by the enemy. He opposed all attempts to create stores depots. When the Germans insisted on carrying out the anti-aircraft defence of Aleppo, he refused, but an order from Vichy soon urged upon him the evacuation of the airfield in Aleppo to leave it to the Germans. He was shocked. On 15 May, in fact, a telegram from Huntziger warned him that '33 German mechanics are going to arrive at Aleppo. They will be in civilian clothes.' This message stated that 'only the airfield at Aleppo is to be used by the Germans and it is the French who will man the anti-aircraft guns.' However, the base must be evacuated by French airmen, with the exception of a security detail and maintenance personnel. That day, 30-odd German mechanics in civilian clothes disembarked from transport aircraft, under the command of Colonel von Manteuffel, and established a camp off the base. They built barracks, were well supplied with equipment, and set up a maintenance workshop; a bomb dump and a supply depot were soon added. In addition, Manteuffel demanded a supply of 10,000 litres of petrol per day, which gradually increased to 24,000 litres per day. Moreover, the number of German mechanics grew to 200 at the beginning of June. With very bad grace, the French put up with these neighbours. Colonel von Manteuffel, who demanded to take his meals in the French officers' mess, was served alone in a side room. Perhaps even more than the number of aircraft in transit, this arrangement was very disquieting.

The German presence having become impossible to hide, the General ended up declaring this half-truth on Radio Beirut: 'Some German aircraft have recently flown over Syria. Fifteen of them have recently made forced landings on Syrian aerodromes. In conformity with the conditions of the Armistice, the French authorities have taken precautions so that these aircraft leave again as quickly as possible.' However, on the BBC, it was too easy for Maurice Schumann to say: 'Dentz lies, Dentz is German.'

The German installations did not, however, spread. If the mechanics in Aleppo carried out aircraft refuelling until 6 June, they were the only German elements to stay in Syria, confirmed General Dentz at his trial.

How many of these aircraft were there? The question is not of great interest; the important thing is that they were there. The figures put forward by various people, and inflated by propaganda, are very different. In any event, there weren't more than those of *Sonderkommando Jung*, that is to say 79 aircraft, plus 15 Italian on 22 May, making a total of 94 aircraft. The number of landings was considerably greater than their basic number. Obviously, there were hundreds of air movements, and as aircraft took off and landed in both directions and on different airfields, it was impossible to count them accurately.

The French octane rating not suiting the German aircraft, they encountered considerable difficulties. Supply by air of spare parts and munitions was an almost insurmountable handicap for them. Reaching Iraq after numerous breakdowns due to the heat and excessively long flights, their military usefulness was almost nil. They carried out six bombing raids against Habbaniya or *Habforce*, and seven reconnaissance flights.[18]

On 21 May, upon his return from Berchtesgaden and on his own initiative, Admiral Darlan allowed the handover to Iraq of three-quarters of the munitions and supplies in Syria. Delivery of weapons to the enemy constitutes a form of direct military cooperation – to be condemned much more than an authorisation for aircraft transit. Here again, Dentz was going to try to limit the consequences of this scandalous decision. He was going to hand over weapons downgraded by the army following its re-equipment by Weygand in 1939. He was even going to sabotage it, as far as possible, by providing incomplete weapons lacking spare parts. In addition, no instructor accompanied them. However, a rifle is a rifle and a grenade is a grenade. If soldiers knew the difference between an old gun and a semiautomatic, the journalists didn't and the propaganda people even less.

This armament was paid for. Germany actually handed over to Monsieur Conty, Political Counsellor at the High Commission, 85 million francs in new notes from the Bank of France (*Banque de France*). The remainder was to be paid for by Iraq by way of food supplies.

The only way to transport them was by the Aleppo-Mosul railway. Now this railway runs along the border inside Turkey for over 400 km, then re-enters Syria at Tel Kotchek where, crossing the Euphrates, it enters Iraq. Franco–Turkish agreements gave France the right of transit through Turkey, but would Ankara, careful of its neutrality, authorise the passage of convoys of armaments to an Iraq at war? Nothing was less certain. It could be made out that this equipment was destined for the defence of the Levant, and this materiel was thus being conveyed by the French Army to which it no longer belonged.

Dentz sent the cast-offs: 'cannon whose firing pins had been "lost", cases of munitions whose fuses no longer existed',[19] cannon without sights, grenades without detonators, Model 1874 Gras rifles, cast-off Chauchat light machine guns from 1915, downgraded Saint-Étienne machine guns [...] General Jacques Méry, then a lieutenant in the 4th Bureau[20] of the High Command of the troops in the Levant, confirmed having received directly from General Dentz in person a written order to sabotage the materiel to be handed over. The order specified: 'All materiel must be, insofar as possible [...] and in a non-obvious way, made unusable. This we did: cannon made more or less unserviceable – firing pins blunted, etc. – grenades without pins, inert grenades, rifles with bent firing pins, etc. Everything was carried out over two nights.'[21]

According to General Albord, 'General Dentz agreed all the more willingly to the deliveries of arms as he was convinced that they were unusable [...]. 'I was absolutely convinced that this materiel would be no good at all', he said 'and the aftermath proved that; in fact, it remained disused. I recall that, in the conversation that I had later with my chief of staff, we said to each other: After all, it would only ever serve to arm the English or the Gaullists!' The English historian Playfair confirmed that these weapons were completely useless.[22] There were arms and there were vehicles. Questioned by General Albord, Captain Gervois, former commander of the vehicle park in the Levant, declared: 'After the Armistice, we had stockpiled all the unusable junk sent from France after the requisition in the Var of butchers' vans, grocers' trucks and soft drinks wagons. In 1941, on the order to send 200 vehicles to Iraq, we sent these cast-off vehicles.'[23]

The dispatch of all this materiel was carried out in less than 36 hours by French soldiers tasked to find the waggons, assemble and load them, and send them on their way. Carried out in the greatest hurry, these operations allowed the worst equipment to be sent. Accompanied by a company of the *16ᵉ Régiment de tirailleurs tunisiens* (16th Regiment of Tunisian Tirailleurs), the first convoy left Aleppo on the morning of 12 May. Davet, who does not contest that the equipment was often unusable,[24] declared that 20,000 rifles, 200 machine guns, 5 million rounds of ammunition, 56 truckloads of aviation gasoline, four 75mm cannon and eight 155mm cannon, were delivered to Iraq. Speaking on oath, General Dentz declared:[25]

> Instead of three batteries, I succeeded in sending only eight short 155mm cannon without telescopic sights or aiming mechanisms, 354 Chauchat Model 1915 light machineguns in service for 25 years, whose magazines or swivel pins for the bipods were broken or twisted. They were of no military value. As for the trucks, instead of the 633 light trucks and 54 heavy trucks which were called for, only 32 trucks were sent, about which I informed Vichy. Rahn asked me to send French instructors. I absolutely refused. He then asked me to accept Iraqi soldiers for instruction. I again refused. In fact, only the weapons and worn-out equipment, without any military value, were sent, along with some trucks barely capable of limited service [...] I succeeded in reducing the requests made by Rahn by three-quarters.

Rahn accompanied the trains in person: he knew the Euphrates region. It was planned that French locomotives would haul the trains as far as the frontier where Iraqi locomotives would take over. On 13 May, no one was waiting at Tel Kotchek. Rahn ordered the two trains to be joined together, and the journey to continue with a single Syrian locomotive. Abandoned by the French escort, he continued his journey on board the locomotive as far as Mosul where a German representative was awaiting the convoy. In exchange for these deliveries, the French brought back wagons loaded with food supplies – wheat, oil, butter, dates, fruit and vegetables – delivered as payment by Iraq. Placed on the market, these supplies caused prices to fall sharply, thus reducing social tension.

To interrupt this traffic, the British, who were well aware of what was happening, sent a raiding party by air on 28 May to blow up the Tel Kotchek bridge, but the damage was minimal and the bridge was quickly repaired. The last delivery, planned for the first fortnight in June, was cancelled as Baghdad fell on 30

May. Unusable militarily, these arms had an important political effect.[26] Although these deliveries hardly seemed to upset Wavell, London found in them the incontrovertible proof that Vichy was compromised militarily.

Alas! There was still another and far more worrying threat. On 21 May, the Admiral authorised 'the use of the ports and transport routes in the Levant by the *Reich*', 'the Germans demanded the use of the ports of Beirut, Tripoli, and Latakia. Kindly let me have your views urgently'. Dentz answered: 'The use of Beirut, Tripoli, and Latakia by the Germans seems to me to be impossible without risk of serious trouble [...] I suggest as an alternative the bay of Chekka where there is a landing stage for barges with a 3.5 metre draught and which is more favourable for secrecy.'

Chekka, approximately 15 km south of Tripoli, is situated in an almost deserted area but on the railway line. This bay was equipped with a 1.5-tonne electric crane. Dentz's reply was thus a rejection: a single landing stage, a small crane, 3.5-metre depth of water could not in any way be a base for an offensive. This suggestion of Dentz's was sharply criticised by judges who were totally ignorant of maritime matters. No Axis ship ever berthed in the French Levant.

In this bizarre Middle East, the British and French had always pursued parallel ambitions. For 20 years, the two mandatory powers cohabited in a polite but distrustful atmosphere. French and British greeted each other without liking each other. The Colonial Office did not forgive France for causing its dream of dominating the Arab world to fail. 'The Intelligence Service continued its covert actions in the mandated states,' noted Le Corbeiller. 'It remained very active, ever-present, and its agents spread by word of mouth all the slogans that served its cause.'[27] A network of local agents kept Cairo informed, and there were also some more highly placed informers. Furthermore, the frontier crossed immense desert areas and, according to Spears, 'a constant traffic was carried on by Jews and Arabs without oversight.' Everyone took advantage of it, the bedouin, the traffickers, the deserters, the spies and even the diplomats. Thus Dentz himself kept secret but friendly relations with the British. At his trial, he said: 'Along the south Lebanon border, very frequent contacts took place between representatives of the High Commissioner and the British mandate. They were always marked by the greatest courtesy and always brought about a favourable settlement of border and commercial questions. The head of the foreign trade service frequently went to Jerusalem to negotiate'[28] Even if Spears protested, Wavell knew very well what was happening in the Levant.

Although officially broken off, relations between Cairo and Beirut never completely ceased. There are witness accounts from both sides. Le Corbeiller, of Dentz's staff: 'Every day at 1300hrs GMT, Beirut contacted Alexandria where Admiral Godfroy commanded the interned ships [of Force X]. Dentz could, no doubt, transmit messages through him to the British high command. Churchill was aware of this link, which operated until the Armistice of Saint-Jean-d'Acre.'[29] Edgard de Larminat, a member of Free France: 'Admiral Godfroy had a direct link with Beirut.' We know that the French admiral maintained friendly relations with his British gaoler, Admiral Cunningham, who was himself closely linked to Wavell. When Dentz finally wanted to send a particularly important message to Cairo, he approached Cornelius van Egert, the American Consul in Beirut, who immediately undertook to transmit it.

Although relations between the Army of the Levant and Free France were non-existent, contacts with the British were never broken.

10

War Clouds Gather

On 15 May, the British Consul-General in Beirut handed the French High Commissioner an official note from His Majesty's Government. By this official action, Great Britain informed France that she regarded the authorisation of a refuelling stop to Germany as an act contrary to its promises. Making France responsible for this situation, she warned there might be repercussions. This communication, stated the Consul, was going to be read in the House of Commons, and be handed to the American Ambassador in Vichy, as well as to Marshal Pétain. Dentz thanked him and reported [to Vichy].

Upon receipt of this warning, Admiral Leahy, representing the United States in Vichy, reacted immediately. He consulted Washington and, 'upon telegraphic instructions from his government', addressed this stern note to Admiral Darlan: 'The help [by the French to the Germans in the Levant] has not been apparent on a large scale until now, but if the use of Syrian territory by the Germans continues, it is clear that such an involvement in the military effort of the *Reich* would go beyond the demands to the Armistice and would in fact constitute active assistance to Germany. This is not in keeping with the past assurances that I have received from His Excellency Marshal Pétain.'[1] On the same day in Washington, in a radio broadcast, President Roosevelt addressed this message to the French people: 'It is inconceivable that the French people would accept, of their own free will, an agreement for a so-called "collaboration" which would imply in reality an alliance with a military power whose essential policy aims at totally destroying liberty, independence and democratic institutions everywhere.' It wasn't only a matter of verbal threats: on 18 May, the US Coast Guard boarded and inspected ten French cargo ships and the liner *Normandie* tied up in New York since the beginning of the war.[2] Moreover, Washington threatened to suspend deliveries of supplies to French North Africa.[3]

The Syrian affair was thus taking on an international dimension whose extreme gravity had not been foreseen by Admiral Darlan. To measure the real size of enemy air traffic and to sound out the state of mind of the troops, he sent the Secretary of State for Air, Air Force General Bergeret, as a delegate, to the Levant from 19 to 25 May. Bergeret noted and reported the reality of the German landings, the British attacks, and the discipline shown by the army and the High Commissioner. He added: 'If the British aerial attacks on our airfields seem to be aimed only at these [German] aircraft, it is nonetheless true that at Rayak Lieutenant Bessi was killed and numerous soldiers were wounded by British bombs.' The death of Lieutenant Bessi could not be a pretext for war, but Vichy decided, on 19 May, to expel the British consuls in response. Endeavouring to diminish the severity of this measure, Dentz transmitted it reluctantly: 'I give every facility to Sir Godfrey Havard, the Consul-General, as well as to all his staff, to leave when they see fit, to take with them what they want in way of equipment, luggage and personal effects.' In response, the French consuls were expelled from Palestine, and British troops ceased using the railway crossing Syria. War, it seemed, was possible, and Dentz, who wanted to avoid it at all costs, implored the British high command, via the agency of Admiral Godfroy, not to cause irreparable damage. On 28 May, however, the British attitude became rather hostile: a communiqué from London announced that henceforth Great Britain 'considered Syria and Lebanon as enemy-occupied territories as regards everything connected with trade and the war economy.'

On 19 May, an astonishing piece of news reached Catroux: the most famous officer in the Levant, Lieutenant-Colonel Philibert Collet, 'Collet of the Circassians', wanted to meet him in order to discuss taking his units over to the British side. Now Collet, who commanded 13 new squadrons of Circassian irregular cavalry, had an important place in the defensive arrangements of the Levant. On the evening of 20 May, the two men met at on the frontier close to the village of Mafrak, where the old Ottoman railway passed by. 'Dusk was falling over the run-down, colourless and bare countryside of the volcanos of the Jebel Druse to the north-west and the peak of Mount Hermon to the north,' remembered Catroux.[4] In the dark under the railway bridge, Collet declared to Catroux that he had decided to join Free France with a maximum number of cavalrymen. Catroux questioned him: how did Dentz's army react to the threat of invasion? Is it falling back, as he believed? On the contrary, answered Collet. In Syria, as in Lebanon, it is moving to its battle stations, and the units have decided to respond to any attempted invasion. No unit will defect. All are hostile to the Germans but all will obey General Dentz in a disciplined manner. Attacked by the British without ever responding, the flyers were particularly hostile to Free France. As for the Navy, it remained Darlan's Navy. Collet convinced Catroux: it was out of the question to attack with only the Free French Division, and the only hope of success was to convince Wavell to mount a large-scale operation.

Collet was an astonishing person. Enlisting as a private soldier in 1914 and becoming a warrant officer in 1918, he arrived in the Levant in 1919. An excellent rider, he raised squadrons of Circassians, making a spirited unit out of these mercenaries who demonstrated their value in many fights. This man with an inflexible courage managed to attach them to himself. A legend grew up around him. His courage and the extraordinary appearance of his men made him a well-known figure. He was untouchable. Did he fit into the officer corps? People were jealous of him for his fame: 'Collet of the Circassians' had been trained only during wartime. He had not graduated from any military school, and his wife, an Englishwoman from Ireland, a former dancer it was murmured, 'exuberant' according to Sairigné, was suspect on several grounds. She belonged to the group of officers' wives only on the surface. In the somewhat erotic memoirs that she published after the war,[5] she appeared as some sort of agent. Sir Godfrey Havard,[6] the Consul-General, had entrusted her with some important missions, telling her: 'You must never forget that you are English. I am going to entrust you with a document of incalculable value. It must be placed only in your Consul's hands [...] you must not hesitate to keep it secret, even at the risk of your life.' The account is rather like a novel, but she described herself in it.

A major in 1940, Collet commanded the group of six 'old Circassian squadrons' at Damascus. 'Outdated, obsolete, and with a storybook appearance, but what an appearance,' admired a tanker watching them leave to go into action. They wore baggy trousers and an astrakhan cap, [armed with] sword and cavalry carbine, with the kit behind the saddle as on manœuvres. The horses, rather nervous, were kept on a short rein. They were unlike ordinary cavalry which are no longer seen in modern warfare. As if on the dusty roads of the Year 1000, when thousands of men were in motion, the Circassians of Colonel Collet marked a turning point in time.'

Was Collet a Gaullist? As early as 1940 he had wanted to cross the frontier but, fearing that his departure would cause trouble, the British had dissuaded him. It was the landings of the German aircraft that had made up his mind to meet Catroux. On 22 May, news of his desertion, with several squadrons the night before, reached Damascus. Two squadrons had been intercepted and brought back, but there had been an exchange of fire. The captain of gendarmerie in Deraa, as well as an engineer lieutenant who tried to prevent them crossing, had been killed at the border.[7]

While three or four squadrons of 'Circassian irregulars' had crossed over to other side, the 'old squadrons' had shown themselves to be less enthusiastic. While most of the officers and NCOs had followed Collet, the majority of the men had balked at leaving Kuneitra where their families lived. Collet finally carried along with him 20 French officers, 16 native officers, 27 French NCOs, 38 native NCOs and 352 men[8] – 453 according to Oddo, including 19 officers and NCOs. Collet's group had an overabundance of officers and NCOs. Cooped up in a camp near Tiberias and briefly threatened with machine guns, they were disarmed, under the pretext of providing them with new equipment, which was a supreme insult. As the officers spoke English badly, conversations were often carried on in Arabic, remembered Oddo. The young officers thought, 'in all good faith, it seemed, they were going to be fighting the Germans in Egypt, so they were dumbfounded to hear from General Catroux, during a visit he made to them on 22 May, that they were going to return to Syria in a few days to reoccupy the positions they had just left.'[9]

Soon, agents from the families came to urge the Circassian irregulars to return; their wives and children in their absence were not able to access French military facilities, their sole source of support. Hunger caused 200 to return. Accepted back, these men fought very well. Fighters by vocation, mercenaries by tradition, cavalrymen by nature, the Circassians served those who paid them, following their chief rather than a flag.

In the sands of Iraq, *Habforce* made slow progress. In temperatures approaching 50°C, the British made superhuman efforts to advance, despite overloaded trucks, bad roads, repeated breakdowns, punctures and being bogged down. The column was attacked by German aircraft, which caused some losses. Destroying the bridges and the dykes and flooding the area around the Euphrates, the Iraqis were solidly dug in to bar the column's way forward. On 19 May, at about 5:00 a.m., in spite of the desultory intervention by German aircraft, 47 RAF aircraft started bombing the area around Habbaniya. The air attacks lasted nine hours, but the resistance collapsed and, in the evening, after an exhausting march, *Habforce* finally reached Habbaniya. On 21 May, after a day's rest, the British broke camp and set out for Baghdad, repelling a rather brisk counter-attack at Falluja; but Baghdad fell on 30 May without a fight. Rachid Ali and the Grand Mufti fled to Iran with 40 companions.[10] 'Rachid Ali and the Forty Thieves', exulted the British. A British column – *Kingcol*, a detached element of *Habforce* – left immediately for Mosul.

The French arms were still on the trains. The British seized them and noted that the equipment had been sabotaged. An English report specified: 'The cannon would have been dangerous for anyone using them. I notified this to HQ 10th Army warning that these munitions were dangerous.'[11]

This brief campaign was thus a great success. By unleashing his affair without consulting Berlin, Rachid Ali had spoiled a fine opportunity. If he had hoped to bring about a general Arab uprising, he must have been disappointed. No one had reacted. Rahn wrote: 'After a short stay in Syria, I suppose I discovered to my great surprise [...] that one could expect everything of the population, except that it would fight.' No one in Germany appeared to be affected by the failure, which seemed to be regarded as of no importance. Summoned by Hitler to the *OKW* at the end of July, Rahn was greeted by the sallies of his staff: 'Well then, it has failed?' The *Führer* himself, not having time to receive him, contented himself with calling out when they crossed in a doorway: 'I left you high and dry over there in Syria!' Caught short, Rahn could only answer '*Jawohl, mein Führer!*'[12]

Wavell therefore was right: the Iraq affair was only a diversion. In ten days, the business had been settled almost without loss. To have become involved in Syria would have only distracted him from the only important threat, the one which hovered over the western coast, that of Rommel and his *Afrika Korps*. The war in the East took a dramatic turning: the day Habbaniya was liberated, 20 May, an unstoppable airborne assault on Crete took place. Germany had attacked suddenly.

On 20 May 1941, an airborne invasion by the *VII Fliegerkorps* – *Unternehmen Merkur (Operation Mercury)* – hit the Greek island. The garrison[13] defended itself with great ferocity, the fighting sometimes being reduced to knives and bayonets, but without assistance and air support, the Germans were absolute masters of the sky. The island buckled under the assault and, on 31 May, it fell. The 96,000 men under the command of General Freyberg[14] – British, Australians, New Zealanders and Greeks – had to fall back and, if they could, embark on ships bound for Egypt. The British lost 17,000 men, including 3,500 killed, five ships including an aircraft carrier, two cruisers and two destroyers. Fifteen ships were damaged, including three battleships, HMS *Warspite, Valiant* and *Barham*. It was a particularly heavy toll. The only consolation – but the British did not know – was that the Battle of Crete was a disaster for the Germans. With 4,300 killed or missing out of 22,000 paratroops, the loss of all its gliders and 170 transport aircraft, *VII Fliegerkorps* had sustained irreparable losses. It was eliminated. Hitler, who totally lacked enthusiasm for the operation in Crete, according to the German General Kurt Student, was very upset by the heavy losses of the parachute units and deduced from them that these units no longer could produce the same effect of surprise. Later on he often said 'the era of paratroops is over'. The *Führer* never wanted to hear them mentioned again. However, the British did not know this. Did the Germans plan on jumping into Cyprus? Syria? Even if this was incorrect, the British could fear it.

At the same time as the loss of Crete, the enemy's pressure on Libya became very heavy. Pushed back over 400 km and partly encircled in Tobruk,[15] the British Army withdrew over a wide front under the German attack. General O'Connor[16] himself, sent as an advisor to his successor General Neame,[17] was captured. Without the unshakeable Wavell, the withdrawal could have turned into a debacle and the Canal could have been reached. Too many men and too much artillery had been lost in Greece, Crete and Libya. In a few months, the Eastern Mediterranean had changed from being a peripheral theatre of operations into an important front. Perhaps the outcome of the war would be played out around Suez. An advanced outpost, Malta still held on, but the passage of convoys to Egypt was a dangerous adventure. The Axis air forces still dominated the waters around Sicily.

Syria was thus on the front of the stage. A new offensive could be feared and the presence of German aircraft perhaps foretold it. 'This Syrian business is very alarming,' Cairo thought. 'The enemy air forces which have been established there are closer to the Canal than if they were at Mersa Matruh, and the Vichy forces at present seem to support the Germans completely,' it was said in British circles.

In German circles, however, the opposite view was held. A landing in Syria was totally outside German thinking. In an important survey following interviews of the major enemy leaders carried out by Liddell Hart after the war, *The Other Side of the Hill* (1948), Syria was not mentioned once, and von Thoma[18] declared: 'That threat [to the Canal] was fortuitous rather than premeditated. The big pincer movement against the Middle East that the British imagined was never a defined plan. It was vaguely discussed by Hitler's entourage, but our Supreme Headquarters never approved it, believing that is was not feasible.'[19] In Cairo, however, the threat of an airborne assault dominated the thinking. A 'paratroop psychosis' took hold of the British. It even affected Churchill himself and it was this, in all probability, which induced him to take an enormous risk in the eyes of his staff. Favouring the hypothesis of an attack in the Levant, Churchill withdrew 30,000 men from Libya to put them into Syria before the Germans arrived. 'Caught short in Crete, he intended remaining master of events in Syria', thought Davet.

For his part, Wavell remained opposed to the plan. For him, to attack the French was an almost suicidal bet. He was 'evidently hard put to find a brigade or even a battalion', he objected to Churchill.[20] Exasperated by the plan, he noted in his diary: 'Why do politicians never learn the simple principle of concentration of forces for the main target and the necessity to avoid dispersion of efforts?' The British general understood perfectly the enemy plan, which was becoming clear; those two offensive pincer movements that, coming from Syria and Lebanon, could strangle Suez. But did he not know, as did Churchill, that Hitler was on the eve of attacking Russia? Did he fear, he who knew them, 'the supporters of Vichy'? The supporters of Vichy were soldiers like him, not a political party as the adjective '*vichyste*' (Vichyite) seemed to suggest. For Wavell, who knew them, these Frenchmen weren't real adversaries. Faced with a German offensive and the Armistice being broken, he thought that they would fight alongside him. The propaganda commotion had not caused him to lose his sense of proportion. The intelligence collected underlined their complete lack of hostility towards England. Their army of 35,000 men therefore ensured cover to the north. For him, the German pincer movement was but a feint. The only enemy was Rommel.

However, surprisingly, all changed on 20 May. Against the advice of Wavell in Cairo, against that of Dill, Alan Brooke and the Defence Committee in London, Churchill, thumping the table, gave the order to get ready to invade the French mandate, with or without the Free French.

How could General de Gaulle not experience great satisfaction? The event proved him right: Vichy had chosen its camp, that of the enemy. Hadn't he hoped and prayed for it?[21] During a speech on Radio Brazzaville, he exulted: 'So, the people from Vichy have handed over Syria to the Germans. They will do the same for [French] North Africa and for French West Africa [...] France crushed, [and] muzzled ascribes this new treason to the guilty men, certain of one day bringing them to justice [...] I confirm that duty consists of rebelling against the traitors who are handing over the Empire after having handed over the country [...]The remnants of the prestige of several important persons is a cover for the designs of the enemy.' Nothing for the General was sufficiently offensive to damn Vichy. Everything was acceptable, even lies. In his *Mémoires,* he asserted that 'if General Dentz received the order to let German troops land, he would not fail to obey, which really came back to meaning that the order had already been given. In fact, the beaches where the enemy was supposed to land were already known in advance.' He even added lies which supported his thesis. According to him, the troops in the Levant 'were taking up positions at the frontier to resist the Free French and the Allies, while behind them, the Germans could move about as they saw fit.' Later, in private during the relief of the postwar period, he answered Claude Guy who asked him it was certain that German airmen were in Syria. 'Yes', he answered, 'a few aircraft [...] On the other hand German ships cruising off the Syrian coast fought in cooperation with the Vichy troops. Oh! It was not said, of course, because it would have made a bad impression, but that is what happened.'[22] Dishonesty or disinformation, the intelligence the Free French had was thus faulty. The reality was already very grave. Vichy was suspect, Darlan guilty. Truth sufficed. Was it necessary to invent these stories that Germans were moving into the region, their ships could intervene? Could a unit of the *Kriegsmarine* sail in the eastern Mediterranean which was completely dominated by the Royal Navy? If Germany had attacked the Levant, she would have broken the Armistice, at the same time delivering the Regular Army from the 'evil curse' that, according to him, bewitched it. Thus hatred led to controversial argument.

Whatever the case may be, on 20 May Churchill forced war on Syria. De Gaulle was thus right and Wavell wrong. *Operation Georges* had another chance. The General congratulated himself: 'The London Cabinet considered that, in these conditions, it was preferable to come around to my way of seeing things that Wavell had tried to dismiss. The turnaround was sudden and complete [...] A message from Mr Churchill asked me to go to Cairo and to not withdraw Catroux, seeing that action was imminent. Very satisfied by the attitude adopted by the British Prime Minister, I answered warmly and, for once, in English. As for General Wavell, his government had commanded him to undertake the action planned by us in Syria. When I arrived in Cairo, I found him resigned to carrying it out.' De Gaulle, happy with this sudden about-face, addressed an enthusiastic letter to Churchill, the only one during the whole war that he had written in English: '1. Thank you. 2. Catroux remains in Palestine. 3. I shall go to Cairo soon. 4. You will win the war.'

On 20 May 1941, the day Crete was attacked, the British War Cabinet sent to Cairo the order 'to prepare to invade Syria as soon as possible' and 'to assemble the elements of as large a force as possible, without the security of the Libyan Desert being affected.' The order also prescribed 'to ensure the transport of the Free French as far as positions close to the frontier and, as soon as Generals Catroux and Legentilhomme decide that it is the moment to act, to bring them all the help possible, particularly aerial support.'

Wavell, surprised by these orders, was furious. His relations with the Chief of Free France, 'awkward and demanding' according to him, had never been good. His composure clashed head on with de Gaulle's impatience. He was ready to fly off the handle. He confided to the British Ambassador in Cairo that 'he had just spent a rather bad night, having been dragged from his bed at dawn by two telegrams, one from the Prime Minister asking him to support at any price the advance of the Free French into Syria, and the other from General de Gaulle "ordering" him to do it.' Wavell, in keeping with his promises, sent his resignation to London! Hadn't he warned Churchill? He telegraphed: 'If the strategy in the Middle East has to be dictated by General de Gaulle, it would be better to relieve me of my command.'

The response from the Prime Minister was blunt:

You are mistaken when you suppose that the strategy outlined in this message has been influenced by the opinion of the leaders of Free France. It is entirely the result of the point of view adopted by those here who have the supreme conduct of the war and diplomacy in all theatres of the conflict. We consider that if the Germans can pick off Syria and Iraq with a few ill-assorted aircraft, some 'tourists' and some local uprisings, we must not hesitate to run small-scale military risks nor expose ourselves to the danger of seeing the political situation deteriorate in case of failure.

And to show his determination, the Prime Minister threatened: 'Of course we take full responsibility for this decision and, in case you are not prepared to agree, we will take the necessary steps to carry out any wish that you may have to be relieved of your command.'

Wavell is a soldier and so will carry out his orders. He will obey, but reluctantly. Churchill will therefore discard him. Churchill's decision being made, Auchinleck, in India, was forewarned that he may be called to replace Wavell in Cairo. The Prime Minister explained to him: 'It is not a matter of mounting [in Syria] a regular military operation. All that one can do is to give the best possible chance to a type of armed political incursion...We take full responsibility for this decision.'

Waiting in Cairo, Wavell did his duty. The same day, 20 May, he ordered General Maitland Wilson to prepare *Operation Exporter*. On 25 May, de Gaulle arrived in Cairo.

11

War Approaches

Weygand in Algiers, Leclerc in Africa, Muselier and Alan Brooke in London, Wavell in Cairo, Dentz in Beirut, whatever their position on the chess board of the war, all the soldiers advised against pursuing this regrettable campaign. All were hostile to a fight that they considered unworthy. But all were officers and had to obey orders. The confrontation will take place, Churchill decided.

Churchill used all the force of his overpowering personality to impose his ideas. Using all the resources of his position, he made the High Command bend to his will, forcing it to abandon its most dearly held convictions including a prudent, defensive strategy and to substitute in its place a somewhat adventurous thrust. Instead of preparing to counter with all his forces the certain enemy offensive in Libya, he gave orders to divert some of them to make a hypothetical attack in Syria. He wanted to attack everywhere, immediately. Here are his orders: in the west, an attack in Libya was to start in three weeks, on 15 June. Following the failure of *Operation Brevity*, a limited offensive in the Sollum-Bardia area against weak Axis forces, *Operation Battleaxe* aimed to relieve Tobruk. The Syrian attack was to start in parallel as soon as possible; it was to be called *Operation Exporter*. Did Churchill impose these two offensives against the advice of all his generals? And was he inspired only by military considerations? He knew that Hitler, on the eve of attacking Soviet Russia, concentrated all his forces in Poland. Probably, he no longer believed in an offensive in the Middle East any more than Wavell did; however, he wanted this war. Wouldn't it be a unique and legitimate opportunity for him to shrink the French territory? To eject the French was a very old English plan. Churchill had already described it: 'There is no question that France should keep the position in Syria that it had before the war.' In September 1939, Havard, the British Consul in Beirut, had declared to Puaux, the French High Commissioner, in the presence of Conty, his Director of Political Affairs: 'England will raise no claim regarding the states in the Levant during the war, but France cannot hope to keep the favoured position it now has after the war. It will receive just compensation.' In June 1940, these conversations convinced Puaux of the aims of the British Colonial Office and, as far as he was concerned, it was clear that a Franco–British condominium could only be a prelude to the eviction of France. 'There is no room in Syria for two [powers] and we are not the stronger', he wrote.[1]

From November 1940 onwards, Churchill harboured this plan. He wrote to Lord Halifax, Foreign Secretary: 'We will certainly have to take control of Syria one way or another in the coming months. The best way would be to do so via the intermediary of Weygand or de Gaulle, but we cannot count on them and, until we have finished with the Italian question in Libya, we do not have enough troops to gamble in the north.'[2] On 8 May 1941, 12 days before his decision, Churchill wrote to General Ismay,[3] his chief military assistant:

> The opinions of the chiefs of staff regarding Syrian affairs must reach me in time for this morning's meeting of the Cabinet. We must do all in our power to prevent the Germans from getting a foothold in Syria with weak troop numbers, and then using the country as a forward base to obtain mastery in the air in Iraq and Persia. Too bad if General Wavell is unhappy with this diversion on our eastern flank [...] We have to bring all our resources, without worrying what is happening in Vichy. I would be very obliged to the staff to see what is the maximum effort we can provide.

Churchill was the successor of Pitt, Disraeli, Gladstone, and a fervent admirer of Lawrence. How could this Marlborough,[4] a Sandhurst graduate born in Queen Victoria's reign, a veteran who had crossed swords with the Mahdi in the Sudan and fought the Boers in the Cape, former First Lord of the Admiralty, and quintessential Englishman, not be satisfied with pulling a fast one on the French? Seize Syria? Parliament would applaud. Churchill had not forgotten the ovation he received in the Commons when he announced the news of Mers el-Kebir. France? The longstanding competition persisted in the heart of this likeable bulldog, stubborn, capricious and tough. Perhaps, under a plausible strategic pretext, Churchill found the unexpected opportunity to recover the conquests that Allenby had had to abandon to the French. Perhaps he could revive the dream of Lawrence, the hero he so admired.

De Gaulle, of course, suspected but, although they did not coincide, the ambitions of both men were along the same lines. For him it was to plant his flag on French territory from which he could speak. With the Army of the Levant and its weapons – if he succeeded in getting them to join him – he could truly stand up, achieve greater stature, and be the embodiment of France to London and, indeed, to the whole world. Until now, was he not only a demagogue supported by foreigners? Syria would be a platform on which he could place his microphone and become a true participant. In Damascus he could be the embodiment of a restored France. But for that, he had to get there. He therefore wished for this conflict as well. According to this logic, it was more pressing to attack the French in Syria than the Germans in Libya.

Who wanted this war? Churchill, quite obviously, because he had the means, but de Gaulle, who called for it, claimed he was its father: 'The initiative for the war in Syria belongs to the Free French.' He wrote in his *Mémoires*, 'It is France which took the initiative of entering Syria in 1941, dragging England along.' He affirmed this in a press conference on 2 June 1945. General Legentilhomme confirmed this statement, as did Catroux who stated that this campaign was 'an undertaking that we had always wanted in the interests of victory and France.'

On the other hand, the Director of Military Intelligence of the Australian Army, Brigadier J.D. Rogers MC accused Dentz:[5]

General Dentz denied several times that German penetration had taken place in Syria but glaring proof of it had reached us [...] Dentz showed as well that his sympathies were entirely with the Axis leaders. Unless he was acting under the orders of higher authorities, it is unquestionably upon him that responsibility rests for the very tough, bloody and useless fighting between the British forces – in great majority Australian – and those of a country which a year or two earlier was still our ally. In spite of Dentz, several of us thought nevertheless that a well-conducted diplomatic approach would have allowed us to avoid this bloody confrontation.

A diplomatic approach? That was an Australian idea. Neither Churchill nor de Gaulle wanted it. That would have been to miss too fine an opportunity. Jim McAllister and Syd Trigellis-Smith – both Australians – wrote: 'Given the profound antipathy separating the supporters of the Vichy government from the Free French, no diplomatic approach could have succeeded, and yet no approach of that sort could have been contemplated that did not involve the Gaullists.'

On 25 May Charles de Gaulle arrived in Cairo, where his presence was unwelcome. Comforted by Churchill's decision, he intended to impose himself everywhere the fate of the French mandate was being played out. Accompanied by General Catroux, he immediately undertook 'many interviews with Wavell', he wrote. 'We pressed him to invade the Levant [...] but absorbed by the operations in Libya and no doubt annoyed by the threatening telegrams from Mr Churchill in which he could see the effects of our own emphasis, he opposed our pleas with good grace. Nothing could persuade him to devote more than a minimum force to the Syrian affair.'

De Gaulle, it seemed, was not worried about Rommel. It was Dentz who concerned him. He asked Wavell for four divisions. For him that was the guarantee of a rapid success: 'Our friends in Beirut and Damascus are saying to us "If the Allies enter Syria in large numbers, there will be only a *baroud d'honneur* (gallant last stand). If, on the other hand, the troops in the Levant come to grips with forces that are weak in strength and equipment, their professional self-esteem will be involved and the fighting will be rough".' Wavell did not have these divisions. Having only 42,000 men and 238 tanks available on the Egyptian frontier, he was fundamentally opposed to breaking them up.

In London at this time, the Foreign Office did not want to favour Free France. For its part, since the indiscretions before Dakar, the War Office distrusted the Free French, who were not regarded as reliable partners. The faulty intelligence that Catroux gave and the aimless conference that he prompted with the British leaders in Cairo could only have reinforced their judgement. These French allies were, for them, more of an embarrassment than a support. Field Marshal Lord Alanbrooke, Chief of the Imperial General Staff, the highest British military authority, did not like General de Gaulle – that is the least that can be said – and he explained why: 'His staff so completely lacked any idea of secrecy that is was practically impossible to contemplate drawing up any plans with it.'[6] General Yves Gras wrote these lucid lines: 'The Middle East Command saw in the FFL (*Forces Françaises Libres*) only a small contingent of foreign volunteers whose boisterous units, demanding and often arrogant, had trouble submitting to the rules of the British Army. It considered them only as a symbolic force whose weak contribution could bring it some extra support in certain circumstances, but which was rather a source of trouble. In any case, Middle East Command intended using the FFL in a clearly subordinate role which would allow the British, as it is said, to "pull the strings". The British command therefore showed little eagerness to equip the FFL and to put them in the front line.'

Amidst the grave concerns of the time, Franco–French quarrels caused bother. The continual abhorrence, the threatening curses, the struggles between a marshal, an admiral and a general in the face of an enemy appeared unworthy to some. The agitation, the outbursts and Gallic arrogance exasperated British gentlemen trained to be restrained and self-controlled. No representative of Free France was invited to participate in the preliminary conferences which took place, before the campaign, in Cairo on 20, 21, 22, 24 and 28 May, and it was not until the final conference on 4 June, when everything had been settled, that they were finally summoned to be among the underlings on the same basis as the Marines. The plan of attack had been settled without French cooperation and the major decisions had been taken in London. The relations with the Free French had been so uncordial that to ease the permanent tension between the Gaullists and the British, Wavell and Spears both asked London separately to appoint a Minister Resident to the Middle East to coordinate opinions and advice and to resolve the differences. Unfortunately, Oliver Lyttelton,[7] the future person in charge of relations with Free France, was not appointed until July.

Tall, calm and competent, enjoying the confidence of his chiefs, and nicknamed 'Jumbo' because of his girth, General Maitland Wilson[8] therefore commanded the invasion of the French Levant. Since his return from Greece where he commanded the British and Polish forces, he was military commander in Palestine and Transjordan. In charge of organising *Habforce* – mission completed – he was now given the job of attacking Syria. Full of common sense, disciplined and respected, knowing his job and his men, 'Jumbo' Wilson lacked that personal magnetism which arouses enthusiasm. He was in many respects similar to Dentz, his future adversary. One had had to hand over Paris and the other had had to hand over Athens. 'Jumbo' would fight against 'the friendly giant.'[9]

As soon as he was appointed, Wilson set to work. On 3 June, Churchill, impatient, pressed him regarding the state of his preparations. 'Kindly tell me by telegram what exactly are the land and air forces that you are using for Syria. What are you doing with the Poles? It seems important to deploy and to use, right from the beginning, the maximum possible air power. Even old aircraft can have a part to play, as they have done so well in Iraq.' General Wilson had no qualms. He was persuaded, like the whole of the British Army, that he was going to fight Germans. Didn't he ask the 5th Indian Brigade to plan special enclosures for 'German prisoners?'[10] The preparatory conferences started on 20 May, the very day of Churchill's decision. General Wilson was in charge of the land invasion, Air Marshal Sir Arthur Tedder commanded the air operations, and Admiral Sir Andrew Cunningham the maritime operations. Assembling an army was difficult. There was a very small number of units. After an extremely careful examination of his strength, Wavell agreed to hand over to Wilson 34,000 combatants: 18,000 Australians, 9,000 British, 2,000 Indians and 5,400 Free French; the last represented a little more than 15 per cent of the total strength and the others 83 per cent.[11] However, he was not given a single suitable tank. Totally outclassed, the small Vickers Mark VI light tanks of the 6th Australian Division Cavalry Regiment were little more than large tracked vehicles armed with a heavy and a light machine gun. The total lack of armoured support was the cause of numerous losses, and the powerful elements of the 9th Australian Division Cavalry Regiment, engaged at the end of the campaign, were too late to be decisive.[12] Nothing had been anticipated to combat the Renault tanks of the opposing forces. Against them, the Boyes anti-tank rifle, that the Diggers called 'the elephant gun', was shown to be ineffectual. Only the 25pdr, the British field artillery gun, was capable of stopping them. It was therefore on foot and in trucks, but with formidable naval support, that the campaign opened. The attacking forces were weak in artillery, signals and transport, 'inappropriate in all regards',[13] but that was all that Cairo could scrape together without weakening Egypt too much.

The effective strength of the RAF was also very modest. It could not do everything. 'Air Marshal Tedder had asked Wavell and Cunningham if his aircraft were supposed to give priority support to the army or the fleet. He could not do both.' It was decided that the air force would give priority to the ships which had already suffered heavy losses in Greece and Crete. Informed of this, Spears later remarked ironically that the air force 'had never dealt a blow which had upset the most emotional supporter of the Vichy government and caused him to spill a single drop of coffee.' The troops on the ground often complained of a total lack of air support. Only 70 aircraft had been dedicated to the Syrian front, including 10 to 12 Hurricane fighters[14] and 8 to 10 Blenheim light bombers, with the remainder protecting the Navy. For reconnaissance duties, the RAF used old biplane Gloster Gladiator and Fairey Fulmar aircraft – easy prey for the French fighters.

These were not the only weaknesses. Spears denounced the poor quality of the British intelligence services. According to him, it was astonishing that more was not known regarding the arrangements of the French forces, the siting of the tanks, and the quality of the forts.[15] There was an important lack of maps: the only map available was on a 1:200,000 scale, on which relief features were indicated very sketchily. French maps with a scale of 1:50,000, on the other hand, showed them with the precision indispensable to infantry.

Finally, these troops were poorly equipped. An order warned each person against wasting equipment:

> Practically everything that you are carrying comes from overseas: your weapons, your clothing, what you eat, your tools, your vehicles and equipment. The majority of these articles were manufactured in factories in Great Britain, which have been bombed. They have been transported in ships that have been attacked by aircraft and submarines. Blood, sweat and tears have been spilled so that they reach you. Are you going to make it necessary, due to negligence, to make and transport more? No, the enemy knows how precious all that is and does all he can to prevent it reaching you, to destroy it before it arrives and after you have received it. You must not help the enemy by using it badly or losing it [...] Take care of all your equipment as if it belongs to you. Keep your weapons, your clothing and your tools in perfect shape. Do not waste anything that can help to win the war.

From gaiters to aircraft, in fact, everything was lacking.

Was this force adequate? Opposing 37,000 men, was Wilson sure of winning? The evidence suggests that he wasn't. On 5 June, he informed the Prime Minister of his concerns: 'The forces that we are committing are in no way sufficient, and the operation is in some ways a wager. Everything depends on the Vichy French.' In the message that he sent to his Prime Minister, Mr Menzies, General Blamey,[16] who was commanding the Australian troops, used the same language: 'The operation is in the nature of a bet.' In an earlier report he was already speaking of a 'risky attempt', and he concluded his recent report on the Greek disaster in insisting that in the future 'no campaign be embarked upon unless success is guaranteed in advance'.

Blamey, like Wavell, regretted having to attack.

Like the Anzacs in 1914–18, Australia had sided with the British from the beginning of the war, but London could not use the AIF (Australian Imperial Force) as it wished.[17] Australia was independent and the agreement of Canberra was required. Yet it was this same Winston Churchill, former First Lord of the Admiralty, who had initiated the catastrophic Dardanelles operation in 1915 in the course of which the losses had been such that the Australian population remained traumatised by them. On 18 May, General Sir Thomas Blamey, commanding the AIF, warned his government that it would no doubt be necessary to send Australian troops to Palestine, and Canberra had agreed. On 20 May, Churchill informed Menzies, the Australian Prime Minister, of the imminent nature of the operation. He warned him the day before the attack, at the same time as Roosevelt. Blamey therefore arrived in Palestine on 30 May. General John Lavarack,[18] his subordinate, commanding the 7th Australian Division, received the order to settle his troops into camp at Hill 95, north of Gaza.[19]

The Australians furnished 18,000 of the 34,000 engaged in Syria and were by far the largest contingent. These men were volunteers. They were relatively old: 50 per cent were older than 25 years, and 30 per cent more than 30, but the enlistment conditions guaranteed high quality troops. Big drinkers and rowdy, used to a rough life, well trained before embarking for Africa, these athletic fighters were sporting, youthful and enthusiastic. In an exotic world, totally foreign to them, there was no possible exchange with the *wogs* (Arabs) or *frogs* (French). They therefore kept all their habits. This war did not have any political motivation for them. They were convinced that they were going to fight Germans. One can read in an interrogation report:[20] 'According to them, Australia's fight against France is shameful, but they thought that they going to fight the Germans first.' Brigadier S. G. Savige[21] himself, at the head of a large unit, asserted later to French officers that he and his men were all convinced that they had 'to fight against the Germans occupying the Levant and that their only goal was to liberate French troops being held prisoner.' 'Many Australian prisoners expressed their deep regret at having to fight French soldiers' was read on a pamphlet printed in Beirut. 'It was a shame' they asserted, 'to fire on their old allies, several of their own fathers or brothers having been killed in the defence of France.' Senior officers had served in France during World War I. Some found themselves on the battlefield where, 22 years previously in 1918, the Australian Light Horse had ridden, stirrup to stirrup, alongside *spahis* and *chasseurs d'Afrique* in pursuit of the remnants of the Ottoman Empire army. Many senior officers wore French decorations won in action in France during World War I. Lavarack knew Dentz personally. These memories were close. Until very recently, relations between Australians and French in the Levant had always been excellent. On 1 June, a week before the attack, the *Sydney Morning Herald* published a report on the visit of a group of Australians to a Foreign Legion camp, and the men in slouch hats had played football with the legionnaires. For them, this regrettable attack could only be explained if there were Germans opposite and propaganda had convinced them that there were.

After the battle, the French Colonel de Bodman drew this sympathetic picture of them: 'The Australian is fair-haired, tall, thin and an individualist. His officers and NCOs are almost all temporary and are recruited, like their men, by enlistment [...] Rather close to nature, very sporting and tough, he is contemptuous of danger and considers war as a sport, simply more dangerous than the others. Violent, not very sensitive, he leaves his dead and wounded on the battlefield for several days. He is the best and bravest of the soldiers of the British Empire.' And Bodman described their methods in this way:

> Their contacts are perfect due to very modern signals, thanks in particular to portable radios which each captain has and which allows the commander to be informed at any moment of the way the battle is progressing and objectives reached. Clad in simple shirts and with light equipment, always without a pack, plus a few grenades, they are remarkably equipped for this war of

movement [...] The leaders do very little. They follow their men and never have to solve battlefield problems other than resuming movement and infiltration. When the position is taken, everyone stops, regroups and reorganises without seeking to push on [...] Typically infantry combat is made up small groups of four to six men, who advance bravely, grouped around a submachine gun or a light machine gun, moving straight ahead towards the objective. They fire while walking, which produces an infernal noise.

This was, in fact, 'the triumph of the light automatic weapon. Easy to transport, it allows the effect of surprise, hence the success of these submachine guns which are not dangerous except at point-blank range but which, especially at night, produce a demoralising effect on the defender isolated in the dark [...] After the battle they are fair adversaries who consider themselves as players who have won or lost a match.' As can be seen, this [Vichy] Frenchman's opinion is very favourable regarding this tough but straightforward adversary.

The Gaullists, however, sometimes held prejudices from another time, speaking in a disagreeable way about 'these Australian convicts', 'drunk from morning onwards', these 'wonderful savages', confusing them sometimes with New Zealanders: 'Wearing their big hats with the brim turned up, some New Zealanders[22] passed through the camp,' wrote a Gaullist. 'They are tall, often with a fine moustache, joking and winking at people. Rather kind. Anyway, no one can understand anything they say.'[23] And Lieutenant de Sairigné wrote in his notebook: 'it is not wrong to talk about their magnificent physique. Invited to dine at one of the battalions, I found a very pleasant atmosphere which almost deceived me by its quietness and its good manners.' This legionnaire, who had fought in Norway, wrote oddly about the men who fought in Greece: 'It is a strange army, without any military training. This explains the terrible and sometimes useless losses they suffered there.'[24]

Don't think for a minute that France's image was entirely positive among Australians. These citizens of a true democracy judged severely the way France acted in the Middle East. 'Syria is the darkest point in the history of French colonisation,' wrote George H. Johnston in a widely read book of the time.[25] Mention the name of General Sarrail[26] to an Arab from Damascus and he will spit on the ground, talking about a butcher and conjuring up the three bloody days in 1925 when the French outraged the Syrians and horrified the world – with the exception of the most hardened imperialists – by firing indiscriminately on Damascus [...] And why Syria, awaiting its independence, has never received anything but vague promises which were never followed up. On the other hand, this sad history of political intrigue and coercion hides economic reasons which deserve to be brought out. As far as Vichy is concerned, the opinion of the Australians was settled: 'Syria is under the domination of Hitler's lackeys, Darlan and Pétain are Axis collaborators, and are hostile to the British.' Another document, also erroneous, wrote: 'The supporters of the Vichy government are now very firmly opposed to their former allies since the Royal Navy was forced to destroy the French fleet at Dakar [*sic*] to prevent it falling into the hands of the Germans. Syria is strongly defended by the French regular army, to which is added the famous Foreign Legion as well as a small German garrison, although its size is not known exactly.'[27] Psychological preparation was intense. Everyone was convinced that they were going to come up against the Germans. Roald Dahl, an English fighter pilot in Palestine:[28] 'Few people were then aware of the chaos caused by Vichy in the Levant, which was a fanatically anti-British and pro-German regime. If the Germans, with their help, had succeeded in getting a foothold in Syria, they could reach Egypt by the back door. Vichy had to be dislodged as soon as possible. The British and the Australians were therefore sent to fight these vile pro-Nazi French. This small war was bloody, thousands of lives were lost, and I will never pardon the supporters of the Vichy government for this useless bloodbath.' The aggressor was of necessity the other side!

However, among the Australians, friendship predominated, which meant that some people counted on it to soothe the French. General Wilson's liaison officer with all the units – Australian, British, Free French, Indian and Transjordanian – Colonel J.P. Buckley OBE ED was a particularly well-informed observer. He wrote: 'The British command considered that the invasion would be simply a walkover, and that, after the frontier was crossed, the troops would be welcomed enthusiastically. It was a terrible error of judgement. With defences set up on the high points and behind rivers with water in them, the Vichy troops had superior air and armoured forces. The Australians had only light tanks, of an outdated model, useless when faced with a hundred or so good quality French light tanks.'[29]

In the House of Commons on 21 May, Anthony Eden levelled this solemn warning at Vichy: 'If, pursuing its policy of collaboration with the enemy, the French government takes or tolerates measures prejudicial to the conduct of the war by His Majesty's Government, this latter would consider itself free to attack the enemy wherever he may be.' Like the world's press, governments were now alerted to the serious risk of conflict. Roosevelt, who did 'not believe the French have a positive view of the Nazis', asked Admiral Leahy, his representative in Vichy, to stress to the Marshal that 'his country was concerned about the consequences of a policy that put the French colonies in a hostile position relative to the United States.' On the other hand, Cordell Hull solemnly warned France 'that a Franco-German collaboration in the form which it seemed to be taking [...] could only be understood as [...] going far beyond the terms of the June Armistice'. During a press conference in Washington on 7 June, Henri Haye, the [Vichy] French Ambassador, answered: 'No German troops are in Syria, and France is taking care to distance those territories from anything that could give the British a pretext for aggression.' But the Ambassador warned: 'France will defend its possessions against any attack, but will never take – at sea, on land or in the air – a military initiative against Great Britain.' This declaration was repeated in the press.

For Darlan, the Syrian business was taking on a worrying, even unexpected, dimension. It fed propaganda and ruined his standing. He wanted to go into reverse gear. Dentz, for his part, wanted to get rid of the German aircraft as quickly as possible, because they were provoking an angry response from Cairo. Rachid Ali having been eliminated, they no longer had anything to do in Syria; however, because of them, war was at the gates. In order to remove any excuse for an attack from the British, the aircraft had to disappear. On 30 May, Dentz telegraphed to Vichy: 'Resistance in Iraq is finished [...] The presence of German elements in Syria can only serve as a pretext for an attack. I ask you to put an end to existing missions and to all transit flights or stays by German aircraft.' On 2 June, Dentz to Huntziger:[30]

> After this ridiculous intervention in Iraq, I long to announce that the Germans have evacuated the airfield at Aleppo [...] the British radio delivers a frenzied propaganda against Syria, supposedly handed over to the Germans, and Collet announces that he will be in Damascus on 10 June [...] I have had them told [...] that if,

for once, they want to fight against the Germans, I know where there are some, near Sollum or Benghazi in Libya [...] With the exception of some key figures [...] the state of mind of the upper classes in the French colony is deplorable [...] I expect an early attack by Gaullists supported by British mechanized troops and tanks [...] the British do not want to make Syria their business, but they would be happy to have it administered by Catroux [...] I really hope the Gaullists find another Dakar.

On the spot, the Germans seemed to want to hang on. On 30 May, Jung came to Beirut in uniform to enquire of General Jeannekyn, commanding the air force, 'the details of a possible Franco-German military cooperation at a local level.' According to him, the OKW had advised France, faced with the British threat, that Germany was ready to provide a massive air support to the Levant, but in Beirut no one was aware of this. Jung asked to discuss this cooperation with General Dentz, but the latter refused to meet him and asked Jeannekyn to get rid of him. It required a lot of insistence on the part of the latter to make up the German's mind to go away, and it was only after receiving a categorical point-blank refusal that Jung finally left Beirut. Informing Darlan of this visit, a worried Dentz commented: 'I do not need to inform you that this collaboration, true or even simply alleged, entails dangers in Syria at a time when I am threatened with British and Gaullist attacks. I keep the army with me by reminding it that it is acting as a defender of the French Empire, but neither for nor with the Germans. If this argument fails, a collapse is feared.' Darlan answered the same day: 'There is no military collaboration agreement against England. The formula "to defend the Empire against all comers with only French means" still holds. It must continue to guide your conduct. I have made an urgent approach to the German Ambassador in Paris so that the German elements in Syria are withdrawn as soon as possible, but I have not yet received an answer.' Abetz, who agreed with it, warned Berlin: 'To remove all pretext for an [British] attack, it is of the highest importance that the German personnel and aircraft returning from Iraq do not remain in Syria.'

And in a surprising way, Hitler accepted it without discussion: the order to withdraw was sent on 3 June. The airmen immediately complied and started to leave Syria. So a British attack lost all justification. In principle, peace was saved. On 6 June, Colonel Montrelay, chief of staff to General Jeannekyn, informed the United States Consul that there were practically no more Germans in the Levant. The evacuation will be total within a few days, he confirmed.[31] He insisted that the British be informed immediately. Beirut transmitted the news to Admiral Godfroy. There is practically no doubt that Godfroy warned Cunningham immediately, who informed Wavell, who in turn alerted London himself. The British had already been warned: at Vichy, a handwritten note had been handed to the American Embassy. The message ended on this conciliatory note: 'The French government will avoid, for its part, until further notice, everything that could be likely to aggravate or spread the conflict.'[32]

Still on 6 June, Huntziger to Dentz: 'Keep a defensive attitude until the [British] forces commence hostilities on territory [under your authority]. You are given full latitude to order [some] air attacks on British territory.' However, even if Vichy authorised it, Dentz would never accept that French aircraft would attack Palestine. Never will they cross the frontier, never will the French attitude be aggressive.

Dentz was very relieved. In a solemn speech on Radio Levant, he spoke to everyone:

> France must live, that is the truth. For that to happen, what is being asked of us? Are we asked to take up arms against anyone? Are we asked to call for help from anyone? No, we are simply asked – here the Marshal demands – to maintain possession of the territories that belong to us or which are entrusted to our care. Nothing more, nothing less. I ask you: is there in that something that can offend the most sensitive conscience, something contrary to the interests and honour of France? No! And I can read this answer in your eyes: to all thoughtful people, keep your eyes on the dial of the radio that brings you my words. The order is clear: to defend our possessions, to defend them with our own forces. I know you will carry out this order because it is as clear as the Marshal's sword. If necessary, we will see your fists clutch the butts of your weapons, the controls of your tanks, the control column of your aircraft, the halyards of your flags. This flag flying here, alongside the cedar of the Lebanese flag and the stars of the Syrian flag, you will keep it there because it is your duty, because it is your honour, because it is the wish of the Lebanese and Syrian peoples who do not want any other liberators than us. You have heard me, you have understood me, now to your posts!

War seemed imminent. On 31 May, the postal service between Syria and Palestine was interrupted. Private communications were forbidden. Intelligence reached the staff in Beirut: 'a military presence made up of armoured vehicles has appeared at the borders of Palestine and Transjordan.'

12

The Free French at Kastina

The agreement between Churchill and de Gaulle of 1 July 1940 stipulated: 'General de Gaulle is creating a force of French volunteers. This force, which comprises naval, land and air units with technical and scientific elements, will be organised against common enemies. It will never bear arms against France.' It was not yet known but, for the General, Pétain is not France.

His decision to create the 1st Free French Division (*1ʳᵉ Division Française Libre: 1ʳᵉ DFL*) was taken on 11 April. He announced his decision to General Legentilhomme, who commanded it from 15 April onwards: 'This division, placed under your command, will combine all the units currently in the Middle East [...] At the request of General Wavell, however, I have agreed that your division will be posted to the Cyrenaica–Egypt theatre of operations, on condition that it be kept together under your orders.' So it was that on 3 May, leaving Eritrea, which had been reconquered, on board the steamer *Président-Doumer*, the French Brigade of the Orient (*Brigade française d'Orient: BFO*)[1] sailed up the Red Sea as far as El Kantara, then reached Tel Aviv by train where, on 26 May, trucks took it as far as Kastina in Palestine.

On the plateau of Judea, between Gaza and Jerusalem, Kastina was the camp that Wavell had allotted to Répiton-Préneuf on 9 May. It was a 'windy and sunbaked area where each stone was ready to cry out.' There was not a spring nor a blade of grass in this camp, isolated in a desert of white sand and stony ground, which was bordered by an orange grove. Under a layer of sand, the ground, in which holes had to be dug for the tents, seemed as hard as stone. The *tricolore* flag marked with a Cross of Lorraine flew over a sea of tents, in the middle of which were a few permanent buildings. On 26 May 1941, following some colourful adventures, the whole of the Free French troops were gathered together there:

six battalions of infantry, a battalion of Marines, a company of 12 tanks, two squadrons of *spahis*, two batteries of artillery, 15 anti-tank guns, and an engineer company. These forces were formed into two brigades.[2] It was an extremely motley crowd in which legionnaires from Eritrea rubbed shoulders with Senegalese from black Africa, sailors from Portsmouth, tank crews from Norway, Colonials from Cyprus, Circassians and *spahis* from the Levant, as well as a few scattered elements who had fled France, like Lieutenant Pierre Messmer or Major René Génin. Under the command of Colonel Magrin-Vernerey, whose *nom de guerre was* 'Monclar', the 13th Demi-Brigade of the Foreign Legion (*13ᵉ DBLE*) formed the hard core of these troops. It had 24 officers and 900 men. Antifascist to the core, these enlistees were mainly former Spanish Republicans.[3] The names of many officers have since become legendary, in particular Kœnig and Messmer. Lost in the ranks, but with a baton in his haversack, Private Jean-Bédel Bokassa later became Emperor of the Central African Republic and President for Life.

For everyone, camp life was rough and austere. For a month the troops underwent further training: firing practice, marching, close-order drill, exercises and field manoeuvres. To weld these troops into a cohesive whole was a pressing task. The big distractions were swimming on the coast, outings to Jerusalem, and pilgrimages to holy places. What thoughts occupied these Frenchmen? Did they know what fighting they were going to be involved in? Were they certain that they had to fight other Frenchmen? Had the people in the Levant truly become traitors, as they were told, traitors in the service of Germany? Certainly, for the men there was no doubt. The atmosphere at Kastina was enthusiastic. To go to war one has to be self-assured. The enemy must be vile; if not, one is simply a murderer. The enthusiasm of the soldiers in the ranks knew no bounds, and their faith was fed with simple truths and, to really hate, contempt was needed. So, in his speeches urging on the troops, General Catroux, usually very measured in his speeches, used very offensive and insulting words: dishonour, treason, ignominy, hypocrisy, lies, trap, infamous, crime [...] No insult was too offensive for him. 'Swine! Collaborators in the pay of Germany,' the Free French soldiers levelled at the others. Since they were traitors, it was important to go to Syria, where they were. In the overheated atmosphere of Kastina, there was no place for hesitation. They had to fight. These men were sincere and sure of themselves.

The officers sometimes seemed a little less assured than their men. Lady Spears, who ran the field hospital of the 1st Free French Division, wrote: 'The Gaullists had the feeling that perhaps they had been traitors to France by joining de Gaulle and the British [...] I think that they were sometimes tortured by doubt about the soundness of their cause, and my impression is that de Gaulle himself did little to help them.' The British did not do much either, noted Fabre-Luce.

For the Free French, the General's decision was tragic. In the opposing camp were comrades from the same schools and often from the same classes. They were often relatives, cousins and even brothers. In any case, people from the same units: the 13ᵉ DBLE (*Demi-Brigade de la Légion Étrangère*; 13th Demi-Brigade of the Foreign Legion) was opposed to the 6th Foreign Legion Regiment; the 1st Moroccan Spahis were opposed to other members of the same regiment; the Colonials of the BIM (*Brigade d'Infanterie de Marine*) were opposed to those of the 24th RIC (*Régiment d'Infanterie Coloniale*), their unit of origin; and the Africans of the 1st, 2nd, 3rd and 4th Marine Infantry Battalions (*Bataillons d'Infanterie de Marine*) were opposed to the blacks of the 17th RTS (*17ᵉ Régiment de tirailleurs Sénégalais*) from which they were derived.

The unit commanders were required to assure themselves beforehand that the officers, NCOs and men were ready to fight against other Frenchmen. 'General de Gaulle's problem', explained Pierre Messmer 'was to ensure that the officers would not play the conscience clause which would allow them to refuse to fight other French troops'. Had not General de Gaulle himself already described fratricidal clashes as 'abominable'? Hadn't he, after the failure at Dakar, declared on 26 October 1940 on Radio Brazzaville: 'Who would not understand what crime that cannot be atoned for was committed by the unworthy chiefs who, at Dakar, had Frenchmen fire on Frenchmen?' And yet that crime today had ceased to be criminal. Here is the reason why: the conscience clause 'in no way signified that they [the enlistees] never had to fight Frenchmen. Alas, the opposite was true, Vichy being what it was and not France at all. But the clause aimed at guaranteeing that Allied military action in which we were involved, even when it came up against the forces of 'official' France, would not be used against the 'real' France [and] would not harm its heritage nor its interests.'

26 May at Kastina remained an unforgettable day for everyone. Scrubbed up, enthusiastic and formed up into lines on parade, the

troops had been waiting since dawn in the burning sun for the legendary chief whom most of them had not yet seen. As soon as he arrived, they recognised him; towering over everyone by a good head, he was impossible to miss. The first recipients of the decoration he had just instituted, the Order of the Liberation, were lined up at attention. First of all, the General solemnly awarded it to General Catroux then, as reward for the operations in Eritrea, to Lengentilhomme, Boissoudy, Jourdier and Folliot. Some men, chosen at random, were also decorated. Followed by his principal officers, de Gaulle moved majestically from battalion to battalion. Saluting the flags, he addressed the troops, outlining the strategic situation and warning: 'Our common cause means that we need to prevent the Germans from getting established in Syria, otherwise the Allies will be attacked from behind. I do not force anyone to fight against Frenchmen under such conditions. I leave it to your conscience to decide. Your enlistment for the duration of the war does not force you to take part in combat against other French military units, even if they have been led astray, you could in all conscience refuse to take part.'[4] No individual decorations, he added, will be awarded for the forthcoming operation if 'by misfortune' it includes fighting against Frenchmen.

Then came the march past. On Radio Haifa, Répiton-Préneuf heard these words: 'Now, under the same sun that made blind Samson's head buzz when he was tied to the millstone, the tall and straight silhouette of de Gaulle could see the march past come towards him, gathered together for the first time, those Frenchmen who, from all over the world, had clung to the idea that he personified.' Heading the Legion and its band, Monclar and Kœnig opened the way, then came the gunners, then Volvey's 12 tanks which, rumbling along, raised clouds of dust. Next were Jourdier's *spahis*, Delange's black infantry, Chevigné's Colonials. Bringing up the rear were Madame Catroux's ambulances and the American ambulance. Legentilhomme's men themselves recognised it was a weak division. The whole group was ill-assorted, but these mixed troops were deeply united: none of those present had been forced to be there. It is generally agreed that there were 5,400 combatants; de Gaulle announced 6,000. According to Boissoudy, 'if one is very generous, there were no more than 4,500 men, including the Demi-Brigade of the Legion. Let's say that there were, at that time, no more than 1,800 Europeans.' According to Yves Gras, 'the 1re DFL was a division in name only. It was especially lacking in vehicles, artillery, and signals. These deficiencies considerably reduced its firepower and ability to operate. It would be able to operate as a large unit only with outside reinforcements.'

The march past over, de Gaulle got all the officers together. 'In my contacts with officers and men, I noted that they had the same state of mind as me: disappointment and disgust at having to fight Frenchmen, indignation at Vichy which corrupted the discipline of the troops, conviction that they had to march, make sure of the Levant and turn it against the enemy.' Some, however, declined to accept responsibility; Monclar, in particular, whom nothing intimidated. Like Weygand and like Amilakhvari of the Foreign Legion,[5] he was a 'son of a king'. It was said he was born to an Austrian prince and a French mother, wounded 14 times during the Great War and had his skull opened twice, he had one arm shorter than the other and limped. But he was a leader of men. 'General' he said that morning to de Gaulle, 'you promised us that we would never have to fight against Frenchmen!' Then de Gaulle, haughty and peremptory, cried out: 'I am the French! I am France!' Monclar was followed by Captain de Lamaze, also a legionnaire, under whose command Messmer had served. 'He was', Messmer remembered 'my own captain, a man for whom I had a very great admiration and who was later killed at Bir Hakeim. He considered that he should not command the company during the Syrian campaign and, as I was the most senior lieutenant, I took command in his place. My colonel [Monclar] did not want to command the Demi-Brigade either, and it was Major Amilakhvari who replaced him.' One cannot determine the number, even approximately, of those who asked to leave the ranks, but there were very few of them, said Gras. When, a distant last, Barberot arrived at Kastina on 9 June he found the camp almost empty. 'The only people remaining', he said 'were a few men who had refused to fight the Syrian French.' Note that, absent at Kastina, were the Free French airmen who, as a group, refused to fight against their own comrades.

Opposite, in the Levant, it was quite different. Oddo:

Having been a participant from one end to the other of this campaign on the side of the FFL, whereas in about a month I would have been on the side of Vichy, I am sufficiently well placed to know the state of mind of the combatants on both sides. There were, as always, a few fanatics who could not be ignored, because their excesses, in words and deeds, were repeated, without variation, in conversations, almost always altered or exaggerated, which deepened the gap between them [...] The general feeling was of embarrassment at being caught up in a terrible but inevitable combat, and solidarity with one's own unit which was going to be in a battle that would no doubt be murderous. There was therefore no question of slipping away. The officers and NCOs, almost all permanent army and very mortified by the defeat experienced a year earlier, were keen to prove their courage and their worth. The rank and file, native in origin, were very well disciplined and followed their chiefs blindly.

How could those Vichy troops imagine that they would be seen in the same light as their only enemy, the Germans? They had not made any choice of sides, and they obeyed their legitimate leaders and fought under their national flag. Lieutenant Simon, Force X: 'Today, not to glorify oneself but simply to admit having obeyed the government's orders, is to expose oneself to disgrace and damnation. Forty years of brainwashing and disinformation have transformed honest soldiers, who were simply wedded to discipline, into henchmen of Hitlerism. However, in 1943–4, these same men very often found themselves in the front line against the Germans.'[6] Robert Aron: 'The honour that Marshal Pétain diminished was the honour of a government which managed to maintain elements of its independence and protect the population. In a word, it was civic honour. The one invoked by General de Gaulle was military honour, for which to admit defeat is always an infamous act [...] Both were equally necessary for France. According to the saying that was attributed in turn to Pétain and then to de Gaulle, the Marshal was the shield, the General the sword.'

If the people in the Levant fought without flinching, it was not therefore for political motives but out of duty. For them, defending Syria was defending France and saving French North Africa. They did not understand they could go against the call for unity. In April 1941, Pétain was France and France was Pétain. To divide the country in the current circumstances seemed inconceivable to them. Their role was to await circumstances which lent themselves to a possible burst of activity. For them, their aggressors were obviously wrong and England wanted to evict France. What doubts did they have? Did they experience hatred of England? 'We were geographically surrounded by British interests – Cyprus to the west, Iraq to the east, Palestine to the south – the British were generally not liked, but fighting alongside them was contemplated if it was the only opportunity for revenge.'

For the Navy, it was different. The costs were already heavy: 1,500 sailors killed at Mers el-Kebir, the *Bretagne* sunk, the *Richelieu* torpedoed, the *L'Audacieux* destroyed, the *Poncelet* sunk and the *Bougainville* destroyed after being set on fire and run ashore, the fleet in England seized, the merchant navy plundered [...] Could this last? Is one supposed to understand and even approve? England invading Syria? All that had the appearance of good old colonial fights.

If 13 aircraft had flown to Egypt,[7] the airmen seemed more calculating. When the airmen saw German aircraft landing, the commanders had a lot of trouble holding back the pilots, especially the fighter pilots of *Groupe de chasse 1/7* (N°1 Squadron, 7th Fighter Group, *GC 1/7*). There were then many who wanted to go and fight alongside the British, but this hesitation was swept aside by the British attack. No Gaullist airman took part in machine-gunning the Syrian airfields. Some simply threw out pamphlets 'at very high altitudes', according to their comrades. When, on 20 May, Air Force Lieutenant Labat came in to land at Kuneitra, abandoning Free France, he confirmed that not a single Free French pilot would agree to fight against the Army of the Levant.[8]

What was heartrending about this unnatural combat was the complete sincerity of the two sides. It was not a question of a crowd of scoundrels facing a handful of heroes. Gaullists and Pétainists were all equally convinced of the correctness of their cause.

It was only four days before the offensive that Generals Catroux and Legentilhomme, with Lieutenant-Colonel Kœnig, were summoned to Nazareth by General Wilson. It was in this village with the venerated name that the British general assembled the chiefs of his main units to tell them the plan of operations decided upon by the British staff in Cairo, and to indicate to them the way to behave with the Army of the Levant. General de Gaulle had had in effect, reluctantly according to Georges Buis, handed over the direction of the military operations to the British. 'Répiton-Préneuf' confirmed Pierre Quillet, 'had little trouble in imagining the thoughts of his chief who was irritated by an excessively heavy British presence in an affair that ought to have been settled between Frenchmen.'[9] However, one fact was clear: the Free French were only providing 15 per cent of the force.

The plan of the offensive was obvious. The Frankish citadels and, before them, the Roman forts, overlooked the three routes that the attackers were forced to take.[10] In the west, the coastal road towards Beirut; in the centre, the path towards Rayak across the Bekaa Valley to isolate Beirut from Damascus; in the east, the road across the plains towards Damascus. Wilson, who had three brigades under his command, assigned one to each route. On the left, the way having been opened by commandos,[11] the 21st Australian Brigade was to progress along the coast. In the centre, the 25th Australian Brigade was to capture the strong point of Merdjayoun, the key to the Bekaa Valley. On the right, progressing both via Kuneitra and Deraa, Lloyd's 5th Indian Brigade and its artillery regiment[12] marched ahead of the 1st Free French Division. Considering the long littoral of the French mandate, a powerful naval support – about 60 guns – carried out fire missions along the coast during the whole operation. If the losses in Greece and Crete had markedly reduced Admiral Cunningham's forces, the units that he detached for this operation, under the command of Vice-Admiral E.L.S. King, were greatly superior to those of the French Admiral Gouton.[13] To minimise demolitions by Vichy forces, the assault was to be simultaneous on all the frontier outposts, followed by a rapid advance towards the three objectives, Beirut, Rayak and Damascus. The campaign was to start before dawn on 8 June, a few days before the opening of the parallel operation in Libya, *Operation Battleaxe*, the counter-attack against Rommel ordered by Churchill.

Having seen this plan, the British and Free French were hardly optimistic. For Legentilhomme, the operation was very risky. Churchill hoped that it would be simply an 'armed political incursion', but according to the British command, to be certain of victory at least three divisions would be necessary, including an armoured one. With only two divisions, 'success seemed quite problematical, remaining dependent on the attitude of the French garrison and the local population.' As this attack was not sufficiently powerful, they would have to 'simulate as large a force as possible.' Hoping that he would not have to fight too much, Wilson wanted to avoid 'useless confrontations and spilling of blood.' 'We will avoid battle' he ordered, 'the weapons at the beginning having to be propaganda, pamphlets and intimidation.'

'Given that we were not at war with the government of Vichy' wrote the Australian Buckley[14] 'it was natural, before attacking, to invite its troops to cooperate with us [...] A slight hope existed that our appeals had been heard, but it is true that the presence of the Free French could exacerbate feelings. Nevertheless, how could we refuse General de Gaulle's troops from taking part in the occupation of what remained, in spite of everything, a territory administered by France? Without the Free French we would have been smaller in numbers. Even so, our forces remained less powerful than what would have persuaded the Vichy troops to accept an honourable surrender, without being tested in combat.'

Catroux, who knew the area, disapproved of this plan for the offensive, but Wilson kept to it. He demonstrated that he did not have enough men, equipment or mobile units to carry out such an enveloping operation. On the other hand, he had other trump cards: Marines landing on the coast would unblock the defensive systems put in place by Dentz along the border, and the Australians would benefit from naval gunfire support as they progressed along the coast. His plan was thus adopted.

Nevertheless, the big question remaining was: what would be the attitude of the [Vichy] French? The Australians thought that the sight of their slouch hats would attract such goodwill from the French that they would not fire. It was therefore decided that, before opening fire, negotiators carrying white flags would walk in front of the forward elements and that, instead of wearing their helmets, they would wear slouch hats.

On the other side of the border, the French were waiting for the attack. On 4 June, the bombing of the Shell petrol tanks covered Beirut with black smoke and alerted everybody. Everyone was ready. In the interior, as along the coast, fortification works had been undertaken during the winter. As soon as the crops had been harvested, fields of fire were cleared. Designed by Fougère to fit in with the terrain, the French set up a plan of static defence: 'Thus far, but no further' and 'combat without thought of withdrawal'. Deemed unfavourable for the use of mechanised forces, the coastal sector was defended only by a battalion placed in a blocking position at the mouth of the Litani river. It had only one battery of 75mm guns but, in front of it and spread out over 30 km, two squadrons of *spahis* were placed in eight positions to act as warning outposts.[15] Behind them there was a battalion in reserve at Sidon.

In the central sector, between the two mountain chains – Lebanon and Anti-Lebanon – the town of Merdjayoun blocked entry to the Bekaa Valley. It was a strongly fortified position. The Palestine frontier, which followed a course shaped like duck's bill towards this position, was barely a few kilometres away.

The main defence effort had been made in the eastern region, in South Syria. Two strong positions had been established at Kuneitra and Sheikh Meskine where, with ditches, zigzag barriers and barbed wire entanglements, the defence works were completed.

In total the French garrison had a greater strength than the attackers[16] and a considerable counter-attack force was in place in the South Syria sector: eight infantry battalions, two Druse squadrons and two Syrian squadrons, a regiment of *spahis*, an armoured regiment and five artillery batteries.[17] The light cavalry squadrons entrusted to Collet had unfortunately gone over to the enemy – along with a precise description of the defence system.

According to Captain Le Corbeiller, a member of Dentz's staff: 'This plan of defence precluded all idea of manoeuvre or mobile defence. The enemy will be held back wherever he attacks, he will be stopped by a position [...] set up in advance, we will counter-attack him. The outdated notion of a front, which was weak everywhere, was retained. The plan was rigid in its conception. No variation was foreseen. All that, he thought, removed all sense of initiative from those carrying out the orders.'

Contact will take place, wherever the enemy penetrated, by delaying detachments made up of horsed cavalry in the mountainous regions of Lebanon and light armour on the Syrian plain. These detachments will fall back on strongpoints manned by infantry in order to force the enemy to deploy and thus lose time. An 'immediate response group' – two squadrons of tanks and a few native units – will be stationed in the centre, in the Bekaa plain. General Dentz will have his Headquarters in Beirut, General Arlabosse will command the South Lebanon sector and General de Verdilhac the South Syria sector.

Under the orders of Admiral Gouton, the small naval division in the Levant had only two destroyers, *Guépard* and *Valmy*, with a single sloop, *Élan*, and three old submarines *Souffleur*, *Caïman* and *Marsouin*. Reserves of fuel oil were stored on board the oiler *Adour*, but there were no ammunition stocks. This force was all that remained of the most powerful squadron in the Mediterranean, the bulk of which had been neutralised by the British in Alexandria. The fighter force was made up only of Morane-Saulnier MS.406 aircraft which had reached Rayak in March 1940, except four which had joined the Gaullists; but, coming from French North Africa, two bomber and one fighter squadrons, as well as a Fleet Air Arm (*Aéronavale*) squadron, succeeded in reaching the Levant. The only available way to bring in possible reinforcements was by air.

Well equipped, but already encircled, the [Vichy] French Army was isolated and could not be resupplied. Its resources were so threatened that General Huntziger considered, as he declared to Benoist-Méchin, that in case of an attack, it could not resist for longer than four days. However, the army absolutely had to fight, even if only to save appearances, since it was known that its surrender would trigger the immediate invasion of the Unoccupied Zone [in metropolitan France] and French North Africa. The Marshal had confided to Dentz when he sent him to the Levant: 'A gallant last stand, nothing more, nothing less!'

In Vichy, people were anxious. 'The Marshal's calm did not hide his emotion', remembered François Lehideux. 'The outcome of the battle was inevitable, he knew it: the disproportion of opposing forces, the difficulty in resupplying the French Army across the Mediterranean dominated by the British [...] Politically, however, it was impossible to resort to a simple sham [...] The Marshal explained to us that is was very painful for a leader to ask his men to carry out a last-ditch mission. In the present case, he was forced to do so. His central plan was based on French North Africa [...] It is there that General Weygand is rebuilding our army [...] This central force had two wings, Dakar and Syria [...] To give it up would be to go in the direction wanted by Germany. "War is merciless" concluded the Marshal.'[18]

Later, Dentz explained:

The orders that I received commanded me to oppose by force any British attack. What was supposed to be my attitude? Obey or disobey? To disobey was to immediately bring about a breach of the Armistice which left France an army and a fleet only on the condition of protecting this Empire [...] a breach would bring about the occupation of the Unoccupied Zone, disbanding of the army, takeover of French North Africa [...] there was therefore only one solution, that was to obey and obey with a conscience which was all the more free as it involved the interests of France. The future was even supposed to show it was that of the Allies as well. My troops understood these reasons, as I had explained them to the soldiers in their fighting positions [...] I have fought against the German ascendancy in Syria, France and French North Africa. That is the basis of my thinking and what I have based my conduct on.

This 'absurd and fratricidal' war was now inevitable. It would be violent from the beginning since it would be frontal: Dentz was waiting for Wilson where he was going to attack. The conflict would have the British opposing the Germans strategically, the French opposing the Australians tactically, the Gaullists opposing the supporters of Vichy politically. On the other hand, it will be clearly colonial, Cairo and Vichy enlisting empire troops commanded by Europeans: Moroccans, Algerians, Tunisians, Africans, Circassians, Syrians and Lebanese, on one side, without counting the legionnaires; Australians, Indians and Transjordanians on the other side, European units being in the minority.

To explain the inevitability of the attack, a flood of particularly alarming false news items spread around the free world. From London to New York and from Ankara to Sydney, war correspondents and press agencies were going to receive and broadcast an uninterrupted flow of messages of doom. Who was spreading them? The British to justify their attack? The Germans to encourage the Allies to fight amongst themselves? The Free French to explain their attitude? From the BBC to *The Times* in London, and from the *Times* in New York to the *Sydney Morning Herald* in Sydney, all collaborated in this campaign. On 25 May *The Times* asserted that 'the Franco-German agreement officially handing over Syria to the Nazis has been signed and promulgated.' The newspaper noted a rumour that 'the Nazis are already in the French mandate of Syria, on their way to Iraq and the Suez Canal'. On 2 June, the BBC broadcast this piece of news coming from Ankara: 'The Germans are carrying out a methodical occupation of Syria. The French regiments are gradually being replaced by German ones.' The Associated Press correspondent in Ankara confirmed that 'Nazi staff officers and motorised troops have landed at Latakia [...] more than 500 men wearing the same helmets and boots as those in Libya [...] A dozen cargo ships flying the Nazi flag have been fitted out to bring other troops and heavy equipment from Romania.' American Associated Press announced from Istanbul that 'Germans dressed in civilian clothes and carrying Bulgarian passports have recently been sent to Syria via Turkey.' The *Daily Telegraph* of 5 June, on the front page: 'Already more than 200 German aircraft in Syria' The correspondent of the American Associated Press in Ankara explained the meeting of German staff officers, in the port of Latakia (Syria), with more than 500 German motorised troops who had landed there last Thursday. On 8 June, the Sydney *Sunday Telegraph*, in a headline: 'According to the British reporter Alan Moorehead,[19] German transport aircraft, carrying tons of tanks, cannon, water, oil, and foodstuffs, landed in Syria. It is by means of retractable ramps that 18pdr guns, light tanks, armoured cars and motorcycles are loaded into the aircraft. Five hundred of these aircraft, he declared, each carrying out two return trips per day, could easily bring a division a week from Rhodes to Syria.' The day the war broke, the same daily stated over seven columns: 'Mammoth German troop-carriers and supply planes arrive in Syria.' A headline in the London *Evening Standard*: 'Two panzer divisions land in Syria.' On the evening of 7 June, Radio Ankara announced that German troops were in the process of building aerodromes in Syria, especially at Latakia. Two hundred aircraft have landed at Aleppo and at Palmyra. The representative of the US National Broadcasting Corporation in Ankara confirmed that 'eight U-boats have been seen near Beirut…German instructors are training Moroccan pilots on behalf of the French High Commissioner in Syria.' Taking up the news broadcast by the Columbia Broadcasting System, the *Sunday Telegraph* of 8 June asserted that 'French aircraft are landing at Rayak bringing, it is believed, crews from the French forces in Morocco, where German instructors are training Moroccan pilots to place them under General Dentz's command.' The American *Times* let itself be brainwashed. It affirmed on 15 June:

A large number of so-called tourists landed in Lebanon. Many pretending to be wounded, laughing as they limped along, came ashore from a hospital ship in Beirut […]Others, fair, burly, standing very upright, entered via Turkey, carrying false passports as Romanian Jewish refugees, their suitcases marked with a capital J[20] […]One can see German officers wearing shorts walking around the streets of Aleppo […] It seems that there are false French pilots. A French fighter that shot down a British bomber had been piloted by a German […] Assisted by paratroops from Rhodes, fake travellers took over French airports.

All over the world, the news was repeated: 'Two German armoured divisions landed in Syria…Sixty thousand German soldiers are massing in Spain.' The British radio asserted that 'the hospital ship *Canada*, which arrived in Beirut to evacuate the wounded, brought 500 German soldiers from Marseilles.'

Fake armoured vehicles, fake aircraft, fake cargo ships, fake staffs, fake aerodromes, fake Romanians, fake Bulgarians, fake instructors, fake pilots, fake wounded, fake passports, fake passports, fake Moroccans and true Nazis disguised as fake Jews; what organisation could have brainwashed the world press in this way in two weeks?

Committed unwillingly by a British staff lacking in confidence, this campaign between recent former allies was carried out without hatred and in a disciplined fashion. 'An unwanted campaign' according to the British, 'a bet' for the Australians, 'an ungodly fight' according to de Gaulle, 'absurd and fratricidal' for François Lehideux, and 'a sad campaign' according to Hilary St George Saunders, the war forced by Churchill and de Gaulle was not won in advance.

Part II

The Rupture

8 June: The Offensive

Dentz, de Gaulle, Verdilhac, Churchill, Wavell, Wilson – General Catroux was the only one who personally knew all the protagonists in the drama, the only one able to understand its different aspects. At the time of the attack, he felt that the gulf separating the two parties had deepened to the point of being unable to be bridged. Two concepts of duty were opposed to each other. The moral conflict would survive physical combat. Underneath the political pretexts, this was a war of religion. On the evening of 7 June 1941, in the car bringing him to General Legentilhomme's jumping off point in Transjordan, Catroux still hoped for 'a winning over':[1] 'The moment was approaching when Frenchmen, weapons in hand, would assault other Frenchmen [...] What would be the outcome of this dramatic meeting?'

While he was driving along, aircraft were taking off to drop pamphlets, calling on the civil population to revolt and the military to rebel against the regime. General de Gaulle: 'French officers, NCOs, soldiers, sailors, and airmen of the Levant, it is time to take up the fight again for the liberation of France. I have appointed General Catroux High Commissioner and Commander-in-Chief of French forces in the Levant. You must obey his orders. This time again we will get the better of them and France will win the war. Until next time!'[2] General Catroux gave an extremely longwinded speech (abridged here):

Officers, NCOs, soldiers of the Levant! Airmen, Colonials, legionnaires, Moroccans, Algerians, Tunisians, Senegalese, our comrades-in-arms from the Empire, in the name of France, in the name of your honour, in the name of your conscience, I address this appeal to you. Side by side, the Free French forces and Allied forces are going to cross your borders. It is not you that they are

waging war on: it is the Germans. [Our forces] are not coming
to fight you. They are coming to attack the enemy and take back
from him the positions that a dishonourable treaty delivered to
him in Syria. Soldiers, an ignominious order commands you to
bar the road to these forces. Understand what is demanded of
you: you, the French, are being required to fight for the benefit
of Germany and to protect with your lives the enemy airmen
stationed in Aleppo, Rayak and Palmyra, and to sacrifice your
lives in order to bring victory to Hitler. Because ignominy is being
heaped on you under the hypocritical and lying pretext of making
you defend Syria. Soldiers, through me, France forbids you to fall
into this trap and carry out this criminal act. It orders you to put
yourselves under my command. I release you from the duty of
obedience to your leaders, and I take you under my command [...]
I forbid all resistance and, in advance, I will court-martial those
who order it. I command you to gather in your positions with
your arms and equipment, ready to take your place in the order of
battle. Follow me! I will lead you along the path of honour, and if
I ask you to die there, you will fall gloriously for France and not
miserably for her enemies. Long live France![3]

These messages convinced only those who wrote them; they did
not elicit any response. On both sides, convictions were firmly
held.

The only important message was that addressed to the local
population on 8 June. Its impact was immense. It confirmed the
solemn proclamation that General Catroux had broadcast the day
before on Radio Cairo:

Syrians and Lebanese! At this moment when the forces of Free
France, united with the forces of Great Britain, its ally, enter your
territory, I declare that I have assumed the powers, responsibilities
and duties of the representative of France in the Levant. I do this
in the name of Free France, which identifies itself with the real
and traditional France, and in the name of its leader, General
de Gaulle. In this capacity, I have come to put an end to the
mandatory regime and to proclaim you free and independent.
Henceforth, therefore, you will be sovereign and independent
peoples, and you can either form yourselves into separate states
or combine yourselves into a single state. In either case, your
status of independence and sovereignty will be guaranteed by
a treaty in which, additionally, our reciprocal relations will be

defined. This treaty will be negotiated as soon as possible between
your representatives and me. While waiting, our mutual situation
will be that of allies, closely united in the pursuit of an ideal
with common goals. Syrians and Lebanese, you will judge by
this declaration that if the Free French and British forces cross
your frontier, it is not to stifle your freedom, it is to drive Hitler's
forces from Syria and to have your rights respected at the same
time as those of France. It is to prevent the Levant becoming a
base for the enemy against the British and us [...] If, responding
to my appeal, you rally to us, you should know that the British
government, in agreement with Free France, has committed itself
to grant you all the advantages associated with free countries.
Thus you will immediately obtain your entry into the sterling
area, which will provide the greatest possibilities for your import/
export industries. Your purchases and sales with all free countries
will be made without hindrance. Syrians and Lebanese, here for
you comes a great time in your history. Through me, France
declares you independent, that France which is fighting for its life
and the liberty of the world!

The declaration seemed clear, but Damascus was not taken
in. The 'I declare you free and independent' was immediately
hedged about by suspicious conditions. What is an independence
'guaranteed by a treaty in which relations between France and its
former colonies are defined'? Is Syria a former French territory?
What is a France 'which would not permit its age-old interests to
be handed over to the enemy'? Are the claimed age-old interests
more than 20 years old? The Syrian parliamentarians were
lawyers and were not taken in. There was nothing new. It was
a formula made up of different parts such as France was used
to employing. Determined to obtain nothing less than full and
complete sovereignty, without limits or conditions, the Syrian
parliamentarians were not swayed.

However, something had changed. This time the French
promise was matched with a solid guarantee by London. Published
simultaneously, a declaration signed by Sir Miles Lampson, British
Ambassador in Cairo, combined in effect with that of General
Catroux. It followed the one on 10 May in which Anthony Eden
had expressed 'the great sympathy [of England] for the aspirations
of the Syrians for independence'. Without contesting, according to
him, the authority of Free France over the Levant, Churchill had
shown 'the wish that the independence of Syria and Lebanon be

proclaimed, and that Dentz's successor bear the title of "Delegate General of France" and not that of "High Commissioner"'. He was also keen that the reforms promised by General de Gaulle be guaranteed by Great Britain.

Even more astonishing, Free France promised that the French mandate would enter the sterling area, that is to say, the sphere of British influence. What could be the secret high-level agreement that resulted in this outcome? Buried in the military proceedings, this is not very apparent. It is, however, determining. By aligning the Syrian currency with the British pound sterling, even before the conflict began, France was fighting *de facto* for Britain and giving up one of the essential bases of its presence in the Levant.

In French on one side and Arabic on the other, General Wavell also sent a message to the French armed forces: 'The Commander-in-Chief of the British Army to the soldiers of France! We have come to Syria to expel the Germans, our common enemy [...] We the British have only feelings of friendship for you. You have fought with great courage and you have demonstrated – which everyone already knew – that you are skilful, brave and worthy soldiers. But are you going to continue to provide our common enemy with a base from which he can attack us?' There then followed an offer of repatriation and, finally, this threatening recommendation: 'Be quite clear that, with or without your help, we have decided not to leave Syria to the Germans. We would have preferred that you help us in this task, but if you do not want to help us, we will do it alone. General A.P. Wavell, Commander-in-Chief, British Army in the Middle East.'

'At the end of May, Monsieur Coulet, a close colleague of General de Gaulle, had had a secret meeting with Monsieur Jamil Mardam Bey, former President of the Council in Syria, in the course of which meeting the requests of the Nationalists had been discussed [...] On 8 May, Coulet had confirmed via this note to Jamil Mardam Bey: 'I have sent you General de Gaulle's letter. I do not know if this document has already reached you. It should answer your wishes.' At the end of his letter, Coulet suggested: 'I think that you could, sometime after 10 June, form a delegation of notables which would ask the Delegate and the General [Dentz] to bring to an end a useless conflict. If needs be, organise some demonstrations.'[4]

Speaking in the name of France, General de Gaulle sent a letter, on 31 May, to Jamil Mardam Bey, in which he defined his role in Damascus and made clear his political plans: 'My dear President,

Entering Syria with the forces of Free France, General Catroux will address a proclamation to the population. This proclamation, whose terms and spirit I have approved, will be made in my name and that of Free France, that is to say, of France. It will bring to the patriots, of whom you are one, the satisfaction of their dearest aspirations by granting the peoples of the Levant, the status, guaranteed by treaty, of sovereign and independent peoples. Thus the success of a cause, to which you have already so warmly and generously devoted yourself, will be established. I am happy to tell you about it and I express the hope that you will find, in this important event, powerful reasons to collaborate with Free France and with its representative, General Catroux.'[5] For unknown reasons, this letter did not reach its addressee until 1 July. Would it have convinced him? Jamil Mardam Bey answered: 'The initial approach of General de Gaulle is a witness to his lack of understanding of Syrian nationalist feelings.'

On 6 June, the eve of the attack, the leader of Free France had in fact made very different feelings known to Churchill: 'I will proclaim and will respect the neutrality of the States in the Levant in return for a treaty with them which will enshrine the rights and special interests of France.' Everyone in this war wore a mask. A. H. Hourani, a clear-sighted Syrian, commented:[6] 'Except among the Francophile elements, local opinion tends to think that, even if the adversaries evoke the noblest principles to justify their belligerency, in reality they are all motivated by their own interests. From the point of view of the exploited nations, there is no choice between two oppressors [...] Moreover, propaganda by the two groups shows the true motives of the opponents.'

It was therefore as onlookers that the local populations were present at the war, without ever becoming involved, and this in spite of the presence of Lebanese and Syrian troops. On 8 June, at 5:30 a.m., at the time of the call to prayer, an aircraft, said to be Gaullist, bombed the Umayyad mosque in the centre of Damascus, a place sacred to all Islam, destroying houses, killing women and children – the number killed, buried under the rubble, was not known. The next day, an identical aircraft attacked the Ferrayin and Sidi Ahmoud quarters, killing survivors of the 1925 bombing. Who bombed was not known, but Damascus did not forget.

'Attacked on the front running from Naqoura-Merdjayoun-south of the Jebel Druse. Armoured cars and motorised infantry are in contact with our forward positions. The battle is continuing.' It was 5:30 a.m. The war in Syria has just started. Dentz alerted Vichy.

It was Sunday. Having received the message, the Marshal had Henri du Moulin de Labarthète, his advisor, awakened, who tells: 'I entered his office. He was in a dressing gown. He had not shaved. His cheeks were gaunt. He held out the despatch to me. It is war!" he said [...] "Warn Darlan!" Darlan, already alerted, joined us. 'We leant over some maps. The Marshal and Admiral reacted rather quickly: 'We have to defend Syria, declared the Marshal. We are at home there. The British had promised not to attack us and if we don't defend ourselves, the Germans will take French North Africa.' 'We must repel the British attack,' Darlan agreed. A protest note was drawn up, but how to have it reach London when relations were broken? The note was given to the US Ambassador, Admiral Leahy, in late morning. The same morning, London published this communiqué:

> In spite of the warning given by His Majesty's Government on 1 July when it declared that it would not permit Syria and Lebanon to be occupied by a foreign power or used as a base for aggression, the Vichy government, pursuing its policy of collaboration with the Axis powers, has placed the Syrian air bases at the disposal of Germany. It cannot be expected that His Majesty's Government would tolerate such acts, in flagrant contradiction of recent declarations by Marshal Pétain according to whom honour would prevent France from undertaking any action against its former ally [...] That is why Free French troops, with the support of troops from the British Empire, entered Syria and Lebanon early this morning.

Du Moulin commented: 'There had been no collaboration between the French and the Germans in Syria. Aviation equipment or German personnel who had been there during the fighting in Iraq had been withdrawn with the exception of two or three damaged aircraft and about 10 men [...] The French government has made up its mind to defend its territories [...] by all means at its disposal. Realising the danger of the current situation, the French government, for its part, while awaiting new information, is avoiding taking measures likely to aggravate or extend the conflict.'

Marshal Pétain immediately wrote this message which was broadcast by Radio Levant during the morning:

Frenchmen of the Levant! The countries where you live and for whose prosperity you have worked for many years are today the subject of an unspeakable attack. This attack was led, as at Dakar, by Frenchmen under a rebel flag. Supported by British Empire forces, they do not hesitate to spill the blood of their brothers defending the unity of the Empire and French sovereignty. To the pain that this observation has caused, France, faithful to its declarations, can certainly take pride in not having been the first to bear arms against its former ally, any more today than in the past, at Mers el-Kebir, at Dakar or at Sfax. Trickery preceded violence. For several days the propaganda which formed the basis for the aggression claimed that German troops were landing in our ports in the Levant in large numbers, and that France was preparing to hand over to Germany the territories whose defence has been entrusted to you. You who are on the spot, you know that that is false. You know that several aircraft, which had stopped over in our territories, have today left Syria apart from three or four that are unfit to fly. You know that there are no German soldiers either in Syria or in Lebanon. You are therefore the subject of a profoundly unjust attack which outrages our conscience. It is only today that French sovereignty in the Levant is threatened for the first time. You can believe me. Your High Commissioner has already told you and I repeat what he said – you are fighting for a just cause, that of the integrity of the territories whose history, confirmed by the mandate of 1919, bequeathed the responsibility to France. You know how to defend them. My best wishes and those of France go with you.[7]

Another message was addressed to the troops: 'Officers, NCOs and men of the Army, Air Force and Navy in the Levant! I am following with [great] emotion the hard fighting that you are experiencing in the defence of those territories that France has entrusted to you. The whole country sends its best wishes, along with mine, to you in your ordeal. France is proud of her children who are heroically fulfilling their whole duty as soldiers in this far-off territory. You can be sure you are not fighting in vain.'[8]

On the spot, the undeclared war started 'in an atmosphere of unreality', according to Colonel Albord, commanding the important position of Merdjayoun. Right until the end, the combatants had rejected the idea of a senseless war. Several did not even believe it: in spite of the order to rejoin their fighting positions, the commander of the Sidon sector stayed home. 'An

English attack has been spoken about for so long' he said. 'The inhabitants travel about on both sides and do not notice any abnormal troop movements [...] There was nothing to suggest the imminent attack that intelligence had announced for a month.'[9] However, war had arrived.

That night, off the coast, in spite of a large swell but in bright moonlight, the Scottish Commando under the command of Lieutenant-Colonel Richard R.H. Pedder,[10] 30 officers and 500 volunteers landed from HMS *Glengyle* to gain a foothold 30 km to the north of the border in order to prevent the arrival of French reinforcements and to capture the bridge over the Litani river, the *Nahr el Kasmiyeh*, the first obstacle on the road to Beirut.

The unit was divided into three groups. After having waited all night for the full moon to set, the first, the northernmost group, under the command of Captain George More, which had landed and settled in just before dawn without difficulty, surprised a group of about 40 men whom they made prisoners and cut the telephone line to isolate the bridge's defenders. Attacked about midday by armoured cars and encumbered by their prisoners, they had to let them escape. Immediately rearmed by their liberators, the freed Frenchmen counter-attacked and the British scattered into the hills. Regrouping at night, they tried to regain the beach but, stopped by barbedwire entanglements, coming under machine-gun fire and having lost too many men including an officer, they had to surrender.

Landing on a broad beach, the second group, that of Lieutenant-Colonel Pedder, was greeted by a murderous fire, including mortars and machine guns, the first of the war. Surprised and without shelter, the Scots hesitated before advancing and, when they rushed forward, they fell in large numbers. Pedder was killed and all the officers were wounded. Led by an NCO, the remainder of the group managed to shelter in a building where they were captured. A few survivors managed to hide in barns. Others succeeded in reaching the *Glengyle*, but many bodies were lying on the beach. Later, an Australian, Captain L.E. Longworth,[11] recounted: 'We passed what remained of the brave commando which had undergone a murderous fire from French 75mm guns, mortars and machine guns. The dead were literally scattered over the beach.'[12]

The third group, the most southerly, that of Major Roger Keyes[13] landed without meeting any resistance, but scarcely had it moved forward when it found: Australians! As a result of a

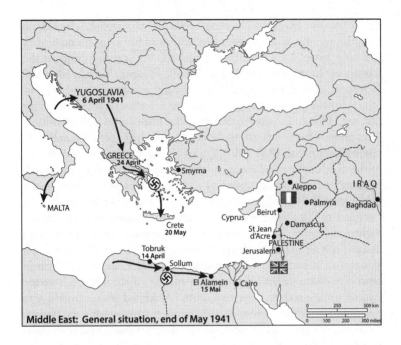

Map 1. General situation in the Middle East at the end of May 1941

mistake, it had landed to the south of the Litani river, the bridge over which had already been blown up. Crossing the Litani by boat, this group also came under heavy fire which, causing losses, delayed it until the afternoon. The commando's failure was significant: 123 men were killed, including two officers, i.e. a quarter of its strength.

That night, behind the commandos, in Palestine after a good dinner at the *kibbutz* in Hanita and guided by Jews, two small Australian units[14] crossed the frontier on foot in dead silence. Their mission was to neutralise the French frontier post at Nakoura, four kilometres away. There was a need to surprise it before mines were set off that could cut the road to Beirut, which hugged the cliff a few kilometres to the north.

Isolated in an Arab world favourable to the Nazis, the Jews were very motivated. Few in number, the members of Wilson's Jewish Brigade were however employed only in ancillary roles such as guides or drivers, or even relegated to logistics duties.[15] No doubt the British did not want to see men, who were already fighting in the *Haganah*,[16] acquire military experience. The Jewish community, moreover, offered to find men for General de Gaulle but the leader of Free France refused, finding the proposition 'compromising' according to Davet.[17] René Cassin stressed however: 'Allow me to note the friendly assistance given to our troops by the Jews of the neighbouring Palestinian mandate. They put the Hadassah hospital freely at the disposal of our wounded. The atmosphere was so friendly towards the Free French that some well-known Jews enlisted and fought in their forces.'[18]

In the dark, crossing a garden zone, the Australians now approached a post occupied by a weak garrison, a troop of the 8th Algerian Spahis. Hearing a noise, an old warrant officer was carrying out a round with two men but he was the first French victim of this war: he was found with his throat cut, his body lying against a wall. Alerted, the post commander, Lieutenant Lalanne, jumped to his telephone to warn Kasminyeh, the main defence position, more to the north, at the mouth of the Litani. Scarcely had he hung up than three men with blackened faces jumped into his office-bedroom. He pulled out his pistol but his assailants, faster, shot him dead. Poor Lalanne. The previous year in Beirut, he played rugby against the Australians. The assailants spread out through the post shouting 'Where are the Germans? Where are the Germans?' A young French NCO replied: 'Germans? We have never seen any here!'

A loud explosion was heard; a Frenchman had set off the mine. The cliff that the road to Beirut followed was made impassable, except for pedestrians, for over 20 metres. In the post at Nakoura, the *spahis,* who were still sleeping, woke up prisoners. Around the post, some were fighting but, overwhelmed, the Algerians fled barefoot among the rocks. Nakoura had fallen but it fulfilled its role. On the French side, the losses were heavy: two officers, 14 NCOs, 143 *spahis*, 11 Lebanese killed, wounded or made prisoner, six vehicles lost including an armoured car, 197 horses and 30 mules. The opposing Australians had only three dead and four wounded, including two Jewish guides. One of them, a certain Moshe Dayan, lost his left eye.[19]

The fighting over, Captain Buis, a Free Frenchman, interrogated the prisoners. The Australians were struck by the attitude of a wounded warrant officer who stared fixedly at this French officer without answering him. When Brigadier Stevens read his report, he was astonished that no Germans had been found on entering Syria.

At day break, at 6:30 a.m., sailing along the coast, the British fleet appeared – two cruisers and ten destroyers.[20] A few small vessels hugged the coast so closely that the French could hear the sailors' hurrahs when they hit their target.

In the interior, in the mountains, the outpost of Bennt-Jbaïl, held by the 8th Algerian Spahis, also reported the intrusion of the 'English' across the frontier with several armoured vehicles. Their mission fulfilled, the *spahis* left the post. Under the command of Majors de Bodman and de Quatrebarbes, these horsed *spahis* undertook a difficult journey. Closely followed, fleeing into the mountains, they had to fight all day to escape from enemy motorised forces which were helped by the local population. 'The overzealousness and servility of those who, as recently as yesterday, were all smiles and bows' disgusted the French. At the end of their tether and scattered, it was not until several days later that the remnants of the unit reached the blocking positions that had been assigned to them at Nabatiye.[21] The losses sustained and demoralisation had sapped the troops' resistance. Rest followed by regaining control were essential.

Behind the frontier of Palestine, the bulk of the Australian forces was awaiting the moment to attack. 'It is the first time that we have hidden like Germans, facing a peaceful border to carry out a surprise invasion,' noted an officer. But these people were optimistic: 'We advance, take our hats off to the Frogs, and push forward.' Before the battle started,' wrote the Australian Colonel Buckley[22] 'the British authorities considered that the invasion would be "an armed political incursion". And that once the frontier was crossed, the troops would be greeted enthusiastically. What a terrible mistake!' The cliff road having been repaired within an hour, the Australian trucks could drive towards Tyre.[23] At about 10:00 a.m. they reached the town, which they passed through: it was not defended. The population greeted them enthusiastically. A second column, coming from Palestine via Bennt-Jbaïl and Tibnine, rejoined the bulk of the Brigade. Driving north, these reunited forces reached the banks of the Litani river about 3:00 p.m. On the road, before the destroyed bridge, concrete blocks stopped the leading elements, the armoured cars of the 1st Royal Dragoons, which were greeted by heavy, precise and dangerous fire. It was the main resistance point. They stopped.

Leaving the deep gorges, the Litani river – 12 to 15 metres wide – spreads out here, gently making its way onto the coastal plain.

To cross it, near the village of Kasmiyeh, the road takes a bend that is overlooked from the north by hilltops where the French had dug in. A barbed wire entanglement prevented all approaches. 'On the evening of the 8th, contact was established with the enemy's main defence line on the Litani. It was obvious that they intended to fight. We did not know about the rapid advance towards Beirut of a force which would have had only to brush aside token resistance.'[23] Night fell. Unable to turn the French positions and the Scottish commandos having been dispersed, Brigadier Stevens, commanding the Australians, had to make up his mind to attack with brute force. Not knowing whether the river was fordable and having only folding boats that could transport only six men at a time, he got his units across the river to the northern bank. It was night and the reeds in the river provided excellent camouflage. Before dawn, a large flotilla, of one cruiser and six destroyers, was in position. Their many guns were trained towards the land and started firing. The naval bombardment was extremely powerful and lasted hours. The town of Kasmiyeh disappeared, pulverised.[24] When the Australian infantry attacked, the defenders, well sheltered, reacted. The Australian front line lost all its officers. The battle which commenced on the morning of 9 June quickly became violent. Opposing the Australians, the 3rd Battalion of the 22nd Algerian Tirailleur Regiment, under the command of Major Le Corné, defended its position 'without thought of withdrawal'. In position since November 1940, they had had plenty of time to set up solid positions with trenches, underground firing positions, barbed wire entanglements, observation posts, etc.; covering an area of four kilometres long by 1,500 metres deep, and supported by a battery of 75mm guns, this 'hedgehog' was defended by nine strong points equipped with mortars and machine guns. Communications were by telephone.

The Air Force intervened to support Le Corné. Old Bloch 200 bombers came to bomb the fleet,[25] but without result: the British fighters reacted and several Blochs were shot down. Crashed into by a fighter, then picked up by a British ship, the crew of one French aircraft found itself nose to nose with its assailant. The French Dewoitine fighters intervened and shot down several British aircraft in a distressing mêlée. Le Gloan,[26] the French ace from 1940, added two Hurricanes to his score. The French fighters machine-gunned the Australian convoy stopped on the road and, if they saw them, the infantrymen hidden in the orange groves and reeds in the river.

Coming from Beirut, Admiral Gouton's powerful destroyers *Guépard* and *Valmy* intervened in turn. Their attack seriously threatened the British units which, forced to spread out, moved away from the coast and suspended firing for a while. An unheard-of spectacle, not seen since the days of Surcouf,[27] a naval battle was going to take place between the Royal Navy and the French 'Royale'.[28] Keyes confronted Gouton. Action was engaged at 14,000 metres. The Vichy French ships, the *Guépard* and *Valmy*, were very manœuvrable and had two advantages: their speed and gunnery precision – a recently installed mechanism that added different colours to the columns of water raised by each ship's shells allowed each ship to distinguish its own fall-of-shot. Green for one, red for the other. This allowed rapid adjustment of range and direction. However, without reserves of ammunition, the French had to be sparing in their shooting. The battle, although rather unequal, was violent and vivid. In a mêlée that lasted two hours, each ship, sometimes hidden in the smoke, sometimes dashing forward before disappearing, firing, then being concealed, tried to destroy the enemy. The British hotly pursued the French but without ever hitting them. However, after eight minutes' firing, three shells from *Guépard* struck HMS *Janus*[29] at the same time, killing some of the crew and destroying the engine room, bringing the ship to a standstill, and staining the captain's beard apple green for several weeks. The ship, after extensive repairs, was eventually returned to service near the end of the war. At 1:56 p.m., the French had already used up half of their ammunition. To continue would be suicidal. *Capitaine de vaisseau* (equivalent to Captain RN) Gervais de Lafont, commanding the French force, gave the order to break off the action. The two ships turned about at full speed and, zigzagging at 30 knots and protected by smoke screens, returned to Beirut. Their only offensive sortie having been too costly in ammunition, they would not be able to attack again. To replenish their ammunition lockers, the French Admiralty sent from Toulon that same day, 9 June, ammunition on board a fast destroyer, the *Chevalier-Paul*, but, until it arrived Gouton's ships would have to avoid battle. Shut up in Beirut and often changing moorings, sometimes going to hide in unexpected anchorages and threatened with bombing, the *Guépard* and *Valmy* were no longer actively engaged.[30]

At Kasmiyeh, Le Corné's men fought all day, repelling three successive attacks preceded by precise artillery preparation, each

10 minutes long. The Australians did not cross the barbed wire entanglements, but the French lost 68 men, and numerous wounded were piled up in the underground shelters. The fleet continued its bombardment, and water started to run out. Sporadic firing took place all night. More and more pressing calls for help were made from the position, and General Arlabosse, commanding the South Lebanon sector, decided to send reinforcements.

Sent by truck from Beirut and Sidon, these reinforcements were large, about 800 men,[31] but no plan of attack had been drawn up and, according to General Albord, Colonel Aubry, who was in command, did not know how to employ them. Departing during the night and so escaping the fleet's bombardment, the convoy came up against an ambush, probably laid by escapees from the Scottish Commando, in the early morning of 10 June. Surprised by the bursts of machine-gun fire, the *tirailleurs* were shot as they jumped from the trucks, many scattered as they ran towards the hills. Some were taken prisoner. An 'Englishman', surprised by their uniforms, asked: 'Are you Germans?' Finding the hideously mutilated body of a French officer, an Englishman, understanding what had happened, said: 'What a stupid war!' British or Australians were still convinced that they were facing Germans. Many said afterwards how sorry they were for having killed Frenchmen.

Frightened by the racket, the horses of the *spahis* bolted towards Sidon, and the 155mm battery was captured after a short resistance. Assembling 14 men, a captain tried without success to recover these irreplaceable guns. During the morning, the guns were removed by French armoured cars but, coming under short-range gunfire from the fleet, they had to withdraw and the finest artillery battery in the Levant was lost without having fired a single shell.

Isolated in his position, an anxious Le Corné felt, about 9:00 a.m., that the end was near. Near midday, the Australian artillery opened fire; then the infantry, accompanied by Bren-gun carriers, commenced the assault. But no one among the French opened fire. 'Fire! Fire!' shouted Le Corné. However, his men did not obey. Through binoculars Frenchmen could be seen walking in front of the Australians as a human shield. Then the enemy reached the barbed wire, cut and passed through it, and overwhelmed the front line. Spreading out through the defences, they reached the command post where Le Corné, unarmed, surrendered.[32]

So the river was reached. The Australian engineers threw a temporary bridge over it and the road to Beirut was again open. The Kasmiych position held up the enemy for only two days. Gavin Long concluded: 'In spite of the destruction of the bridge and the failure of the ill-prepared landing by the commandos, the self-control and initiative of the [Australian] officers and NCOs, the skill and dogged courage of the men, had forced a passage across the river, [and] captured a skilfully prepared enemy position that was well defended with mortars and machine guns.'

What remained in front of the Australians that could delay them? The machine-gun section of the Algerian *tirailleurs* under the command of Lieutenant de Mesmay[33] made its way south along the coast road, followed by an ammunition column. Attacked by the British fleet since daybreak, several trucks had already exploded. When Mesmay reached Adloun – seven kilometres north of the Litani – he received the order to stop, to leave the road and to take up a blocking position facing south at the exit from the village. Kasmiyeh was thus abandoned to its fate. In the village which overlooked the road, Colonel Mocquillon installed his command post in a big building that was easily recognisable. The lieutenant dug trenches and set up his guns. Reinforced by three 25mm anti-tank guns which could take the road under enfilade fire, and joined by three tanks during the night, they made up a solid blocking force. At dawn five British ships appeared; at 6:00 a.m. they opened fire. The command post became untenable and the Colonel retired by car at full speed towards Sidon. Neither the *tirailleurs* nor the *spahis* in the village, nor the blocking force on the road, received any orders, but seeing the cars dashing off, many disappeared. Well dug in, Mesmay remained alone with a few men, his machine guns and two cannon. In the village of Adloun, the *tirailleurs* decided to retreat into the mountains. Famished, shivering at night in their light clothes, they started off on an exhausting and difficult march, poorly led, which ended three days later with bitterness and disillusion. The *spahis* didn't do any better. Their captain brought back only about 60 cavalrymen on foot, the others having got lost.

Abandoned without directives, almost without men, did Mesmay have to stay? The order being 'to defend without thought of withdrawal', he stayed with a handful of Algerians and, under fire from the British fleet, held on for two days with incredible fortitude. Destroying several carriers, he kept the enemy pinned down all day. On the evening of 11 June, at about 6:00 p.m., a Legion lieutenant finally appeared. Having left Damascus the day before, he was preceding a weak battalion – two companies. At midnight, the legionnaires were in place. Their mission? 'Resistance without thought of withdrawal'. The formula was much in fashion at the time.

Mesmay had more trenches dug, positioned his remaining two cannon and two machine guns, and laid mines along his front. At 11:00 p.m., a section of legionnaires appeared and the 30 men took up positions. On 12 June, at daybreak, an incredibly violent bombardment commenced, which overwhelmed the positions. As soon as it stopped, Australian infantry appeared on the side of the mountain and started moving forward. The defence positions were hastily moved. At 6:10 a.m., an assault was repulsed thanks to a counter-attack by the three tanks. It was then that an astounding message arrived from Sidon: the three tanks had to leave. The naval gunfire continued; the ships were so close inshore that the 'hurrahs' of the gunners could be heard ashore. The situation worsened by the hour. At 10:00 a.m. there was a new attack. The enemy flanked the village of Adloun, which was taken from the rear. An extremely murderous infantry battle started. The Australians overcame the French defence posts one by one. Out of ammunition, Babonneau's company was overcome.[34] On the road, there was no more than a handful of men left. Sergeant Forgerit continued to serve his machine gun and it was he who described the end.

Now installed in the village, the Australians started to attack with mortars. In the fray, communications between Mesmay and Forgerit were broken. Soon the carriers moved forward, firing on and moving across the French trenches. Forgerit, wounded three times, was taken prisoner. While he was being taken away, gasping for breath, he saw the lieutenant's body at the bottom of a hole. Allegrini, a Free Frenchman acting as interpreter, asked him to go and make sure that he was dead. The officer's helmet had two bullet holes in it. An exemplary hero, Mesmay and his men did their duty until the end[35]; at Sidon, 60 years afterwards, people still speak about the French lieutenant who held his ground until killed.

Ill-conceived, badly organised and badly commanded, the plan of the French counter-attack ended in a fiasco. Positioned one behind the other, the troops were sacrificed without any benefit, used up in a static defence against a mobile enemy who was nimble and provided with powerful and coordinated means. 'As mortifying as it may be for the reputation of the French Army, one has to admit that these badly conceived operations were the late result of prewar mistakes', concluded General Albord.

Let us now return to politics: there was much agitation in the capital cities at the same time as there was fighting on the ground.

London's response to Vichy's protest of 8 June, reached France on 10 June. Its tone was very precise: 'In its declared policy of collaboration with the enemy', France was accused of 'having taken or permitted measures prejudicial to the conduct of the war by His Majesty's Government'. London therefore threw the responsibility for the attack on Vichy. It noted the 'wish of the French government to not see the conflict spread' and suggested 'that it not oppose the entry of Allied troops into Syria'. It repeated that 'England has no territorial ambition either in the Levant or in any French colonial possession throughout the world and that her intention is to restore the independence and greatness of France after victory.'[36] The Marshal took note of it but held firm on the principle of resistance.

The same day, 10 June, Darlan sent a telegram to the French Ambassador in Spain asking him to contact his British opposite number in order to be reassured that the conflict would remain localised. The two diplomats met several times and the Briton confirmed that it was a limited conflict. To prove it, he added, Britain would not oppose the resupply of French North Africa by American ships. Also on 10 June, Churchill gave this speech in the Commons:

I am coming to the Syrian operation. Allow me to repeat that we have no territorial ambitions, either in Syria or any French territory whatsoever. In the current war, we seek neither colonies nor any sort of advantage. Let none of our French friends be fooled by the screeching propaganda from the Germans and Vichy. On the contrary, we intend doing everything that we can to restore to France its liberty, independence and its rights [...] There can be no doubt that General de Gaulle is much more zealous in defending France's rights than are the men in Vichy whose policy is to submit obsequiously and unreservedly to the German enemy. One does not have to be very shrewd to understand that, by infiltrating into Syria and the intrigues that they committed in Iraq, the Germans were endangering the whole eastern wing of our defensive system [...] Was it necessary to encourage the Free French to try a counter-attack alone or to prepare ourselves, as we have done – risking greatly, given the inevitable delay – a rather large expeditionary corps formed from our own troops? [...] As a result of our relations with the government of Vichy and the possibility of open rupture, the movements became of the very greatest consequence from both the military and strategic points of view [...] The formidable threat facing Egypt of an invasion by the German army from Cyrenaica, supported by considerable Italian forces [...] remains, in the Middle East, our main preoccupation [...] We have had to take into account all these factors, and I was very happy when General Wavell announced to me that he was ready to carry out the advance which began on Sunday morning and which, according to intelligence received, is progressing favourably and is meeting very little opposition. The situation in Syria was almost desperate. The German poison was spreading throughout the country [...] However [...] we do not know [...] in what way the Germans are going to react.

On the same day, General de Gaulle gave a speech on Radio Cairo:

Free France is at war. And yet, with the consent of Vichy, the Germans have started gaining a foothold in the Levant. Militarily, it is an immense danger. Politically, it means handing over to the tyrant peoples whom we have undertaken for all time to guide to independence. Morally, it means that France will lose all of what remains of its prestige in the Middle East. We do not want that. That is why we have entered Syria and Lebanon with our British allies. It is unfortunately true that our advance can meet resistance by our comrades in the troops of the Levant. Some of them, ill-informed, reluctantly consider that they have to oppose us by force. We will never fire on them first, but if several clashes result from their conduct, we will do our duty. Moreover, how many others come and join us! I can reveal that [in the Free French Forces] at the present time [there are] 63 officers who came from Syria [...] Vichy has sent to Marseilles or to prison more than 200 others. France does not want a German victory. France wants to be freed. We are carrying out the will of France.[37]

On 11 June de Gaulle left Cairo for Jerusalem where he put up at the King David Hotel in the strange surroundings of a British peacetime mess. On 12 June, he left with Brosset to visit the troops, in particular Legentilhomme who had just been wounded – slightly wrote Brosset, seriously wrote de Gaulle. During his stay in Jerusalem, Brosset visited the front several times, finding himself in the evening back at the dance at the King David Hotel. He said everything seemed illogical to him in this conflict in which he was opposed to the army to which he belonged.

For the Australians, the next stage on the road towards Beirut was Sidon, the ancient Sidon of the Phoenicians, the former capital of King Louis IX of France (also known as Saint Louis), today buried under native markets but still largely intact. Opposite the harbor, at the end of a causeway, the castle built for him, almost in ruins but easy to defend, recalls the sovereign's love for this land that France had never quite forgotten. The commander of the Sub-Sector was Colonel Aubry, commanding the 22nd Algerian Tirailleur Regiment. Some people held him responsible for the loss of the reinforcements sent to Kasmiyeh. For him the town was only a stopping place. On the evening of 11 June, after the fall of Kasmiyeh, members of units that had been scattered and then came flooding back towards the town, told of the terrible firepower of the enemy's ships. Colonel Aubry suddenly became aware that he was going to find himself in the middle of an offensive. The enemy could turn up any day. But nothing had been planned for war in Sidon. Clearing the ground, preparing firing positions, laying of mines and installing barbed wire, everything had to be done in a hurry. What means did he have? A battalion of Colonial troops which had not yet been under fire,[38] a company of Lebanese Chasseurs, three artillery batteries. Three of Major Lehr's[39] six tanks, which were fighting at Adloun, were recalled immediately by Colonel Aubry.

On the evening of 12 June, Adloun having fallen, nothing separated Sidon from the enemy except the 14th Company of the 6th Foreign Legion Regiment which was still holding Hassaniyé, eight kilometres south of the village. To defend the position Aubry gathered all his forces behind the Nahr Saitanak, a dried-up river bed, scarcely a gully, to the south of the town, the last obstacle before Sidon. In the town, the only remaining troops manned his command post.

Under the command of Major Lehr – who escaped from Dunkirk and who had conducted himself brilliantly in France – this improvised defence was supported on the left, on the top of Miyé-Miyé, by an excellent observation post at the base of the mountains. It was there that he set up his command post. On the right, overlooking the road and the coastal plain which here extended over a depth of about 1,500 metres, he set up camouflaged machine guns, mortars, anti-tank guns and, opposite cleared ground, his six tanks. To prevent any flanking movement, a group of *spahi* squadrons, which had successfully carried out a withdrawal, was sent into the mountains on the Jezzine road. In the town, in the Château Saint-Louis, the Algerian *tirailleurs* who had escaped from the fighting at Adloun were reorganised.

The 21st Australian Brigade showed itself next day at about 10:00 a.m. Impatient, always up forward, Brigadier Stevens pushed his artillery forward behind the infantry.[40] Showers of shells started to fall on the French defences, but the 75mm guns replied. An Australian gun was destroyed, and there were wounded, including Brigadier Stevens. The lead company, which was marching under cover in the orange groves, suddenly broke into open country. Waiting until it was well in the open, Lehr, who was observing from his command post on Miyé-Miyé, ordered firing to commence. It was 12:45 p.m. Machine guns and mortars began firing, and the tanks broke cover and advanced. The R-35 tanks were specially designed for infantry support. The effect was instantaneous. The Australians fell back. In a growing confusion, which turned into a headlong flight, the leading company ran into the company following, dragging it into flight. The panic carried away some of the artillery. Two captains were killed trying to restrain their men. Lehr then launched the Colonials and the attack was brought to a halt. An officer was sent to Sidon to give the good news to Colonel Aubry. He was back in an hour, shattered. There was no one in the town, Aubry himself had left. Only a Lebanese gendarme was there to welcome the enemy. Everywhere was disorder. The Army warehouses had been pillaged; some were burning. More importantly, the telephone exchange was destroyed. There were no longer any communications with Beirut. The commander in Sidon had abandoned his post without warning the neighbouring units. This conduct was a disaster. Communications had to be re-established with Arlabosse's staff as a matter of urgency. This was soon carried out. At the Grand Serail, the news of Lehr's successful counter-attack was greeted with immense relief. 'Lehr is the saviour', wrote Albord. At 5:00 p.m., General Dentz appointed him commander of the Sidon sub-sector in place of Aubry, and ordered him, as usual, to defend 'without thought of withdrawal'. Gathering his officers together, Lehr tightened his defences and organised a counter-attack. About 6:00 p.m., accompanied by infantry who were heartened by his attitude,

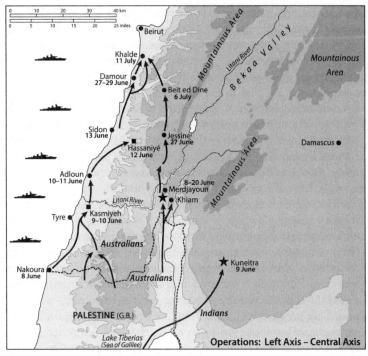

Map 2. Operations: Left axis – Central axis

the R-35 tanks emerged. The surprised enemy fell back and the French occupied the retaken ground.

Naturally, the British fleet resumed firing, both on the battle front and on the town, which bore scars from it for a long time; the firing could be heard in Beirut. To relieve those fighting, the Navy was called upon. About 4:00 p.m., Admiral Gouton ordered the destroyers to sortie forth and attack the enemy. The *Guépard* and the *Valmy* immediately got under way, but scarcely had they moved away from the coast and increased speed than a message recalled them: they had to turn around. The sailors were dumbfounded. What had happened to Gouton? Henceforth the British fleet had absolute freedom to fire.

During these actions, the Air Force was very active.[41] From dawn to dusk, the air battle was incessant. The clashes were frequent and bloody. British, Australians[42] or French, the airmen were pugnacious. Among these combats, two are noteworthy, one because it was significant and the other because it was worrying.

In order to relieve Sidon, French fighters attacked their adversaries on the ground. 'One can't stress enough', wrote Ehrengardt, 'the stupidity of missions in which vehicles were bravely machine-gunned by French fighter pilots who, in a hostile environment and flying aircraft not set up for this special sport, were exposed to the worst for mediocre results. The loss of experienced pilots was a waste at a time when the French Air Force could not easily replace such precious aircrew.' The death of Captain Jacobi illustrates this situation. At 4:00 p.m., he took off from Rayak leading a pair of aircraft from N°3 Squadron, 6th Fighter Group (*GC III/6; Groupe de chasse 6*), tasked to machine-gun an enemy column on the coast. In preparation for an aerial attack, the Australians had dispersed their vehicles so that they did not present a grouped target. At the controls of his fighter, Sub-Lieutenant Blondel was Captain Jacobi's wingman. He said: 'There we were, having great difficulty in finding targets. The Australians had used the rugged country admirably to disperse their vehicles and they were waiting for us unwaveringly. I dived behind the captain and the trap closed on us. Automatic weapons opened fire on us from all sides. In front of me, the captain flew in a straight line, without worrying about the shell fire concentrated on him. He was hit a number of times, his Dewoitine pulled up slightly, and then sideslipped to the left. No doubt he was hit because he made no effort to recover, hit the ground at full speed and exploded.'[43]

The second engagement was ever more disturbing. At 2:50 p.m. British fighters, which were continually flying over the fleet, suddenly found themselves facing eight German Junkers 88 bombers. Three were shot down and two were damaged, but who were these intruders? Where did they come from? Who ordered them to come and take part in a fight that did not concern them? Their intervention, about which the French troops were ignorant, seemed to prove Franco–German collusion. These aircraft from X *Fliegerkorps* were operating from Crete in the general framework of the Battle of the Mediterranean which extended from Malta to Suez. Their action was thus foreign to the Syrian operations in which they had just become involved, and the French were the beneficiaries. This intervention by the *Luftwaffe* continued over succeeding days. Sixteen aircraft from Crete laid mines along the Palestine coast on 13 and 14 June; and up until 25 June there were four bombing raids on Haifa, by about 40 Ju-88s. The last attack took place on 8 July with

21 aircraft. Moreover, on 15 June, two squadrons of the French Fleet Air Arm (*Aéronavale française*) flying Glenn Martins – 13 aircraft from Algeria – reached Rayak at 2:35 p.m. and, the same evening, attacked the British fleet, seriously damaging the destroyers HMS *Isis* and HMS *Ilex*. Added to the elimination of the destroyer HMS *Janus* by the French Navy, these attacks caused serious damage to the British fleet.

Let us not imagine however that the bombing raids on Haifa were comparable to those that later flattened Le Havre and Hamburg. They were restricted to the naval base. Life in Palestine flowed peaceably along. The military threat seemed non-existent there. The staff were so far from the front that they worked 9–5 in a peacetime routine, with weekends off.[44] Social life continued and, from Mount Carmel, the journalist Alan Moorehead could see the fighter combats.

The French command was aware of the German intervention. On 15 June, the *Luftwaffe* warned Damascus that *stukas* from Rhodes or Leros were going to attack the British fleet. Although out of sight of troops on the ground, who were totally ignorant of it, this attack did in fact take place. A communiqué from Berlin confirmed it: 'A formation of German aircraft attacked a British naval formation abreast of Beirut. A direct hit was observed on a heavy cruiser.' Another message announced an attack on Haifa. The German attacks on Palestine had the effect of a cold shower on Dentz and his staff. Politically, they were catastrophic. How could one not believe that the *Reich* would support the French? How could one imagine a coincidence? These simultaneous attacks reinforced Cairo's ideas that German forces were present in Syria. De Gaulle wrote in his *Mémoires*: 'The whole world learned with horror that the Vichy government made its soldiers fight alongside the German Air Force.'

Evacuation of the outposts, withdrawal along the Litani, withdrawal from Adloun, withdrawal from Sidon: until now, Dentz had suffered only defeats. Although total in the early days, Vichy mastery in the air diminished. Piloted by Australians, the new American P-40 fighters, more powerful than the Dewoitine D.520, started to dominate. If the morale of the Vichy troops remained high, there were signs of fatigue. Due to lack of reliefs, the troops were worn out by continual fighting. The wounded flowed into the hospital in Beirut in large numbers. The Commander-in-Chief did not feel that he could sustain the tempo of the battle for long. Did he not have to consider an armistice before being crushed? On 12 June, Dentz asked himself the question, and also asked Vichy, which answered: 'For general political reasons, you must remain for as long a time as possible [...] in the States of the Levant in order to confirm our resistance to British aggression and to maintain our authority over the country [...] Resist as long as possible [...] When you are forced to give up, destroy all your military equipment and anything of military value.' Faced with an increasingly probable defeat and his duty to resist, Dentz was confronted with a moral dilemma. Keime wrote: 'General Dentz is now fighting without a hope of winning, but he wants to persist and to preserve honour in order to be able negotiate acceptable conditions.'

To push back the enemy, more powerful means were necessary. Rahn the German and Giorgis the Italian invited the French command to call upon the Axis. On 9 June, Giorgis offered Dentz the intervention of the Italian Air Force. The Frenchman refused. He responded to this unilateral offer by saying 'the Italians were free to attack the English everywhere, but on condition that they do not use Syrian airfields.' Dentz informed Vichy. The Germans, for their part, via Rahn, offered him the support of *stukas* from Crete. The same day, an identical offer was made at the Armistice Commission in Wiesbaden. Abetz, supported by Benoist-Méchin, this 'enthusiastic collaborationist',[45] intervened in the same direction in Vichy. On 10 June, Darlan declined the offer: he did not want the participation of the Axis in the Syrian conflict at any price. On 10, 14 and 18 June, Abetz returned to the charge, but the Admiral did not change his mind: this conflict must remain localised and, especially, must not degenerate into a generalised conflict with Britain. A military alliance having no relation to an authorisation for landing rights, nor the delivery of arms already in the possession of the enemy, the intervention of Axis forces would inevitably lead to such a conflict.

For Dentz, receiving anguished appeals from his men and finding himself facing the threat of defeat, the temptation was however strong. *Stukas* or no *stukas*? The idea persisted. Dentz resisted at first, but then he hesitated. On the morning of 11 June, he summoned his principal assistants to the Grand Serail: General Arlabosse, commanding the coastal sector, Admiral Gouton, commanding the Navy, and General Jeannekyn, commanding the Air Force. Arlabosse was pessimistic:. 'Impossible to hold on if the troops continue to be shelled as they are the moment by the British ships, all my unit commanders tell me. They complain

of never having the support of a French ship and wonder what
the sailors are doing.' Very angry, Admiral Gouton explained:
hunted by the British at sea, threatened with being torpedoed
in port, without sufficient ammunition, the two surface ships
were powerless to confront the opposing fleet. At night, they
have to hide in small harbours or coves, where they can't be
seen very easily. The arrival of the destroyer *Chevalier-Paul* with
ammunition, which has been announced, will not of itself re-
establish the balance of power. 'I can only bring you my support
if the British fleet moves away from the coast', he affirmed. 'For
that I see only one solution', he went on, 'a massive and continual
intervention by *stukas* of the German Air Force! Knowing their
range of action, they cannot operate from Crete. The obvious
conclusion: we have to accept that we see them operating from
Syrian airfields!' On 12 June, at 1:15 p.m., Admiral Gouton
confirmed this in a telegram to his chief, Admiral Darlan:[46] 'I
insisted yesterday morning with the Commander-in-Chief to
authorise the *stukas* to use airfields in the Levant to relieve us
from the shelling of the British fleet, moving each day further
north, the only effective method in the current state of affairs.
I am sure that this measure, rejected before the British attack,
would be welcomed by all troops. I press upon you a rapid
and continued action which could have a great influence on
the situation.' Admiral Gouton thus openly declared himself
favourably disposed to collaboration. For his part, the airman,
General Jeannekyn, was absolutely opposed. If the airmen agree
to fight and die, he said, they would not agree for this to be in
the company of the *Luftwaffe*. The presence of aircraft bearing
swastikas on French airfields would be considered as treason.
The conference broke up in bitterness and acrimony.

In the evening, at 7:50 p.m., having made up his mind alone,
General Dentz sent telegram N°1425 to Vichy, for which he was
bitterly reproached later. He asked for German help:

> [I] am in an unstable position, particularly in Damascus where
> this morning I found very tired troops. [A] threat was confirmed
> on my right flank where the Gaullist forces were reported. On the
> other hand, [we observed] a noticeable strengthening of the British
> fighter force. In these conditions [an] immediate intervention of
> *stukas* based in Syria and acting against [targets] on the ground
> and additionally against the [British] fleet would be decisive [...]
> The bombardment of the fleet and the rapid wearing down of

the troops has changed my views. [I] ask that [some German] squadrons [which will be employed] against the [fleet] and [the] ground [forces] can use the airfield at Aleppo. Rahn confirms that the visitors [that is to say the *stukas*] will depart immediately after the business is settled.

This appeal was dramatic and contrary to all previous undertakings and assertions. It embarrassed Vichy. Kept up to date by Rahn, Berlin was becoming impatient. The offer of aerial help had a certain imperative character.

France was flirting with the devil. Darlan telegraphed Dentz:

1. [Your] request must be examined by the government because of probable repercussions.
2. General Bergeret will be with you Tuesday afternoon, 17 June. After [a] discussion with you, he will telegraph the results.
3. Waiting for the [German] Air Force coming from Crete can obtain appreciable results on [the] fleet. [For that] you have to ask Rahn to intensify that action, that I will ask for from here.'[47]

Huntziger's response, which reached Beirut in the middle of the night, was just as compromising: 'A group of torpedo aircraft of the French Fleet Air Arm (*Aéronavale*) will arrive in the Levant on 13 June. Other aircraft will reach you later. The aid of *stukas* must be asked for only if it can be rapid, massive and continuous. Make sure that these three conditions can be fulfilled technically. We await your further requests.'

Dentz, however, remained undecided. During the night, he thought the matter over. If the aid was massive, he feared seeing Germany get settled in Syria and so losing the moral benefit of his attitude, without changing the outcome of the campaign in any way. He therefore changed his mind. On the morning of 13 June, at 9:15 a.m., he telegraphed Vichy: 'Received your telegram, I withdraw my request.' This indecision was a measure of the crisis of confidence that the Commander-in-Chief was going through and the anguish it caused him. Later, this weakness weighed heavily at his trial. Only Collet, who did not like him, nevertheless confirmed: 'General Dentz refused to accept the offer of help from the German Air Force which was suggested to him by Vichy.' Vichy, in any case, understood the urgent need for powerful help.

The next day, 17 June 1941, was the first anniversary of the request for the Armistice in 1940. The Marshal gave a solemn speech in which he launched one of the famous formulae invented for him by Emmanuel Berl: 'Frenchmen, you have a short memory!' He wanted to reassure them: 'You have been neither sold out nor abandoned.' Finally, speaking of the 'hard fighting' in Syria, he added: 'France is proud of her children who are heroically carrying out their duty as soldiers in that far-off land.'

16 June, 7:30 p.m. At Sidon, the fighting was continuing. To the left of Lehr's positions a new threat was becoming clear: armoured elements were reported on the Jezzine road and in the mountains. The French positions were at risk of being turned. A series of '*colombogrammes*'[48] warned Beirut at 9:00 p.m. that Miyé-Miyé was under threat of encirclement. This news had the effect of a 'last will and testament': for staff officer Captain Le Corbeiller, Sidon was lost. It was then – a theatrical effect – that the arrival was announced of a liaison officer carrying intelligence. Once more, a counter-attack by tanks saved Sidon. Sent to meet the enemy in the mountains, the R-35s pushed them back. The atmosphere relaxed. At 11:00 p.m., Major Brygoo, deputy chief of staff, received orders to go there, taking supplies of food and ammunition. A convoy set off rapidly. Wasn't it too late? Towards midnight, it was learned that numerous enemy forces were moving along the coastal road and that broad flanking movements had taken place in the mountains. The enemy would be at Beit ed Dine. A broad flanking movement therefore threatened to reach the coast ten kilometres behind the French positions. Brygoo, his mission accomplished, returned to base exhausted at dawn on 17 June, aware that his presence had cheered up the French garrison. However, immobilised by naval gunfire, threatened by both a frontal attack and a flanking movement, without support and without reserves, Lehr understood on 17 June that he was no longer able to fight and that he would have to withdraw. On the other hand, judging from the lack of drive from the forces in contact that, for the moment, the Australians were not able to attack; he therefore decided to slip away as quietly as possible. He had his tanks withdraw and, as soon as night fell, he left his position, passed through Sidon and, moving up the coast 15 km, reached Damour with his troops, escaping from the trap.

Geographically very favourable for defence, the ravines of Nahr el-Damour were the last positions suitable for a serious defence before reaching Beirut. The river, dry in summer, opens onto the seashore after emerging from deep gorges which traverse the mountains in a stretch of country that is very difficult to cross. There are high summits. The flanks of the enormous winding fault-line were sometimes bordered by rocky walls and sometimes by sheer cliffs, which were free of vegetation in the north with wooded slopes in the south. The broken country reaches almost to the sea. The coastal plain here is very narrow. The road coming from the south runs along the shore as far as the mouth of the river, which it crosses via a large twin-arched stone bridge, before rising, where it was under observation from the Vichy defensive positions. Reinforced by Lehr's tanks and the men from Sidon, the 2nd Battalion of the 6th Foreign Legion Regiment, supported by strong artillery elements, were getting ready for the inevitable fight. Protected by barbed wire entanglements, the positions were dug in, and fire plans were in place. The strong artillery presence was effective against land forces, but remained ineffective against naval gunfire from the British fleet. Nevertheless, on 15 June, the Damour position seemed impassable.

The Australians had seemed blocked for the previous two days. What were they doing? In this very rough terrain without roads, vehicles were of no use. Weapons, ammunition, water, rations, everything had to be man-carried. Like the French, they would come to understand the importance of the mules they managed to capture and the donkeys that they requisitioned. Soldiers from the bush taught the others how to harness, load, lead and feed them. It took only a day or two, and these Australian mule drivers became extremely popular.[49] As the very light-coloured coat of the Lebanese donkeys made them easy targets at night when they moved around, they were painted. Dissolved in water, disinfectant crystals[50] produced a violet mixture which was used to paint them. Their odd colour blended in well with the surrounding countryside. But the donkeys hated artillery fire. During the coming battle, they often stopped, stubborn, all together, refusing to move down the steep slopes, especially at night. Sometimes they fell to the bottom of the slopes. One therefore had to avoid loading them with weapons. Each muleteer had his own method of making them move forward. Sometimes the first one in a file could be seen being carried on rifles passed under its belly, in the hope that the others would follow. Often they had to be unloaded, pushed forward and then reloaded after passing through difficult stretches. Often everything had to be man-carried.

It is impossible to grasp the logical development of a battle if one does not follow it from beginning to end. It is necessary therefore to follow the Australian offensive along the coast until 15 June. This war, however, developed in parallel in other areas. Each one was different from the others. If the first thrust – Stevens – moved along the coast at the foot of the high country, the second – Lavarack – attacked a fortress in the mountains and the third – Lloyd – progressed along a plain where mechanised units could move freely.

Let us return to 8 June, in the centre of the attack, the area of the second thrust. Emerging from the plains of Palestine, the road leading to Lebanon passes a short distance from the town of Merdjayoun, an isolated strong point in the mountains held by the [Vichy] French. The tortuous border allows the attackers to get close to their objective. Facing them from its hilltop position, Merdjayoun overlooks the region. From the French fortified barracks, the view extends as far as the Golan Heights. The road leading to the Bekaa Valley, the objective of the attack, passes through the town. Merdjayoun cannot therefore be avoided. This blocking position, which closes off access to the Bekaa Valley, is strategically important. Forced by the nature of the country, this is an ancient invasion route. To the west of Merdjayoun, the old Frankish citadel of Beaufort, today in ruins, has played the same role in the past, and to the east, in direct sight, set firmly on the summit of a small hill, the fort of Khiam also rests on the foundation of a Frankish citadel maintained by the Turks and kept by the French. Khiam overlooks the Jordan Valley. Whoever holds these positions controls entry to the Bekaa Valley. Colonel Tony Alford, commanding the position, had carefully prepared his defences. Faced with the threat of attack, he obtained the reinforcement of a battalion of his regiment which, until then, had been left in the rear[51] at Jezzine, a Lebanese battalion, and three artillery batteries. Setting up a command post, pushing ahead with the defence works, and sharing out the supplies, he had considerably improved his position. Suspecting the pro-British sympathies of the Druse and having little confidence in the value of the Lebanese battalion placed in the front line, he prepared for the worst. Visiting the most forward posts, he had kept his troops on the alert for several days. Linked to all position by telephone, 'he stood out by the speed of his decisions, his ability to size up a situation at a glance, and his courtesy' said Lieutenant Ortoli. In addition, he was supported by a team of young officers for whom this attack was a 'crime', and whose fieriness was 'unleashed by rage', On the evening of 7 June, the bugles sounded the assembly. Put on alert, the units left to occupy their posts. Merdjayoun would not be surprised.

At dawn on 8 June, the Australian infantry crossed the frontier. Emerging from the lowlands, they moved forward over stony, semi-desert country, where more or less ruined low walls marked out small rundown fields. As soon as they came within sight of Merdjayoun, heavy firing broke out. The men stopped, put on their helmets and three men, two flags in their hands – a white one and a *tricolore* – stood up and moved forward to parley. They were a Free Frenchman, Captain Garbit, an Australian captain whose Christian name was Ben, and a Jewish NCO. Garbit tells:[52] 'At first light we reached a village [...] We were greeted at short range by heavy firing from infantry weapons. The men took shelter and the company commander decided to ask for artillery support. While waiting, I tried to parley. I therefore moved forward waving a *tricolore* flag and shouting "Frenchman" with all my strength! I reached a small wall. I climbed up on it and waved my flag.' Fifty metres away he saw some black infantrymen who clearly did not wish to fire. He then heard a very French voice shouting 'Shoot, shoot this fool with his flag!' A few rounds rang out; one of them went through the collar of his sweater. He didn't persist and returned to the rear. Behind him, the Jewish guide was staggering, seriously wounded in the head. Only Ben remained standing. The contact was a complete failure. 'The firing started up again,' said Garbit. 'The artillery joined in [...] It could have been 7:30 a.m.'[53] The battle before Merdjayoun had started.

In front of Khiam, it was already almost over. As soon as the Australians appeared at the border, the Lebanese cavalrymen bolted, shouting 'English! English!' Panic immediately gripped the citadel and the troops fled, leaving their French officers and NCOs behind. When a handful of Australians appeared, the latter opened fire. 'Just like in a Western,' an Australian remembered, 'an infernal fusillade took place between the combatants without a single one being hit!' Nevertheless, Khiam was overrun and fell. Recovered later, the runaways from the two Lebanese squadrons were sent a short way to the rear, to the banks of the Jordan, to prevent any breakthrough, and the arrival of two Circassian squadrons allowed this approach to be sealed off.

In front of Merdjayoun, it was quite a different matter. The French fire was impassable. Firing positions had been carefully placed to allow enfilade fire. Although, facing the attackers, there was only a single company of Algerian *tirailleurs* spread out over 1,500 metres, the barrage fire was precise. At regular distances – 100 metres, 200 metres, 500 metres [...] – the gunners had placed small piles of stones which allowed them to know the range and to immediately fire effectively. As soon as the tanks appeared on the road from Palestine, they were forced to withdraw under fire. When, reported by the outposts, the infantry came within cannon range, they were stopped. The Australian history: 'Violent cannon, mortar and machine-gun fire fell upon the Australians who were now moving through bare countryside.' This avalanche of fire caused 'paralysing' losses and halted the advance. During the day the Australians tried to resume their forward progress but in vain. 'Far from being a thin shell likely to be broken by a night attack [...] the French defence, set up in a well-prepared position, showed itself to be tough.'

Not only did the French resist, but they counter-attacked. Captain Ortoli, of the 22nd Algerian Tirailleurs: 'At 2:00 p.m. I received the order to get ready for a general offensive in the direction of Palestine, supported by a platoon of five R-35 tanks under the command of Lieutenant Leclères.' The objective was the heights overlooking the Palestine plain. The attack started off at 3:00 p.m. The advance was easy at first, then the leading units[54] were considerably slowed down by the Australian resistance. Ortoli, moving ahead of them, dragged them forward. Further on, greeted by very heavy fire from automatic weapons in a strong position, the Algerians at first had to throw themselves to the ground; then, supported by Leclères' tanks, they moved forward by crawling or taking very short bounds, and when night fell, they jumped on to the objective that they overran, taking about 20 prisoners and picking up some weapons. From this position, Ortoli went on, 'we could see the roads running south, being used at that time by English convoys which were moving fast. On my right, the tanks had regrouped. Leclères, severely wounded by a shell splinter in the face, died several days later.' Thus, resisting any advance, the French held out. The only position which had fallen was the small post, at the bottom of the gorge beneath Beaufort, which was ordered to blow up the bridge over the Litani.

Faced with the impossibility of capturing Merdjayoun, General Lavarack[55] decided to call off the attack and, to 'crack the nut', leave his artillery to do the job with a powerful bombardment. But the guns were in Palestine, and it would take two days to

bring them up with ammunition, to pinpoint targets, to register
the guns and to start shelling. Albord reported to Beirut and, faced
with the strength of the attack, called for more reinforcements. A
battalion of the Foreign Legion was despatched to Merdjayoun.[56]

On the evening of 10 June, the British had 40 guns in position.
To observe 'the first attack of the campaign supported by such a
powerful artillery concentration', two generals and two brigadiers
came to watch. In front of them a 1918-style major attack would
take place, with artillery preparation, a rolling barrage and an
infantry advance in two waves to capture two successive objectives
– to overcome the outlying defences and, finally, capture the town.
On 11 June, at 2:30 a.m., the artillery bombardment started.
Well dug-in in their outposts, the Algerians awaited the attack,
and when the Australians advanced, firing submachine guns and
throwing grenades, shouting, they encountered a fierce resistance.
The fighting became hand-to-hand, and with knives. The
Algerians, finally overrun, succumbed. On the left, the Lebanese
battalion was overcome by panic and fled. The Australian assault
reached its first objective. After regrouping, evacuation of the
wounded, and resupply, the assault started again. Under such
a bombardment and faced with such rapid progress, Colonel
Albord can imagine what awaits him: a massacre. To hang on
to Merdjayoun would mean being overwhelmed in a hopeless
battle, heroic but useless, in the manner of the infamous 'without
thought of withdrawal'. And yet, 1,800 metres to his rear, he
noted a rocky hill strewn with fallen rocks which also barred
the road to the Bekaa, a 'magnificent blocking position to the
valley with fallen rocks like a petrified sea' which he called 'the
rocky crest'; a '*jebel*' to the Algerians. He was convinced that
they could very well take up positions in the rough country and
among the rocks. He was therefore going to set up a position
there, leaving Majors Dilleman and Sirot[57] at Merdjayoun with
full permission to withdraw when they thought fit. He left his
position and settled in again on his deserted *jebel* with the bulk of
his forces. He thus saved them and continued on with his mission,
but lost control of the other road, the one which was henceforth
out of sight and which, heading west, passes through the low
country beneath Beaufort and makes its way to the coast, making
it possible for Lavarack to join up with Stevens' brigade. Upon
learning this, Dentz criticised Albord and telegraphed him: 'The
defensive position specified by the army can be abandoned only
after authorization by the Commander-in-Chief.'

If he could not enter the Bekaa, the enemy was now installed in Merdjayoun and Khiam. For the chief of Native Affairs, Captain Hébrard, 'a tall lanky *spahi* with a bushy moustache', Khiam was vital. It had to be retaken. He appealed to Albord to permit a reconnaissance, but alas, there were no troops to give him. Hébrard set off with only six cavalrymen. He knew the mountains perfectly and made his way to the totally deserted town, then advanced to the postern gate, which he found open. The town square seemed deserted. Then Hébrard, with a drawn sword, galloped in with a few men. Surprised, the few Australians who were guarding the square did not have time to react. One of them was killed, the others disappeared. Hébrard sabotaged, with a grenade, the 90mm gun which had been abandoned when the post was evacuated, then slipped away. He returned to take stock. This feat of arms encouraged the French to try to recapture the fort permanently. An operation was mounted under the command of Captain Ortoli. The approach was quiet but when, after reaching the walls, he set up his two machine guns, there was a strong explosion and part of the wall collapsed. The occupants had just blown up the installation before escaping. This is what Ortoli hoped for. He settled into the fort upon which an artillery bombardment immediately fell. In the closed courtyards of the little citadel, the noise was deafening. Shell fragments and pieces of stone went in all directions, to the extent that Ortoli was astonished to have survived. It was untenable with so few men. During the night, Khiam was evacuated without, it seemed, the enemy being aware of it.

Ordered to retake Khiam from the French, the Australian Brigadier Berryman[58] was going to concentrate such large forces[59] and amass so much ammunition that Lavarack was astounded, paying homage to the defenders: 'In fact, in less than 24 hours, the French counter-attack had drawn around Merdjayoun the largest force in the three sectors of the attack west of Damascus!'

If Merdjayoun was in the hands of the enemy,[60] Albord, who was isolated on his 'rocky crest' nearby, continued to carry out his mission, i.e. to block entry to the Bekaa Valley. On 13 June, the central thrust of the British attack had thus found itself at a standstill for almost a week, at a time when Stevens was progressing along the coast towards Beirut and, on the right, Lloyd was advancing to Damascus. To make up for this delay, Wilson decided to leave only a covering force in front of the French position, which was now isolated, and to resume his offensive towards the north by moving around the French. With this in mind, he formed two columns. The first, moving to the left to the depression of the Litani and under the Beaufort citadel, a route that was out of sight of the French, would leave at night moving towards Jezzine, 30 km to the north and, once there, having made up for its delay, could join forces with those on the coast. On the right, the second column, made up of fast mechanised troops, would force its way along the road and, pursuing the advance initially planned, would drive towards the Bekaa Valley. Doubtless Wilson thought that the French, isolated on their 'rocky crest', were now neutralised, and he believed that the way through would be easily forced. For this operation, he gave Lavarack his fast-moving units,[61] a squadron of English cavalry – the Royal Scots Greys (whose motto is 'Second to None') – in trucks, and a squadron of the 6th Cavalry Regiment and the Staffordshire Yeomanry, mounted on carriers. 'The enemy is somewhere in the region in weak numbers and his morale is low,' Wilson made clear in his orders.

Confident, the British moved off on 15 June, but scarcely had they gone 1,500 metres past the ruins of Merdjayoun, than they ran into aggressive defences, almost invisible against the grey of the hills. Moreover, a lethal machine-gunning by six French aircraft stopped them. Progress resumed but the road a little further on was blocked by the collapse of a cliff that had been mined by the French. It took four hours to open a passage and, when the first carrier moved along it, heavy firing broke out and its tracks were broken. The French kept the block in place. Lavarack did not press on.[62]

The loss of Merdjayoun would be catastrophic for the French: with the Bekaa Valley reached, Damascus would be isolated from Beirut and turned. But it was impossible to remain for very long on the 'rocky crest'. It was therefore necessary to retake the town. General Dentz therefore decided to urgently send a strong column in order to retake it. With this aim, a task force was assembled under the command of Colonel Amanrich, including the Legion, tanks and three squadrons of Circassian cavalry.[63] His mission was to recapture the fortified position, and then work towards Metulla in Palestine and Kuneitra in Syria. The Circassians acted as a covering force to the east and the battalion of Lebanese *chasseurs* remained in reserve; the attack was to be led by two battalions of *tirailleurs* from the crest and a squadron of R-35 tanks. The attack started at 3:00 p.m. on 15 June, and drove towards the city, which it reached. There was shooting through windows, at point-blank range and from floor to floor. A section of the Legion saw all its men killed at their post. The fighting lasted long hours but, on 16 June, the town was reoccupied and the leading elements reached Khirbé on the border. Care of Merdjayoun was entrusted to the 3rd Battalion of the 6th Foreign Legion Regiment which, for two days, searched the houses and gardens. The Australians remained at a standstill. Inactive for three days, they only prodded the Vichy defences, and this respite allowed the French to improve their positions, to dig new fighting positions, and to establish fire plans meshing with the barbed wire entanglements.

Faced with these unfavourable developments, on 18 June Lavarack undertook a major reorganisation of his forces. The commander of the Merdjayoun sector, the Australian Brigadier 'Tubby' Allen, handed over his charge to Major-General J.F. Evetts,[64] commanding the British 6th Division which had just arrived from Egypt. Allen could thus rejoin Stevens' forces on the coast and help him to continue his progress towards Beirut, the main objective.

In front of Merdjayoun, Allen reorganised and divided his forces into three, and decided to return to the attack. The capture of Merdjayoun, which was supposed to have been completed on 9 June, became an important battle. On 19 June, at 5:00 a.m., supported by a powerful artillery barrage, five battalions,[65] who took up positions during the night, unleashed a violent attack. The surprise was complete. The advanced French elements were overrun, but Colonel Albord launched his reserves,[66] supported by the tank squadron, and repelled the attack, retaking the lost ground. The attackers withdrew three kilometres, to the village of Kfar Kila, which had been deserted by its inhabitants. If the ground separating the two villages was bare and out of machine-gun range, the French guns followed them and commenced a severe bombardment which continued intermittently for a long time. At nightfall, the clearing of the terrain was complete. The Australians lost 82 prisoners. The positions remained unchanged for four days. Albord had behaved magnificently.

'Tubby' Allen nevertheless definitely wanted to reach the Bekaa Valley. On 24 June, at daybreak, after an intense artillery preparation, the Australians unleashed a new offensive all along the front of the position, from the outskirts of the town to the 'rocky crest'. At 10:00 a.m., their efforts were concentrated on the Jebel es Saqi, to the left of the position that was held by the remnants of the 2nd Lebanese Chasseur Battalion. Less sturdy than the Algerians, especially in the early days, the Lebanese nonetheless held the position courageously. In the evening, after several incidents in which the enemy thought that he had carried it, the French forces were still holding on. On 25 June, pursuing the attacks of the day before, and increasing the pressure on the Lebanese *chasseurs*, the Australians however, after a powerful attack, succeeded in pushing them from their position. Nevertheless, Merdjayoun had still not fallen. A static battle settled in. Colonel Albord, supported by the Amanrich group, blocked the access to the Bekaa Valley until the end.

Let us go back chronologically, to dawn on 8 June, the day the war started.

On the right, the 5th Indian Brigade of Brigadier Lloyd[67] crossed the Syrian frontier a few hours before the Free French. The Indians were not concerned about political questions and there was no fear of fraternisation. According to Tony Albord, these old warriors were 'experienced veterans of Keren and Sidi Barrani – in Cyrenaica – used to the heat and thirst, and to being on the receiving end of brutal attacks that make faint hearts give way.' They have their own customs. They live apart and, wearing turbans, fight in their own way. The long screeching cries that they give vent to when attacking, disconcert their adversaries. They have nothing in common with the other units.

That night, a swift surprise attack was carried out on the metal bridge at Tel Chehab,[68] a great work of art that is used by the Transjordanian railway where it enters the Syrian plateau. In 1918, T.E. Lawrence had tried unsuccessfully to destroy it. It was essential for the future of the campaign that trains could cross it. The ravine that it crosses is broad and deep, and it was certainly mined. Under the command of Captain Murray of the Rajputana Rifles, a small commando made up of a Free Frenchman – no doubt a renegade who knew the country – and a *havildar* – an Indian sergeant – was ordered to take possession of it before it was blown up. Behind a barbed wire network, the viaduct was guarded by only a single sentry on routine guard duty, half-dazed by the monotonous noise of the waterfall flowing beneath it. Crawling at night up to the barbed wire, the Indian cut it, got through and killed the man.[69] Alerted, the Tunisian section on guard awoke, seized its weapons and started firing but, being the better trained, the commando neutralised it before defusing the charges. The success was strategic.

Followed by an artillery group, the truck convoy of the Indian brigade entered the French mandate at dawn. The turbaned Punjabis assaulted the customs office and killed an employee who was trying to flee in a car. With two posts no longer responding, Deraa became anxious and three armoured cars, detached from Damascus, were sent on a reconnaissance. Sub-Lieutenant Lambert, who commanded them, said:

> With my two Dodge armoured cars, I fell into an ambush on a winding track with high rocky borders. A difficult path ahead became apparent after rounding a bend. Turning around I saw my motorcycle liaison officer fall to the track and remain still. Getting out of my vehicle, I noted that he had received a bullet in the back. No doubt the noise of the engine had masked the sound of the shot. Suddenly, I found myself facing a submachine gun, surrounded by Indian soldiers under the command of a British officer. Charging down the track behind me, the third armoured car, probably stopped to observe, was put out of action by two armour-piercing shells [...] The time to write these lines is doubtless longer than the business took.

The Indian convoy advanced as far as Deraa where, according to the rules, an offer was made to the garrison to surrender before being attacked. Tony Albord:

> A group of envoys – a Free Frenchman, Surgeon-Captain Maurin, an English major, and a public servant from Transjordan – went forward in a car. Just outside the town, they came under fire and the vehicle was hit. They continued on foot, but the request for surrender was rejected at 5:30 p.m.[70] The French refused to fraternize. At 7:30 a.m. the artillery opened fire, at 8:30 a.m. the Punjabis surrounded the barracks, took possession of it and 250 prisoners: two companies of Syrian infantry and a cavalry squadron.[71]

At 8:30 a.m. Deraa was in their hands. At 10:00 a.m., the Indians continued along the Damascus road towards the following town, Sheikh Meskine, 25 km to the north. At 3:00 p.m., the Punjabis reached the town, defended by a company of Senegalese *tirailleurs*[72] and a platoon of armoured cars. Here there was no longer a question of a diplomatic approach. After a seven-minute artillery preparation, the Indians walked towards their objective behind their weapons carriers.[73] They had to cross a broad slope planted with cereal crops whose stalks in that season were tall and dry. When the Indians were well advanced in the area, the defenders set fire to the crops. Caught in the flames and under mortar and automatic weapons fire, the Indians withdrew in disorder. French aircraft appeared which machine-gunned them. Several carriers were destroyed. At 4:30 p.m., the attack was driven back. The frontal assault of the Punjabis having failed, the Rajputs, who had not yet been engaged, carried out a broad sweeping movement to take shelter on a hilly area on the other side of the centre of resistance. However, it was so late when they were in place that Lloyd decided not to attack with his two battalions until the morning of 9 June. Damascus, which had been warned, during this time gave the order to the French garrison to evacuate. Supported by the platoon of armoured cars, Major Boyer carried out a night sortie in force, but he had to fight hard to get through. He got clear only at the price of half of his troops and his heavy equipment. When the Hotchkiss tanks of the Free French Forces entered the town next day, the men came to examine 'the more or less destroyed French equipment at the exit from the town, two

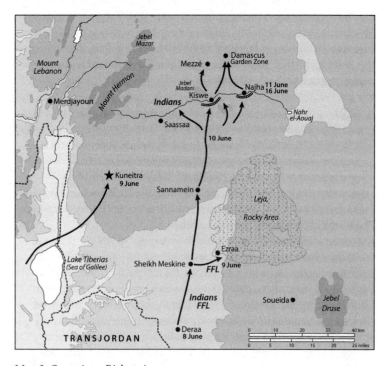

Map 3. Operations: Right axis

armoured cars, including one that was burned out, a 75mm cannon
which seemed intact and a big pile of light equipment.'[74]

By a miracle, the Senegalese who escaped ended up reaching
Damascus, after a great deal of walking, slipping away under the
nose of Collet's horsemen who were operating in the area.

After having crossed the frontier at the Jisr ben Yacub[75] post
to the north of Lake Tiberias, the 1st Battalion of the King's Own
Royal Regiment, under the command of Lieutenant-Colonel Orr,
accompanied by an Australian artillery unit,[76] marched towards
Kuneitra. The King's Own was, with the Royal Scots Greys, one
of the few British units engaged in the struggle. On its flag could
be read the battle honours 'Guadeloupe 1759' and 'Corunna
1809': fighting against the French was a tradition. At 9:30 a.m.,
the King's Own was in front of the town. But Kuneitra was not an
ordinary town, for it was there in the nineteenth century that the
Ottomans settled Circassian families driven from the Caucasus by
the Russians. These were a warlike people who had come to enter
the service of the Turks. Moreover, Kuneitra had been fortified
that winter by the black *tirailleurs* of the 17th Senegalese Tirailleur
Regiment who had installed barbed wire entanglements, anti-tank
ditches, road barriers, and firing positions, making it a strong point.

At 5:00 a.m., obeying the orders that obliged them to parley
before attacking, an English major and a Free French soldier,
Surgeon-Captain Rédinger, presented themselves before the
defences, preceded by a bugler carrying a white flag who, in a
loud voice, made contact with a French officer, Captain Dewatre.
The latter invited them to follow him to the command post of the
commander, Lieutenant-Colonel Milliet,[77] where discussions were
commenced, interrupted by a long conversation on the telephone
with Beirut. The English soldiers had the impression that he was
trying to gain time. The envoys walked backwards and forwards
from one command post to the other. Finally a truce was decided
to allow the evacuation of the civilians. The envoys withdrew. At
the end of the morning, a French officer came out of the lines,
moved forward and, in a loud voice, announced, like a herald in
the Middle Ages, that the position refused to surrender and that
hostilities would recommence at midday. Heralds, messengers,
trumpeters and white flags, truce and verbal understandings, the
whole process entertained the Australians whom it reminded of
novels about knights in armour and the operas of Gilbert and
Sullivan.[78] At midday, the truce came to an end, and the English

opened fire. The cannon thundered, the infantry advanced and, without encountering any resistance, entered the town. It was empty! The garrison had slipped away. To receive them there were only two *riz-pain-sel* (rice-bread-salt)[79] men, and a gunner without a gun. Kuneitra was British.

During the night of 8 June, troops from the French outposts in Southern Syria, which had fulfilled their mission, made their way towards Damascus in a disorderly fashion. This was not an orderly march by a cohesive group. The withdrawal took place, according to some witnesses, in an 'incredible shambles'. In scattered groups, a more or less disorganised mass of runaways was walking through the night, wavering, fearing the threat of an attack by Collet's cavalrymen or the enemy's carriers which, here and there, appeared unexpectedly, progressing along mountain tracks where the Lebanese villagers had guided them in a servile fashion. On the plain, among the shadows, rockets and flares, there was confusion. By the light of the moon, each person was trying to find out where he was and to recognise the people around him. Who was walking there, in front? Are they speaking French, English or Indian? It is not sure that, during the night, Boyer's men who were leaving and those of Chevigné who were arriving, did not meet: soldiers speaking the same language and wearing the same uniforms were not inclined to kill each other [...] Nevertheless, in the confusion, Collet's cavalrymen took a few prisoners.

If the withdrawal of Dentz's troops was disorganised, the assailants' attack was also carried out in some confusion: units became mixed up, overlapping of authority and translation faults caused friction. In addition, the procedures of the two armies were different. Grasping, on this first day, to what extent these factors were the cause of incidents, Wilson entrusted the command of all the troops to Lavarack. Legentilhomme and Lloyd were therefore subordinate to him. However, battling with Merdjayoun until 20 June, the Australian surrendered the initiative to the Frenchman. For the attackers, the gains were significant. Deraa, Ezraa, Sheikh Meskine, Kuneitra and the outposts in Southern Syria were all swept aside. In their rapid advance, the Indians captured 30 officers and 300 men. For their part, the Free French had suffered their first casualties. Everyone took note that the French regular army was not going to let itself be pushed around. The expedition was not the 'armed political incursion' that Churchill had hoped.

For the defenders, the results were not catastrophic. Certainly, the south of Syria had been evacuated, 513 men had been lost, but orders had been followed. The communiqué broadcast by the staff was rather optimistic: 'The units to which a delaying action had been assigned carried out their mission well, inflicting heavy losses on the enemy. The majority of attacks have been repulsed and artillery has scattered the Gaullist units with heavy losses [...] Our defence has been greatly helped by the almost total absence of enemy aircraft.'

Free French troops left Kastina on 7 June, the day before the attack. Their convoy entered Transjordan, travelling north, crossed the frontier, entered Syria, and pushed on towards Deraa. The entry into the French mandate was peaceable for everyone. 'One would have thought we were out for a drive.'

Getting off a train at Deraa, the Marine Infantry Brigade[80] boarded trucks. They were attacked on the way by two waves of aircraft – 'Glenn Martins, Potez, and Messerchmitts', confirmed Freitag who was impatient to catch sight of the Germans – two attacks which killed or wounded a dozen men. These were the first Gaullist losses. Panic ensued and the black *tirailleurs* had to be rounded up before they could continue on their way.

At dawn on 8 June, General Legentilhomme went to Brigadier Lloyd's headquarters to follow the progress of the Indians at Deraa. At the beginning of the afternoon, still being at his side near Sheikh Meskine when the attack failed, Legentilhomme offered to capture Ezraa, approximately ten kilometres to the northeast. Lloyd, who agreed, lent him an artillery battery. It was therefore at Ezraa that the Free French carried out their first attack against a French position.[81] 'It seemed incredible to us to be *attacked* [sic] by Vichy troops', wrote Freitag, of the Free French Division, oddly.[82] Ezraa, already evacuated, was easily occupied by Chevigné's Marine Infantry Brigade. The most active unit in the Free French Division was naturally at the front. The Tunisians who were occupying the place had already been ordered to leave, and the Special Railway Sapper Company, a Lebanese unit barely trained to fight, surrendered. Its commander, who fled, reached Damascus on a horse after a solitary ride that was long spoken about in the messes. A Gaullist prisoner, who was captured by prisoners he was supposed to be guarding, was taken to Soueida, where he maintained he believed 'the town to be occupied by the Germans. He asked if these latter were numerous in Syria, showing great astonishment upon learning that there weren't any.'[83]

On the right of the Syrian plain, Collet was advancing with his cavalry, 300 Circassians and 100 *spahis* on horseback or in trucks.[84] They left the *kibbutz* of Geva in Palestine on the night of 7 June, and occupied Naouah,[85] where a section of Senegalese surrendered without a fight. In the evening, they returned to Sheikh Meskine, which was being besieged by the Indians. During the night, they patrolled on the plain looking for garrisons which were retreating but, without maps and guides, they were wasting their time. Not being able to outflank the Vichy troops who were retreating, Collet and his men rejoined the Free French troops on 9 June at Sannamein, halfway to Damascus.

Coming from Kastina by train, the 12 Free French Hotchkiss tanks and their two tank recovery vehicles arrived at Beisan railway station in Transjordan, at dawn on 8 June. The same evening, they set out, moving on their caterpillar tracks, for Deraa in Syria, 60 km away. Moving along rocky tracks, they progressed along a chaotic path through narrow gorges where, in the moonlight, the walls seemed breathtakingly high. There were breakdowns, sometimes serious. These vehicles had already covered 1,500 km and were showing serious signs of fatigue. During the night, however, they reached Deraa; then, passing through Sheikh Meskine at dawn, they had a short rest before joining Legentilhomme's convoy which was moving forward ahead of them. Yves Gras[86] described the column on the march:

A long column of trucks and buses stretched out along the road in a cloud of dust. It was moving slowly, with 150 metres between vehicles, with the units widely spaced. This plan was quickly upset. Some wheezing vehicles broke down. Enemy aircraft flew overhead; they attacked, bombed and machine-gunned several times. Trucks and buses had to stop. Everyone jumped out, spread out and lay down in the fields, then reboarded the vehicles and set off once more. On the road there were no Army Service Corps personnel to restore order in the column and to give directions to those who were lagging behind or were lost. Everyone was looking after himself, trying to catch up with the others or find his unit. The procession, which started off in a proper fashion, turned into a car chase. However, late in the evening, the brigade managed to regroup.

It had covered 60 km. 'Still escorted by French Marines, the divisional headquarters was set up at Sannamein, in the Syrian gendarmerie post where there was a telephone [...] Tents were erected around it. Numerous vehicles were driving around and becoming bunched up. There was much toing and froing [...] The British liaison officer, Major Hore-Ruthven,[87] considered that the Free French camp was more like a wedding party than a staff on campaign.'

The day before at his headquarters in Damascus, learning of the invasion, General de Verdilhac, commanding the South Syria sector, sent a strong armoured force south accompanied by two sections of legionnaires[88] in order to determine the position of the enemy and to recover the retreating garrisons. On that night, at 3:30 a.m., these troops came face to face with Chevigné's motorcyclists, the vanguard of the Gaullist forces. 'Don't shoot, we are French!' they shouted. But quickly realising who they were dealing with, the two groups opened fire at the same time. The motorcycle troops abandoned their machines, the opposing troops turned around and the Marine Infantry Brigade troops, who were following with their headlights blazing, came to a halt in order to take up positions. It was the first encounter. No one had hesitated.

The convoy had thus halted. The men dismounted and waited in the icy conditions. The tanks were called up so that that they could go in front. Trucks, infantrymen, command cars, everyone took measures to overtake the column. The Hotchkiss tanks now were at the head of the column and soon the battle resumed. A tank crewman: 'A few hundred metres further on, an artillery barrage opened up [...] The shells rained down, first of all 300 metres away, then quite close, a few metres in front or behind. A shell fell just under the front of the tank lifting its 13 tonnes [...] Inside, the two crewmen were dazed, but unhurt.' Another: 'The road was blocked by heavy and accurately directed shelling. A small truck burst into flames. Shots were coming every now and then, which came closer as if invisible observers were guiding them in the smoke of the early morning.' A third said: 'For the tanks, there was only one way forward: the road. It was impossible to go into the loose stones. The cross paths were made for flocks of goats, not tracked vehicles. The rocky conditions were not for them. A turn that was too sharp, a large rock, the tanks could lose their tracks all too easily [...] and the engines stalled as soon as the effort was too great. In the potholes along the road, the tanks moved forward in second gear, if not in first [...] The artillery fire continued but was not as well aimed.'

Behind, the infantry were not following: the Senegalese, as
the Saras of Chad and the Bayas of Ubangi are wrongly called,
of the 1st Marine Infantry Battalion, and the Marines of the
Marine Infantry Brigade, were still a long way behind. The tanks
were waiting. It became relatively calm. The men were stretched
out and sleeping between the tanks. Finally, at 1:00 p.m., in
Indian file on either side of the road, the infantry arrived. The
column started off again. Realising that the retreating garrisons
were going to get away from him, Legentilhomme ordered the
advance to be speeded up. Followed by the infantry a short
distance behind, the tanks entered the village of Deir Ali. Heavy
firing started again. Barely protected by their helmets, the
Marines seemed to pass through the barrage without a problem.
Having moved through the town, progress halted and, in spite of
sporadic firing, the tired men set up camp: camouflage, listening
posts, defences, sleeping positions and a meal. Two tanks were
broken down, one having lost a track, and the other caught in
mass of rocks.

Coming from the direction of Damascus and proceeding
towards Deir Ali on reconnaissance, a Vichy armoured column
with tanks and armoured cars was stopped by a 25mm gun. It
turned around, with one tank being towed, and abandoned two
armoured cars. Further to the east, in the semi-desert zone, another
reconnaissance force of R-35 tanks detected Collet's group and
forced it to withdraw. These were not only reconnaissances, but
the first sign of a stiffening of resistance. The military parade
was over. In front of Damascus, there would be a battle: the
real war was about to start. As the effect of surprise was no
longer operating, one had to wait for the bulk of the forces to be
assembled in order to attack. On 10 June, the Free French convoy
which, for three days, had been advancing without meeting any
enemy of similar size, stopped. Although, in spite of the machine
gun and aerial attacks, 30 km had been covered, there were still
20 km to go before reaching the capital. They would be the most
difficult: the defences started there.

During the night of 11 June, Jourdier and Collet succeeded in
getting this note – by what means? – to La Boisse, a lieutenant
in the 1st Moroccan Spahi Regiment, one of Dentz's units:
'Jourdier to La Boisse. Follow Ménétrier and meet me at Nagha.
Collet is here.' And Collet: 'My dear de La Boisse, I am waiting
for you. I hope that you are not one of those who wish to be

the advance guard of the Boche. We are coming only to prevent those Boche who are already in Beirut from taking over all Syria. Affectionately. Collet.' La Boisse did not accept. Did Collet believe what he wrote?[89]

Learning from the experience and noting the distance of Lavarack who was entirely occupied by the attack on Merdjayoun, Maitland Wilson decided, before attacking Damascus, to place all his forces – the Free French and Indians – under the sole command of General Legentilhomme from midnight on 13 June. The new unit was called *Gentforce*.[90] 'I admit that as a Frenchman,' wrote Legentilhomme 'that I received this news with emotion. It proved that the British high command had not lost all confidence in the French command.' But if Maitland Wilson wanted it, the gods of war decided otherwise: at Sannamein, during the day on 12 June, Vichy aircraft bombed Legentilhomme's command post three times and, on the evening, at 7:00 p.m. during the last attack, he was severely wounded in the left arm. He had to be urgently evacuated to hospital in Deraa[91] on the frontier, more than 100 km to the rear. Before leaving, he ordered his chief of staff, Colonel Kœnig, to make plans for the impending attack: he planned on being back the next day. However, having spent a disturbed night, the surgeon refused to let him leave and he had to stay in hospital.

For his part, Lloyd considered the opposing position to be too strong to be able to be tackled with the current state of his forces. A solid artillery support was needed to carry it off, and he decided to go and speak about it with his new boss, appointed that very morning, General Legentilhomme. On 13 June, at the Ambulance Unit, the two generals came to an agreement: the offensive could not be launched until 15 June, two days' time. It would be directed by an Englishman.[92] So Brigadier Lloyd and Colonel Kœnig drew up the details of the planned offensive, and it was Lloyd who signed the order for the attack on Damascus on 15 June.

The main line of defence at Damascus was established to the north of a river which was almost dry at that time of the year: the Nahr el-Aouaj, a broad ditch with edges that were sometimes steep in places, sometimes stony, sometimes damp and muddy, which, from west to east, barred the roads coming from the south. Two bridges crossed it, the one at Kiswe on the left and the one at Nehja on the right. Placed in a state of defence, the towns barred access to the bridges. Beyond and behind them, a short distance away, the hilly country becomes more prominent. The hills bear marvellous names – Jebel Maani, Jebel Kelb, Jebel Abu Atriz – but they are only large hillocks with difficult approaches, sometimes with rocky areas favourable to defence, a terrain so suited to manoeuvres that the Damascus garrison had carried out training there for a long time.

A forward position had been set up to the south of the river on a sharply rising hill, Jebel Maani, which, being between Deir Ali and the bridges, could observe the road for over four kilometres. Formed from enormous rocks, the cliffs could not be crossed and were devoid of vegetation; it was, according to Hugo of the 1st Marine Battalion, 'a real high wall'. From the top of its 1,000 metres, Damascus could be seen 15 km away. A battalion of Moroccans,[93] supported by artillery, occupied the crests. To take Kiswe required that the *jebel* be captured. The attack on the *jebel* was entrusted to the 1st Marine Battalion,[94] while the 2nd Marine Battalion, on the far side of the hilly country, continued north on foot across a desert zone as far as the bed of the river. Launched at dawn on 11 June, the first attack, attempted an exhausting climb, did not succeed. It had to be repeated in the middle of the day, in sweltering heat, but following a course that was both less difficult and less exposed. The battalion carried out this assault in overwhelming heat and in conditions made particularly difficult by intense, never-ending thirst – a one-litre water-bottle between two men and no resupply. It wasn't a last-ditch stand, but a stubborn, long and bloody struggle. According to Yves Gras, the Free French, whose first engagement it was, were 'painfully astonished' and this fight had serious psychological consequences. The feelings of the Gaullists were suddenly marked by a violent animosity. 'We fought henceforth with the passions of a civil war', affirmed Gras. The fratricidal aspect of this fight to the death now appeared clear. Killed at the head of one of the Moroccan companies, Captain Perdrix was an intimate friend of Amilakhvari at Saint-Cyr and it was said that the news of his friend's death affected him greatly. After an initially stubborn resistance, the Moroccans' defence suddenly weakened when, its two officers having been killed, a company withdrew without fighting, abandoning this important position and dragging two others along with it. The news caused consternation in Beirut. The question was asked: did Dentz overestimate the reliability of his troops? Speaking of fraternisation, Gaullist propaganda exploited the incident.

While the 1st Marine Battalion was fighting at Jebel Maani, Major Roux's 2nd Marine Battalion had moved towards the northeast in dreadful conditions – rocky terrain, furnace-like heat – as far as the river bed where bursts of machine-gun fire brought it to a halt, wounding Lieutenant Faure, who had to be evacuated. Legentilhomme had thus made contact, finding himself alone in a forward position. The Indians were still 60 km behind at Deraa, where they were joined by 350 men of the Transjordan Frontier Force,[95] ordered to guard the town of Ezraa occupied by the Free French the day before. Situated at the foot of the Jebel Druse, Ezraa monitored this massif, still occupied by the Vichy French and threatening the roads used by the resupply convoys.

Accompanied by its quick-firing Bofors guns – anti-tank and anti-aircraft – and its field artillery regiment, the convoy of Lloyd's Indians drove north in a cloud of dust which largely camouflaged it. This was the reason that Free French tanks, on watch, fired on it in error.[96] Without there being any real combat, the Indian Bofors opened fire.

In front of the Nahr el-Aouaj, the forces were soon lined up. In the centre were the three infantry battalions, the Marine Infantry Brigade on the left, the 1st Marine Battalion in the centre, and the 2nd Marine Battalion on the right facing Nehja with the tanks and Collet's group. On the left, Lloyd with his Indians would take care of Kiswe. Thus, on 12 June, the attacking force was in place along a front of approximately ten kilometres.

Before launching the offensive, Legentilhomme asked for a reconnaissance by tanks of the principal objective, the bridge at Kiswe. Two Hotchkiss tanks were designated. The one commanded by Tresca and driven by Rouard, went in the lead, followed by Lacoste's, which was driven by Floch. All men were very young, still almost adolescents. Tresca was a seminarian in Beirut; Lacoste had fought in the Saar; Rouart had taken part in the Norwegian campaign. They had scarcely gone 800 metres when artillery fire opened up; probably 75mm guns, firing over open sights. Lacoste's tank reared up, turned over, and lay still, a track blown off. Behind it, Tresca's exploded – its turret was torn off, pieces flew in all directions, enormous flames rose up and ammunition exploded. Collapsed in his turret, Lacoste was stunned but was in one piece. Floch, however, had a leg torn off and one eye was nothing but a bloody hole. When he recovered consciousness, Lacoste dragged him from the wreck, applied a tourniquet made from electrical wire and, under fire, dragged him, gasping for breath but conscious, into a ditch where he took shelter. Later, at night, people came to get him. He survived.

The battle for Damascus was, quite obviously, going to be hard.

14

The Battle for Damascus

What was known in Damascus about the enemy, except that he was close? Having come on a reconnaissance mission to the Jebel Krim, to the west of Kiswe, the *spahi* platoon under the command of Lieutenant de Chillaz, saw some men stand up and, as they approached, waved. It was an outpost of the Marine Infantry Brigade, which had been there since the morning. On both sides the Frenchmen chatted in a friendly fashion, then Chillaz departed as he had arrived, peacefully. On 12 June, two Hotchkiss tanks on reconnaissance had been destroyed to the south of Kiswe, and a reconnaissance repulsed at Nehja. On 14 June, aircraft had reported large movements over 18 km of front. Faced with this threat, General de Verdilhac, commanding the South Syrian sector, had only three infantry battalions, the 1st Moroccan Spahi Regiment, a few Circassian units with a wavering morale, and two artillery groups. Opposite, there were six or seven Gaullist battalions, three Indian battalions and the Collet group. Intelligence gathered by the *Deuxième Bureau*[1] from the few prisoners taken was scanty. Captured on 16 June, three nurses, from a Gaullist ambulance which had become lost, had not told much. One refused to speak and the other two had seen only the tanks and Indian reinforcements. 'According to them, the morale of the Gaullists was not very good. Some had refused to fight against [Vichy] Frenchmen.'[2] Interrogated the same day, some Free French[3] captured near Sheikh Meskine by Michelet, declared 'that they were convinced that they would find facing them in Syria German troops mixed with a few Frenchmen who were partisans of the alliance with Germany.' The author of the interrogation report noted in his own hand: 'They added that they had been convinced that the majority of the French in the Levant were awaiting the arrival of the Gaullists and the English to free them from the German yoke.'

On 15 June, the offensive started. At daybreak, the Punjabis crossed the dried river bed of the Wadi Nahr el-Aouaj, brushing aside the enemy, entering their lines and, without difficulty, captured Kiswe and moved through it. They had benefited from an unexpected piece of luck. The [Vichy] French battalion holding the village was waiting for its relief but, instead of this taking place at night, by an inexplicable fault – inexcusable said many – it was carried out in broad daylight, in sight of the enemy. The relief force had, in fact, arrived at the moment of the attack. Surprised, not knowing the layout of the defences, it was driven from the field. Panic-stricken, it fled, dragging with it the unit being relieved, which was in the process of regrouping. In the great disorder, there was no one in command. Only a company of Algerians, which was departing, and a company of Senegalese, which was arriving,[4] tried to resist. Seizing the occasion, crossing the ditches and barbed wire entanglements on ladders, the Indians captured the village. Kiswe and the hill overlooking the village were thus lost. Regrouping the units, and assembling the men wandering about the battlefield, [Vichy] French officers tried about 2:00 p.m. to mount a counter-attack, but in vain. They succeeded only in pushing back the enemy into the town which would never be recaptured. 'So things go in war,' noted Yves Gras 'Careless mistakes were seen which no one would dare commit in the training area.' For Verdilhac, in any case, the setback was serious. A battalion having left three days earlier for Sidon and the armour being in the process of learning to manoeuvre in squadrons in the south, there were no longer the means to counter-attack. After the loss of Kiswe, Damascus could never again take the initiative.

In the centre, facing the Jebel Kelb, the failure was immediate. Major de Roux's Gaullist black Africans (2nd Marine Battalion) found themselves facing Major Rollet's Vichy black Africans (1st Battalion, 17th Senegalese Tirailleur Regiment). Having moved off very smartly, an advance, after crossing the Nahr el-Aouaj, was blocked by very heavy fire coming from the crest of the hills. The climb up had barely started but two section commanders having been killed, the Gaullist blacks, deprived of their officers and without artillery support, had fallen back. Whether by losses or desertions, at 4:00 p.m. their effectives had been reduced by half. Major de Roux therefore decided to call off the attack and, during the night, the 2nd Marine Battalion withdrew to its start line. Who would know what these combatants, coming from villages in Africa, would feel if forced to kill people often from their own ethnic group, from the same tribe or even from the same family? Did the quarrels of the whites involve the Africans?

On the right, Collet had under his command eight Free French tanks, eight armoured cars of the Yorkshire Dragoons, and three French armoured cars that had been recovered, but no artillery. Six kilometres from the start line, the approach march ended behind a hill which hid the armoured vehicles from the enemy's sight. A Transjordanian Arab battalion, as well as Jourdier's *spahis*, arrived by truck. The Circassians hobbled their horses to attack on foot. Had the enemy been warned? His artillery fire had been heavy for the past two hours. The tanks would attack in two waves, a section of three tanks in front, another 200 metres behind, with two tanks remaining in reserve. The objective, the Nehja bridge, was at the far edge of a desert plain, strewn with large stones, where the armour, moving with difficulty, could deploy.

At 8:15 a.m., the tanks moved out. As soon as they were sighted by the Vichy troops, heavy artillery fire opened up. The roar was impressive. Raising enormous clouds of sand and dust, the tanks drove forward in the midst of the din in a countryside that was barely discernible through the driving slits. Everything seemed confused, nothing was like what they had been told, but 'as long as one is advancing, there was no fear, nothing is more invigorating that an assault!' said Hébert, a driver, who added, 'We had to descend into the wadi and climb out the other side without stalling or overturning, a difficult manoeuvre when under enemy fire. As soon as we had crossed the wadi, we moved around the village to attack it from behind, but the manoeuvre had, of course, been foreshadowed by the defence.' The tank commander, suddenly shouted: 'Gently, Hébert, I am firing!', when he saw a cannon camouflaged among bales of straw, but as he fired, he saw a shot from scarcely 50 metres away. The first projectile blew off the machine-gun housing, the second pierced the turret. Miraculously, no one was hit. The driver trod hard on the accelerator and pushed forward. Suddenly, the soil became soft and the tank sank in, then stopped, its nose in a marsh. He had to withdraw quickly. But where were the other tanks? The tank commander saw one, then another. Further away, the Circassians were digging in. 'Let's go!' he said to the driver. The hull was holed, the turret jammed, the cannon was unusable, but the engine roared and the tank, freed from the mud, rushed forward again. Alas, hit by a bullet, Robédat, the tank commander, collapsed and, immediately afterwards, there was an explosion. Everything blew up. His face covered in burning fragments, the driver could no longer see. The tank rolled over, fell back and stopped, lying on its side. Only Hébert, severely wounded, succeeded in reaching his lines after a painful walk in the middle of the battle.

What happened? As a result of a mistake by the staff, the tanks attacked alone, without artillery support. The attack finished in a catastrophe. Pierced through and through, the first Hotchkiss was destroyed on the bridge and the tank commander lost both legs and the wounded mechanic was taken prisoner.[5] Two tanks were destroyed on the road; in the first, the crewmembers were burned to death, in the other, the two men were mortally wounded. The tank commander, paralysed in the legs, committed suicide to avoid being taken prisoner. Facing an entrenched enemy, well equipped with anti-tank guns – 25mm and 47mm – and supported by two batteries of 75mm cannon, one 105mm battery and a 155mm battery, the assault became a catastrophe. Breakdowns, becoming bogged, destruction: the unit lost half its tanks. The British also had heavy losses. In total, eight tanks and ten armoured cars were put out of action. Behind the armoured vehicles, *spahis* and Circassians, advancing on foot with fixed bayonets, were also stopped very quickly. Their losses were also heavy. A nephew of Clemenceau, Sub-Lieutenant Bensa, was killed. Villoutreys' squadron lost all its European officers and NCOs, and 37 *spahis* out of 95. Villoutreys himself, his body pierced by a bullet from one hip to the other and left for dead on the field, was taken prisoner. After receiving basic treatment, he was evacuated to hospital in Damascus.[6] Eliminated, the Collet column played no further part. The attack on Nehja had failed.

When, on 15 June, General Legentilhomme, his arm in a sling, returned from hospital to his command post to learn of the failure of the offensive, he was extremely unhappy. The attack had been badly planned. 'The armour had been engaged,' he thundered, 'without his knowledge, [and] without artillery support, which was a serious mistake'. He severely criticised Major de Roux, who was in charge. He wanted to relieve him of his command, but deferred it in the face of the unanimous protests of the officers of the 2nd Marine Battalion.

The attack would be resumed the next day, 16 June.

15

Kuneitra: The Counter-attack

Let us return to 12 June, to the Grand Serail in Beirut. Dentz, who had been ordered to resist, knew that he could not await sizeable reinforcements in either men, equipment or munitions. On the coast, the Australians had reached Damour; in the centre they had reached Jezzine and, ten kilometres from Damascus, the adversaries were in contact. Even if his troops were motivated and his forces still powerful, his position was threatened. He had to fight alone and without a hope of winning. 'He wanted to hang on, save honour, and to be in a position to negotiate in acceptable conditions,' said Colonel Keime. Moreover, the situation was not yet desperate. If up till then it had only endured, Damour seemed able to resist and Merdjayoun was still holding. In front of Damascus, the enemy was more than 100 km from his bases, and his supply lines were very drawn out.

No doubt inspired by Keime, commanding the cavalry in the Levant, Dentz understood then that a fast powerful mobile force could, by means of a well-led strike towards the frontier zone of Palestine, cut his adversary's communications and disorganise his offensive. One year to the day previously, the Germans had won the war in France by slipping behind the Allied forces. Tony Albord:

> Facing a wall map, sitting astride a chair in a familiar pose, Dentz spoke his thoughts aloud in front of a few close friends: 'We are still holding on [...] Obviously this hasn't happened according to our predictions [...] The threat is not to Damascus but to Beirut [...] We have to do something [...] Impossible on the coast under naval gunfire [...] The two axes Damascus-Kuneitra and Damascus-Ezraa remain [...] To act on one with a maximum effort would be to get caught in the flank on the other [...] We have to act on the two'.

So a plan was drawn up. As soon as he launched the armoured attack, all the troops would resume the offensive. An infantry force under the orders of Colonel Barré would force the enemy from Jezzine, then, moving towards the sea, would harass his rear, cutting the coast road before it runs into Beirut. New life was breathed into the army. The battle was going to change its rhythm.

On 12 June, Dentz developed his plan and, on 13 June at 8:30 p.m., he called in Keime: 'I want to go on the offensive, penetrate deep behind the enemy, attack Sheikh Meskine or Sannamein on the one hand, Kuneitra on the other. Taking these positions will cut the enemy's communications [...] I order you to organise and command the whole show. Come to an agreement with Verdilhac to get the necessary troops.' Keime, who was languishing in Beirut, was delighted. He had already stressed his interest in this vast operation. At 9:00 a.m. he left Beirut for Damascus. A father of armoured units and producer of the White-Dodge and the Dodge armoured cars, he had already studied the problem. He knew the operation: simultaneously, two armoured groups would attack the two places overlooking the invasion routes, Kuneitra and Sheikh Meskine, while a mounted cavalry group would advance behind them in order to block a possible counter-attack. Priority would be given to the fastest vehicles, and aerial patrols would cover the columns. To guarantee surprise, they would pass to the right and the left of the enemy installed on the Nahr el-Aouaj, via Mezzé on the west and via Hijjane on the east. With success depending on surprise, it was forbidden to use the telephone before the force moved off, and the troops would not be informed of the objectives until they set out.

As soon as he arrived on 14 June, Keime organised a secret meeting at the Grand Serail in Damascus. Only four officers took part: himself, who would direct the operation, General de Verdilhac, who would supply the troops, Lieutenant-Colonel Le Couteulx de Caumont, commanding the 7th African Chasseur Regiment, and his chief of staff, Major Simon. 'It was hoped that the secret was well guarded, because in Damascus we lived in an atmosphere of treason. It was felt that there were spies listening everywhere,' Keime remembered.

Under the command of Lieutenant-Colonel Le Couteulx de Caumont, the first group, the largest, comprised 35 armoured vehicles, about 200 men, some artillery and a cavalry squadron.[1] Passing via Saassaa, a town situated 35 km from Damascus that the Vichy French were still holding, he would sweep towards his objective, Kuneitra, 60 km to the south. It was not Le Couteulx's first offensive. The year before, he commanded the armoured cars in General de Gaulle's armoured division at Moncornet, where had been wounded. His artillery was very weak and his infantry insufficient, but his units were well commanded. Keime accompanied him, as well as Lieutenant-Colonel Milliet,[2] who had set up the defences at Kuneitra and who knew better than anyone their weaknesses and the least well defended angles.

The second group was commanded by Major Simon, chief of staff of the cavalry in the Levant. With ten armoured cars, five tanks and 120 men,[3] it would wend its way along the track which, via Hijjane, passed to the east of the rocky area of Leja. Arriving from the east, reinforced at Mezraa by troops who were still occupying the Jebel Druse, it cut the enemy's supply line, the road from Transjordan. Following hazardous tracks, he took advantage of the reconnaissance work that had been undertaken for several months by Keime, thanks to which the cavalry had detailed maps showing routes and the availability of tracks in dry weather and wet weather. Under the command of Captain de Carmejane, a third group, would travel across the plain between Saassaa and Sannamein in order to sow disorder in the enemy's rear. Its mission – 'not very well defined, it must be acknowledged', said its chief of staff – would be to cover the rear areas especially. Refuelling would take place at Saassaa for Le Couteulx and at Mezraa for Simon. Starting at dawn, Dewoitine fighters would ensure aerial protection. Moving off the following night: at daybreak they had to be far away. They therefore had only a few hours to get ready.

On 14 June, when the operation was announced to the troops, it caused lots of enthusiasm. All were happy to take part in a large-scale operation. At 8:00 p.m. the Le Couteulx group left Mezzé. Three Dodge-White armoured cars, followed by five Renault tanks, led the group, followed by the trucks carrying the African *tirailleurs*, a 47mm cannon, the headquarters section, two platoons of armoured cars and the bulk of the tanks. About midnight, the convoy stopped at Saassaa. British units, it was learned, had just arrived a few kilometres to the south. Before moving off, they had to remove the mines and the barricades which blocked the road. Two 75mm cannon were recuperated but, equipped with wooden wheels, they could not move at more than 10kph. Finally, in the dark of night, the convoy set off once more.

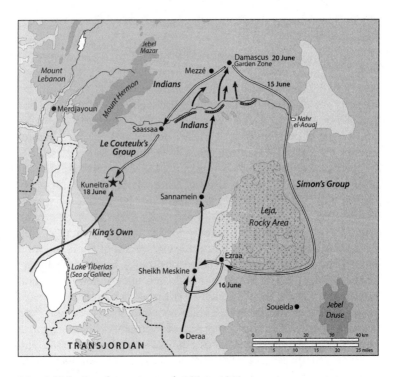

Map 4. Vichy French counter-attack 16 June 1941

Suddenly, after having gone six kilometres, firing broke out and tracer rounds streaked through the darkness. Firing from all guns and with headlights blazing, the armoured vehicles at the head of the column rushed forward. A lucky shot lit up a petrol tanker parked at the bottom of the slope and its light illuminated the countryside. Captain Quarez, commanding the Senegalese, followed on foot. For him, as for his 80 men, including ten white officers and NCOs, it was his baptism of fire. Deployed as skirmishers in a night pierced by tracer rounds, some became frightened and withdrew. A group returned to the trucks driven by locals, turned them around, and fled towards Saassaa. Quarez took charge of his men energetically, but his task was difficult: although he had good NCOs, he had been in command of these men for only two days and they did not know him. However, following his example, with a light machine gun on the hip and

Plate Section

Plate 1. General Lavarack inspecting the troops in Beirut, 1941.

Plate 2. Commemorative tablet with inscription.

Plate 3. General Catroux and Field Marshall Wilson, Cairo, May 1941. Wilson in foreground, Catroux in background, partially obscured.

Plate 4. Generals Spears and Catroux, Beirut 1943. Spears in civilian dress, Catroux in uniform.

Plate 5. Photo with dedication from General Dentz to General Keime, April 1942.

Plate 6. An Australian Vickers Light Tank Mk VI and crew at rest during the advance into Syria, 11 June 1941.

Plate 7. A 15-cwt truck passes a sentry as it leaves Fort Weygand at Palmyra, Syria, 12 July 1941.

firing blindly, they moved forward again. The Circassians joined them, but the enemy resisted. The battle lasted a long time. For four hours, a confused battle raged through the night, sometimes with handtohand combat. It was surprising both in its scale and its duration. Finally, a green rocket was seen and the enemy broke off the engagement. The road was open.

Isolated on a hilltop, an officer and 20 men of the King's Own were taken prisoner. According to them, the unit was getting ready to attack Saassaa at dawn the next day. 'These prisoners were young. One had fought in France, others in Eritrea and Egypt. Some had arrived directly from England. All were surprised at not fighting Germans,' said their interrogation reports.

Sent out that night on a reconnaissance, an armoured patrol found Kuneitra already on alert. Knowing that the element of surprise was gone, Colonel Le Couteulx decided nevertheless to push ahead and, before dawn, accompanied by his officers, he went to reconnoitre the town's access roads which were blocked by barricades. Each ravine, each path was examined carefully with binoculars. The plan of attack was drawn up. The north, which was rocky, was inaccessible for armoured vehicles, so infantry would take up positions with the 75mm guns, which would be able to fire on the town. The armoured attack would come from the east and south, where the terrain was open. However, the two 75mm guns recovered at Saassaa, indispensable for attacking the defences, had not yet arrived. The Circassians' horses, their heads lowered, registered the effects of the 24-hour march, and units which, during the night had covered 70 km and had had a hard fight, needed to rest. All therefore stopped at Khan Arembe, in the shelter of the hills. Tanks watched the roads: the Palestine frontier was close by.

On 16 June, at 4:30 a.m., the attack started. The artillery opened fire, the tanks moved out, the din was overwhelming. After a moment of hesitation, the defenders recovered. A cannon duel started. A deluge of fire fell upon the attackers. On the northern outskirts of the town, the Senegalese gave way before the heaviness of the firing. They could no longer summon up the physical and nervous effort that an assault demanded. However, they were going to be asked to carry out three! Captain Quarez spoke of 'the apathy of his exhausted blacks.' 'A single company', he said, 'was insufficient. It would have needed a battalion.' Whatever sorrow he caused himself, this desperate officer understood that his unit 'as well as its officers and NCOs moreover, brought up in the religion of defence, materially inadequately armed and equipped[4] was far from being the troops best suited to carry out a mission as motorised infantry'. The inferiority was obvious. Guided by an observation post outside the town, an English mortar caused large losses and, in spite of the efforts of the officers and NCOs, some Senegalese fled. The section of 75mm guns supporting them also disappeared. 'The last assault, at 9:00 a.m., with European officers and NCOs leading, was the most pitiful of all', wrote Quarez. 'We were moving forward 50 metres at a time, under the cover of machine-gun fire, but the mortar shells were following us step by step. When we turned around, we were alone. The men had not followed!'[5] He returned to the rear: 'I looked at these fine blacks flattened against the ground, their toy-like carbines trembling in their hands. Their big eyes followed my every gesture fearfully.' But their captain understood them; they had reached the limit of their physical and mental strength. In the preceding 33 hours, they had spent 15 in combat. 'They were at the end of their tether, I could feel it. Wasn't I exhausted myself, not having closed my eyes since the night of 12 June at Saassaa? And here we were 16 June!'

Where the terrain was easier, Gastine's tanks used their mobility, occupying the ground, driving around, looking for weaknesses. From time to time, they stopped and fired on excavated areas, a rock or the top of a wall where a weapon was seen. The vigorous resistance gave no sign of let-up and, if the attack lasted too long, it risked failure. Knowing that it was the key to the whole battle and that the encircled enemy could not be reinforced, Keime did not want to give up at any price. He asked Damascus for reinforcements, which he did not obtain. Invited to have bombing missions, Colonel Le Couteulx refused, the town being inhabited by numerous Circassian families.

A tank – a single one – succeeded at last in entering the town, that of Warrant Officer Hocquaux, a large man who could scarcely fit into the confined turret of the little Renault, but who fought for close to four hours with unfailing aggression. Roaming through the streets, machine-gunning what he saw, turning around like a bear in a cage, looking for a way out of the town, he finally escaped towards the south at the moment when, crossing the ditch, a tank patrol succeeded in joining him. Not everyone had his luck: when he got out of his armoured car to remove a barricade, a long burst of fire mangled Major Gaillard-Bournazel, commanding the Circassians. Finally, at 11:30 a.m., the enemy, weakened by his losses, seemed in disarray, and Le Couteulx decided to mount a decisive assault. Two sections of Senegalese and a platoon of Circassian cavalry, which had been waiting without fighting since the morning, were going to attack at the same time as the tanks.

Thin and done up tight in his uniform, cold, sitting upright in his saddle, Captain de La Chauvelais was in command of the Circassian cavalry. This former member of the *Cadre noir*[6] commanded his troops by his example. Le Couteulx called him and explained his mission. He had to reach the defences to the east as quickly as possible and to attack them on foot. Returning to his unit, Le Chauvelais drew his sword, explained what had to be done, and attacked at the head of his shouting men. Fire was concentrated on him and Le Chauvelais, struck by a bullet, tumbled off. The death in the sun of this exemplary rider, killed in a charge such as Murat[7] led, became part of legend. His riders continued galloping through the fields of barley and joined the tanks which were coming up to the first houses. The Senegalese were following. Quarez, speaking about these fighters overcome with fatigue after the morning assaults: 'These are the same men who, towards midday, alongside the cavalrymen on foot and the tanks, fought from house to house with grenades, barricade by barricade [...] At 1:00 p.m. the centre of the town was reached, and mopping up continued until 6:00 p.m.'

Here is the end described by the English:[8]

> At 6:20 p.m., accompanied by an English prisoner, a French officer approached the town in an armoured vehicle, waving a white handkerchief. Taken to the battalion command post, he explained that the defenders were surrounded by a greatly superior force [...] He hoped for a surrender as he hated firing on the British. The English commander asked him for a half-hour to think things over and, having consulted the second-in-command and as well as the Regimental Sergeant Major,[9] he decided that surrendering was the only way to avoid a massacre of the remainder of his men [...] When he came out, he saw 11 tanks grouped near the closest houses. He surrendered at 7:00 p.m.

Colonel Le Couteulx de Caumont then courteously greeted Colonel Orr, King's Own, who was in command of the place. Very politely the Frenchman congratulated him and announced that he was his prisoner.[10] Three hundred Englishmen according to the French, or 13 officers and 164 men according to the British, were assembled at the exit from the town. The recapture of Kuneitra and the capture of the King's Own was the greatest Vichy success of the campaign. The summary of the prisoner interrogations concluded with these words, repeated by all the British who had been deceived by propaganda: 'All were surprised to not be fighting against Germans.'

Le Couteulx immediately reorganised the defences. Unfortunately he had to abandon Kuneitra that he had reconquered. On 17 June, obeying an order that astonished and disappointed his men, the Le Couteulx group set out again with the prisoners who hampered its progress, leaving the area under the guard of a delaying detachment. The sudden worsening of the situation in Damascus demanded it.

Sent during the night, on Wilson's orders, at the head of a small force[11] to retake the town, but dissuaded by an officer who had escaped, the Australian Colonel Blackburn[12] observed the departure of the Vichy French, and it was in the evening, following an exchange of machine gunfire, that a British battalion[13] reoccupied the town, losing only a single man. Following a difficult withdrawal under fire, the covering force reached Saassaa. By this time, the prisoners had been evacuated to Beirut.

Entering Kuneitra on the evening of 17 June, Blackburn described the town:

> A tank, almost red-hot, was burning in the centre of the town. The streets were cluttered by overturned French and British trucks. There were three destroyed armoured cars, bodies of horses, piles of ammunition, papers, clothing, guns, rifles and vehicles riddled with bullets. In spite of this spectacle, the majority of shops were open. The Australians, if they were free, wandered about the streets and shopped. The inhabitants were calmly putting things in order, sorting out their belongings, going about their business, apparently indifferent to the war.

Roy Gordon, a machine gunner: 'We equipped ourselves from the loot. All the tools and equipment that we lacked seemed to be available here. We found a complete tool kit for the vehicles, camouflage nets that we might need, a few anti-tank guns, a vehicle for the workshop, three motorbikes, stoves and all sorts of other equipment.'

While the Le Couteulx group was driving towards Kuneitra, to the east Simon's group was progressing towards Sheikh Meskine.

Its route was longer and more difficult. To get round the rocky area of Leja, it had to carry out a very long detour. Past Hijjane, 35 km from Damascus, the bad track that it took crossed 75 km of desert.[14] Progress was slow. Finally, after 110 km, it reached Mezraa, where there was a refuelling point. It was then – 'Aircraft warning!' – five or six enemy aircraft 'of a relatively old type' attacked, machine-gunning in a line astern formation. There were wounded. The White-Dodge armoured cars replied, and four were shot down by the Dewoitines covering the column.[15] A link-up was effected with the Vichy French garrison of Soueida, capital of the Jebel Druse. That night, a company of Tunisian *tirailleurs*,[16] bringing two 75mm guns, reinforced the column. At daybreak, the group set off again. The villages that it passed through were empty. At 2:20 p.m., they were quite close to Ezraa. The column stopped out of sight. On one side backing on to the rocky area of Leja, Ezraa is bounded on the other side by a vast, flat area scattered with large rocks. The approach was to be made in the following manner: while the R-35 tanks, accompanied by Moroccan *spahis*, would overwhelm the village from the right, the platoon of five armoured cars under the command of Sub-Lieutenant Michelet, crossing the rocky ground, would reach the embankment of a disused railway track and, to the south-west, would block the road from Sheikh Meskine occupied by the enemy. Stationed at Ezraa during the previous winter, Michelet knew the area well. They were to move out at the sound of a mortar shell. The heat was overwhelming, the extremely hot armour plate burning those who touched it.

How long it took to get everything in place! Finally, the sound of the mortar round. The vehicles moved into the rocky expanse, while opposite, numerous automatic weapons began firing. Even at very low speed, the vehicles were shaken severely. 'The armoured cars jolted terribly' remembered Michelet, 'so that it was thought the suspensions were going to break.'

On the approach to Ezraa, bullets rattled on the armour plate and the shutters had to be closed. Looking through the driving slits made driving difficult, and the first vehicle struck a rock. The engine stalled and the vehicle was stuck. Seeing the lead vehicle stop, the others did likewise, hosing the edges of the town with their guns. Bullets banged on the armour, Michelet, wedged in by bursts of firing from the sheltered side, signalled to the following vehicle to come and fetch him. He climbed aboard and it was then that he saw in front of him several dozen vehicles going flat out along the road in a cloud of dust, making for Sheikh Meskine and firing all their weapons as they did so. With the heavy vehicles on the stony area, it was impossible to follow them: in Ezraa, which was deserted, there were only bodies and several Arabs wearing English uniforms with a pink *keffiyeh*[17] and red leather cartridge belts, the remains of Colonel Kerkelly's Transjordanian Frontier Force's two companies equipped with fast trucks, and armed with heavy machine guns and anti-tank rifles. The Vichy French, who had lost only one man, took 17 prisoners, recovered a radio truck, weapons, including a 37mm cannon, 1,000 litres of petrol, and a large quantity of ammunition which was immediately sent to Soueida by a fleet of trucks. It was a success but only a step along the way. The objective was Sheikh Meskine and, to attack this larger target, the Tunisians were needed. Simon shot up a large vehicle park to the north of the town, the fire from which could be seen for a long time. The armoured car which had ended up in the rocky area was recovered and repaired at the village forge.

We are now at 16 June. The next objective was Sheikh Meskine. Alerted by the Transjordanian Frontier Force, the town had certainly reinforced its defences, but the Vichy French had been joined by a company of Tunisian *tirailleurs*. Simon's plan was a follows: the bulk of the armour, followed by the infantry, would attack Sheikh Meskine from the east and north, while the Michelet platoon, approaching the town from the south, would cut the road from Palestine. Brought by truck to the scene of the action, Moroccans and Tunisians moved into the sloping area where the enemy was waiting for them. Crushed by artillery fire, the armoured vehicles could not move forward, and the infantry, fired on from all sides and pursued by machine guns, was very quickly brought to a halt. The assault was repulsed. A second attempt was equally unsuccessful. To get through, aerial support was necessary. Simon telephoned to Damascus, but the Vichy Air Force did not have any available aircraft. Knowing that the Glenn Martin bombers of the *Aéronavale* (Fleet Air Arm) had arrived the day before, Simon contacted Admiral Gouton. Failure at Sheikh Meskine would imperil the whole offensive, he argued. The Navy did not have a mission to support Army units and Admiral Gouton had, since their arrival, sent his aircraft to attack the British fleet. Nevertheless, he agreed to send them, even without fighter escort, this one time only. The action would not be renewed. The bombing took place, but its effect was fleeting.[18] Hampered by the presence of the hospital, the bombers attacked the truck park and, as soon as the aircraft had departed, the enemy's fire recurred, as intense as before: the air attack did not help. Simon understood then that he did not have enough forces to capture the town and, at sunset, having collected his wounded, he gave the order to withdraw.

As far as Michelet was concerned, he started out at the time ordered, but if Sheikh Meskine was only 11 km by road, the track was longer for him since he had to bypass the town and move across the desert. Finally he reached the road from Sheikh Meskine to Deraa, and proceeded north. Reaching 2,000 metres from the town, he stopped and observed. No noise was heard, no sign of battle. No friendly element was visible. Where were they? He gave the signal for battle and, with a group to the right and another to the left, moved forward. Soon, well directed artillery fire forced him to fall back into the shelter of a hill, but when he wanted to resume his approach, increasingly accurate firing recommenced. He was alone. Should he carry on? His mission not being to capture Sheikh Meskine all alone, he gave the order 'About turn!' and withdrew towards the south. And yet, he could see in the distance a convoy coming from Palestine. He deployed his armoured cars and, 300 metres away, stopped the first truck. Some 'Englishmen' jumped out and dived into the ditches where they were taken prisoner. These 'English' were Gaullists, members of a tank unit to which they were bringing petrol. Michelet: 'The prisoners were placed on the rear deck of the first two armoured cars and were covered by the guns of the third and, the trucks following the three leading armoured vehicles, the two last bringing up the rear, they set off again for Ezraa.' Upon arriving, the officer learned of the failure of the main attack. The road from Transjordan was not cut. Could the attack be resumed? Could reinforcements be received? Damascus, upon being questioned, gave the opposite order: during the evening, Simon received the order to let the Tunisians alone occupy Ezraa and to go himself to Soueida. At Damascus, the position became serious and Verdilhac wanted to concentrate his forces. Moreover, Simon, his radio having broken down and his last carrier pigeon sent, could no longer communicate.

It was at about 3:00 p.m. on 15 June that the news of the fall of Ezraa and Kuneitra reached the Free French headquarters. While he was attacking northward, Legentilhomme had turned south. The two adversaries had acted at the same time. Suddenly, the situation became very grave: if Sheikh Meskine fell, the supply lines of the forces attacking Damascus risked being cut. Legentilhomme, who did not have any reserves, telegraphed Lavarack and Wilson to ask them, with extreme urgency, for one or two battalions of reinforcements as well as an artillery battery. But how would they go about it? Threatened in the same way on the road from Palestine, Lavarack, for his part, assembled another force, an artillery group and the 1st Battalion, Queen's Royal Regiment. Sent by train to Deraa, they had to recapture Kuneitra. Legentilhomme, from his own troops, got together a fast column under the command of Lieutenant-Colonel Génin: two Free French companies and a British artillery group.[19] As soon as it was assembled, the convoy set off towards Sheikh Meskine. Driving as fast as possible, Génin reached Sheikh Meskine about 9:30 p.m. – in June it was still daylight – early enough to organise the defence of the town with the Transjordanians. Thus he could repel the attack on 16 June by Simon's troops.

His next mission was to retake Ezraa. In the evening, Captain Le Roch, Génin's deputy, went to spy out the land: 'Impossible to take the village in force', he said, 'we have to strike at dawn, surprise the armoured cars while keeping our positions.' At 1:00 a.m., the advance started. There were 100 men of the Marine Infantry Brigade with Lieutenant de Laborde. A Vichy soldier: 'During the night, some signs seemed to show enemy infiltration around the town. During a patrol in an armoured car, Lieutenant Touya, seeing some silhouettes, approached them. "Don't shoot, we are French" was heard. At the same time an anti-tank shell blew a rivet from the turret which cut his throat.' Another report, from the Free French, by Le Roch, Génin's deputy: 'Laborde's company came upon armoured cars patrolling two kilometres from the village, where horses neighing would have given the alert. A few were wounded, but they were scattered [...] The section regrouped under Laborde's orders and attacked the village. It entered the village but was shut up in a house, surrounded by an enemy ten times more numerous, and held on with difficulty.' The fight dragged on.

No one had had news of Colonel Génin since 4:00 a.m. Le Roch: 'I risked a quick look over the edge of the ditch. Almost in front of me and 30 metres away, on the other side of the road, I saw Colonel Génin's body stretched out on his back, seemingly asleep. I rushed up to him. He was dead from a bullet in the heart. Alongside him was the body of Boisredon, a soldier of the Marine Infantry Brigade [...] The colonel had walked towards the village by following the edge of the road,[20] accompanied by a single man, although Laborde's section had already entered. They were hit 50 metres from the village and killed outright [...] It was 8:00 a.m. and our men were fighting very well.' The chaplain came and gave a short absolution, then the body was buried under a pile of stones surmounted by a cross.[21]

At about 11:00 a.m. on 17 June, the fighting continued. Le Roch, who was standing around, went with Sairigné to give a report at Sheikh Meskine and to look for reinforcements. To win the day, Major Garbay, who replaced Génin, decided to organise a stronger force. Major Hackett[22] of the Transjordanian Frontier Force, the Glénat company of the 3rd Marine Battalion – less than 100 men, Senegalese – and a group of 12 Englishmen having two carriers and an anti-tank gun, were going to resume the attack. At 2:00 p.m., a vigorous assault took place against the barracks in Ezraa. 'Firing off VB grenades,[23] firing into rifle ports, attacking', wrote Sairigné in his notebook, 'we were firing as best we could into the windows opposite which gradually fell silent', The garrison finally surrendered. The final results: 168 prisoners,[24] a 75mm cannon, three 25mm guns, 16 machine guns and a mortar. The attackers lost 14 men. The three days of fighting at Ezraa cost, in killed and wounded, 71 British and Free French and probably 120 combatants from the Levant.[25] The fighting at Ezraa was amongst the most violent of this French-on-French war. Le Roch, wounded in the wrist, noted in his diary: 'We were all disgusted by this struggle against Frenchmen [...] Our dead were killed by Frenchmen [...] However, we did not think for a minute of slowing down or being sorry because we were convinced that we are doing our duty. But what a painful duty!'

While Le Couteulx was attacking Kuneitra and Simon was attacking Sheikh Meskine, the third group, the mounted cavalry of Captain de Carmejane, was advancing by squadrons on the plain beyond Saassaa and was pushing on as far as Sannamein, which it entered without fighting. About six kilometres before reaching Kfar-Cham, the Circassians seized some vehicles belonging to General Legentilhomme's command post. They took possession of baggage, notably his tin trunk, whose contents – papers, letters and passports – were later carefully analysed in Damascus.

On 19 June, after a few contacts in the Jebel Druse, the Simon force started off again for Damascus. On the long and bad track, the vehicles overheated dangerously. This return took place in a dangerous atmosphere. With prepared positions for mines, sporadic mortar and machine-gun fire, the approaches to Damascus were hostile.

When he arrived, Michelet received the order to take three vehicles and reconnoitre the Sheikh Meskine road as far as possible, with strict orders to avoid all combat. The same order was given to Weil on the Kuneitra road. Careful advances and halts to scan the countryside with binoculars: scarcely had he gone four or five kilometres past Kadem, than Michelet observed, 1,500 metres away, a large number of infantry, on both sides of the road, moving towards the capital. In the currents of hot air, he could make out turbans: they were Indians. Michelet then withdrew. Weil saw the same thing. The staff learned in this way that the advanced defence line of Damascus had fallen.

The results of the counter-offensive? From the point of view of the Vichy French, they were very mixed. Kuneitra, captured, had been abandoned, Sheikh Meskine had not fallen, and the road from Palestine had to be evacuated. Many people were severely critical of the rapid return of the Le Couteulx force. Why didn't he exploit his success by pushing on towards Merdjayoun, which was no further than Saassaa? Many were ignorant of the fact that Le Couteulx, like Simon, returned under orders. Very early on Verdilhac wanted to recover his forces and that is why, only two days after their departure, he asked Keime to have them return. Even though accompanied by a message of hearty congratulations from the general in chief, Dentz, – 'Thank you to the cavalry!' – he ruined the operation.

From the point of view of the Allies, it was different. If Sheikh Meskine, in dire straits, had been saved by the arrival of the 3rd Marine Battalion on the night of 15 June, its vehicle park had been burned. The Vichy French had cut communications with Palestine, Kuneitra had fallen and hundreds of prisoners had been captured. On the other hand, Merdjayoun still held. Thus, behind the back of his attackers, Dentz still preserved the capacity for an attack. His army remained aggressive, his reserves were still powerful and capable of large-scale operations. There was not therefore an outpost that was not threatened by a surprise attack and the situation remained very serious. Beirut and Damascus were supposed to be reached in two days? It was much too optimistic. The 'armed political incursion' showed itself to be a war. Did Wilson advance too quickly? In Cairo, the radio lowered its tone and stopped announcing unlikely people joining Free France. Nobody spoke about the Germans any more. The troops understood that they were fighting Frenchmen. In London, the staff became aware of the risk of seeing its forces thrown back to the frontier. Gavin Long: 'The stubborn [Vichy] French resistance in each sector had been causing great concern in London, and General Dill proposed to General Wavell, first that mobile columns from Iraq be sent to Syria – a project that Wavell had already decided on – and that bombers from Egypt be used to add weight to the attack.'[26]Alan Brooke noted on 17 June: 'At midday, meeting of the commanders in chief with Churchill [...] The Prime minister started with an interesting general survey of the world situation. To my horror, he informed us of the powerful offensive he planned to launch in Libya! How could we announce such an attack on two fronts simultaneously at a time when we did not have the means to mount one? From the moment when we decided to invade Syria, we should have concentrated all our forces together to bring about victory in the shortest possible time. If the operation was not finished rapidly, it could have serious consequences in the long run.'

The British in fact did not have worries only in Syria. On 15 and 16 June, in Libya, *Operation Battleaxe*, for which very large forces were mobilised, failed. Rommel gave nothing away. It was thus that, by a strange turn of events, this failure caused the loss of the Vichy French. All idea of a new offensive in Libya being put aside, extra British forces became available again. 'The failure of Great Britain in Libya forecast Dentz's defeat', noted Davet correctly.[27] Cairo, trebling troop numbers, was now going to devote sizeable forces to the war in the Levant. The 7th Australian Division went from two to three brigades, the 6th British Division and the 10th Indian Division, as well as *Habforce*, reinforced Wilson's troops which thus went from three to ten brigades.[28] In addition, a part of the RAF would become available again. The war in Syria thus took on quite another dimension. In this new set-up, the Free French would represent only about 8 per cent of the whole. Their influence and their opinions were going to become secondary. Since the failure of 15 June, moreover, the influence of Legentilhomme had not increased.

Promoted lieutenant-general on 18 June, Lavarack commanded the whole of the Australian forces, and it was Major-General A.S. 'Tubby' Allen[29] who took command of the 7th Division.

Leaving behind them the impregnable Merdjayoun, Lavarack's Australians decided on 12 June to push on to the north, towards Jezzine, by crossing the mountains. Twenty kilometres as the crow flies – much more by road – Jezzine, where immense ravines meet, occupies a damp area between two parched mountains, which are rugged and virtually impassable. After some complicated twists and turns, the road crossing the little town leads to Sidon in the west and Beit ed Dine in the north. Now, if Beit ed Dine were to fall, Beirut would be threatened. Nabatiye, half way, was occupied by Bodman's *spahi* cavalry who, five days previously, had, following a tiring withdrawal, evacuated the outposts. They lost two-thirds of their men and horses which, in this type of country, are confined to the roads. Now, this is not the case with mules or donkeys. The face of the war was about to change.

Equipped for fighting in Egypt, the Australian Army was not prepared for mountain warfare, but its men from the country adapted to it immediately.[30] Leaving their carriers, which could not be used in the mountains, they rode on horseback to form a flying column, the 'Kelly Gang', from the name of a famous Australian gang of bandits.[31] Gavin Long stated:

> To go towards Jezzine, it was necessary to substitute ancient methods for technical equipment. The use of mules became commonplace, and visual signalling replaced the telephone. Both by night and day, on faint tracks or even with no track at all, rations and ammunition had to be painfully carried forward by animal convoys. Only patience and an enormous capacity of endurance allowed one to advance and to repel the enemy. The war, then, became individual. Fighting in this ravine here was quite different from fighting next door. General advances consisted of dozens of little clashes in which only one, two or three sections were involved. The road itself was sometimes so steep that the artillery could only advance at walking pace. The hairpin bends demanded endless toing and froing, often under enemy fire. Certain points on the road to Jezzine became so dangerous that they were given familiar names such as the 'Mad Mile' or 'Hellfire Corner'. Every run drew fire, they had to be crossed all alone, at full speed, along the edge of deep ravines.

Progressing along the peaks, keeping the roads under fire from their machine guns and mortars, the Australians quickly pushed back the *spahis*. Moving along the road, the Australian artillery submitted the town to a heavy preventive bombardment and, on 14 June, the attackers entered the abandoned town. For them it was a great success: from Jezzine, Lavarack could stretch out his hand to Stevens on the coast and, especially, advance towards Beirut via Beit ed Dine by bypassing the Damour defences. It was a very grave threat.

To recapture Jezzine, a 'Chouf Force' was then formed[32] under the command of Colonel Barré of the 6th Foreign Legion Infantry Regiment which, on the ninth day of the battle, had still not been engaged. The staff had kept this strong unit in reserve until now, but being suspected of Gaullism, for fear that it went over to the enemy! The other troops in the Force were less reliable: the Senegalese had already suffered heavily and Bodman's *spahis*, very shaken by their retreat, were only dismounted cavalry, not real infantry soldiers. Well trained and still fresh, the Legion was therefore the nucleus of the Force. It would benefit from a strong artillery support.

The attack by the Vichy French against Jezzine on 17 June, in a countryside with steep-sided ravines and insuperable cliffs, quickly ran up against a powerful barrier. The Legion was caught in the stony country and the enemy immediately mounted a counter-attack. An account, coming from the opposing forces:[33]

About 8:30 a.m. on 17 June, the Thomson and Robson companies reached, via a twisting route, a point only 70 metres from the Vichy French positions. Major Robson then launched two sections into an assault with fixed bayonets, the third section acting as a covering force. There was a violent hand-to-hand combat. Several Australians were killed or wounded but the surviving French – two officers and 65 men, Senegalese – surrendered. These prisoners were exhausted and demoralised. They declared that they had been marching for four days and were dying of hunger. They were, apparently, so tired as to be incapable of fighting. In spite of this setback, the enemy, supplied by mules across the very broken terrain, continued his efforts all day to move forward and threatened to overrun the two companies from the east. Captain Thompson's company, which had reached Hill 1332, was dislodged by an infantry assault. The Australian progress then had to stop, with considerable losses. In the evening, the men were exhausted, hungry and frozen. They wore only a cotton shirt and shorts or long pants. On Hill 1377, they looked for food on the bodies of the French dead which were lying in front of their positions, and the Australian stretcher bearers picked up the Vichy French wounded and, although they had very little water themselves, the bearers shared it with them. During the night, the Vichy artillery fired on the positions at frequent intervals and, at daybreak, they could be seen gathering on a high point for a new attack.

In spite of heavy losses, the assault was resumed the next day at dawn. Gavin Long:

> The enemy attacked at 10:50 a.m. with artillery support. When he was no more than 80 metres away, Houston fired a rocket to stop the Australian artillery fire and fixed bayonets to counter-attack. He was no more than 50 metres from the Vichy French when these latter opened fire. Houston, an excellent leader, Lieutenant Coakley and five men were killed, and there were 22 wounded. This was, in this sector, the unfortunate end of a resistance that was successful elsewhere. The enemy had had many more losses than us [...] Later in the afternoon, after a long battle, six bombers, escorted by fighters, dropped twenty bombs on Jezzine. The 'Hotel Egypt', where the ration store and kitchen were installed, was hit several times. Forty men were buried in the rubble. Seventeen died and ten were wounded. The terrified population fled to take refuge in caves in the surrounding hills. Some were carried away to other villages in military trucks, and the force had to find men to police the town against the Arabs who crowded in from the outlying areas looking for loot.[34]

Mortar and machine-gun duels, attacks by both sides under an overpowering sun and among extremely hot rocks, very hard fighting continued for several weeks. On this static front, Australians and legionnaires fought with staggering fierceness. Exceptional in its violence, the battle of Jezzine was engraved in the memory of all participants. Attacks and counter-attacks followed one another without coming to a conclusion. Immediately it was detected, the slightest movement was attacked with artillery and automatic weapons fire. Huddled up amongst the stones, facing all the assaults, each person was coated with dust and this fighting, eyeball to eyeball, went on for almost three weeks. Heroism was found equally on both sides. Pte J.H. Gordon[35] won the Victoria Cross: over ground swept by fire – grenades and machine guns – he charged alone, in a frontal attack, an enemy position that he captured.

The 'Gaullist' battalion fought with the same fury. Pépin-Lehalleur, a former lieutenant in the 1st Battalion, 6th Foreign Legion Infantry Regiment:

> Our intention, which was that of all the lieutenants of the 1st/6th, was to only pretend to fight, to have a gallant last stand, and then to cross over. Now, in approaching Jezzine, the battalion found itself caught in violent artillery fire which forced us to dig in among the rocks in extremely hard conditions. In this trackless terrain, everything had to be brought in on men's backs. The losses were very great, resupply did not arrive and the evacuation of the wounded posed particularly difficult problems [...] Daily resupply was carried out across the mountain by fatigue parties on foot carrying ammunition, tins of water, and rations. The rations brought by the first convoy had to be thrown out. Rotting during transport – it was extremely hot – they were inedible. People had to feed on canned goods. For several weeks, the Legion ate only tinned sardines and canned fruit in syrup [...] The frequent and steady mortar bombardments projected flurries of stones and shell fragments everywhere. The men were sheltering behind piles of rocks and, as it was impossible to dig in the soil, the dead had to be buried under piles of pebbles and rocks near the fighting positions. During the course of the battle, the 1st/6th lost two-thirds of its strength killed or wounded.

Hit in the legs on 4 July, Pépin-Lehalleur was evacuated at night in a litter carried by a mule across the mountains; the trip to Beit ed Dine was long and agonising.[36] The result of the battle of Jezzine was that the situation became static, with excellent troops tied up until the end of the war.

In Damascus, mistrust, spy mania and indecision reigned. 'Was there a spy or a traitor on the staff? wondered Le Corbeiller [...] The Levant was, it seemed, teeming with German agents who were trying to stir up the Arabs, English and Gaullist agents being much more numerous [...] The civilians who worked until the end behind the army carried a terrible responsibility.'[37] In Beirut, General Dentz considered that this all smacked of a novel.

On 18 June, the command changed hands: recalled to be with Dentz in Beirut, General de Verdilhac left command of the Damascus sector to Colonel Keime. The front that he took over was now very extensive but shallow. Somehow or other, he was going to have to face three concentric assaults. In the west, leaving

Kiswe, the Indians would want to advance over the rough ground towards Mezzé. In the centre, between Kiswe and Nahja, the 1st Marine Battalion was going to try to conquer the Jebel Kelb before pushing on towards Kadem, the southern suburb of the capital. On the right, having bypassed Nehja, the remains of the Collet group hoped to push on towards Jeramana, to the east of the city. If the heights overlooking the Ghouta[38] area were captured, the fall of the city would be only a matter of days.

Jebel Krim, Jebel Madani, Tel Kiswe, Jebel Kelb, Jebel Abu Atriz – the chain of mountains which, to the south of the capital, extend from west to east above the Wadi Nahr el-Aouaj, thus making up a defensive shield. In the extremely hot rocky area, under artillery and mortar fire which produced stone and shell fragments, the combatants on both sides showed surprising rage. Speaking the same language, fighting under the same flag, all assured of fighting with honour, they showed an equal will to win and reciprocal detestation. The worn-out French of 1940 showed themselves to be furious fighters in Syria. They would have added a glorious page to the book of French courage if it hadn't been in these frightful fights. Let us consider only one because it is a good example, that for Jebel Kelb, but in these hills similar acts of courage were repeated. Roger Barberot, a legionnaire: 'Jebel Kelb was the last obstacle before Damascus. From the summit, the view is over a green plain surrounded by a setting of reddish hills, a sort of Normandy *bocage*[39] with fields edged with high embankments and hedges, with clumps of trees, poplars in a row. Palm trees and olive trees remind us that we are not in France. At the far edge of the greenery, the houses in Damascus can be seen as well as the slender towers of the mosques.'[40]

To capture the summit – Hill 748 – assaults occurred one after the other from 15 to 18 June. On the day after the failure of 15 June, Boissoudy's company of the 1st Marine Battalion,[41] resumed the assault. It fought from 9:45 a.m. until the end of the afternoon. Freitag: 'Boissoudy charged through the firing, a light machine gun under his arm, with his two lieutenants and a brilliant band of NCOs. They looked like bandits. Shells and grenades exploded all around them. They charged ahead, in front of their *tirailleurs* from Chad (Saras, Adjerais and Mossis) who, brandishing their machetes, bounded ahead, shouting savage cries. All followed like a single man.'

Opposite, the Moroccans had relieved the Senegalese. Sheltering in deep trenches dug between the rocks, these North

Africans fought like tigers. At about 5:00 p.m. the battle was still raging. There was no wind, not a scrap of shade, not a blade of grass. Thirst became a torture. Opposite, held in reserve, Rougé's company – the 2nd Company of the 1st Marine Battalion – had just replaced Boissoudy's, which moved to the left to try to cut the road to Damascus behind the Jebel. About 9:30 p.m., out of 250 men, there were only about 100 left. Boissoudy regrouped and charged once more before nightfall, but a counter-attack forced him to fall back. Not being able to break through, the two companies returned to their start positions and settled in for the night. Ninety-eight exhausted soldiers sprawled on the rocks. At midnight, Rougé's company got ready to attack the summit of the Jebel alone at first light on 18 June.'

That morning of 18 June was the most drama-filled for the 1st Marine Battalion. Opposite, during the night, the two companies of Moroccans were relieved. Rougé and his Africans moved off and the artillery, which was waiting for them, started again. Under a leaden sky, the fighting recommenced. The Free French progressed, among the projectiles, from rock to rock. Assaults, counter-attacks, there was fighting all day without a decision being reached, but after hours of fighting, at a time when Rougé, at the head of his men and shouting as he led them on, collapsed, shot in the chest. His deputy took his place, stood up and fell in his turn. The distraught *tirailleurs* wandered in circles around the battlefield and then fell back: the attack was repulsed. Captain Langlois, commanding the Support Company, assembled the men in the rear. Two volunteers rushed through the firing and brought in Captain Rougé's body. Night fell. Fighting would resume the next day.

19 June, 6:00 a.m. The stench of decomposing bodies filled the air. Leaping from rock to rock, the Moroccans counter-attacked. A Free Frenchman, Lieutenant Colonna d'Istria, a light machine gun under his arm, led his *tirailleurs*. Freitag: 'Soon there was hand-to-hand fighting. Shouts of "Death to the Gaullists!" and "Death to the murderers!" could be heard. The fighting was fast and furious. Frenchmen versus Frenchman, African versus African, with bayonets and machetes.' The Moroccans were repulsed. Called up as reinforcements, Brousset's company – the 3rd Company of the 1st Marine Battalion – continued the attack. Behind them, in the confusion, the entire battalion – drivers, clerks and cooks – regrouped and started firing with submachine guns and mortars. The Moroccans were stopped. The Free French, who held the

summit, could not leave it. However, all the available fighters were up there, in the firing line: the 1st Marine Battalion had no more reserves and the men were exhausted by the fighting. All day long, stretcher bearers brought dead and wounded to the doctors who cleaned, sewed up, amputated and bandaged. The chaplain comforted and consoled the wounded and dying. Finally, in the evening, Amilakhvari's 3rd Foreign Legion Battalion relieved Major Delange's severely mauled 1st Marine Battalion on Jebel Kelb.

When night fell over the battlefield on 19 June, the attack had failed all along the line. Yves Gras: 'At Legentilhomme's headquarters, there was great anxiety. It had been thought they would enter Damascus the very next morning and they were in a much graver situation than the day before, with two battalions less.'

The Legion was therefore going to intervene but with restraint, said Pierre Montagnon: 'Did the higher command detect some reluctance on the part of the legionnaires and their officers and NCOs to open fire on Frenchmen? It is not impossible,' he wrote, 'even if no one dared admit it'. It was on 19 June, in any case, that the Legion took part in its first battle to capture the road separating Jebel Kelb from Hill 748 held by the *tirailleurs*[42] the access to which was blocked by two Renault tanks of the 7th African Chasseur Regiment.

Do we have to talk about this succession of battles all of which were fierce? To overcome the defences on the Nahr el-Aouaj, Colonel Kœnig sent his five remaining tanks. From 17 to 20 June, the battle raged around the town in the complicated pattern of orchards and interlinked alleyways of Arab villages. Dentz's troops still fought with the same obstinacy but, for lack of reserves and reinforcements, they gradually became exhausted. Weakened by losses which often reached a third of their strength, Keime's units found themselves scattered over very broken ground, blocked by walls, concealed by clumps of trees, orchards and gardens. Carrying on a hopeless fight, without contacts, not knowing who was guarding their flanks, nor even, for lack of maps, knowing where they were, they fought with a feeling of isolation. Capable of defending themselves with undiminished fierceness, even of counter-attacking, they let go only step by step but, progressively disjointed and incapable of operating together, their struggle continued in increasingly tight positions. The fighting for Damascus, always stubborn, lasted a further three days.

On the opposing side, on the contrary, the Free French were boosted by the conviction that they were winning. Yves Gras: 'The taking of Damascus was no more than a matter of days away.' This prospect galvanised everyone. In the ranks, no one was tired any longer. There was no longer any complaining about resupply or thirst, although since 8 June the whole division, from the general to the private soldiers, had been eating only bully beef (corned beef) and Army biscuits from the British Army Service Corps.

On the left, Lloyd's Indians had met a dramatic fate. Leaving Kiswe at dawn on 16 June, the two battalions – Punjabis and Rajputs – had entered the range of hills which extended towards Mezzé over six to eight kilometres. Almost a suburb of Damascus, Mezzé was a particularly important objective: the area overlooks the city, the airport and the road to Beirut. If this last were cut, there was no route to allow crossing the Anti-Lebanon Mountains. Colonel Péfontan, of the 24th Mixed Colonial Infantry Regiment (*Régiment mixte d'infanterie coloniale*), was defending the town. Gathering everyone he could find, Algerians, Circassians, legionnaires, *spahis*, even Service Corps personnel and prisoners, some armoured cars and a few tanks, he hastily formed a small battalion with two companies.[43]

In the afternoon of 17 June, after violent fighting, the Indians and Free French marines reached and cut the road to Kuneitra. Not moving all day on 18 June, they resumed their advance in the late afternoon. Michelet, you will recall, had reported their advance. 'During the night of 18 June, strong enemy elements had gained a foothold in the village of Mezzé,' he reported to the staff in Damascus,[44] 'the assault was led by infantry attacking shoulder to shoulder with very many submachine guns, directing their aim by means of red tracer rounds. The firing was intense, but localised to Mezzé and in the area of the forts.' At about 11:30 p.m. the Indians broke into the Aujac barracks, Péfontan's command post. The *spahis* who were guarding it having scattered, Péfontan and his officers only had time to disappear through a concealed doorway. To escape, they walked all night through the mountains. On 19 June, at dawn, moving carefully through the deserted streets, the Rajputs entered Mezzé without encountering any resistance. Isolated from the bulk of their unit, they were however at the doors of the capital. At daybreak their carriers reached the racecourse, close to the Hamadiye barracks, Colonel Keime's command post. Their arrival caused considerable consternation.

The situation had become catastrophic. About 10:00 a.m. Keime realised that he could no longer exercise his command from Damascus. He informed Beirut of this and asked for authorisation to move his command post to Khan Meissaloun, on the road to Beirut in the gorges of the Anti-Lebanon Mountains, a defensive position from which he would be able to take things in hand again. Dentz gave his authorisation. 'I prefer to lose Damascus than the army!' he said. The staff then left the capital in cars in a way that some considered precipitous. The troops, who were still fighting, received no more orders and no further supplies. At the time the Staff was evacuating, the Beirut road had come under enemy control. It was impossible to use it. To reach his new position, Keime and his staff had to undertake a very long journey by car northward via Douma, Nebek and Homs then, having skirted the mountains, come back down again towards the Bekaa Valley. Even though carried out with all possible speed, this journey of about 230 km took half a day, during which there was no one in command of the South Syria sector. The only remaining staff member in Damascus was Chaléon, who henceforth was in command there. He then gave the order to all the depots, parks and services to leave the city, then went to the citadel where he summoned the colonel commanding the Syrian police and gendarmerie: order must continue to reign in the city. At 6:00 a.m., he received reports: the evacuation was being carried out calmly and in good order. The remaining troops moved out in the direction of Beirut. The armoured cars withdrew northwards. Not much was known about the battle front. The small detachments and stragglers passing through the city, coming from the south, gave contradictory intelligence. Isolated rifle shots and bursts of firing could be heard from Mezzé. The atmosphere was unsettled. At 4:30 a.m., Lieutenant-Colonel de Chaléon was at the Grand Serail where 'an obsession with espionage had taken possession of the coolest heads'. Were they mistaken?

Alone with a few officers, he had no more than a few remaining armoured vehicles. Via the civilian telephone system, General Dentz ordered him to stay put, to resist with all available means, and to hand over the command of the Damascus sector to Colonel Le Couteulx as soon as he could contact him. The order was repeated to the troops still in position at Kadem, Achrafieh and Boueida. The remnants of a Circassian squadron reoccupied the western outskirts of the city, facing Mezzé. Everything now seemed quiet. At about 11:30 a.m., Le Couteulx arrived and Chaléon handed over to him the command of the troops.

Until the end, Colonel Keime and his men held on 'enthusiastically' according to Le Corbeiller.

> They broke up powerful attacks by night and day by an enemy who left about 300 prisoners in our hands. Facing a spirited infantry who were skilled in night attacks, Senegalese, marines, Moroccan *spahis* and *tirailleurs*, African Chasseurs, sappers, all fought as infantry in the battle, well supported by excellent artillery, and tried to outdo each other in courage under the orders of energetic and passionate leaders. Their morale was higher than ever, and if the general in chief had asked them to continue the fight, by leading a retreat over the 400 km separating Damascus from the Turkish frontier, they would have carried out his orders joyfully.

Around Damascus, which was emptying, fighting continued. Only the guns in the forts overlooking the city, which should have been firing, remained oddly silent.

Damascus seemed lost, but Le Couteulx was a great soldier. Taking charge, he started by appointing a worthy fighter, Cadet Montuis of the 1st Battalion 29th Algerian Tirailleur Regiment – already decorated with the *Médaille militaire* and *Croix de guerre* – to lead a miscellaneous group of 25 men that he managed to collect – *tirailleurs*, legionnaires, *spahis*, sappers – and ordered it to defend the approaches to Mezzé. His small group had only a single light machine gun served by a legionnaire, but all evening of 19 June, it fought successfully.

Instead of charging ahead for Damascus to cause confusion there, Lieutenant-Colonel Calvert-Jones, commanding the Indians, decided on the morning of 20 June to set up defences in the village and to base his two battalions there. He placed his command post in a big building surrounded by solid walls, called the 'Maison Rondeau' where the command groups of the two battalions joined him. From up there they overlooked the road to Beirut and the entry to the Barada river gorges.

On 17 June, after evacuating Kuneitra, the Le Couteulx column once more took the road to Damascus around which the noose was tightening. He stopped for the night off the road at the village of Katana, 22 km from the capital and, on the night of 18 June, on Colonel Keime's orders, he advanced towards

Mezzé, behind the Indians. On 19 June, at daybreak, supported by artillery, Gastine's tank squadron, accompanied by horsed cavalry,[45] attacked Mezzé to clear the town. This vigorous and unexpected counter-attack surprised the Indians. Shells falling on its non-camouflaged vehicles caused significant losses. The Vichy French who passed through Mezzé were impressed:[46] 'The road to Mezzé was littered with wrecked and burned-out British trucks and armoured cars. An Army Service Corps team, without a medical orderly, took inventory of these vehicles filled with dead. "Come and see! There is one moving!" cried a terrified soldier. The sight was dreadful: four bloody bodies were covered with flies. One of them moved or seemed to move [...] an Indian.' Another account: 'On the edge of the road, a tragic sight: a convoy of burned-out Marmon Herrington armoured cars and Bedford trucks had been recently pushed to the side of the road to clear a passage. As a further horror, the bodies were still in the vehicles, eaten by vultures. Indians mainly. Our fellows were indignant at this lack of respect for the dead.'

Le Couteulx's artillery was extremely accurate and decimated the Indian troops who did not have time to dig in. Calvert-Jones tried a manoeuvre which failed, faced with the resistance of a group of infantry and *spahis* posted on the mountain slopes. All day long, fighting continued in the maze of narrow and twisting alleys in Mezzé. At nightfall fighting continued, but the Indian units were by then completely scattered; only a few isolated groups were still fighting. The 5th Indian Brigade was destroyed. On the evening of 19 June, the road to Beirut was again open. The warning had been warm, but the retreating Vichy French troops could reach Mount Lebanon where they could fight again.

Be that as it may, Lieutenant-Colonel Calvert-Jones was still installed in his command post in the 'Maison Rondeau'. At dawn on 20 June, a hail of bullets rained on Cadet Montuis' small group patrolling in Mezzé. The firing came from an isolated house that Montuis decided to capture. It was the command post but he did not know that. Now, Montuis was a fighter. An attempted assault had been beaten back, Montuis returned to the attack from behind. By a coincidence, one of the few cannon-trucks, produced that winter in Beirut that had reached Damascus, was passing by. Montuis requisitioned it. There was no accompanying crew. The gun, removed from the platform, was set up 350 metres away. Making himself the observer, loader and firer, a *spahi* captain, Chaumeil, transmitted the corrections to a sergeant who, not being otherwise engaged, trained the gun. The cannon fired 18 times. In the opposing camp, it was a slaughter. In that house there were more than 200 men, who were guarding about 80 Vichy French prisoners. One of them, Ségur, an artillery lieutenant, was on the ground floor at the time of the attack. He said: 'The English colonel had his bedroom on the first floor. At the beginning of the barrage, a shell tore away part of his side. The projectiles caused frightful damage to the interior. There were about 30 killed or wounded. I pressed the English to surrender and they decided to send me to parley. After the last shell, I therefore left the house with a handkerchief in my hand. The bullets were still whistling by.'

Chaumeil, then, reached the house. 'A great number of officers and men, about 30 in all, were killed or wounded. The interior of the house was an alarming sight.[47] More than 200 Indians, including 12 officers, surrendered. The Vichy French prisoners were overjoyed. The disorder was immense. Wounded were lying about whom we tried to bandage with dressings made from torn-up bed sheets. Among them was the dying Lieutenant-Colonel Greatwood, of the Punjabis.[48] All these men were exhausted. They were dying of hunger: their rations, like their ammunition, were in the destroyed vehicles. To guard so many prisoners and stretcher so many wounded, a platoon of *spahis* had to be called for. The Indians soon placed an engraved marble plaque on the house:

> In this house and its surrounds, several hundred officers and men
> of the 4th Battalion, 6th Rajputana Rifles and the 3rd Battalion
> of the Punjab Regiment, elements of the 5th Indian Infantry
> Brigade, surrounded by superior Vichy French forces, defended
> themselves with great tenacity and courage from 6:30 a.m. on 19
> June until 2:30 p.m. on 20 June. Taking into account their heavy
> losses and lack of ammunition, they finally had to surrender. This
> plaque was erected by the survivors of the 5th Infantry Brigade in
> memory of this splendid action.

Captain Chaumeil, for his part, estimated that, on the contrary, the fighting took place with one Vichy Frenchman against 13 Indians. Isolated, without orders, Montuis broke off the action the next day with an extremely narrow margin, a British brigade having come from Egypt to replace the Indian brigade that was now eliminated. The fall of the 'Maison Rondeau' was thus much more than a battlefield incident. It ended a very great success:

after having captured the King's Own at Kuneitra and annihilated the Punjabis and Rajputs at Mezzé – with the exception of two companies which had remained in reserve – Lieutenant-Colonel Le Couteulx de Caumont, in five days, had totally destroyed the Indian brigade. 'I have no more than two captains and six lieutenants under my command,' stated Brigadier Lloyd soon afterwards. This very brilliant success, from the military point of view, was never inscribed on any page of glory: it is the victors who write History.[49]

Out of the eight small forts that overlook Damascus, seven had been abandoned: Andrea, Sarrail, Vallier, Weygand, Goybet, Guedeney and Gamelin were all empty when the final fighting took place. In Beirut where the battle was being followed anxiously, the catastrophic news seemed incomprehensible. It was even doubted. Le Corbeiller noted on 20 June: 'The forts which protected Damascus were abandoned on the evening before on an order whose origin could not be determined.' Only Fort Gouraud, manned by a sergeant and a few Senegalese, had to be abandoned on 19 June following a long fight by only a few combatants. A first attack was beaten back with large enemy losses. Surprisingly, it was an officer under arrest, Sub-Lieutenant Sentis, who directed the defence. This Gaullist, in prison since 22 May for having sought to go to Palestine with his squadron, had been freed from his cell for the occasion. Fighting effectively, he did not seek to flee. In the afternoon of 20 June, a sergeant attempted a sortie, bringing back arms and ammunition, but in the evening the enemy attacked. Overwhelmed in numbers, subject to a brisk automatic weapons fire, the sergeant destroyed the weapons and fled with his men and Sentis. He reached the city by a covered route. From then on, all the forts in Damascus were in the hands of the enemy. Later, an enquiry found the author of the evacuation order but, on Dentz's order, his name was not revealed.[50]

At Vichy, as in Beirut, the evolution of the battle was followed anxiously. The fall of Damascus could only presage a defeat. Moreover, people were already preparing for it: on 18 June, Air Force General Bergeret had taken the gold reserves of the High Commission back to France in his aircraft.[51] He had come from Vichy to examine the possibility of strikes by *stukas*, an intervention to which he had showed he was strongly opposed. During his visits to the air bases, he was very pessimistic about the outcome of the fighting. Received by the Marshal on his return to France, he explained his position. In his opinion, the intervention by German aircraft was both morally and technically impossible. For these reasons, their help had to be refused. Supporting his views, General Jeannekyn sent this telegram next day to the Marshal: 'The French aircrews operating in Syria prefer to die alone rather than have to cooperate with the German Air Force.' Two days later, Vichy informed Berlin that it abandoned the idea of any German intervention, and confirmed that the French Air Force would carry out the defence of the Levant alone.

Each day, at the radio contact time of 1:00 p.m. GMT, a radio exchange took placed between Beirut and Force X interned at Alexandria. Via this special channel,[52] General Dentz begged Admiral Godfroy to make the English understand how obnoxious these battles were to him. All the evidence suggests that it was an overture on his part for negotiations, but Godfroy, who could only pass on the message, could detect no echo from the British. On 20 June, judging that the situation was hopeless, the High Commissioner decided to make a final gesture. Calling in M. Conty, his Director of Political Affairs, he asked him to sound out the British via the intermediary of Mr Van Egert, the US Consul-General in Beirut: 'What would be the Allies' conditions for the cessation of hostilities?' Relayed by Washington, and probably dictated by Churchill himself, London's reply reached him the next day at 1:00 p.m.:

> Far from wanting to impose degrading conditions on General Dentz, His Majesty's Government is absolutely willing to accord all the honours of war to him, as well as to his officers and public servants who have only done what they consider to be their duty with respect to their government. In consequence, there can be no question of condemning General Dentz or any other officer or public servant to the death penalty or any other penalty. The High Commissioner, his staff and all officers and public servants who do not wish to remain in the Levant will be repatriated to France as soon as conditions permit. The negotiations for a cessation of hostilities will be conducted by General Maitland Wilson, as representative of the Commander-in-Chief of the British forces, and by representatives of General Dentz. Hostilities will cease immediately, and the honours of war will be accorded to the military forces.

Dentz was disappointed. In a tone of voice which surprised his staff, he gave his opinion to General Huntziger in Vichy:

Some people delude themselves on the possible conclusion of an agreement [...] The British conditions envisage the repatriation of public servants and officers, but not the men. It is obvious that the British will never agree to having the troops from Dakar and in Africa facing them again [...] There is nothing but to fight to the end [...] There, General, is where we are today [...] I questioned a lieutenant-colonel [English prisoner and I asked him] 'What do you want in Syria?' His answer: 'Aerodromes to defend Cyprus so that the Germans do not use them.' The English ask us, as a minimum, for the control of the aerodromes and that we can't agree to. It would ruin us irremediably in the eyes of Germany. We would have lost on both counts. There is nothing but to hold on, to hold on. But for that, send me as soon as possible some men and let the staff be a little more imaginative. For the moment, I am enemy number 1. After the destruction of the Residency, I slept one night at the Hôtel Normandie. On that night it was bracketed by two bombs. We are surrounded by treason and spies. I have to look after myself carefully because they are capable of anything. What a flattering tribute!

The war, therefore, was going to continue on, as fiercely as ever. To the north of the Nahr el-Aouaj, the capture of the hills had destroyed the last defensive obstacle. The road to Damascus was open. Supported by strong artillery, General Legentilhomme was going to launch an attack that he hoped would be decisive. The Free French Division started to advance towards Damascus that is protected only by its broad garden belt, the Ghouta. The legionnaires of Free France ran the risk of finding themselves face to face with those of Vichy. When, having passed the town of Kadem on a superb moonlit night, Amilakhvari's men suddenly ran into a post manned by the 3rd Battalion, 6th Foreign Legion Regiment, on the edge of the gardens, and shots rang out. A Gaullist legionnaire fell dead and, opposite, there was one man wounded. The feared drama has just happened. Progress stopped and, under protective fire, the leading section deployed. Captain Saint-Hillier was there: 'To assemble his legionnaires scattered around, Major Amilakhvari had his bugler sound the beginning of *Le Boudin*.[53] Opposite, a bugler played the following bars. Standing up immediately, Amilakhvari ordered a cease fire and, in company with his deputy, walked towards his adversary. The Legion does not fight the Legion, Monclar had said. He found a post opposite held by a few legionnaires commanded by a NCO.[54]

Amilakhvari asked him in a severe tone: "What is your mission?" "To resist until 1:00 a.m." answered the post commander. "Good" said Amilakhavari. "Have a rest. We will not advance until 2:00 a.m. If you need anything, come and get it from us." And the group disappeared.'[55]

The incident was not unique. At nightfall, Captain de Bollardière[56] had a similar experience. Approaching the Ghouta, the advance was carried out in the following order: the Senegalese on the right, the Legion on the left. Behind the leading section, as silently as possible, the vehicles moved slowly, at walking pace, with headlights extinguished. Bollardière and his leading section commander, Barberot, were behind the forward scouts. Damascus, a few kilometres away, was twinkling from all its lights. In the background, there were scattered points of light on the mountain. 'We were plunged into a feeling of great excitement as we undertook that romantic march towards the illuminated city,' remembered Barberot. Suddenly, there was a burst of firing. Everyone went to ground. After a moment's observation, the men started off again, carefully. Suddenly, a shout in the shadows: 'Who goes there?' 'Foreign Legion' answered Bollardière. 'And you?' 'Foreign Legion!' 'What company?' '7th Company'. He knew that his side had only four companies. It was therefore someone from the Vichy forces. Then, in a warm and commanding tone, he stood up and said: 'Well, you old bugger! You are in the Legion and you fired on the Legion? Come forward!' Tall, fair, well-built, holding a submachine gun by the sling, a man stood up, walked forward in the harsh moonlight, came to attention and saluted. Bollardière, as if it were the most normal thing in the world: 'Get behind and follow me!'The legionnaire, without hesitation, obeyed. He was in the Legion? He was still in the Legion. What did Pétain and de Gaulle matter? It was the Legion that counted. *Legio, patria nostra.*[57] The advance continued.

Amilakhvari considered that there were too many risks in entering the Ghouta at night; this area, under trees and between walls, that was so well suited to ambushes. Bollardière had already warned his men: 'Be very careful: never go into the gardens in Damascus. In 1925, lots of people had their balls cut off there. Therefore, do not lose sight of the other men!'

The companies regrouped and formed a square guarded by sentries for the night. Rule N° 1, protect yourself first. Officers in the middle, sentries around, helmets on, weapons and equipment set up, eat a little and sleep a little. Suddenly, 'in the middle of the night', said Barberot, 'a noise was heard. We woke up. There, around us, were armed men. A whole section. An officer was asking his way. Astonishment! It was a section of the Vichy Army, complete and fully armed, in the middle of the battalion! Amilakhvari was awakened who, 'in his falsetto voice' bawled out the opposing officer: 'Listen, old boy! It is unbelievable! You are not likely to find your way! We don't need people like you in the army! If you continue, you are going to have worse hassles. I think you would do better to give me your revolver and go and sleep [...] Dismiss! Pile arms!' 'Yes, Major' answered the fellow. And he settled in. 'There was a comic side', commented Barberot, 'all the same! We had had a narrow escape! The troops were wearing British helmets, with British equipment. There was a very bright moon and the battalion had allowed itself to be surprised. Guarded on all sides by sentries, the Legion had allowed an armed section to enter! No one had seen it!'

In the Ghouta, other odd encounters took place between Frenchmen dressed as British and Frenchmen dressed as Frenchmen. Barberot again:

> In the evening, we found ourselves a certain number of prisoners, mainly a company of Tunisian *tirailleurs* with their officers [...] I put them in a farm courtyard and, to guard them, I posted some Senegalese machine-gunners on top of the walls. In the courtyard there were 250 men. What made a big impression on me, and which really upset me, was that we looked like foreigners, wearing British helmets, in our British uniforms (shorts and shirts), and that we holding prisoner people who were wearing French uniforms. They had French helmets, they had cloaks, French weapons, and the officers were themselves French. It was an extremely unpleasant impression. I invited all the officers to come and eat at my table. I do not think, searching in my memory, that a single one refused, which would not have been inconceivable. During our conversation, we carefully avoided sensitive subjects, but the atmosphere was nonetheless very heavy. The meal lasted a short time and in inviting them to go and rest, I reminded them that they were my prisoners. A nasty moment.[58]

The next day the Legion entered Damascus, and then was not further engaged.

The Senegalese also felt the absurdity of this fratricidal combat. A report seized at the 'Maison Rondeau'[59] noted their lack of enthusiasm. On 20 June: 'The Gaullists being stopped by tanks [...] [Major Howard] received the order to move ahead'. The detailed history of his action ended thus: 'In this way, Major Howard gave a fine example to the Gaullists troops [...] forcing them advance.' According to Gavin Long: 'General Evetts was convinced that the Free French units were tired and low in spirits. He wrote on 20 June to Brigadier Rowell[60] 'that they have little or no wish to kill their compatriots. One can doubt being able to persuade them to advance even against weak resistance.'[61] On 18 June, a company of Australian machine-gunners[62] was attached to the 1st Marine Battalion to support its advance. When, north of Kiswe, it rejoined French units, it found them motionless on both sides of the road. Captain R.R. Gordon:[63]

> At 5:00 p.m., the machine-gunners advanced towards rather demoralized black troops and set up firing positions [...] Lieutenant-Colonel Blackburn then brought the order to try to lead the Free French forward and push them ahead. Lieutenant T. A. Gilpin moved his N° 6 section more than 1,200 metres forward. He set up his guns and started firing in spite of constant machine-gun fire from the Vichy defences. His action had an effect. Led by Colonel Cazaud, the [black] infantry advanced as far as the machine-gunners but, having joined them, stopped again. Advances were made in a concertina fashion: the machine-gunners advanced, the infantry joined them. The Australians repeated this over about five kilometres. At nightfall, the Free French had reached the Ghouta, but it was clear that their heart was not in their work.

The Free French were tired. General Legentilhomme had declared to General Evetts, who arrived with his British 6th Division as reinforcements, that only the sight of British troops would induce his men to move again. After seven days of exhausting fighting in the heat and dust, they ought to have been rested.

For their part, the Free French called into question these accusations that they considered defamatory: 'The Australian assertions giving a gloomy picture of Free French morale were contradicted', affirmed Yves Gras, 'by all the accounts of French officers who took part in the Syrian campaign in the ranks of the 1st Free French Division'.[64] Duly noted. Nonetheless, the Australians did not value the Free French. They were suspicious of them. In a unit history: the unit 'was supposed to be relieved by the Free French who, as one may expect, arrived several hours late.' Unjust or not, this unfriendly feeling was nourished by the conviction of having been manipulated by these Frenchmen, who made them believe that they were going to fight against Germans during an easy campaign. And yet it was the Australians who provided by far the strongest contribution to the overall effort and who suffered the heaviest casualties.

Whatever the case may be, the Franco–British forces were at the gates of the capital and unfortunate incidents multiplied. Mutual hatred brought about unfortunate deeds. Accusing each other of treachery, the Gaullist and Vichy troops killed each other until the end of the war.

At 7:30 a.m. on 21 June, Major Delange, promoted lieutenant-colonel that very morning, gave the order to the 1st Marine Battalion to advance and take Damascus. From the top of the Jebel, he pointed out a rallying point, a characteristic olive grove. At 8:00 a.m. the battalion set off, rushing down the slopes. At daybreak, after its night in the Ghouta, 'the 13'[65] also started its advance, moving in well-grouped fashion through the maze of gardens, embankments, walls and groves where it took several prisoners but, when Damascus was close, the Franco–French conflict took a dramatic turn. Yves Gras: 'On the edges of the village of Kadem, Senegalese *tirailleurs* of the Guéna company [Free French] advanced towards other black *tirailleurs* of the Baud company [of the Army of the Levant]. "Don't fire, we are French!" they shouted.' Baud's *tirailleurs,* surprised, let them approach. At the same time, heavy firing broke out to the north. It was the legionnaires of Lieutenant Messmer's[66] 3rd Company who were attacking the Kadem mill, a large building to the north of the town. As soon as the firing broke out, the two groups of Senegalese quickly became mixed up in the confusion. No longer understanding anything about this business of Frenchmen shooting each other, they turned around and, mistaking their unit, fled. During this time, the legionnaires were advancing. Suddenly, they were brought to a standstill. It was impossible to move. A particularly violent fight started. Simon: 'Two Hotchkiss armoured cars, camouflaged in the middle of flowers, began firing. I found myself stuck with all my men. Impossible to move [...] We were like condemned men facing a firing squad [...] I took a submachine gun to fire on a machine gun. I wanted to crouch down, there was a burst of fire.' Simon, who was hit in the face, collapsed, disfigured. Installed on the top of a water tower, a machine gun forced the legionnaires to squash into the smallest hole. An aircraft machine-gunned them. Time went by. Bollardière ended by silencing the machine gun, doubtless with a mortar, but behind, more firing resumed, coming from a big building overlooking the countryside that had been bypassed, the Normand barracks. Many people were already hit. Bodies were lying on the ground. The firing finally slowed, became more irregular, and white flags finally appeared. Captain de Boissoudy: 'A white flag appeared, held by a lieutenant. He shouted to me: "Send a negotiator!" I went. I was no more than 20 metres away when they started firing at me. The firing went on for two hours. Two hours! I received nine bullets in the leg and one very large wound along the thigh. I had to have my leg amputated. That day was particularly difficult.'[67]

Shooting to kill a negotiator? Treachery! Opposite, of course, things were seen differently and, in the turmoil, each was going to accuse the other. In any case, the battle resumed. The 1st Marine Battalion being blocked, Delange had the artillery brought up. The Legion, which tried to capture the barracks, was beaten off by grenades thrown from ditches and blind angles. It was a brutal siege. At 9:00 a.m., the small Vichy garrison had one killed and five or six wounded. At 9:30 a.m., the encirclement was complete and the cannon started to breach the perimeter wall. The siege, however, lasted a further four hours. At 1:30 p.m. there were two killed, 14 wounded and the ammunition was exhausted. Lieutenant Morand, who withstood the encirclement, decided to surrender. The firing stopped. At Kadem, 70 men fell! Among them was a particularly popular motorcyclist scout, Legion Warrant Officer Tartière, a French actor who had come from Hollywood to fight – his movie name was Jacques Terrane. Some said he was murdered by a Vichy soldier.

The crisis was now going to take a nasty turn. Brought in for interrogation and accused of having fired on a negotiator, Morand was shot four times. A witness, Coursan, wrote a detailed report on the affair. Some did not admit that armed soldiers were negotiators, others asserted the contrary, that it was murder. Outside these cases between Frenchmen, no other treachery was revealed. The Australians, it was known, roughed up prisoners, but no serious crime was committed.[68] These armies were professional. In a note on 29 June, Colonel Keime recalled, for example, that 'prisoners must not be stripped of their personal effects [...] Any plundering of this sort will be severely punished.

The good name of the French Army demands the maintenance of its traditions of discipline, military integrity and humanity.' On 3 July, another note ordered that 'military identity discs taken from the bodies of enemy soldiers must be carefully collected and sent to the *Deuxième Bureau*[69] in Beirut so that the Red Cross can notify the families and that, in reciprocity, the reverse can be carried out.' In this resolute fighting, apart from these exceptions, the rules of war between civilised nations had been respected: neither gratuitous abuses nor violence.

Dentz's troops were driven back. They had no more reserves and were withdrawing everywhere. Le Corbeiller: 'Night fell over the battlefields. In the gardens of Damascus, with the sweet smell of flowers, each person watched and looked, straining to see in the dark, listening to the silence. Fruit fell from the trees with a dull sound [...] Bullets cracked here and there. Shells ripped through the silence with their thin noise and burst with a horrifying crash [...] Sometimes in this heavy silence, a cry arises, a wounded man who is dying or who is calling for help [...] who shouts his fear of dying under the knife.'

Towards the east on 21 June, Collet's detachment was pursuing the retreating Senegalese,[70] who, after having stood up to him for so long, pulled back that night. He inflicted 150 casualties on them – dead, wounded or prisoners, including Major Rollet. Lieutenant Volvey, commanding the Free French tanks accompanying this advance, was seriously wounded and had to have a limb amputated. Divry, his deputy, replaced him at the head of a company that was now no more than a large section: five tanks out of the 13 that had left Kastina. Towards 11:00 a.m., Collet reached Jeraman; the village was empty. From then on, he advanced without meeting any resistance. Isolated, having remained in the rear and receiving no further orders, elements of the 29th Algerian Tirailleur Regiment were the last to pull out. Damascus was now defenceless.

On 21 June in Damascus, Chaléon and Péfontan had not slept. All night, meetings and visits had followed one another. To avoid street fighting, it had been agreed that all troops ought to have left the city before the enemy arrived. Units returning from the front were guided by a few officers who had remained on the spot and a few civilian volunteers. The Syrian Gendarmerie guarded the barracks that were at risk of being looted. It maintained order, watching over the main arterial roads while awaiting the arrival of the Franco–British forces. As soon as contact had been established with them, Damascus would be declared an open city.

The order to evacuate was given about 8:00 a.m. The Army of the Levant, as it withdrew, benefitted from widespread esteem. Although in 1918, the inhabitants of Damascus had massacred the Turkish rearguard evacuating their city, their sons guided the Vichy French through the streets, alleyways and mosque courtyards. The Syrians had never shown hostility to the soldiers during or after the battle. 'During all the time that we had been on operations and were driving along the roads,' testified a French officer, 'we had never experienced a bomb attack. Never had a telephone line been cut nor railway lines damaged. Even so, we had the impression that we were supported by the friendship and brotherly loyalty of the people. That relieved our distress during that affair.'

At 10:00 a.m., the evacuation was complete. The main roads were clear. When the last armoured cars under the command of Sub-Lieutenant Michelet left in the direction of Homs, the city was absolutely silent. There was an impression of absolute emptiness.

An hour passed. Chaléon sent policemen to Kadem and Mezzé to announce to the Franco–British that the city was henceforth empty of troops, and had been declared an open city. Overlapping arrivals and departures took place without incident, even as he arrived. When Saint-Hillier, at the head of one of the first Gaullist units, entered the city, the last Vichy unit was leaving it. A Vichy rearguard detachment was withdrawing on the right side of the main street, while the Gaullists were marching in single file on the left. All were marching in silence, he remembered. When Captain Amiel's Free French company reached the Hamadiyeh barracks, one of the biggest in the city, it found only a few Syrian guards. The staff archives were there, intact. Barberot: 'The city was deserted when we entered [...] The inhabitants were shut up at home. The legionnaires reached the Hamadiyeh barracks which was in a mess when they entered. The men light-heartedly ransacked the place for what they could find, emptying out trunks, parading around in boots, pyjamas, and dressing gowns without any respect for these spoils, whether they were Italian or German. Our entry into Damascus marked the end of the war in Syria for us, members of the 13th.'[71] Pierre Messmer, commanding a company of the Foreign Legion: 'My unit was the first to enter Damascus. It was I who received the members of the Municipal

Council when they appeared carrying a white flag in order to contact the commander and ask that Damascus be declared an open city.'

The Australians: 'About 11:00 a.m. a line of vehicles appeared, the first one flying a white flag. It was the mayor and officials who had come to offer the surrender of the city and the police. Colonel Blackburn, the highest ranking officer present, accepted the surrender at the Town Hall, where there were several speeches. Congratulations and thanks all round! We also had something to eat.'

The Free French staff warned Lieutenant Divry, Volney's successor at the head of the remaining tanks:[72]

> Damascus will not be defended. Tomorrow make your way in convoy towards the city, be on your guard of course, but avoid fighting. 'Have they asked for an armistice?' asked Divry. 'No', he was answered. 'The agreement is valid only for the city [...] It will be up to us to maintain order [...] You will cross the city via the *Place de France* and occupy the Cavalry Barracks on the Mezzé road [...] There will be people watching you. Don't look too much like pirates!'"

After having made slow progress and being parked on the roads in the Ghouta since dawn, the company entered the city. At 10:00 a.m., Divry sent his five motorcyclists to patrol the streets in the centre. The barracks and administrative buildings had been evacuated. In the *souks*,[73] everything was calm. The inhabitants were going about their business, unconcerned. Neither rebellion nor acclamations. The five tanks reached the barracks where there was an indescribable mess: looting had been instant. There remained a dozen R-35 tanks, in good to bad condition. The company was going to be able to be re-equipped, but certainly not with new vehicles!

In a city relieved to escape the war, life picked up again very quickly. Pierre Iéhlé, of the 1st Marine Battalion, in the afternoon:

> We reached Damascus crammed into trucks. We passed through the streets where, my God, the traffic seemed almost normal [...] It was very astonishing to find a city: we had been in the *bled*[74] for more than three or four months, and our Sara *tirailleurs* who had come directly from Chad, were seeing a big city for the first time. We rushed and occupied the

barracks which had housed a regiment of Senegalese. I entered with my company. The men spread out everywhere, finding themselves in familiar territory, that is to say, finding clothing and *tirailleur* equipment. I raced into the colonel's office to put my hand on whatever was there. He must have left in a hurry. There were all his belongings, his *képis,* his uniforms and his papers. In a locked drawer, I found the reports on the officers of the regiment.

In the centre of the city, the mood of the people was warming up. Indifferent to the fact that the occupying forces had changed their name, the Syrians were enthusiastically cheering those who were bringing them independence. They came out into the streets, restless and surrounded the troops. The turmoil in the centre of the city was general. In spite of the presence of a guide, the convoy of six trucks filled with Australian machine-gunners almost split up. Filled with shouting soldiers, covered in dust, it passed through to general jubilation. The trucks passed through the redlight district. Scantily clad women on the balconies and at the windows watched them go by, inviting them up. A captain said: 'I must admit that I prayed to Heaven that we were not stopped by a traffic jam. Not a man would have remained. It had been months since they had seen women. Praise God, the traffic did not stop.'

Contact with the Vichy authorities was established about 1:00 p.m. when, accompanied by Colonel Blackburn and two other officers, Lieutenant-Colonel Cazaud drove to the Grand Serail. After introductions and given the time, the report specifies strangely, it was decided by common accord to meet again at 2:30 p.m. It was then that the handover of power took place. Chaléon stressed the importance of having the military establishments guarded immediately with a view to avoiding looting. During the conversation which followed, Cazaud declared to Chaléon that the Free French Division did not expect Damascus to be abandoned that day. It was following receipt of his message that it was decided to enter.

A journalist, Alan Moorehead, did not feel, upon entering Damascus 'anything comparable to the excitement caused by Lawrence's army 24 years previously'. He was disappointed: instead of the dream of the city, where gardens and cool water awaited the traveller. 'I could see dusty and dirty streets and dilapidated buildings. We made our way to the Orient Hotel and reserved rooms

as we would have done in Marseilles or Bayonne before the war.
Everything was very French, but the crowd swarming on the square
was essentially Arab: the French had taken the road to Beirut [...]
There was a curfew but no blackout during this first night. For the
first time in a year, I could see from my window a city glittering
with light. Like *carnevale* in Venice, the electric light globes gleamed
weakly all over the oasis picking out, with their warm colours, the
heights overlooking the city, where fighting was still going on.'

The Gaullist prisoners were liberated at 5:00 p.m., and painful
scenes took place when some, who had been in garrison there
since before 1940, intended re-occupying villas in which they
had lived. Some demanded the keys. There were altercations. The
atmosphere was tense.

At 3:00 p.m., in an open car escorted by a detachment of
Circassians, General Legentilhomme, his arm bandaged, made his
entry into the city.[75] At that hour, the heat was torrid. Received by
the Syrian government, he now represented France. Coming from
Palestine that very morning, Catroux joined him at 4:00 p.m. at the
Residency, rue Salieh, that he knew well. He had come there for the
first time more than 20 years previously, in the time of Gouraud.[76]
Today there was no cavalry guard in full-dress uniform, presenting
arms standing in their stirrups, no more *chaouch*[77] or even an *aide
de camp*. The offices were empty. The doors were open, it was
'Sleeping Beauty's castle'. When, a few minutes later, Captain Buis
entered to ask for orders to go to Nazareth to look for the British
tanks, he found no one. He wandered about, calling out, looking
for someone. A door opened: it was Catroux, who recognised him.
In Cairo, in the presence of de Gaulle, he had invited him serve in
the *Troisième Bureau*[78] but Buis had refused, preferring to fight.
Catroux, tight-lipped, had noted this without saying anything. Buis
introduced himself but Catroux interrupted him: 'You have served
in this country. You know it. Sit down: you will be the head of my
private staff.' Silence, then: 'Believe me, dear boy, I am taking you
because I have nobody else!' Buis, waylaid, had to obey. He sat
behind a desk and signed himself the mission order he had come
to get. At Nazareth, he could obtain only 'clunkers' that were no
longer usable, and took up his post upon his return.

Damascus resumed its daily life.

Moorehead:

On the morning of 22 June, we drove around the city looking for the
famous 'Street Called Straight', watching the endless bazaars and

alleyways where one could see hideous prostitutes that Lawrence described with the disgusting but very evocative epithet 'made-up meat' [...] Later, we climbed to the top of a hill to observe the city. Returning home, we entered a Catholic church where Collet's Circassians had come to hear a Requiem Mass celebrated in memory of one of their comrades. A white wooden coffin was placed before the altar. These wild men, stinking of the stables, wearing leather accoutrements and bedecked with knives, occupied the seats. They carried the coffin outside, placed it on an Army truck, and set off for the cemetery, with the men walking in front. I then got into my car again with Christopher Lumby, of *The Times*. On the road a little further on, an Australian soldier shouted to us: 'Piss off! Get out of here!' We had stuck our nose into the frontline! Here, three minutes from the centre of the city, two minutes from the pathetic funeral, bullets were sweeping the road, dead and wounded were lying in the hills. Sited close to Mezzé, [Vichy] French guns were still firing on British transport driving along the road.

It was at that moment that I learned of the invasion of the USSR by Germany. Compared to such a piece of news, my reporting on the fall of Damascus was of no further interest! I left again immediately for Cairo.

Damascus had in fact fallen on the day of *Operation Barbarossa*.[79] The Germans invading the USSR! The world scene was suddenly drastically changed.

Having come from Jerusalem, General de Gaulle made his entry into Damascus on 23 June. It was a great day. De Gaulle could confer upon it all the solemnity that could be desired. Appointed 'Delegate General and Plenipotentiary, Commander-in-Chief of France in the Levant', General Catroux held, as a high commissioner, all powers but, at Churchill's request, independence having been promised, this title was suppressed. A letter from General de Gaulle laid down his mission: 'To direct the re-establishment of an internal and economic situation as close to normal that will allow the prosecution of the war; to negotiate, with qualified representatives of the people, treaties with France that will institute independence and sovereignty of the [Levant] states; ensure the defence of the territory against the enemy; cooperate with the Allies in military operations in the Middle East.'

As soon as they were published, these directives aroused British anger: to designate Catroux as commander-in-chief in the Levant was completely contrary to the Franco–British agreement whereby military responsibility was supposed to lay with General Maitland Wilson for the complete duration of the war, but, for de Gaulle, it was important above all to reaffirm French sovereignty over the mandate in the Levant. A few days later, on 28 June, he explained, almost menacingly, his attitude to Churchill: 'If to the satisfaction of Vichy, Berlin and Rome, our common action in Syria and Lebanon seems to have resulted in a diminution of France's position there and to have introduced strictly British actions and leanings, I am convinced that its effect on public opinion in my country would be disastrous. I must add that my own effort, which consists in maintaining, morally and materially, French resistance alongside England against our enemies, would be gravely jeopardized.' So he faced off against the Allies whom he suspected of aims foreign to the current conflict.

By giving his first speech in Syria, de Gaulle thought first of all about the nationalities with which he wished to get on without giving anything away. For him it was a question of prestige, his only concern. Following his arrival, he had received political, religious and administrative notables – 'and there were many of them' – he noted with a sigh. All told him of their wish to see the instrumentalities of the State function and, especially, a government installed.

Contrary to what one might hope, the occupation of Damascus did not progress in an atmosphere of hearty rejoicing. Incidents were frequent. In a report, dated 4 July and sent by an informer to Military Intelligence in Beirut, we read: 'The tension reported in the city continues. Armoured car patrols travel around the streets and market places, machine guns continue to keep watch over intersections [...] Real discontent accompanies the occupation of the city. Soldiers, both Gaullists and British, treat the population without tact and consideration, and several brawls and scuffles have been reported.' Was it more than drunken fights? In the city, muggings were mentioned. Even if the authorities assert that they were baseless rumours, these incidents were, in any case, sufficiently grave to justify the presence of armoured vehicles. On 7 July, a Syrian delegation made up of 'numerous personalities representing all classes of society' went to see the head of the government to 'inform him of the situation following incidents which had taken place in Damascus'. The latter answered 'that he has already been in ongoing contact with the military authorities to study this situation and to prevent any repetition of such acts'.

Without knowing their exact nature, these incidents seemed to cause the military some concern. They were ongoing, since on 12 July a note from General Legentilhomme reported again that 'some regrettable incidents have happened in Damascus through the fault of a few soldiers.' The town major, Colonel Collet, confirmed that 'measures have been taken to avoid any repetition'. Stating in a note that 'some regrettable incidents have taken place in Damascus', he made it known that 'any aggression against persons or property will be punished with the greatest severity. Any soldier convicted of having committed an attack will be immediately court-martialled. Instructions have been given to the [civil] police, the gendarmerie and the military police.' Finally, the town major asked the population to keep calm and reminded it that 'demonstrations are forbidden'. Moreover, relations between the two French groups were difficult. At the Officers' Club, the women were from one side and the men from the other, and they did not speak to each other. Propriety? Not at all! The men were Gaullists and the ladies were wives of Vichy officers. Sometimes they recognised one another, but still ignored each other.

Militarily, a threat continued to hang over the city. On the night of 23 June, aircraft bombed it. No military target was hit, but the damage was great. There were hundreds of victims in the Christian quarter. The deed was attributed to the Germans by the Free French, who found in it proof of Vichy's collaboration. The Vichy histories bear no trace of such an operation and General Jeannekyn himself identified it as German. This bombing took place without consultation with the Vichy authorities, but weighed heavily in the case against Vichy. General de Gaulle, present during the bombing, also saw in it proof of military collaboration.

No doubt as a reprisal, on the following night, British bombers attacked the *Résidence des Pins*[80] in Beirut where the High Commissioner and his wife were staying. There were five killed, seven wounded and the building was heavily damaged. Some bombs also fell in the city. General Dentz, absent from the *Résidence*, was not hurt but he wrote to General Huntziger: 'They are getting worked up. Destruction of my residence, senseless bombing of Beirut [...] By bombing mosques and *souks* they hope to stir up the population against me. They are already calling me "the butcher". People find this resistance ridiculous, etc. You see the tactic. One has to protest strongly. Do I bomb Damascus where there are 10,000 men and a staff? Do I bomb Jerusalem where there is also a staff?' he reminded officers who suggested reprisals on the residence of the British High Commissioner: 'One does not bomb Jerusalem, a city holy for the three religions.'

At the announcement of the fall of Damascus, the atmosphere in Beirut suddenly changed. Unrest grew. In the city for several days, the roar of guns could be heard to the south. The British naval squadron gradually moved closer and the morale of the civilian population started to drop. Lies circulated that women especially liked to repeat: the British had decided to destroy Beirut by shellfire; new weapons, terribly destructive, were going to be used; Officers who fought will all be shot ... Overall hostile to the Mandate and favourable to independence, the Christian population, without saying it, hoped for the success of Free France.

Rahn continued to offer the services of German units allegedly ready in the Balkans, Dentz continued to refuse, the German brought pressure to bear and threatened. Dentz continued to dodge. He had other worries: on 20 June, the day Damascus fell, a new front opened in Syria: *Habforce* crossed the Euphrates.

In fact, on 2 June, suddenly appearing from the Iraqi desert, coming from Baghdad 350 km away, two columns of British armour and trucks crossed the Euphrates.[81] It was estimated that it contained about 800 vehicles. The first column, coming from the south, entered Syria at Abu Kamal and moved along the pipeline from Mosul to Tripoli; the second came from the southeast, from Rutba in Iraq. Both advanced towards Palmyra. It was a threat of primary importance. If Palmyra fell, the British would continue on towards Homs, Tripoli and Latakia, thereby invading Northern Syria, a zone practically devoid of troops. Taken from behind in this way, the army would have its flank turned. The most southerly column had already penetrated 65 km and reached Pumping Stations T2, and then T3 130 km further on, where it met the first resistance, at a small post manned by a very small garrison – a warrant officer, 22 legionnaires and 10 days' rations – much too weak to stop it. However, when the 45 British vehicles came in sight of the post, the legionnaires, refusing to surrender, barred the way. An infantry assault, supported by artillery, was launched against the post but failed. Leaving a group watching the T3 post, the bulk of the troops carried on towards Palmyra, 70 km further on. It was then that an aerial reconnaissance by Captain Tonon sighted the 150 vehicles. Raising a great cloud of dust, they were visible from

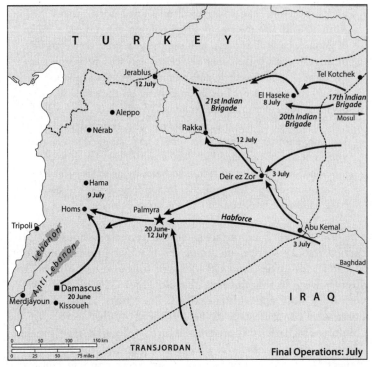

Map 5. Final operations July 1941

afar. To counter-attack rapidly so deep in the desert, there was only the Air Force. Beirut decided to engage all its aircraft. Late in the morning General Jeannekyn sent four bombers escorted by fighters then, at 3:00 p.m., six others.[82] The next day, 22 June, all available aircraft, even those of the *Aéronavale*, were despatched.[83] One hundred and twenty-two sorties took place during the day. Captain Menu of *GC II/3*:[84]

> 11:30 a.m. It is hot. The engines were whistling [...] T4 passed by under the wings – four walls, two buildings, three tanks, an airfield, then it is Palmyra [...] Heading south, following the track, a light streak against the brownish soil. Waggled wings, the other flight members closed in. Each one has seen, 20 km away, black spots and clouds of dust [...] Down-sun approach, reduced engine revs [...] Armoured vehicles, trucks [...] Waggled

wings: everyone has understood and lined up to attack [...]
Altitude 200-300 metres. A small column was raked, a burst
of gunfire, bank to the left, pull up, the gruesome conveyor-belt
of attacks against the other vehicles. I can see one burning on
my right [...] Each vehicle gets a burst of fire. Six cannon shells
and 20 rounds – see 15 or 20 men lying on the sand. We have
overshot the column in ten seconds. We climb to have a look.
On the ground, all around, men are running, terrified. A truck is
burning, another is on its side, others have stopped in disorder
and some are still moving [...] A new short pass. Am now out of
ammunition, it is time to return to base, flying at tree-top level:
we are now defenceless prey [...] In a half-hour we will back at
base, mission completed [...] 15 km from Palmyra.

The Vichy French air attacks were extremely serious: GC II/3
carried out 26 sorties, including 17 machine-gunning missions,
EO 595[85] 28 sorties, and GB I/25 sent four aircraft. All available
aircraft were in the air, even the old Potez 25[86] biplanes which
were very slow and vulnerable. All the efforts of the Vichy Air
Force were concentrated, to the detriment of other sectors, on the
columns which each day progressed further along the Iraqi pipeline.
Although defensive fire was precise and plentiful, the RAF did not
protect *Habforce*. Major-General Clark, commanding *Habforce*,
demanded urgent and massive support, without which, he said, he
would not be able to take Palmyra. The nine Gladiator biplanes
sent to him were not up to the task of facing the Vichy Dewoitines
and, far from their base, their maintenance was impossible. They
departed the very day of their arrival. The sky was thus clear for
the Vichy French. On 23 June, 63 bombers and 36 fighters were
engaged,[87] with impunity.

Since the RAF could not intervene above the battlefield, they
were going to counter-attack aircraft on the ground: to cut off
the Vichy French at the knees, they were going to attack their
airfields, which were poorly protected. The rugged countryside,
which masked the aircrafts' approach, the absence of listening
posts, and the weakness of the Vichy anti-aircraft defences,
all favoured this tactic which showed itself to be particularly
effective. The British attacks were not, as in the past, entrusted
to bombers alone, but also to fighters attacking with machine
guns. Ehrengardt and Shores considered that the consequences of
this tactic were incalculable and that they weighed heavily since,
according to them, 'the repeated machine gunning of [Vichy]

French airfields constituted the principal cause of the collapse of Vichy forces in the Levant.'

Now that Damascus had fallen, and the Australians were halted at Merdjayoun, Jezzine and, it seemed, at Damour, it was at Palmyra that a battle that would take place both on the ground and in the air. This battle took place on two parallel fronts, the land one at T3 and Palmyra, the other on the air bases and dispersal airfields. It all started on 23 June when ten Hurricanes, flying very low, suddenly appeared over Baalbek airfield without having been detected. On the ground, surprise was complete. The damage was impressive. Six aircraft were destroyed, and a number of others damaged. Five Glenn Martin bombers, which had just landed, were rocked severely. One caught fire and another, laden with bombs, exploded, a third was severely damaged, a fourth put out of action. Three aircraft from the *Aéronavale*, which were about to take off, were also damaged. The capacity of *GR II/39*[88] to operate was so seriously reduced that it could not take to the air again until 27 June. The ten Hurricanes continued on their mission towards Rayak which, happily, had been alerted. The aircraft of *GC III/6* had already taken off when the British arrived. It was 2:30 p.m. From the sky, the Vichy French had seen the smoke above Baalbek. Scarcely had the first Dewoitines taken off than the Hurricanes arrived, guns blazing. The Vichy fighters engaged them. The battle whirled around. Le Gloan shot down an enemy aircraft. A returning patrol joined the battle, which turned in favour of the Vichy French. The intense and generalised air activity was marked by pursuits, flights, dummy moves and meeting other aircraft with other missions, notably over the fleet. The Dewoitines of *GC III/6* were themselves credited with five victories; only one was damaged, Le Gloan's aircraft. Was it over? At 5:20 p.m., 12 Australian Tomahawk fighters attacked Qusayr, near Aleppo, an almost empty airfield. As they were returning, Vichy fighters from Rayak, to the south, took off to block their return route. The battle extended over Zahleh, on a level with Beirut. The fighter that made its appearance in this battle, the American Tomahawk, was a powerful aircraft[89] and the Dewoitine, although more manoeuvrable, started to be outclassed. Two Vichy French aircraft were shot down and, more or less damaged, all the Tomahawks returned to base; one crashed on landing. If the bombers and fighters were working independently, the appearance of the Tomahawks forced the Vichy fighters to change their role to bomber protection. However, by mobilising almost all available aircraft, carrying out 419 sorties – 258 bombing and 161 fighter missions, plus numerous reconnaissance missions – the Vichy Air Force provided a considerable effort. Meanwhile, at T3, the 22 legionnaires were still holding on.

At Palmyra, the core of the defences was Fort Weygand, north-east of the ancient ruins, on the other side of a palm grove. It was a stone-walled enclosure, such as is seen in the Sahara, behind a barbed wire network that was impassable even for light armoured vehicles. Moreover, scattered support positions were set up in the oasis, in the ruins and in the mountains overlooking the fort, in particular in the medieval Arab castle. The garrison was reduced: Major Gherardi, in command, had only a company of the Legion – 15th Company of the 6th Foreign Legion Regiment, 187 men – the 1st Light Desert Company[90] made up of bedouin, and a few Air Force ground staff – inexperienced infantrymen: in total, about 300 men.

When, on 22 June, the leading element of the British column – 30 vehicles of the Household Cavalry – emerged near Palmyra, they came up against impassable resistance. At 4:30 p.m., Gherardi sent this message: 'Are [at] first contact with [some] armoured cars and 30 enemy trucks on our southern defences.' At 5:45 p.m.: 'Very violent shelling. Fear being overrun.' At 9:45 p.m., Dentz replied: 'The Army of the Levant is counting on the Legion to hold Palmyra as at Camerone.'[91] On 23 June, the whole of *Habforce* having joined – four cavalry regiments, including the Arab Legion, and an infantry battalion – the encirclement was complete. The artillery ranged its shots. Land communications were no longer possible, and resupply and evacuation of the wounded could no longer be considered. Henceforth, the evolution of the battle was followed by radio. The siege started. Faced with the violence of the fighting that commenced, the Light Desert Company scattered almost completely, and the Legion company found itself alone with a handful of Air Force ground staff, strongly supported by the Air Force which tried to break the enemy's stranglehold. Gherardi, 23 June, 3:47 p.m.: '[We] are holding [the] centre of resistance [at the] southern outskirts of Palmyra. [We] are holding [the] Pass of the Tombs and [the] Pass [of the] Castle. Intense bombardment [of] Weygand post. Morale excellent.' On 24 June, the garrison, which was giving as good as it got, counter-attacked at some points. 25 June, 6:25 a.m.: 'Two attempts supported by heavy automatic weapons fire [were] repulsed. New arrival of about a hundred vehicles coming from the south.' Beirut's answer:

'Bravo Palmyra!' In return: 'Respectful thanks.' On 26 June, the pressure increased. New message at 12:20 p.m., the pressure was increasing: '[A] large movement of vehicles [has been] observed from our position. 16 vehicles coming from Iraq arrive in the region [of] Tel Ouaner. [A] column of about 40 vehicles [was] sighted coming from T3 to Palmyra. [A] column of 20 to 25 vehicles sighted coming from the south and making for Palmyra. Request energetic intervention [of the] Air Force.'

This 26 June was a dark day for the Vichy flyers. In ten seconds, Australian fighters devastated the airfield at Homs, destroyed four Moranes, damaged six other aircraft, and blew up a train carrying ammunition and fuel in the railway station near the strip. There was considerable damage and several men were killed. Continuing their fast flight and, attacking from the north-west where they weren't expected, the Tomahawks again strafed Rayak where they destroyed a Dewoitine and three Potez 25. The growing losses were irreplaceable.

With burned out fuel tankers, destruction of an artillery battery, and troop losses, *Habforce* was also suffering greatly. A report from the 10th Indian Division confirmed that 'even if the number lost is not great, the effect on morale of frequent bombing and machine gunning is disturbing. All units, English and Indian, are fairly shaken up, and administrative sections, made up of recent enlistees, poorly trained and sometimes without weapons, will be hardly able to continue the war in several days.'[92] On 28 June, installed on the steep peak where the medieval castle stands, Blockhouse N° 13, held by about 20 legionnaires repelled several assaults. In the palm grove, riflemen, waiting in ambush, prevented infiltration. Bullets whistled in the ruins. At 3:10 p.m.: 'Intense and unceasing artillery fire on our posts. Violent shelling.' The garrison abandoned some posts in the palm grove, but the legionnaires counter-attacked, driving the English from the gardens which they had infiltrated and in which they abandoned, in a hasty retreat, equipment, weapons and vehicles. Nevertheless, the enemy was advancing. 29 June, 11:40 p.m.: 'Enemy occupies the castle and [the] southern Pass, [as well as] western end [of] Pass [of the] Tombs.' 30 June, 6:55 a.m.: 'Reinforced enemy artillery opened fire on us at 4:30 a.m. Request immediate neutralization.' 7:30 a.m.: 'Enemy has succeeded in infiltrating into the western part of Palmyra. Our troops still holding on southern edge.' 11:30 a.m.: 'Shelling continues with same intensity. Fighting in the ruins continues. Very serious enemy losses.' 3:25 p.m.: 'Enemy has been driven from ruins and pushed back into the gardens where he is being pursued. [We] have captured some machine guns, [much] ammunition and grenades.' 2 July, 6:35 a.m.: 'Enemy has ceased all contact with our positions. Attacks in preparation. All western heights [are] strongly occupied.' The British forces were regrouping, obviously to carry the position, and the Vichy French were becoming exhausted. 11:12 a.m.: 'Village shelled. [Our] positions towards Zenobia [are] turned. We have no more ammunition for [the] mortars. [We] are firing our last 80mm rounds.' 11:30 a.m.: 'Enemy pressure increasing. [We] have some losses.'

In *Gringoire*[93] on 25 June 1941, Roland Dorgelès, author of *Les Croix de bois*,[94] conjured up Gherardi's men: 'The ground, underfoot, burns the like the breech of a machine gun. The sandy wind gusts dry out the lungs, tear the eyes with their millions of pricks, coat the mouth through the *chèche*[95]: the sun burns you with its red fire between the shoulders and blinds you with its reflection: you are fighting in an oven and your temples become tight enough to burst. However, you have to hang on, gasping for breath, burned [...] The spirit of Verdun sustains the combatants in Syria.' France was indeed following the various episodes of the siege. Marshal Pétain cabled to Dentz: 'Let all those who are fighting beside you know that the whole of France is following them with emotion in the battle. With her, I salute the valiant handful of defenders of Palmyra [...] Their sacrifice remains an example of strength for the country.' On 2 July, at 1:25 p.m. Beirut signalled: 'Palmyra no longer answers', but at 6:27 p.m., 'the radio link with Palmyra has resumed.' The fighting was thus continuing, but if Gherardi was still hanging on, his end seemed inevitable. All day and night, the British artillery continued firing. At 1:00 a.m. on 3 July: 'Situation at 8:00 p.m.: [the] enemy attacks are continuing. [We] have only evacuated the Temple of Baal. The enemy is shelling the village.' Finally, at 2:40 a.m., at the end of his strength and out of ammunition, Gherardi sent his last message: '[I] am forced to surrender the position. Stop all air activity [in the] region of Palmyra. [The] radio is put out of action. Long live France!'

Seeing 88 cadaverous survivors walk out of the fort, the only ones fit to stand, Major-General Clark marvelled: 'That's all?' He thought he was dealing with a battalion. He congratulated the survivors and rendered military honours. There were only 165 prisoners.[96] Out of 300 combatants, 135 were dead. As for the

English, they had lost 85 men, generally from aerial bombardment. The fall of Palmyra brought about that of T3. In learning of the fall of Fort Weygand, the warrant officer and his 22 legionnaires surrendered in their turn. On 24 June, coming from Deir-ez-Zor, a small friendly Vichy column – eight armoured cars and four trucks – tried to relieve the post but the English repulsed it. Sustained by the Air Force, but very alone, the besieged men put up with ten days of assaults and bombardments, but on 6 July, out of rations and ammunition, the warrant officer in command of the post agreed to surrender but not unconditionally. The British besieging force agreed that all weapons be destroyed and that the men keep their belongings. T3 and Palmyra had brought the Kingstone column to a halt. Without artillery, without armour, without resupply of any sort, but sustained by the Air Force, the Legion had held on for 13 days in the face of 1,000 men with carriers and strong artillery. 'Camerone, Tuyên-Quang, Bir Hakeim, Diên Biên Phu, the history of the Foreign Legion is rich in fine defences,' wrote Pierre Montagnon, 'but a discreet veil covers those of Palmyra. Had the attackers been German and not British, the glory of the defenders of Palmyra would also have been eternal.' Glory, everyone knows, is the offspring of politics.

The north of Syria, practically devoid of troops, was already potentially lost: while there was fighting at Palmyra, a flood of British units crossed the frontier, but the resistance of almost two weeks at Palmyra allowed the reinforcement of Homs. When the Arab Legion resumed its advance towards the west, it came upon an armoured group 160 km further on.

On 1 July, about midday, coming from Iraq, two motorised brigades of the 10th Indian Division[97] reached the passages across the Euphrates. Mayadine[98] fell. At Abu Kemal, 130 km further on, the column came up against a strange group supported by French armoured cars. Its resistance caused very serious damage until it was scattered by artillery.

As soon as this resistance was overcome, the British 'flying column' moved along the Syrian bank of the river in a northerly direction, and Deir-ez-Zor, the regional capital, risked being taken from behind. Now, the commandant of the place was absent at the time of the attack. All the exits were under fire by British guns and confusion reigned. Abandoning its artillery and leaving the bridge intact, the garrison[99] scattered. One hundred men, nine guns and 50 trucks were captured. Throwing away their uniforms, Syrians and bedouin in large numbers melted into the civilian population, a part of the garrison fled to the north, another towards the west, towards Palmyra where fighting was going on. Coming by surprise up against the rear of the Arab Legion which was fighting, and counter-attacked by Glubb Pasha's men, the convoy lost 11 dead, 80 prisoners and six armoured vehicles. For Beirut, this general retreat, without a leader and without orders, was a debacle. The loss of the big bridge at Deir-ez-Zor, the only practicable means for mechanised vehicles to cross the Euphrates, was a catastrophic event for the Vichy French. The door to Syria was now open. It was a strategic turning point. The event was so important that General de Gaulle himself, generally laconic about military operations, wrote in his *Mémoires* that the structure had probably been abandoned: 'On 3 July, on the bridge at Deir-ez-Zor which had remained intact, thanks to a piece of luck that I can say must have been well planned, an Indian column coming from Iraq crossed the Euphrates and advanced towards Aleppo and Homs.' That was not all. At Tel Kotchek, in the 'duck's beak', the north-east corner of the mandate, another British column – the 20th Indian Brigade – reached, on 3 July in the late afternoon, the railway bridge where the defence by the small [Vichy] French garrison, although vigorous, did not succeed in blocking its passage. Driving more than 600 km – more than 1,200 since Baghdad – the British Army could now develop behind the [Vichy] French Army one of the most extensive strategic movements of World War II. Three columns, moving at breakneck speed, came up to the Turkish border and then moved back to the south in a mechanised drive that brought to mind Guderian's strike towards the English Channel or Rommel's thrust in Cyrenaica. On 10 July, the enemy threatened Aleppo.

Wasn't the ostensible aim of the war to ensure the protective zone north of Egypt? It was now achieved. It was time: on 18 June, Turkey signed a treaty of friendship with Germany, whose armies, advancing across the Russian plains, now threatened the Carpathians.

The resources of the Vichy French were becoming exhausted. To hang on, Dentz needed reinforcements in men and armaments, but how to bring them to Syria? If Vichy had refused the help of the *Luftwaffe*, the outcome of the battle nonetheless depended on Berlin's goodwill, as it was impossible to bring in reinforcements without its consent. The intention of the government was to send Dentz a half-brigade of three battalions of Algerian *tirailleurs*, a Legion battalion, a battalion of colonial infantry, a group of self-propelled 75mm guns and a company of nine tanks. Just before the attack on 8 June, talks had been started at Wiesbaden aimed at sending weapons stockpiled in France by the Germans, without the request being met. Therefore Admiral Marzin[100] again sought authorisation to send these troops to Syria, and this time he received authorisation. From the beginning of June 1941, a recruiting campaign had been launched in France, and fund-raising had taken place in favour of the soldiers in Syria. The *Légion française des combattants*[101] organised the sending of parcels bearing this message: 'We are thinking of you. We are proud of you.'

Authorisation having been obtained from the Germans for transit by rail across occupied Europe as far as Salonika, the reinforcements, given the urgency, were embarked on trains without delay. From 11 June onwards, batteries of anti-aircraft and anti-tank guns, with their crews and ammunition, were loaded on trains at Chalon-sur-Saône railway station.

On 14 June, there had been talk of transportation by the fleet and Admiral de Laborde, commanding the fleet, had met Admiral Darlan on this matter, but to have the fleet set sail in the Mediterranean without air cover would have been extremely risky; it would have been necessary to obtain from the Axis, apart from fuel oil, air protection. Questioned, the Germans were astonished: Does the French government realise that such an operation could bring about an open conflict with England?' In the following days, Darlan thought about the matter, consulted, restricted the extent of the operation and then, finally, abandoned the idea. The risk of a widespread war was too great. There remained only the land route, except for the sailors.

To resupply the *Guépard* and the *Valmy*, the French Admiralty sent the destroyer *Chevalier-Paul* from Toulon to Beirut but, off Cyprus, it was attacked by a British Swordfish aircraft on 16 June. Although greatly outdated,[102] this torpedo aircraft had already demonstrated, at Mers el-Kebir, Taranto and Matapan, its feared effectiveness against ships, even those under way. The big biplane succeeded in hitting the *Chevalier-Paul* at full speed. An officer and seven men were killed by the explosion of the torpedo but the vessel remained immobilised for long enough for the crew to escape from the wreck. Coming from Beirut, the *Guépard* saved the men, but the ammunition went to the bottom. Avoiding the cheers of the crowd and movie cameras, another fast destroyer, the *Vauquelin*, carrying munitions, left Toulon afterwards and succeeded in reaching Beirut discreetly on 20 June, but its contribution was slight. No other ship ever succeeded in reaching the Levant.

For lack of a maritime solution, and since the Germans were in agreement for the passage of seven trains, the transport of reinforcements had to be envisaged between the Greek port – now German – of Salonika and the Vichy Levant. To obtain authorisation from Ankara to cross Turkey by train ought not to have been too difficult since, on 18 June, Turkey had signed a friendship pact with Germany.

At Ankara, negotiations were commenced. They lasted two days but ended without success.[103] The French Air Force reinforcements remained blocked at the Turkish frontier. The only elements which reached the Levant before 4 July were brought by 43 rotations of transport aircraft stopping off at Athens. The British holding Cyprus, these aircraft – three-engine Dewoitine D.338 of Air France and four-engine Farmans – had to fly at night. In spite of the effort involved, the transport capacity remained much too weak. Only ten tonnes of materiel – two anti-tank guns, about 100 machine guns, spare parts and ammunition – and 500 troops could be transported.[104] The Germans, more convincing, had obtained permission for a train loaded with aviation fuel to be sent to the Levant.

But how could the reinforcements blocked at Salonika get to the Levant? To examine the problem, Darlan called a conference, on 29 June, at the Navy headquarters at the Hôtel Helder in Vichy. Two Air Force officers, sent on a mission by Dentz, Majors Gaudillères and Tézé, were present and were extremely surprised that only the question of transports was dealt with, and not the conditions of a possible armistice. After the conference, Darlan decided: under the protection of the three destroyers *Guépard*, *Valmy* and *Vauquelin*, the two cargo ships present in the Levant, the *Oued-Yquem* and the *Saint-Didier*, would go to Salonika to pick up the reinforcements. The convoy of five ships immediately set sail, ran the blockade and reached Salonika. On 4 July, the troops embarked on the two cargo ships. As there were not enough lifejackets, everything that floated – pieces of wood and barrels – was piled up on deck. On the evening of 5 July, the flotilla set sail and was immediately chased by the Royal Navy. The *Saint-Didier*, loaded with men, weapons and ammunition,[105] was sunk at anchor in the Turkish port of Adalia; nine officers and 37 men died, and 266 survivors, including 22 wounded, were interned by the Turks.[106] The *Oued-Yquem* took shelter at the island of Castellorizo which was controlled by the Italians. The destroyers which were cruising about, trying to avoid the British fleet, soon found themselves facing seven destroyers, two cruisers and a submarine. On British orders, they had to return to Salonika. As can be seen, the Franco–British war was not total. To avoid the massacre spreading, Darlan did not involve his cruisers, and Britain held back the full force of its Navy. The Royal Navy left these ships to France: on 18 July, the *Guépard*, *Valmy* and *Vauquelin* returned to Toulon.[107] No reinforcements reached the Levant by sea.[108]

Dentz, after 28 June, no longer believed that the situation could develop in a positive fashion. On that day, he dictated his instructions: 'At this time, it is a matter of hanging on. Consequently, to go easy on the infantry and cavalry, and to give maximum artillery support in order to allow us to await the arrival of the reinforcements that have been announced. To hold on grimly to the current positions. To restrict ourselves to counter-attacks that are strictly necessary to maintain the essential points.'

There was only one essential solution: ask for an armistice.

16

Negotiate?

Did the war in Syria still have the slightest importance?

On 22 June, at 3:15 a.m., exactly 100 days to the day after the French collapse, the *Wehrmacht* invaded Russia: it was *Operation Barbarossa*. Involving three million men, 3,600 armoured vehicles, and 4,200 aircraft, the operation was colossal. The war had suddenly changed its mood and its centre of gravity was moved sharply to the Soviet Union. On 22 June, the Franco–British conflict showed its absurd nature to the eyes of the world.

It was urgent to stop this conflict in Syria, a waste of excellent soldiers and precious equipment, this Franco–British clash which cost the Germans nothing, which weakened the Allies and distracted them from the sole important objective, defeating the *Reich*.

Dentz considered that it was time to stop the fighting. This was also the opinion of the British and, on 23 June, approved by Wilson, Lavarack had the following message handed to Dentz via the intermediary of the United States Consul-General at Beirut: 'Dismayed and shocked that the French and Australians, allies during the Great War, can clash in a combat causing a useless waste of brave men, convinced that the idea of conflict between two former comrades of the last war disgusts and shocks the French as much as the Australians, General Lavarack, commanding the Australian forces in Syria, offers to send by plane, to Rayak or any other suitable airfield, an envoy so that he can meet General Dentz's delegate and hand him a message from General Lavarack capable of bringing an end to the disastrous conditions obtaining today and avoiding further bloodshed.'

So, neither of the two adversaries wanted to carry on any longer a conflict whose causes, good or bad, had disappeared. On 27 June, being bound by the decisions of Vichy, Dentz decided to send Major Tézé, the chief of his military cabinet, to Vichy so that he could explain the position to the government and the need to stop the fighting. The General called in Tézé and gave him a note for General Huntziger, his Minister:

> General, The situation is grave. Taking into account the fuel train held up by Turkey, there are ten days' supplies of fuel for the Air Force. The battalions that have been announced can permit resistance continuing if they reach Beirut, [but] they cannot allow me to renew the offensive for lack of armour. On the other hand, Homs has fallen. There will no more than a fortnight's supply of wheat in Lebanon. I am coming up against the hostility of people who are already getting restless. I do not believe that the situation will get better. The troops, who have fought magnificently, would no longer understand the aim of their total sacrifice [...] If the government wants to talk to the British, it is the moment.

In that note General Dentz then proposed a plan for negotiations. In order to protect the French presence as much as possible, while giving the British 'maximum guarantees concerning their military mastery', he proposed that 'an occupation zone be established on the current frontline, France retaining the use of one aerodrome in Lebanon and two others in Syria, their operation being restricted to police operations, commercial traffic and flights to metropolitan France. Other airfields would be made unusable. French numbers remaining in the Levant would be fixed by mutual accord, the others being repatriated. French public servants would continue to work with the local authorities.' In the case of a total military reverse, 'the only measure to obtain would be the repatriation of the army and families'.

After having received Tézé, Dentz called in Major Gaudillères, an airman who had come with Bergeret and remained on the spot to represent him. Dentz asked him to accompany Tézé and 'to guide him in his dealings if possible'. That very day, Tézé and Gaudillères took off for Vichy.

As soon as they arrived, Bergeret took them to see Darlan, who listened to them. Handed to General Huntziger, the note displeased him. The Minister suspected weakness in General Dentz who deserved, according to him, a call to order. He cabled to Dentz: 'The gravity of the situation has not escaped the government. You are not authorised to begin conversations whose automatic effect would be to upset the resistance that is your duty to pursue with determination. Better results from all points of view can be obtained by prolonging resistance.' On 28 June, Marshal Pétain and Admiral Darlan received Gaudillères and Tézé who set out the situation and the wish of their chief to open discussions via the intermediary of the Americans. The conversation, which lasted four hours, ended with the conclusion that discussions were necessary. However, the next day, 29 June, at 10:00 a.m., during the conference that the Admiral had called at the Navy Office at Vichy, there was only talk about sending the reinforcements. Gaudillères was astonished that the vital subject of his mission, the conditions for an armistice, was not touched upon. To the entreaties of the two delegates – 'There are Frenchmen dying on both sides! It has to stop!' – the Admiral answered haughtily that they are 'perhaps two officers qualified to speak on military matters, but who understand absolutely nothing about diplomatic customs' and he brought out of his pocket a note that had already been drawn up: 'The French government is inclined to authorize General Dentz to enter into relations with General Wilson in order to examine the conditions for a cessation of military operations. It goes without saying that the projected negotiations imply the recognition by the British government of the maintenance of all the rights and prerogatives that the mandate assures France over the whole of the territories of Syria and Lebanon.' Tézé, having become aware of this note, expressed doubts about the way in which the proposal is likely to be taken. The Admiral put him in his place, ended the session, and left. Tézé said: 'I left absolutely downhearted, absolutely disgusted and convinced that Admiral Darlan had sabotaged in advance the attempt by General Dentz to put an end to the war, an attempt in which I would have been extremely proud to have taken part to the best of my ability.'

The same evening, Dentz received a telegram encouraging him to not put an end to the resistance. 'Our position will be all the better', he read, 'if our resistance continues to be asserted. A few days gained can be of major importance. It has therefore been decided to speed up the despatch of reinforcements.' It was only ten days later, on 8 July, that Dentz was finally authorised to negotiate.

On the ground, fighting continued but, until 26 June, the fighting in front of Damascus remained sporadic. Only mortar or artillery duels were reported, along with clashes between patrols. The English batteries, probably motorised, moved very quickly, and Vichy French counter-battery fire usually landed in empty gaps. For Dentz, his losses were appreciable. On 27 June the fighting moved northward, towards Nebek and Homs, which, being defended by a weak native garrison, Lavarack had ordered a rather small Free French column to occupy.[1] In addition, *Habforce*, freed by the fall of Palmyra, was now approaching from the east.

At Homs, the Vichy French had now regrouped. The town was full of troops: Senegalese, *spahis*, Circassians and battalions of the Levant cluttered the streets, as well as numerous officers and NCOs who had just arrived from France. The will to fight had not diminished. Captain d'Ornan, a *spahi*, was ordered to mount a counter-attack.[2] His intention was as follows: at daybreak, after having carried out a broad flanking movement through the mountains at night, a mixed mobile group – horses and armoured cars – would attack Nebek from the rear and, at the same time, infantry and seven tanks would launch a frontal attack. However, he was ignorant about espionage activity. The intelligence that the British already had was both precise and recent: they expected the next day a powerful offensive supported by artillery. Seventeen Vichy tanks, they were told, would appear at Deir Atiye, approximately ten kilometres to the north of Nebek. This intelligence was exact, although preparations for the attack had been kept secret. The presence of high-level traitors in the Army of the Levant was confirmed.

All night, the progress of the mobile column was carried out over terrible paths but incomprehensibly, at 5:00 a.m., the order reached it to stop, to suspend the attack and to withdraw. Only the Tunisians and the tanks would attack. It was never known who had sent this order. At midday, the Tunisians, supported by the tanks, pushed in the Gaullist defences and penetrated deeply into the town; then a counter-attack from the flank, led by blacks from the 2nd Marine Battalion, pushed them back under an avalanche of fire. The tanks withdrew. At Homs there was consternation – the general feeling was that the enemy had been warned of the attack. Everyone was convinced of it: by means of spies, the enemy knew the Vichy order of battle and its plans, even the secret ones. The defeat was bitter and the morale of the soldiers was severely dented.

At the end of June, General Wilson was marking time and reorganising. Changing his strategy before the final thrust, he was going to rearrange his forces.[3] Since the fall of Damascus on 21

June, his troop strength was increasing each day. His forces were now about three times greater in number than they were on 8 June[4] whereas the Vichy French were worn out. If, at the time of the invasion, three columns of comparable power had been engaged in parallel, the British strategy would have consisted in concentrating its efforts on Beirut. The interior fronts – Merdjayoun, Jezzine and Homs – would have become secondary. 'A British military principle,' explained Gavin Long, 'is that victory can only be obtained by the offensive, but that attacking everywhere and all the time – the French theory in 1914 – can be disastrous [...] The attack on Mezzé had cost a brigade and that on Merdjayoun almost a third of the total losses. In the light of these experiences, one could conclude that the return to a plan originally conceived of concentration of forces in the direction of Beirut ought to have been adopted earlier.' On 28 June, obeying this new notion of the Commander-in-Chief, Lavarack therefore gave new orders: reinforced by Brigadier Savige's 17th Brigade which had come from Egypt,[5] the 7th Australian Division would concentrate its efforts on Damour, while Major-General Evetts' 6th British Division, also from Egypt, would look after Merdjayoun and Damascus. Thus freed from the interior fronts, the Australians could concentrate all their efforts along the coast.

'From this viewpoint', Gavin Long continued, 'Lavarack was therefore going to have to watch at containing the ambitions of the only one of his subordinates from whom he could expect an attack on a secondary front', that is to say Legentilhomme. The task of the Free French being to protect Damascus against possible counter-offensives, perhaps he wanted to launch a spectacular and politically beneficial offensive in the direction of Northern Syria. On 2 July, Lavarack therefore sent the Frenchman precise instructions, drawn up with tact: 'The force high command does not wish to uselessly reduce your freedom of action in your interpretation of your mission, but it is keen to specify that, for the moment, it would not approve an advance past Nebek.' Lavarack also suggested to Legentilhomme that a senior Australian officer, Lieutenant-Colonel Rogers, 'join his staff and that other British liaison officers be placed under his authority'.

On 28 June, although fighting was still continuing at Jezzine, the invader gave the overall impression of waiting, except at sea where his fleet had reappeared. Its bombardments, added to those of his batteries ashore, had resumed on Damour with the same devastating accuracy. According to the wounded who were evacuated, it was impressive. Constantly battered, Damour and the road north from Beirut were in ruins. Hit by a shell, an ammunition dump blew up, adding even more to the devastation. In an increasingly tense atmosphere, everyone was getting ready for battle. Each person knew that it was there, on the Nahr ed Damour, only 18 km from Beirut, that the war was going to be decided. If Damour fell, Beirut would inevitably fall afterwards. It was the last rampart.

Happily, the position was very strong. To prevent use of the road whose bridge had been blown up, the defence had been entrusted to two particularly tough units, a battalion of Algerian *tirailleurs* and a Legion battalion.[6] Settled in since 17 June, the legionnaires belonging to Major Brisset, an old firebrand, had shifted a lot of earth, using cracks and blind spots to dig in among the natural defences. With covered trenches, shelters under rocks, camouflaged observation posts, barbed wire entanglements swept by automatic weapons, and fire plans drawn up, the position was strong. The gunners had carried out ranging fire on the ravines, observation posts, obligatory crossing points and all other possible targets. From their elevated position, machine guns, mortars and cannon could sweep the countryside. In the background, dogs warned of suspicious movements. More to the left, clinging to the mountains and extending the natural big trench formed by the Damour river, defensive positions facing south[7] defended Beit ed Dine. They had also been reinforced. In front of them, on 29 June, Vichy batteries opened fire on a convoy of 37 trucks which, 2,500 metres from the outposts, unloaded a battalion. About 50 men were mown down. No further doubt was possible: Australian troops were massing for an assault.

The assaulting troops, for their part, were getting ready, destroying everything that they could see opposite them, firing on the Vichy French with all their artillery, trying to overwhelm the Vichy positions. The enemy seemed to see everything. The accuracy of his fire, both on land and from the sea, was astonishing. Infantry position, artillery posts, approaches, reserves, everything was targeted. Camouflage was of no help. Everything seemed to be known to the enemy; it could be said that he had, hour by hour, exact information. No doubt observers with the fleet, using powerful telescopes, informed the gunners ashore and, on the mountain tops, observation posts constantly scanned the countryside, but who knows if spies were active, furthermore, the British fleet, in any case, was firing salvoes with complete impunity, like in an artillery camp, and the battering resumed each day. On land, mobile guns added to it. The Vichy French fire power decreased progressively. Their guns were gradually silenced. As at Saint-Jean-d'Acre in 1799, as in Egypt in 1800, and as in Palestine in 1918, victory in the Middle East was snatched by the sailors.

On the morning of 4 July, in front of Beit ed Dine, the Vichy French had to give up Gharife, their most distant outpost, but it was only a realignment. It was on 5 July that the real battle commenced. At 8:00 a.m., just like the big battles in France in 1918, a general offensive commenced all along the front. Suddenly, the whole line lit up. A bombardment of untold power fell on the Vichy lines. Heavy shells overwhelmed everything, opened up the barbed wire entanglements, and destroyed rebuilt trenches, shelters and firing positions. In the din of the enormous detonations, the roar of steel and stone fragments, the whistling of bullets, the Vichy French had to go to ground. The sheer hell lasted for three hours. Nothing seemed able to stand up to it. How many would survive to face the following assault? Finally, the firing became less frequent. In the bottom of the narrow valley, the first bursts of firing could be heard: having taken up positions during the night, the infantry attack started to climb towards the Vichy French positions. Five battalions in total.

The assault demanded exceptional physical and mental qualities from the Australian soldiers. Few troops would have been capable of such a climb. The edges of the Nahr ed Damour are incredibly steep and the firing was coming from almost at right angles. Grenades, tumbling down the hill, caused havoc far and wide. This battle around the ravine was one of the toughest of the whole campaign. For the Australians, it was Gallipoli over again, that battle that they had fought in similar country in 1915 against the Turks in the Dardanelles. Covered by their machine guns and mortars which had remained on the hilltops, shouting war cries, the Australians nevertheless reached the Vichy French positions which had been practically destroyed, the barbed wire cut to pieces. The Vichy French batteries were almost silenced. Their weakened fire was not sufficient to support the defence. The fighting became hand-to-hand. Two lots of elite troops clashed in a struggle where each person gambled with his life and fought as if he were alone. Grenades, bayonets and automatic weapons were all used to kill each other. In the suffocating heat, the water tanks having been destroyed and the slight trickle of water at the bottom of the ravine being inaccessible, it was very thirsty work. The Australian Lieutenant Roden Cutler[8] received the Victoria Cross[9] for repeated feats of arms. It was the second time that Great Britain had awarded this supreme decoration in Syria.[10]

Gradually, the assaulting troops penetrated the Vichy French positions. The command post of Major Brisset was threatened and he himself was firing. However, the Legion held firm: orders passed and Brisset kept control of his men. During the afternoon, the Australians reached the heights where the tracks were and approached the artillery positions. It was then that, against all odds, they were attacked at the same time by tanks and the Legion. In the centre, the 6th Legion company repulsed the attackers, regained the ground lost and reoccupied its positions. 'While the enemy was withdrawing, the bugler, at the request of Major Brisset, played *Le Boudin* and, standing on the parapet, legionnaires sang the *Chant du départ*[11] loudly.'

Alas, the same thing did not occur on the flanks. The company which, close to the mouth of the river, was defending the approach to the bridge, had been decimated by direct fire from the British fleet. Only a few soldiers managed to escape by climbing the cliffs. In spite of the stubborn resistance of the Algerians holding the mouth of the river, British tanks succeeded in infiltrating along the northern bank of the river. There was the risk that, by following the coast, they would turn the Vichy French positions.

On the left, after a particularly steep night-time descent, followed by a climb between the cliffs, following narrow paths which separate the impassable overhangs, the Australians succeeded in reaching the heights where they took the hamlet of El Boum and, continuing their advance, they even reached a peak which, from three kilometres away, overlooked Damour in ruins. The Vichy French position was practically turned. There were very numerous dead and wounded. Brisset, however, felt that he was still capable of hanging on. To protect his flank, he recalled the garrisons from the posts which, on his right, overlooked the banana grove. During the night, they reached the crest which, behind him, towered above the village of Damour. The enemy would not surprise them. About 8:00 p.m., he reported, in writing, his situation to the colonel commanding the sub-sector. Brisset did not at all care for the attitude of this officer who had never come to visit his posts nor, at any time, had telephoned to encourage his men. In his message, Brisset gave assurances that he could hold on if he was resupplied with water and if ammunition could be brought to the nearest posts. But, at 9:00 p.m., to his consternation and horror, Brisset received an order to leave and go and set up new positions 15 km to the north, at Kfarchima, a village close to Baabda, that is to say at the gates of Beirut! Brisset did not understand. He was master of his defences. Wasn't he blocking the Australians? The Legion was holding firm. If he withdrew, what good would have been the dead whose bodies were there, visible on the barbed wire, on the slopes and at the bottom of the ravine? An indignant Brisset sent the courier back with an explanatory note and a request for confirmation. The orderly left and was soon back, bringing the answer. He had to carry out the order. Brisset was furious and left his posts in which his unit had lost 65 per cent of its strength.

'During the night, a long line of shadows, haggard, covered with sweat, dust and blood, because many of the wounded continued to fight, started its retreat. A succession of small columns of dispirited men, carrying their weapons and ammunition, climbed into the mountains, scaling cliffs and then moving down the slopes. As if by chance or as if they knew, the Australians interrupted their artillery fire. The quietness surprised. The disengagement took place without a rifle shot. Nothing replied to the stone that was dislodged, the noise of a water bottle that was knocked, or the curse of a fellow who tripped in the darkness. Pain, thirst and fatigue suddenly weighed very heavily. Fatigue hit men crushed by disappointment and bitterness. Their resistance was broken.[12] The withdrawal of the Legion left the Australians practically free to advance. Between the Australians and the capital, the road was no longer guarded except by Captain de Lanlay's battalion of Algerians, who were overlooked by the crests that Brisset had just abandoned, and who remained on the lookout in the ruins of the village.

In Beirut, the general staff had followed the fighting anxiously and then with consternation. The order to disengage given to the Legion surprised everyone. It did not come from Beirut, and Captain Le Corbeiller, a staff officer, attributed the responsibility for the catastrophic abandonment to the colonel commanding the Damour sector, without naming him. Dentz telegraphed France: 'The situation is very grave. I am heavily threatened at Aleppo and Beirut [...] The loss of one or the other would bring to an end all serious resistance [...] We can no longer count on [...] the reinforcements arriving in sufficient numbers to redress the situation [...] I ask you to let me know on the one hand where we are as regards negotiations being opened, on the other, if the situation here became hopeless, on what bases and directions I would be authorised to enter into contact with the British.'

Now, it was no longer a case of hanging on as long as possible. General Dentz took the telephone himself and spoke to Lanlay who was in command of the Algerians who had remained on the Nahr ed Damour. Gravely, he ordered him to hold the village 'without thought of retreat' and to defend it to the death.

After having counted the remaining units, there was no other solution than to recall troops from Damascus. He therefore ordered Keime, who was in command there, to send to Beirut a battalion of the 29th Algerian Tirailleur Regiment. Driving all through the night, a column of trucks left for Khan Meissaloun to pick up the unit, which had descended with great strides from their positions in the mountains, and then took them with all possible speed to Ain Traz, five kilometres to the north of Damour where the approach of the Australians was already reported. These men were exhausted. If their mission was to counter-attack, were they still capable of it?

As soon as the Algerians reached the last positions of the Brisset battalion, on the morning of 5 July, the Australians reacted. The artillery – both land-based and the guns of the fleet – started firing again, with all its power concentrated on them. Pounded, massacred, unable to move, they remained there, hacked to pieces, useless. Their sacrifice was in vain, dead and wounded were scattered all over the area where, as soon as the firing stopped, the Australians advanced and moved through. Imploring help from those passing by, the wounded, said the survivors, often received only kicks, blows from a rifle butt, and sometimes a bullet to shorten their suffering. Dying without water, without shade, without help under a burning sun, some remained there for three days before anyone came to look for them.

On the afternoon of 6 July, the colonel commanding the Damour sub-sector reported to Beirut about his situation which was henceforth hopeless. For him, it was over. The Australians, he said, had surrounded his command post. He was going to have to surrender. Dentz, once more, took the telephone to tell him that they were going to do their utmost to extract him from there. Major de Carmejane – from Sannamein – was rushing towards him with three armoured cars. He reached the ruins of Damour that he passed through and, on a moonlit night, spoke to the *tirailleurs* of the 22nd who, calmly and in good order, were setting up fresh positions to face the new threat that had appeared on their left. Oddly, the withdrawal by the Legion on orders had not been exploited on the coast: the Australians had not even established contact. So where were these enemy soldiers who had threatened the colonel's post so closely? Moreover, where was the colonel himself? He was soon picked up by the sailors from the observation post set up to the north of Damour to keep an eye on the British fleet. Pushed, urged on, and brought back, at the double, a kilometre behind the lines, then hidden in a hole awaiting rescue, he had been surprised there by the Australians. Taken to Palestine, 'he was one of those who preferred not to return to France at the end of the fighting', indicated Le Corbeiller who had the delicacy not to mention his name.

To try to recover the troops still in place, everything had to be sent, even the old FT[13] tanks dating from the previous war, which were so slow. Six of them left Khalde, three broke down and the three remaining took four hours to cover the last 800 metres over difficult terrain, with ditches and low walls. Two turned over and had to righted, another lost a track, but at nightfall, these few vehicles were behind the Algerians. Naval gunfire killed their commander and forced those who remained, after this last-ditch mission, to destroy the immobile hulls, which were out of ammunition and without communications. Under fire from the Australians posted on the hilltops, the Algerians, who were still trying to hang on close to the mouth of the river, were soon killed by naval gunfire. Only a few scattered groups managed to return. Carmejane and his armoured cars attempted to cover their withdrawal. All night long, his vehicles patrolled the road looking for stragglers, finally reaching a small defensive position set up at Khalde.

Ordered on the evening of 7 July to replace his faltering predecessor, Colonel Georges-Picot immediately set out for Khalde – only six kilometres south of Beirut – to regroup those who had escaped, reorganise them, pass out the remaining weapons and, with the remnants of the Legion and the two remaining FT tanks, set up a defensive position. But Khalde was on the plain, without reserves and without artillery, and the men were exhausted: what hope could be placed in this weak plan?

As day broke on 8 July, everything was quiet. In their holes, close by their weapons, automatons rather than soldiers, the men were sleeping, tired out after a horrible night. Would the position hold if the enemy approached? Where are they? What are they waiting for? The news was confused, often contradictory. Explosions were heard. Some of the Vichy French artillery batteries which remained, it was said, would undertake counter-battery fire, others would withdraw, but which ones? Where to?

Opposite, Lavarack felt that the Vichy French had reached the limits of their endurance, but his troops were also very tired. 'While withdrawing', he said, 'the enemy is resisting stubbornly on all fronts and our progress is slow. If one considers that the two adversaries are equally exhausted, one must conclude', he wrote surprisingly, 'that today's disappointing results are due more to our troops' lack of offensive spirit than to the enemy's will'. The Australian therefore halted the advance. On 9 and 10 July, the Australians were only in evidence by their artillery fire, especially on Khalde, over which the French flag still flew, but on 10 July at 9:00 a.m., Georges-Picot realised: The Australians have been on the tops of the hills for about an hour. They did not advance along the road but via the heights. About midday, from his outpost, a number of small columns could be seen in the distance moving towards the sea. The Australians were coming closer. About midday, protected by armoured cars which, on the road, attempted a delaying action, Georges-Picot and his men had just enough time to break off smartly and withdraw to the *caravanserai* of Chouaïfète, five kilometres from the capital. So Khalde was lost. It was the end, in an atmosphere of going in for the kill. With the exception of Merdjayoun and the pocket of defence at Jezzine, Lebanon was lost. Le Corbeiller: 'A simple push by the Australian infantry and everything would collapse since the Vichy French troops were exhausted.' Only the action of the officers and NCOs kept the troops on the alert and, without them, there would be a headlong flight, known only too well to those who had fought in France in 1940. 'During these few days, the officers and NCOs showed exemplary courage, an unshakeable will, and an energy worthy of the highest praise.' No matter that: 'The Australians were at the gates of Beirut. Faced with the decay of the [Vichy] Army, it seemed useless to carry on a fight which, sooner or later, would inevitably end in defeat. Thus the decision was taken to ask for an armistice.'

During the night of 9 July, Dentz sent two telegrams to Vichy and received authorisation to enter into negotiations, as soon as he judged it necessary, with the 'local' British authorities, with a view to stopping the fighting. Darlan's agreement was matched with a formal condition: to negotiate only with the British, to the exclusion of the Gaullists.[14] Upon receipt of this message, Dentz submitted a request to Mr Van Egert, American Consul-General, for a ceasefire to be sent to Cairo, containing the following sentence: 'Let England not impose upon us unworthy conditions, we will not accept them, such as installing the Gaullists in our place or forcing us to deal with them.' Van Egert sent the message. The answer came the next day.

The High Commissioner's office informed the Italian Armistice Commission that it was no longer able to guarantee their safety. General de Giorgis, their chief, tried to obtain the destruction of the refinery in Tripoli, the pipeline from Iraq and some railway lines, but Dentz refused. The Italians then disappeared on the last trains leaving for Turkey. It was now a matter of saving the jewels, the Air Force and Navy. The following order was sent to General Jeannekyn: 'Upon reception of the present order, the general commanding the Air Force in the Levant will send away his flying units. No destruction will be carried out.'[15] On the afternoon of 11 July, all aircraft able to fly, about 50 in number, took off for French North Africa, via Athens, carrying with them the flags and banners, as well as a contingent of English prisoners, 39 officers and 13 NCOs, who were sent to Salonika to be despatched to France by train.[16] A similar order for evacuation was sent to the Navy. Admiral Goujon carried it out.[17]

Having received the request for an armistice, the British consulted General de Gaulle about a response. Their planned answer sprang from the conditions that de Gaulle had indicated just before the conflict broke out and that, in a letter of 7 June to the leader of Free France, Churchill had accepted. He declared himself in favour of an 'honourable arrangement' with the High Commissioner of Vichy in the Levant: 'All military men and public servants who wish to, may remain, as well as their families, the others being repatriated later [...] All arrangements must be carried out by the Allies so that this choice is truly free [...] Never having put on trial those of my Army comrades who have previously fought me in carrying out orders they received, I have no intention of doing so in the present case.'

On 3 July, Mr Anthony Eden, British Minister of Foreign Affairs, nonetheless wrote to Mr Oliver Lyttelton whom he envisaged sending to Cairo as Minister of State, that 'the British government has never promised to substitute the Free French for the Dentz administration nor to govern Syria in the name of France [...] His Majesty's Government would not accept such a policy of the Free French which would contradict its major decision, to permit Syria and all people to attain independence [...] As long as military operations continue and probably until signature of the necessary treaty is accepted by His Majesty's Government, British martial law, already in place, will continue to be applied.'[18] Thus Great Britain secretly reserved the right to limit the powers of Free France. From just before the Armistice, the rot had set in.[19]

On 9 July, Mr Van Egert brought General Dentz the British response to his request for a suspension of hostilities:

> The Allies had no other goal in Syria than to prevent it serving as a base for enemy forces. The Allies have no resentment of any sort against the French in Syria and are willing to agree to a full armistice regarding the recent fighting. They have no grievance against any of the leaders, authorities or troops in Syria. General de Gaulle, who has never dealt ruthlessly with any of his Army comrades who have fought against him in the execution of orders they have received, has no intention of doing so in the present circumstances. Full liberty must be given to French troops in Syria to join the Allied forces. Those of their number who are not disposed to join the Allied cause will be repatriated with their families.

Transmitted immediately to Vichy, the text was accepted and Dentz given the power to negotiate.

The announcement of the request for an armistice incensed General Lavarack so much that he sent a disapproving note to his superior in Cairo, General Sir Thomas Blamey: The BBC in London had announced this very morning, he said, that Canberra had already openly reported the [Vichy] French request. He considered that it was premature and likely to decrease his men's energy. 'The proximity of an armistice can hold back the troops from producing that little extra effort which so often makes the difference between success and failure. No one likes to risk his life if he knows that the campaign is coming to an end. I can't stress enough that any negotiation of an armistice must be kept absolutely secret until the last possible moment. The question must be submitted to the Prime Minister in such a way to ensure that no indiscretion of a similar magnitude can be committed by a member of his cabinet in the future.'[20]

The French request, in fact, did not remain secret for very long. In a speech given on the same day, 9 July, in the Commons, Churchill declared:

We have just received from General Dentz an official request asking for armistice talks. I scarcely need to say with what satisfaction His Majesty's Government will see the end of this distressing conflict in which 1,000 to 1,500 British, Australian and Indian soldiers have been killed or wounded, soldiers who voluntarily joined the army to defend France. It was French bullets which shot them, a consequence of the deplorable disarray in which so many worthy people in so many parts of the world have found themselves following the victories of Hitler's armies. For my part, I will open these discussions willingly, and I like to believe that they will end quickly. But in waiting for a military agreement in accordance with the relevant rules, military operations will naturally be continued with undiminished energy.

The day went by. In front of Damascus, at Merdjayoun and Jezzine, fighting continued but, at Beirut, everything was quiet. On the night of 10 July, a message from General Maitland Wilson arrived by radio at the Grand Serail in Beirut. There was no question of negotiations: on the contrary, it was an ultimatum. The Englishman demanded, under threat of bombardment, that Beirut be immediately declared an open city,. On 11 July, Wilson renewed his demand: 'I repeat my call to you. Withdraw your troops and declare Beirut an open city.' Dentz, who only a year previously, on 13 June 1940, had already lived through the drama of having to surrender a capital to the enemy, did not answer this message. He was right: it was intimidation. Abandoning this demand, Wilson, still by radio, announced that his command did not have any reservation regarding the choice of plenipotentiaries. If they presented themselves before 9:00 a.m., local time, with a white flag at the British outposts on the Beirut–Damour road, hostilities would cease at midday. Two hours later, Dentz responded by the same channel: 'Kindly wait until 6:00 p.m. [...] I will then contact in clear the Commander-in-Chief of the forces in the Middle East via the intermediary of Admiral Godfroy [at Alexandria] [...] I will then reply to the memorandum of His Majesty's Government concerning the cessation of hostilities.' At the appointed time, the Commander-in-Chief of the [Vichy] French Forces in the Levant announced that he would agree to negotiate on the basis of the memorandum that had been handed to him by Mr Van Egert, the American Consul-General. He proposed that a ceasefire come into effect at midday on 12 July. He would send a negotiator, being understood that it was not a plenipotentiary, who was authorised to deal only with a military representative of the High Command. Wilson agreed and, at 11:45 a.m. via the intermediary of the United States, London had handed a new memorandum to Vichy at the same time as at Beirut. The Free French were associated with the British request:

> The Allies have committed themselves to the Arab population by giving it [...] a guarantee of independence [...] The representation of the French in the Levant will be carried out by the Free French authorities within the framework of the promise of independence that they have given to Syria and Lebanon and in which Great Britain herself is associated [...] The British do not have any resentment regarding the French in Syria and are willing to accord a full amnesty as regards recent hostilities. They will not embark upon any legal proceedings against the French command, the [Vichy] authorities nor against the troops [...] The [Vichy] French troops in Syria [...] must be allowed full latitude to join the Allied forces. The Allies reserve the right to take all measures necessary to assure themselves that each man's choice is truly free [...] All combatants who are not inclined to join the Allied cause will be repatriated with their families if and when circumstances allow [...] Equipment and naval units will be handed over intact in order to be interned. The restoration of these units at the end of the war or payment of damages to France are guaranteed, provided friendly relations are in place. All British prisoners will be released.

Dentz informed Vichy that, in the absence of instructions to the contrary, he was inclined to hold discussions and proposed that a ceasefire come into force that very day, at midnight on 12 July. He specified that he intended 'to deal only with the British military authorities to the exclusion of the Gaullist representatives.'

Vichy's response reached Beirut via the intermediary of the cruiser *Duquesne* interned at Alexandria. Admiral Godfroy: 'The British Commander-in-Chief cannot accept any, I repeat any, reservation concerning the [Allied] plenipotentiaries. Unless General Dentz's present themselves [...] at the British outposts on the Beirut-Haifa road [...] at 9:00 a.m. local time, 12 July 1941, offensive action will resume.' Darlan replied: 'The French government cannot lend itself, under any pretext whatsoever, to negotiations with Frenchmen who are traitors to their motherland such as de Gaulle and Catroux.'

At 3:10 a.m., only six hours before the meeting, General Huntziger dictated to Beirut the bases of the discussions which must be adhered to.

> The principal aim to pursue must be, by keeping the army in good order until the end, to take advantage of the magnificent morale that it has shown to avoid large numbers joining the Gaullists, at the same time bending to the conditions imposed by the British concerning the free choice to be given to the troops between loyalty and rebellion [...] The convention that you are authorised to sign can deal only with military and technical matters. It must not contain any political element that could involve the future.

The objectives are the following:

> Solemn recognition of the rights of France in Lebanon and Syria, the wish to see her authority recognised 'symbolically' over a fraction of the territory. Return of the troops with their equipment, maintenance on the spot of public servants with technical skills and even in positions of authority under the authority of the British occupying power [...] The negotiations must not involve any compromise with the rebels. Weapons which will not be removed, must be destroyed [...] to refuse all support by public servants to an administration by the rebels [...] to demand from public servants who are kept in office a declaration of loyalty to the Marshal's government.

On 11 July, Admiral Gouton had already made known to the French Admiralty that it had to envisage the repatriation of about 32,000 people, made up of 25,000 servicemen and 7,000 civilians.[21]

The battle continued nevertheless. The British wanted to finish with it, and the French troops were aware of the request for an armistice. It was thus more necessary than ever to struggle to keep them fighting. It was particularly important for them to be able to say that they weren't beaten in the field. Although Beit ed Dine had been captured, the Legion was still fighting at Jezzine. At Merdjayoun, on the other hand, all resistance having become futile, Albord was at the end of his tether when he received the order to withdraw his troops. Patrols from the Border Regiment and the Durham Light Infantry discovered one morning that, on the heights above the Litani river, the Vichy French had disappeared from all their positions. Albord had kept the doors to the Bekaa Valley closed until the end, but now they were wide open.

In front of Damascus, under the command of Colonel Péfontan, the Vichy French remained solidly entrenched in dominating positions which they defended grimly, notably on the hills of the Jebel Mazaar whose tops overlooked Damascus and the Ghouta. On the right, somewhat lower, rose the Jebel Habil, at the base of which stood Khan Meissaloun, Keime's command post. At the beginning of July, reconnaissance by the RAF had revealed that the defenders had probably not reduced their defensive power in machine guns, mortars and cannon. On 23 June, during a first attack against Georges-Picot's men at Dimas,[22] the English of the 6th British Division had lost an entire company. The same failure was repeated on 26 June. After several other attempts, Lavarack telephoned Wilson on 9 July that 'the enemy is still resisting and everywhere is trying to counter-attack'.

On the night of 10 July, Major-General Evetts launched what he hoped would be a decisive offensive by the 16th Brigade which had just arrived from Egypt. The unit was fresh. Under the command of Brigadier Cyril Lomax,[23] it would be its first attack, with strong artillery support. The Queens would have to reach the summit to the west – 1,427 metres – and the King's Own the two others – 1,455 and 1,404 metres respectively. The Free French of the BIM[24] would attack the Jebel Habil in parallel. Launched at night, the attack developed well but, as soon as day broke, the Vichy cannon fire erupted and blocked all assaults. Pinned down by fire and counter-attacked in the early dawn by Moroccans of the 5th Battalion, 1st Moroccan Tirailleur Regiment, the Free French rapidly found themselves in such difficulties that Evetts withdrew them. The 2nd Leicesters replaced them. On the left, the 2nd King's Own and the 2nd Queen's climbed in a lively manner the barren and broken slopes of the Jebel Maazar. Going all out in a violent storm, the King's Own reached the summit which it captured at bayonet point at the end of the morning. At the top, Captain Allan Murchison[25] discovered a French officer hiding under a ground sheet and pointed his pistol at him. 'It is useless,' said the Frenchman, 'there are no Germans here'. 'Well then' retorted the Australian, 'what of it?' The Frenchman, taken aback, said 'But..then..why are you fighting?' 'Because I've been told to!' replied Murchison.[26]

Was the scene invented? One might think so, the setting, the situation, the storm, everything seemed prepared for this brief dialogue which epitomised the drama. The discipline, the good and bad reasons, the ambiguity of this futile war, the spirit of sacrifice, everything was said by these two officers who were subject to the same ethics and who were ready to kill each other.

Under artillery and machine-gun fire, many officers fell. The King's Own was disorganised. Counter-attacked by the Vichy French, it could not hold on and, at 4:45 p.m., judging the situation dangerous, General Evetts gave the order for a general withdrawal. Not easy to do, under fire. It was impossible to extract two companies of the Queen's from the hills, who, isolated, were captured. For this battalion, from which the Vichy French had already captured 80 prisoners the day before, the losses became disquieting. A relief was obviously needed. A unit which had fought in Crete and which had also come from Egypt, the 14th Brigade, then came to relieve the 16th.

On the road out of Dimas, at the entrance to the Barada gorge, an armoured element of the 9th Australian Division Cavalry, equipped with Mark VI tanks, tried to force its way through, but the Mark VI was not up to the job. It was only a type of large carrier equipped with a turret. Everywhere it had been engaged, it had suffered heavy losses. The unfortunate crews, however, advanced courageously under intense fire and scarcely had they entered the gorge than a tank was destroyed. Taken prisoner, two members of the crew – the third, wounded, was sent to hospital – declared that they had arrived, with 35 other tanks of the same type, from Palestine eight days previously. It was their first attack. Progression was therefore impossible along the road. To prevent a return of the Vichy French who had retreated into the Anti-Lebanon Mountains, a Free French section of R-35 tanks, recovered at Damascus and painted with a Cross of Lorraine, was sent to watch the exit from the gorge. To enter would have been suicidal.

The fighting on the Jebel Maazar, the last, was a remarkable success for Dentz's troops. For his resistance until the last day, Colonel Péfontan received an exceptional citation in Army Orders: 'A superior officer of very great bravery, a remarkable organizer [...] Commanding the resistance at Dimas [Jebel Maazar] on 10, 11 and 12 July 1941, was violently attacked all along the front of his sector by an enemy with large mechanised forces and an overwhelming numerical superiority [...] Kept the position intact, inflicting enormous losses on his adversary, taking more than 300 prisoners, including ten officers.'

And what was the view in the opposing ranks? Christopher Buckley: 'The enemy had unleashed heavy gunfire without following it up with an infantry attack. The reality was that his gunfire was covering his own withdrawal. His troops were extremely tired and weakened by our attacks. This last day, the Vichy artillery began to suffer greatly from our gunfire directed by the RAF. When, after the fighting was over, we could inspect the [Vichy] French positions, we noted that four 75mm guns had been destroyed by the intense firing, lasting 20 minutes, by eight of our 25pdr guns. The French command could moreover allow itself a retreat: a series of equally strong defences was already prepared behind. While we were withdrawing towards the plain, the Vichy troops were doing the same towards a line of hills about ten kilometres away.'

These were the last hours for everyone.

A ceasefire was ordered on 12 July. At one minute past midnight, all fighting stopped. The war in the Levant had lasted 34 days.

17

Armistice at Saint-Jean-d'Acre

At 8:00 a.m., the July sun, already high, cast its light over the bay. Under the direction of General de Verdilhac, the file of cars of the High Commission and the Military Staff left Beirut, carrying the French negotiators. The delegation counted a dozen people, high-ranking public servants and officers of the three services, including Captain Le Corbeiller. Barely a few kilometres away, to the south of Khalde, on the front line, Australian motorcyclists were awaiting them, to flank them as they made their way to Palestine, going in the reverse direction back along the road where, for more than a month, so many fierce battles occurred. On the right, the sea glittered, on the left, life resumed: shepherds had brought out their flocks. Everywhere, military equipment could be seen, with wrecks and traces of battle. They often had to slow down to get around the ruins, avoid holes and cross temporary bridges. All looked on in silence. There was Damour, shattered; beneath the bridge, wrecked tanks could be seen. On the seafront at Sidon, the people were moving about and ruined buildings could be seen. To the south of the city, at the beginning of the road that goes to Merdjayoun, the burned-out shells of the trucks of the Bocquillon column were lined up one behind the other, then they came to Adloun, the Litani river where Le Corné sacrificed himself, and finally Nakoura, the stages of this hard fighting in reverse order. Everywhere, the cars received military honours.

After Nakoura, it was Palestine. Twenty kilometres further on and they came to Saint-Jean-d'Acre. The cars left the highway and stopped in the courtyard of a barracks, the Sidney Smith Barracks.[1] The Vichy French got out and entered a light room whose bay windows looked on to a lawn. In the distance, the sea sparkled. The big T-shaped table, which occupied the centre of the room, was covered in military blankets: paper and pencils were placed in front of each seat. General Wilson, who was president of the Allied delegation, was waiting, surrounded by officers. At the entry of the Vichy French, all rose. They saluted each other. The reception was imposing. To the strong annoyance of the delegation from Beirut, some representatives of Free France were present, standing alongside the British. Churchill had imposed their presence at the last minute. There were General Catroux, Colonel Brosset, Colonel Vallin and Captain Répiton-Préneuf. Catroux was on Wilson's right. All sat down. The delegations were facing each other.[2] Le Corbeiller, who was watching the Free French, felt 'their dull hatred'. Répiton-Préneuf, who was opposite him, also remembers: 'They were looking at us and we were looking at them. Their eyes avoided Catroux and those surrounding him to fix their gaze on Wilson, Lavarack, the officers of the Royal Navy and the RAF, but they could not stop their gaze sliding towards us.' Conty, Director of Political Affairs at the High Commission, and Répiton-Préneuf, of the Free French Forces, acted as interpreters.

At the time the conference opened, General de Gaulle was taking off from Cairo for Brazzaville. He suspected a dirty trick. He did not believe that Churchill was sincere. He feared that the British would take possession of the Levant. He preferred to distance himself: 'I had no other way to limit the damage than to leave space and rise above it, to find a cloud and to melt from there on to an agreement which did not commit me and that I would tear up as much as possible. The cloud was Brazzaville.' Aware of his suspicions, Churchill had written a personal letter to him on 6 June, sending de Gaulle his best wishes for success in the war and confirming that Great Britain 'does not seek any special benefit in the French Empire'. The Prime Minister had repeated these remarks in the House of Commons on 10 June, maintaining that he would do 'all that is in his power to restore the independence and rights of France'. All the same, de Gaulle did not believe him. He had already returned several times to this point, essential in his eyes: it was that Free France which, in the name of France, must exercise authority over the mandate. On 19 June, in a letter addressed conjointly to Sir Miles Lampson, British Ambassador in Cairo, and to General Wavell,[3] he stressed again the political independence of the representatives of France in the Levant. On the eve of the talks, he reaffirmed once more 'that he considered it necessary that his representative takes part in the negotiations and that the response given to Beirut be in his name as well as in that of the British authorities'.[4] And he again recalled 'the guarantee given by Great Britain that the rights and interests of France in the Levant will be maintained, the representation of France in the Levant being carried out by the Free French authorities'. In a note left before his departure on 13 July, de Gaulle hammered out the same theme: 'The supreme authority in Syria belongs to France and does not belong in any way [...] to a foreign commander-in-chief [that is to say General Wilson]. The British troops do not occupy Syria as a conquered country, but collaborate in a battle on allied territory.' Will this essential demand be heard and agreed to?

On the eve of the talks, relates René Cassin, a telegram from Mr Anthony Eden to the British Ambassador in Washington did not contain the slightest mention of any participation by Free France in the next round of talks and, when General de Gaulle drew his attention to the gravity of this omission, the British minister did not modify his instructions in any way. The diplomats were evidently reluctant. The British military were, moreover, no more anxious than the diplomats to see the Free French control the Levant. They were career soldiers. They obeyed their government and did not care for rebellion in a regular army. They distrusted rebels, even when they were allies. In London as much as in Washington, General de Gaulle's initiative in starting a fratricidal war was not greatly appreciated. Churchill himself doubtless regretted it: 'In putting up a fierce resistance, the French army in Syria clearly indicated on what side, according to it, was the legal government of its country and that it intended remaining loyal to it.'[5] Although suspicious of their adversaries, it seems that sometimes the British had greater esteem for the Vichy troops than for the Free French. Nevertheless, could the Vichy troops become allies after what had just happened? The British did not want to encourage the coming over of the Vichy French troops to the Gaullist side.

Addressing Wilson, Verdilhac avoided looking at Catroux. At first the tone was courteous and simple.[6] The English showed themselves to be conciliatory right from the beginning. General Wilson: 'Do you agree that the troops take with them into the collecting areas all the weapons that they had on the battlefield?' "Of course," Verdilhac agreed, the concern of both leaders being to maintain order. The Englishman then worried about the recovery of weapons held by the Arab reserve troops.

Verdilhac: 'I agree, all the more as I have always had a great deal of apprehension in giving weapons to the natives.' Maintenance of law and order in the cities was then envisaged, in order to avoid disturbances, looting and acts of violence. Wilson showed himself to be particularly cooperative. 'What are your suggestions? What is the best method?' and the Englishman called to mind his bad experiences in Libya. Verdilhac: 'I do not think that there will be trouble. Everything is quiet.' Nevertheless, a protocol was hammered out: timetables, handover of powers, resumption of posts, etc. Verdilhac added: 'General Wilson has spoken of Libya. I would like to stress that over there it was the Italians and here it is the French. There is a difference [...] [Laughs from the British delegation, noted the stenographer]'. It can be seen that they were men of the same world. Catroux then started to speak. Faces hardened on all sides, looks became tense, and the atmosphere became hostile. If the British proposal for an armistice was broadly inspired by General de Gaulle's note, it seemed to ignore the essential point in his eyes, the solemn recognition of the rights of Free France in Syria. Catroux then asked the question of Wilson, who avoided answering him: 'I have decided not to broach this question which is not part of the remit of this conference.' Répiton-Préneuf then read aloud in English General de Gaulle's memorandum asking the French public servants to remain in place. Verdilhac fell into line with Wilson's attitude: 'I am a soldier. I deal only with military questions. I can't know the proposals contained in this document, but I will send their terms to my government.' Pretending to be ignorant of his presence, Verdilhac did not address Catroux. He then informed Wilson that [Vichy] France could pay for the repatriation of members of the French Army who do not want to join the Gaullists. The safety of ships sailing under the French flag must obviously be guaranteed. The military equipment would be left in Syria. The local units would be placed under the command of Free France, reminded General Catroux: these are absolutely essential conditions laid down by General de Gaulle.

The conversation then became heated. Verdilhac:

> Our weapons are reduced in quality and quantity. We have fought honourably with very little. Our weapons are worn out. The [Vichy] French command understands clearly that all the weaponry cannot follow the French troops in their repatriation, but it earnestly requests, very insistently, that it not return home

like a dishonoured army, and that the troops keep at least a part of the weapons which will serve as badges of honour [...] The weapons that we do not take with us will be destroyed. If you take our weapons from us, if you do not give us the responsibility of destroying them, under your control, we will be dishonoured.

Wilson: 'I understand perfectly [...] I agree to leave your soldiers their rifles [...] Your flags will be left with you.' Verdilhac: 'Our flags have left for France, but I thank you for your thought.' If individual weapons were left with the [Vichy] French, Wilson on the other hand made the surrender of crew-served weapons a matter of principle: 'We could have need of them to fight the Germans.' This condition was so non-negotiable that the Englishman refused the Frenchman authorisation to consult Dentz on the telephone. Verdilhac found the solution: the weapons retained by the British Army *for its own use* will be handed over to it, the [Vichy] French will destroy the remainder themselves. Wilson agreed. Then came the important question of the way that Vichy troops could join the Free French. The memorandum stipulated: 'Complete liberty [for each member of the Army of the Levant] to join the Allied forces in their struggle against the Axis forces, the Allies reserving the right to take appropriate measures to ensure the liberty and the sincerity of each person's choice.' Probably at the request of General Catroux, General Wilson asked that the following be added to the text: 'To ensure that each individual is free, it will necessary that representatives of the Allied forces [that is the Free French] have direct access to the troops.'

That was the crucial point. Verdilhac immediately objected to this clause, that was not in the memorandum, that was so foreign to his instructions that he threatened to break off the talks if it were kept. 'It would be a dangerous thing', he stated, 'if representatives of Free France could come into the lines to carry out direct propaganda to the men [...] Serious incidents would be sure to occur'. Catroux, who had until then avoided from intervening too much, answered him directly. General de Gaulle, hoping to find in the Levant a large source of recruits, the question for him was essential. How to avoid a confrontation? Catroux and Verdilhac, who knew each other, faced off. Verdilhac: 'I am keen to ask a last question on the manner in which the representatives of Free France intend to act in carrying out their propaganda among our troops.' Catroux: 'Our action will be carried out without any pressure whatsoever. What we want to do is to enlighten the troops. We will set out the goals of Free France, without any partisan remarks, and the necessity of continuing the struggle against Germany.' Verdilhac, who was still controlling his emotions: 'I would like to have precise details about the way that you will act in practice among the men in the lines and bivouacs.' Catroux: 'I remain the judge of the ways and means for that, and I decline to give you any precise details on the matter! Will you admit to us that we will meet your officers and that we will say to them: here are our goals, here is what we want?' The tone of voice was now serious. Verdilhac: 'This army has as its head Marshal Pétain [...] I cannot admit that other officers wearing French uniform come into our units to say: "You must no longer obey", disparage the leaders of [Vichy] France, perhaps attack the person of the Head of State!' Catroux: 'We will make no personal attack against any member of the government. The devotion to the person of Marshal Pétain will not be called into question [...] We will not exert any pressure [...] We want to make our aims known [...] We want people who rally to our cause of their own free will.' Verdilhac did not give way. The exchange became more acrimonious. Catroux ended by declaring: 'If you have obtained the conditions that you wished from the British high command, you owe it to Free France!' Verdilhac then exploded. Red with anger, he stood up, walked towards Catroux, stopped two metres from him and retorted: 'I cannot listen to more of this! I won't! I admit that a British general can say such things but not you, General. The Army of the Levant recognises only one head, Marshal Pétain. It is entirely devoted to him. [The Army of the Levant] has proven it during the course of these 35 days of fighting which unfortunately ended badly for it but in which it has shown magnificent bravery. It is in the name of this army that General Dentz asked the British authorities, and not others, for a cessation of hostilities [...] For me, a French officer, when a Marshal of France orders me to do something, I salute and I obey!'

And looking daggers at Catroux, Verdilhac, clicked his heels and saluted. Then Catroux, ever the diplomat, calmed the situation: 'Given the position taken by General de Verdilhac', he said, 'I withdraw the extra sentence proposed for the text'.

The British were stupefied by the spectacle. To cut short the exchange, Wilson asked that they return to the problem of the propaganda. The two Frenchmen sat down. After long exchanges, polite but very tense, it was decided that there would be no personal contact between the Free French and the others. The Gaullists could use pamphlets, loudspeakers and the radio. The choice of each soldier will be strictly personal. No pressure will be exerted on anyone. And Wilson, who feared further incidents between these quarrelsome Frenchmen, added: 'The intervention of British officers can be requested by the [Vichy] French authorities if these latter consider it necessary.' When the negotiations ended, it was 10:50 a.m. The heads of the two delegations initialled the text that had been drawn up, and agreed to meet again in two days' time, on 14 July, after having consulted their respective governments. The British knew that the [Vichy] French were stuck and that they were in no position to demand.

'In a general manner', wrote General Wilson later, 'the discussions took place calmly, although on one occasion I was afraid that the war would start again when Generals Catroux and Verdilhac launched into a furious discussion'.

Consulted, Darlan agreed overall and asked only for changes in the wording. [Vichy] France not being at war with Great Britain, the word 'armistice', in particular, did not suit him. He asked that it be replaced by 'Franco-British accord on the cessation of hostilities in the Levant'. The Admiral also asked that the term 'occupation forces' replace that of 'Allied forces' which, according to him, 'may suggest that the French government recognizes the Free French'. As for the right to incite defections from among the [Vichy] French troops, the Admiral objected strongly against this. Without opposing it formally, he recalled that soldiers who chose Free France would fall under the weight of the law for desertion, at the same time risking the loss of nationality, the confiscation of property and possibly the death penalty.

On 14 July at 10:53 a.m., the talks resumed. Verdilhac presented the wishes and remarks of his government. Wilson agreed to substitute 'accord' for 'armistice', but refused to change 'Allied forces' which for him covered the British, Australians and Indians. He was keen on it. The word was thus retained. Finally, the accord was concluded on the following bases: grouped together in assembly zones, the units of Dentz's army would be repatriated to France on French ships with their personal weapons. The civilians who so wish would be able to return home with the army. No soldier will be able to leave the Levant if he opted beforehand for a return to France. The heavy weapons and transport will be handed over to the British. The [Vichy] prisoners will be handed back by the British as soon as all those held by the

[Vichy] French have reached Palestine. The British Army and the Free French will occupy the mandated states conjointly. Under the presidency of the English General Chrystall,[7] a tripartite control commission will oversee the application of the Armistice convention. Sitting at Aaley, near Beirut, it will comprise General de Verdilhac for the [Vichy] French Army and Colonel Kœnig[8] for Free France. General Wilson assured General Catroux, who did not sign, that the accord conforms to General de Gaulle's wishes. Catroux believed him, and it did, but with the exception of one principal clause, the solemn recognition of French sovereignty over the territories of the mandate. In the treaty of Saint-Jean-d'Acre, there was no question of victory or defeat. Verdilhac did not capitulate, but handed over his powers to the British. London, all things considered, was not fully aware of the part played by the Free French Division in the conflict.

In the evening, the final text was drawn up, re-read, corrected by an editing committee, and then typed. When everything was ready, it was almost night. The doors were then opened wide so that the reporters – press, radio and movies – could be present at the final signing. They all rushed in in a disorderly fashion. Alan Moorehead:

> Edward Genock, the Paramount cameraman, remarked that there no longer was enough light to shoot. Having obtained several office lamps in the building, his assistant had made a cluster of them in such a way as to be able to turn them all on together by plugging them into a single power point. As soon as the press was admitted, the assistant rushed in, his lights at arm's length, to be beside General Wilson. The latter – who was seated – gave an astonished look at this sudden intrusion, then dipped his pen in the inkwell to start signing. The assistant then switched on his lamps and, suddenly, it was dark! Total darkness. All the lamps went out.

It was a short-circuit. In the dark, there was a general commotion. Everything that could be found was turned on, pocket torches, kerosene lamps and, finally, the headlights of a car were aimed through a picture window. Someone suggested bringing a motorcycle. A dispatch rider ran down the steps, brought his machine into the room to where the assistant had been, and under the stunned gaze of those nearby, started up his machine. The backfiring was deafening. 'I can't turn on the headlight if the motor is not running' stated the unhappy soldier in justifying his action He was asked to turn off his engine and leave; storm lanterns were brought. It was then noticed that a certain number of those filling the room, who had come from the barracks to take advantage of the spectacle, had entered without authorisation. They had to be removed. Wilson and Verdilhac finally signed in surroundings of complete disorder. Wilson, having signed, observed: 'This text is final. We are happy and relieved that the spilling of blood is finished.'

Against the advice of his generals, Churchill had thus won this war. Raising his voice in the general hubbub, Wilson and Verdilhac then exchanged a few pleasantries. The Englishman: 'I am anxious to thank General de Verdilhac for his understanding. I am keen to add that during the operations which have just come to end, the fighting qualities displayed by the [Vichy] French forces have been worthy of their finest traditions.' And the Frenchman, in the same manner: 'There are in the life of all men painful periods [...] I would like to thank you for the comradely language you have used [...] A few months ago we were allies. A few days ago we were adversaries. We hope with all our strength that the future will be better for our two countries.'[9]

Thus the name of Saint-Jean-d'Acre, already so rich in memories, entered history again. Its memory, glorious for the British, remained sad for the French. 1941 marked the 750th anniversary of the capture of the city by Richard the Lionheart; it was here in 1291, after a presence of two centuries, the Franks, following a heroic siege, had to abandon the Holy Land, and it was again at Saint-Jean-d'Acre in 1799 that Bonaparte's eastern dream came to an end.[10] It was here on 14 July, France's national day, that at last the harrowing conflict came to an end.

Immediately after the signing, the delegations went their separate ways. Verdilhac left for Beirut where the festivities for Bastille Day had been forbidden. Catroux got into his car, where his *képi* adorned with oakleaves had been stolen, and set out for Damascus where a big celebration awaited him.

London broadcast a prepared communiqué: 'The armistice in Syria shows that Hitler has missed a stage on the road to the oilfields of Iran and Iraq.' The correspondent of the Australian Press Agency in Palestine sent this message: 'A bitter feeling of misunderstanding, unreality, and waste has permeated the whole of the campaign, its relative slowness has demonstrated that the clash was political rather than military [...] Until the very last day, many thought that they were going to come up against Germans or Italians.' The correspondent of the *Sydney Morning Herald* wrote: 'The end of the fighting answers the wishes of all the combatants, even those of Vichy. This war has not been one in which people on both sides can take part with pride or even with a sense of adventure. For most, it was only an inevitable continuation, a dark appendix to the fall of France in 1940.' Although he claimed to have initiated this conflict, General de Gaulle also expressed a feeling of bitterness during an apologetic speech:

> In Syria, this army [*Forces Françaises Libres*] has just undergone fighting no less hard but infinitely more painful [than that in Eritrea]. The ambiguity created by Vichy had to be resolved with a sword. The scandalous war that was imposed upon us was necessary, but we cannot rejoice with the success obtained against our brothers. Even after the victory we will continue to wear mourning for our people who fell in Syria, as much for those who fought in our ranks as for their adversaries, victims of the treachery of a few men who sacrificed France to better serve Hitler [...] Having remained faithful to ourselves, we are thereby certain of being loyal to France, to its mission and to all the traditions that have made its greatness in the past and that cannot be denied without making it unrecognisable.

The magic of words! To engage in a fratricidal war, wasn't that going precisely going against 'all the traditions that have made the greatness of France in the past and that cannot be denied without making it unrecognisable'?

On 15 July, Winston Churchill announced the news in the Commons:

> The Chamber will have learned, I don't doubt, the good news from Syria. A military convention has just been signed which puts an end, in a cordial atmosphere, to a period of fratricidal fighting between the [Vichy] French on the one hand, and, on the other hand the [Free] French, and soldiers from Great Britain, Australia and India who had spontaneously drawn swords to defend the soil of France. That our relations with the government of Vichy, however precarious that they were, did not deteriorate during these weeks of painful fighting in which, on both sides, the troops exhibited so much discipline, skill and bravery in carrying out their duty as soldiers, this proves that the French people fully

understand the struggle that is going on all over the world. The manner in which this brief Syrian campaign was brought to an end honours the leaders responsible, General Wavell who firstly found the troops to snuff out the revolt in Iraq, then to act in Syria and all that at a time when he was standing up vigorously to the German–Italian army whose powerful armoured units had been vainly seeking for months to invade the valley of the Nile; to General Sir Henry Maitland Wilson, to whom was entrusted the local conduct of that campaign. It will be remembered that it was he who managed to withdraw our expeditionary corps from Greece at a time when terrible danger threatened it from all sides. He has showed himself sparing of reports in both of these campaigns which constitute admirable examples of skill in military art.

We can say that, for the moment at least, our situation has improved considerably in the valley of the Nile. If anyone had predicted two months ago that, from the middle of July, we would have cleaned up all the Levant and re-established for the moment our authority in those countries, such a prophet would have been accused of foolishness at least.

At the same time, Marshal Pétain was addressing the Army of the Levant: 'After a month of bitter struggle that was too uneven, we have to lay down our arms. France, which has continued to follow you in that unjust war with love and pride, bows before your sacrifice. You will continue displaying to her, during these days of mourning, the unshakeable loyalty that you have immortalised with your blood during the fighting. The nation will be grateful to you.'

Dentz broadcast this message to his troops:

Officers, NCOs, soldiers, airmen and sailors of the forces in the Levant! Since 8 June, you have been slugging it out toe to toe to resist the British forces [...] Everywhere the enemy came up against your stubborn willpower to hold on until the end to the positions which were entrusted to you. You had to fight against superior forces, strongly supported by artillery and armour. On the coast, you found yourselves without any possible defence against the violent and murderous bombardments of the British fleet. At Kasmiyeh, Sidon, Damour, Khalde, Merdjayoun, like at Jezzine and Beit ed Dine, the *groupes mobiles* (paramilitary police units) from Lebanon, mingling Lebanese blood with

French blood, forced the enemy's admiration. They gave back hope and pride to the French army [...] Faced with much superior forces, the Army of the Levant was forced to ask for an armistice. The adversary today grants us the honours of war, retrieval of prisoners, repatriation. What you can be proud of is not only the fierce fighting that you withstood alone, without help. It is also, and especially, for having shown the world that, 3,000 km from the mother country, when the government of France gave an order, it was obeyed until the end.

This war involved not only the mandatory powers, British and French, it was a conflict between two dominant powers. Apart from the coastal towns which were often devastated and, in the interior, Merdjayoun, Kuneitra and Jezzine, the country had suffered little. The victims were almost all combatants on the battle front. The civilians did not feel involved. On 4 July, Michelet was passing through Zhale: 'I was impressed by the carefree atmosphere of this summer resort frequented by Lebanese high society, where nothing suggested that a war was being carried on nearby. Young Lebanese people crowded in the streets, laughing and exchanging pleasantries. The hotels were full, and a table had to be reserved for lunch.' Already on 24 June, during his passage at Aleppo, Dentz had confided to Benoist-Méchin: 'My soldiers are enraged at having to go to war on foot, while the Lebanese and Syrian gilded youth disport themselves in American cars!' Syrians and Lebanese politicians and ordinary citizens were present at the conflict without ever becoming involved. They waited for the end without showing any commitment. Dentz confirmed at his trial that during the fighting there was no reaction among the populace. Not a telephone line was cut, not a rail was unbolted, not a nail was thrown on to the roads. On both sides, the two belligerents declared themselves delighted with the support shown to them by the local population. Some people recovered a few weapons, several acts of espionage were reported, but the local gendarmes were always cooperative. Order therefore continued to reign.

It was not until 15 July, on entering Beirut, that the Australians, seeing thousands of inhabitants leaving their homes to cheer them, understood that the war was really over. Alan Moorehead accompanied the troops:

We progressed slowly along the coast through rich plantations that had been devastated by the fighting. I counted about 50 houses in the village [of Damour] that had been hit by a shell. The big bridge crossing the river had collapsed, here and there shells of tanks and armoured vehicles could be seen. A funeral parlour, in which the [Vichy] French had hidden a tank to bar the road, was completely destroyed. While we were making our way to Beirut through immense olive groves, the villagers came out of their houses to applaud us and congratulate us [...] In the city's suburbs, as they were running along, girls were waving Free French flags that had been hastily made, with the Cross of Lorraine on them. We finally reached the *Place des Canons* (Cannon Square)[11] where, in bright sunlight, a compact mass of 10–12,000 people thronged the footpaths, balconies and roofs. In front of us, a military band started playing 'Mademoiselle from Armentières'.[12] A long column of infantry[13] and Bren carriers followed it [...] We were all, that morning, extremely relieved that this war in Syria, with all its implications of civil war, was over. We were sincerely willing to forgive, forget and fraternize with the people on the other side. I was staying at the Saint George's, a luxury hotel which rose from the sea like a Chinese pagoda. The bar was packed and, in front of the windows, ravishing Lebanese girls were lazily swimming in the water. One could have said that the war had never taken place.

The atmosphere was, as it happens, festive. An Australian field newspaper: 'At 10:30 a.m., escorted by 24 carriers and field guns, Generals Wilson, Catroux, Lavarack, Allen and Evetts, made their solemn entry into Beirut. The inhabitants, overexcited, cheered them, convinced that they were bringing independence.' Welcomed at the gates of the city by Lebanese officials, the key figures made their way to the Grand Serail in front of which was a large crowd.' Buis:[14] 'Generals Catroux and Wilson made an entry that I would call triumphal. Not that it had been organised with great pomp, but by the simple fact that a war was finishing, a war that had worried many Lebanese.' This arrival of two generals in a small procession of two cars – Generals Wilson and Catroux in the first, Captains Répiton-Préneuf and Buis in the second – had attracted a large gathering of people with all that Mediterranean joy that was given free rein. We arrived with that group at the Grand Serail. There was just a section of marines, under the command of Burin des Rosiers, with a priest wearing a white soutane with a shoulder belt. With Répiton and myself, that was all that was surrounding General Catroux.'[15]

The correspondent of the *Sydney Morning Herald* described the event with more enthusiasm:

> Generals Wilson, Catroux and Lavarack were greeted by a dense crowd on Martyrs' Square where a guard of honour of mounted gendarmes, Lebanese, presented arms with drawn swords. British aircraft flew over the city. French and Lebanese flags flew over numerous buildings. Some bore the Cross of Lorraine. Spread right over the bonnet of a car, an Australian flag could be seen. It had been given to a South Australian chaplain by some veterans, with the hope that it would be used on great historic occasions. The generals and their aides crossed the square quickly and went to the Grand Serail. When they got out of their cars, young Lebanese girls bowed to them and offered each one a bouquet. The generals were received by a guard of honour of British Yeomanry, Free French marines, and helmeted cavalry.

General Wilson seemed rather embarrassed. Swagger stick under his arm, he glanced at the imposing building, mounted the steps and entered. At the foot of the staircase, Monsieur Conty, Director of Political Affairs at the High Commission, greeted him. Ignoring the Free French, he moved towards the British general and asked him to follow him to General Dentz's office in order to carry out the handover of powers. Dentz, as a matter of fact, refused to do it himself. To surrender Beirut after Paris was probably beyond his strength, and to recognise the authority of the Free French was forbidden. General Wilson seemed to hesitate a moment, and then followed Conty. The 'real' French for the British were thus the Vichy representatives. 'In a vast marble room', went on the Australian reporter, 'the generals received bearded notables, clad in a picturesque fashion, who had come from different regions. In their full regalia, representatives of the Orthodox Church, carrying icons heavily ornamented with precious stones, monks with shaved heads, and Muslim imams, about 50 representatives of all religions made up a picturesque scene [...] The clergy from the Beirut mosque expressed their gratitude to the Allied command for not having caused victims among the people or damage to property. They finally expressed a wish for the next British victory.'

In a general fashion, a warm reception was reserved by the population for the Allied forces, particularly the Australians, considered the reporter of the *Sydney Morning Herald* who added: in spite of this reception, General Wilson did not want to take any risks and a curfew was decreed. All over the city, posters were put up warning that any threat to the Imperial troops was punishable by death.

Beirut changed masters and life resumed, but when the Australians, Indians and British in impeccable uniforms marched through the streets with perfect dignity, the Gaullists displayed a joy that soon bordered on curses, jeers and hostility, noted Le Corbeiller. Very rapidly, they began to act as if they were in an enemy city that they had conquered after a heroic struggle.

Whilst some were settling in, others, on the contrary, were leaving. All the information coming into Catroux's office confirmed that, in the whole of Syria and Lebanon, the [Vichy] French military and civil administration was withdrawing, taking its files. 'The cupboards were bare and the archives had disappeared. Had they wanted to hand over this territory to the British, they would not have acted differently.'

Who was responsible for this success? The power of the weaponry? There was no doubt that the Army of the Levant had fought with a fierceness that none of its adversaries, British, Australian or Free French, would dispute. Its courage surprised, there were innumerable testimonies to it: 'The [Vichy] French fought with all the skill and knowledge of old professional soldiers', noted George H. Johnston, an Australian journalist.[16] 'The [Vichy] French fought like madmen all along the line', stated a British historian.[17] 'There was no evidence of any German aid whatsoever during the whole campaign.'[18] 'The Vichy troops, from start to finish, fought like tigers until the Armistice. It is almost a miracle that the AIF and other Allied troops managed to bring down such an enemy,' said Colonel Buckley in an official history.[19] 'We had to face a skilful, courageous and stubborn adversary, knowing every inch of the terrain, knowing how to make excellent use of his weapons, and counter-attacking vigorously each time that the situation was favourable to him, reported his adversaries. It is remarkable that, in spite of the weakness of our forces, the lack of armoured vehicles and modern weaponry, that we managed to drive the enemy to surrender in the relatively short space of time of five weeks.'[20] Even though systematically matched with political reservations, the Free French too did not stint in their praise. On 21 June, on entering Damascus, Colonel Cazaud did not hide from his Vichy opposite number, who was handing over the city to him, 'his admiration for the resistance of the [Vichy] French troops to the south of Damascus, in particular for the very effective action by artillery and bomber aircraft which caused numerous and appreciable losses in Gaullist ranks, whose officers and NCOs were particularly distressed'.

'As unpleasant as this whole affair has been, it also left the memory of one of the last colourful British military campaigns,' remembered one of the British.[21] The commandos advancing through the orange groves along the Litani, the cavalry charge by the *spahis*, the siege of the Indians at Mezzé, the attack of the Yeomanry and the men of the Essex Regiment among the shattered columns at Palmyra, the picturesque citadels overlooking the deserts in the east, the young Australians, stealthily climbing down the cliffs at Damour by moonlight, greeted by the growling of [Vichy] French guard dogs on the banks of the river [...] How could one not remember the brave French officer in an impeccable uniform who defied us from the top of the walls of a fort, emptying his revolver at our guns? It was only with the greatest tact on our part that we managed to secure his surrender. A *jemadar*[22] confided to a British officer: 'I was so afraid that the French gentleman would be hurt!'

It seems beyond doubt that among the very staffs, behind the soldiers who were being sacrificed, moles had worked for the enemy. Too many disastrous orders had been broadcast without their origin being able to be traced. If the relief in broad daylight of the troops at Kasmiyeh was perhaps a fortuitous mistake, the abandoning of Sidon, the forts in Damascus, and the bridge at Deir-ez-Zor, the order to the mobile column at Nebek to withdraw, the order to abandon Damascus, all those catastrophic decisions surprised the staff. It was dishonourable to betray one's men. No reasoning could justify it. Whatever the excuses that were made, those who agreed to act in this way sacrificed their dignity. Keeping on trotting out justifications, they will have to forever put up with their perverted patriotism in silence.

'The happiest of all at the announcement of the Armistice seem to have been the wounded Australians, cared for in hospital at Beirut, taken prisoner at Merdjayoun, Jezzine or on the coast. Escorted by two smiling nurses, 'I was able to visit,' said the *Sydney Morning Herald* correspondent, 'a vast modern hospital where I met some Australian officers and British Yeomanry officers, as well as about 50 Australian soldiers. All gave the highest praise to the manner in which they had been treated.

Whether it be food or care, they asserted that they had received the same, or perhaps even more, attention than the French wounded. They had been shown the greatest kindness and all possible consideration. I lunched with the wounded officers. Some had a leg in a plaster cast or a bandaged chest, others, who were limping, had crutches. The food? Soup, salad, meat, vegetables, bread, butter, and as much wine as one wanted. They confirmed to me that it was an ordinary menu.' An Engineer officer, who had distinguished himself in the attack on Merdjayoun, said he was the happiest of men. 'The Armistice is a great relief for all of us', they told me. 'You can't imagine our joy yesterday when our men came to visit us!'

The Australians were soldiers. If they were ignorant of everything about the Levant, its past, its inhabitants, Franco–British relations, it was they who had won the war. Victory owed almost everything to them. However, were they satisfied? 'This campaign had been very trying', wrote one of them. 'Even success had a bitter taste. How could we rejoice after having fought the French, who were allies the year before?'[23] This war seemed to them like a type of undignified fist fight fought by contestants who were all equally suspicious. Keen on boxing, they considered it a slogging match, one of those fights where two clumsy adversaries beat one another up until there is a victory without panache. If, for them, Marshal Pétain's men had given signs of collusion with Germany, the Gaullists, however, were none the less suspected of fascism in their eyes. In addition, they were soldiers by chance. According to them, the Free French profited more from their allies than they helped them. Furthermore, noisy and blabbermouths, they exasperated the Australians.

Adopting a more general view, likening it to the world war, Gavin Long concluded in his brilliant work, *Greece, Crete and Syria*:

> Since it was necessary to attack simultaneously in Libya and Syria, the two offensives should have been entered upon with sufficient forces. The Syrian campaign was too long and too costly. An unexpected event, the German attack on Russia, proved that the attack had been premature. One could have attacked later with the necessary forces, but it was above all a political gesture and the political factors were badly evaluated. The Allied advisors could not assess the feelings of the Vichy forces. Wanting the invasion to take place, impatient to play a leadership role to

enhance their prestige and to assert their interests, the Free French also underestimated the probable resistance. More than any other factor, it seems that the presence opposite them of the loathed Gaullists provoked the solid resistance of the Vichy troops who treated them as renegades. France was in a state of civil war, and the two parties were opposed with all the resentment and reproaches that are favoured by this type of conflict. The presence of the Free French Forces contingent also complicated the control [of operations] for it was not under British command, but acted 'in cooperation', a procedure that is always disagreeable, especially when it was a matter of troops made up of soldiers who were more or less mercenaries, the black Africans and legionnaires.[24]

He went on: 'Well commanded, in an inventive way, the French [of General Dentz] fought in a country they knew very well and in which the defenders had the advantage. In addition [...] they had 90 tanks whereas we had none [...] They could thus launch counter-attacks across the fragile lines of communications of their adversaries, and threaten Jordan and Palestine, which were then almost empty of troops. Their counter-attacks obtained bigger results than their forces deserved, or even when their command did not expect it [...] It is probable that the Allied inability to concentrate their forces on a single objective [...] was the result of a faulty concept of operations controlled from Jerusalem by General Wilson and a staff, which was especially preoccupied by political and administrative problems, that were too far from the battlefield [...] The invasion forces benefited from the important advantage of mastery of the sea and, later, the air, as well as a slow increase in their forces and equipment, a more powerful artillery, although the excellent French heavy mortar outclassed the Australian guns in the mountains [...] The Allies had a superior morale. The French [of the Levant] and the colonial troops drew their determination from their pride as professional soldiers – many thought that the British despised them because of their defeat in France – in their hatred of the Gaullists and in their resentment against the British who attacked them under the pretext that they were protecting them from the Germans. However, on their side, the Allies were inspired by a pride much greater than partisan animosities. Finally, the Australians, in particular, were much tougher and showed more resilience.'[25]

The war being over, it was going to be hidden from sight. It caused shame. In England as in France, censorship intervened after the conflict was over to maintain silence on this disastrous blunder. Gavin Long:[26] 'A political as well as a military censor was given supervision of reports of the campaign. The censors were instructed by Wavell's headquarters that they must delete references to fighting. The first communiqué issued in Cairo stated that "only slight and often no resistance" had been met from the French [...] following which General Lavarack's chief Intelligence officer informed Middle East headquarters that his chief was worried about the effect on his troops of BBC broadcasts that the [Vichy] French were not resisting [...] The fiasco of the British censorship in the early stages of the fighting, as well as the vigorous protests of American press correspondents against manipulation of information, however, led to changes in Wavell's censorship staff and the appointment, as Cairo spokesman, of Major Randolph Churchill, the Prime Minister's son.

In a surprising but significant way, the overshadowing persists. Even after 60 years, this war remains hidden; no doubt it damages too many legends. In his monumental history, published in London, *The Second World War*, Liddell Hart does not speak of it. The *Men at Arms* series by Osprey in London, although so extraordinarily verbose on all aspects of military history, and World War II in particular, ignores it completely. Published in Paris in 2005, the important *Dictionnaire Perrin des guerres et des batailles de France* (Perrin Dictionary of French Wars and Battles) does not mention it. In his very thick *War Diaries*, Field Marshal Lord Alanbrooke, who was very opposed, does not speak of it. Censored in history books, the memory of this conflict remains alive only in the hearts of those who took part in it. It is only on Anzac Day – the ex-servicemen's day – when in Australian towns and villages, veterans march past when age permits, behind banners showing their campaigns, that the name of Syria is brandished under the eyes of those who understand.

For the French also it was a time for appraisal of the results. For them it was, from all aspects, a catastrophe. Everyone can debate the question whether this war was just or not, necessary or not, justifiable or not, but everyone admitted that it was distressing. 'This Syrian affair has added nothing to the glory of the French, whatever side they are on,' judged Diégo Brosset, who was very close to General de Gaulle. 'Its most lasting effect will have been to insert a Franco–French civil war into the heart of the world conflict,' wrote Georges Hirtz, a member of General Weygand's staff. 'It was certainly my worst memory of the war,'

declared Pierre Messmer. And de Gaulle in his *Mémoires*: 'The
campaign in which we had had to take part evokes cruel memories
in me [...] I feel, regarding those who opposed us out of honour,
mixed feelings of esteem and commiseration [...] these losses [...]
impress as being a horrible waste'.

By creating discord among the enemy – France and Britain
– almost without any capital outlay, Germany had succeeded in
carrying out an amazing feat. By simply uttering threats, Hitler
had succeeded in getting his enemies to kill each other. That is
what General de Gaulle stated in his speech of 15 August 1941
in Beirut: 'The enemy has managed to work it so that Frenchmen
were opposed to other Frenchmen and France's allies.' Only
Britain derived clear profits from this campaign: the occupation of
the buffer zone north of Suez, domination of the French mandate
and – this was not the least of them – that of having strengthened
Turkey in its neutrality.

The losses? On both sides they were severe. In this highly
controversial area, it is difficult to estimate them, because the
figures differ so much from different sources. We will therefore rely
on indications given at the time by the best informed authorities.
According to the 1st Bureau[27] of the Staff in Beirut, the Army
of the Levant lost 66 officers, 281 NCOs and 2,124 rank-and-
file killed in action, including the missing. The *Service historique
de l'armée* (*SHA*; Army Historical Service) indicated 1,066 killed
and 5,400 wounded. Gaujac gives 839 killed, including 76
officers and 1,790 wounded. With 92 pilots killed, the Air Force
sustained very heavy losses. According to the report of General
Legentilhomme on 5 August, the Free French had 156 killed, 450
wounded, 21 missing. Yves Gras gives different figures.

It is impossible to know the figures of 'British' losses, the term
often covering the Australians, Indians and Transjordanians.
Five Ventures,[28] published by Her Majesty's Stationery Office,
the official British publisher, indicates the Commonwealth troops
lost a total of 4,700 combatants, including 1,800 Indians. For
the Australians, Gavin Long[29] gives: 37 officers killed and 87
wounded, 379 NCOs and men killed and 1,049 wounded. The
7th Australian Division lost a total of 1,519 men in Syria, which
is more than in Greece and Crete.[30] It also had an abnormally
large number of sick: 3,150. In total, the losses were thus a little
more elevated among the [Vichy] French than the Allies. Davet
estimates that there were, in total, more than 6,000 dead or
wounded, and 10,000 men put out of action. Taking into account

the variations in the data, the average figure is 7,000 dead. The equipment losses were equally very heavy: the [Vichy] French Air Force lost 179 aircraft, mainly on the ground, and the Royal Air Force 41. In total, 220 aircraft were destroyed. Three British destroyers were eliminated, generally for the duration of the war. [Vichy] France lost the destroyer *Chevalier-Paul*, the submarine *Souffleur* and the cargo ship *Saint-Didier.*

There have been bloodier and much more destructive wars, but surely none that caused a mental wound that was so hard to heal. When all is said and done, the Allied forces were missing 10,000 men, 200 aircraft and six ships when, in 18 months' time, those calling themselves followers of Vichy, Gaullists and British found themselves shoulder to shoulder in battle.

Britain recouped its outlay. It occupied the country, controlled the petroleum refinery in Tripoli, and took charge of all its infrastructure. The British were installed everywhere as masters. Officers of the Political Service took over the public service, police, transport, customs, posts and telegraph, and telephones. The transfer of powers from French public servants did not give rise to any incidents. The Union Jack flew over Palmyra, Jebel Druse and Jazeera. No contact occurred with the Free French. The 'basic principle, the favoured and pre-eminent position of France' demanded by General de Gaulle was totally ignored. Having trouble admitting that the Free French wanted to occupy a country that they conquered, Commonwealth troops felt at home. The Levant became British. Oddly, it was the situation in 1919 that was starting all over again, but in reverse. Didn't Allenby have to leave to France an area that he had conquered with the support of a French contingent?

General Sir Alan Brooke, Chief of the Imperial General Staff, stressed in his *War Diaries* the extreme importance for England of this highly strategic region: 'It is in the Middle East that the overseas British forces are mainly situated [...] Since 1940, a continuous flood of reinforcements, both troops and equipment, has been directed there, not only from England but also from India, Australia, New Zealand, South Africa, Rhodesia and the African colonies. By the end of 1941, the forces in the Middle East will have about 250,000 men, only a fraction of whom, about 100,000, will be in contact with the enemy in Libya, the remainder being scattered over immense areas.'[31]

The co-presidents of the Control Commission, set up at Aaley,[32] were Brigadier Chrystall for the Allies and General de

Verdilhac for the Vichy forces. Relations between the British and [Vichy] French were, in spite of numerous incidents, marked by good manners. The community of thought between career officers, who had been moulded by the same experiences and the same traditions, was complete. Ties of esteem, and soon personal friendship, developed between General[33] Chrystall and General de Verdilhac. In spite of some friction, their courtesy facilitated the easing of a delicate situation. 'The sessions always took place in an atmosphere of complete correctness', can be read in the Frenchman's account. 'The English delegation', he stressed, 'strove very loyally to check the execution of the clauses of the Saint-Jean-d'Acre agreement but, from the beginning of August, the consequences of the accord signed on 25 July in Cairo between de Gaulle and the British government, represented by its Minister, Oliver Lyttelton, were felt strongly'.[34] An unsparing game was then played between the British delegation, which was supposed to apply the Cairo accord, and the [Vichy] French delegation, which 'wanting to ignore officially this latest accord [of which the British did not whisper a word and whose existence had only been learned of in a round-about way] to keep to that of Saint-Jean-d'Acre'. Verdilhac went on: 'It must be said in defence of General Chrystall that he truly did all in his power to satisfy the [Vichy] French delegation. To his credit, he had General de Verdilhac informed "that he sometimes could not sleep at night from the shame at what he was forced to do".' Because, on 13 August, when the [Vichy] French command learned via the newspaper *L'Orient*, that General Catroux proclaimed that the Army of the Levant was dissolved and its members placed under his command, General de Verdilhac immediately went to Chrystall's office to ask him 'if the British authorities were covering up [...] "such an infamous deed"'.[35] Verdilhac asked to meet Wilson who refused to see him, arguing that the Cairo accord was 'perfectly valid'.

Nevertheless, Verdilhac granted that, 'in spite of his protests each day, the [Vichy] French delegation [...] found an almost constant support from the British delegation which, very often, allied itself with it to dismiss the Gaullist claims [...] It is nonetheless true, concluded an outraged Verdilhac, that 11 days after the solemn signature of the Saint-Jean-d'Acre agreement, the British government delivered the Army of the Levant to de Gaulle, and that General Wilson, signatory to that agreement, refused to recognise his legal obligations.'

Incidents, sometimes serious – thefts, insults, brawls and threats – took place due to the position of the troops who were stationed close together; the surrender of weapons, prisoner exchanges, the encroachment of Gaullist propaganda, forced recruitment, repeated efforts to impede departures, etc., gave rise to heated exchanges. Free France increased its efforts to attract as many troops as possible. 'Mister Kœnig', as General de Verdilhac wrote, 'will do his best to delay embarkations, to disperse them and to "control" them in place of the Australians'. 'On 27 July', he recalled, 'Colonel Kœnig declared for example that "all [Vichy] French troops who have not embarked by 22 August will be considered as prisoners of war".' Verdilhac was incensed and Chrystall agreed. Bitter conflicts occurred and, until the last day, there was fighting over the 55 Special Service officers – intelligence and local administration – whom the Free French wanted absolutely to keep. They were of vital importance for the maintenance of the French presence. The quarrel was so intense that on the eve of his departure, 'General de Verdilhac informed General Chrystall that he himself will not embark if the last Special Service officer does not leave with him.' On 27 September, apart from nine who joined the Gaullists, the Special Service officers were repatriated.

The Resident British Minister in Cairo noted that Wilson's officers are on better terms with 'the officers of the Army of the Levant who respected their oath of loyalty to the Marshal at the cost of their country, than with the Free French who fought alongside them for the greatest glory of France'. This was particularly true for the Australians. Lavarack, who had met Dentz during World War I, ordered his troops 'that all possible courtesy and consideration be shown towards an enemy who had carried out a very courageous defence'.[36] Keime also confirmed it: 'Correct relations were established with the British. They showed their esteem for those who had obeyed, without hesitation or murmur, the orders of their government. Only the absolute discipline of the armed forces makes great nations. They [the British] showed a certain respect for the combatants, who were few in number, but who had dealt them rough blows until the very eve of the Armistice.'[37] They themselves, often hostile to aggression, hadn't they obeyed in a disciplined manner? Without doubt, professional solidarity also played a part. The scrubbed appearance, tight-fitting uniform and stiff style of the two former enemies reinforced their respective dignity.

The relations between the members of Dentz's army and the Australians were correct. When they met, they had discussions, compared recollections, and sought to understand the reasons for a war against the Germans whom the French detested! 'At no point in the campaign had the slightest sign whatever of German help been found', repeated the Australian Press Agency on several occasions. The Australians understood that they had been deceived: not only were there no Germans facing them, but their adversaries had not surrendered without fighting as had been asserted to them. Now, it was they who had borne the weight of the hard fighting. If the Army of the Levant had earned their esteem, the Free French had deceived them. Their enmity was sincere; for them 'FFL' meant 'French Felon'.[38] They felt that 'the Free French had not played an adequate part in the campaign.' In a battalion history,[39] Ken Clift[40] expressed feelings that were suppressed by reports from a higher level: 'The High Command and the Australians harboured grave doubts about the value of the Free French troops [...] neither from the point of view of morale nor training did they show themselves, in the event, to be up to the test. At no point in the campaign did we consider them to be reliable.' Relations between the two lots of troops were, in reality, very rare except at Damascus, but Ken Clift maintained that in the Mezzé region 'the FFL [Free French Forces] had "thrown in the sponge", frankly admitting to the High Command that they were not prepared "to kill compatriots". They were nothing more than embarrassment for the Allied forces'. It was brutal and unjust, but this conviction of the rank-and-file explains an almost irreversible hostility. Exceptional but significant, this sign on the door of an Australian mess: 'Forbidden to Indians and Free French Forces.'[41] Vichy naturally exploited the photograph. The Free French, conversely, took the Australians to be uneducated brutes incapable of carrying out military manoeuvres. They considered them as brave but mediocre soldiers. Thus, without esteem, no friendship.

The Official History erased all that. In Australian public opinion, no discredit for the memory of the war in Syria is laid at France's door, and the fraternal feelings born in the 1914 war remain. In the eyes of Australians today, the French in Syria were not truly French but 'Vichy French', a separate species, which has disappeared in the incomprehensible twists and turns of time. For their part, the French are ignorant of the role played by Australia in this war: indifferent, they think it was the English.

It was on the morning of 15 July, in Brazzaville, that General de Gaulle learned via Radio Cairo of the main thrust of the Saint-Jean-d'Acre accords. He was outraged. In this text, there was no mention of Free France. The treaty did not take his wishes into any account. It was not to him but to the British that the Levant surrendered. Was he only a back-up? 'The content and form of this went further, in the wrong direction, than I had feared,' he wrote. 'In effect, the accord amounted to a handover, pure and simple, of Lebanon to the British [...] By signing this capitulation, Vichy has shown itself faithful to its sad vocation, but the English seemed to lend themselves to it with all their ulterior motives.'

Considering himself swindled, the General flew into a violent rage and, without waiting for the full text of the accord, he telegraphed Catroux that he refused this agreement absolutely: 'I hope that you have not been induced to sign this armistice convention contrary to my intentions and instructions,' he cried. He denounced 'the ill-will of the British plan'. Unlike Catroux he was convinced that England wanted 'to try, sometimes silently and sometimes bluntly, to replace France in Damascus and Beirut'. Catroux explained in his *Mémoires*: 'if de Gaulle was on the lookout and was observing the behaviour of our Allies with a prejudiced eye', Catroux himself 'did not share, at that time, his anxieties. Not that I was not very well informed about the old dispute in the Levant, but because I trusted Churchill. I considered that the Prime Minister was a prisoner of the solemn promise he had made to restore, after the victory, France in her grandeur and territorial integrity.' Was Churchill truly sincere? The future would show that he was[42] but his aim, in engaging in this battle, was different to that of the French: his was basically strategic, whereas de Gaulle's was basically political. One wanted to secure his rear and the other wanted to hoist his flag.

The chief of Free France sent a formal protest to Mr Anthony Eden, Minister for Foreign Affairs in London, warning him that he did not consider himself bound in any way by the Armistice convention. He kept to the conditions accepted on 19 June 'without recognizing any others'. At the same time, the Free French intelligence services in London sent a protest note to the Foreign Office[43] on 17 July complaining about the repatriation of the Army of the Levant 'capable of attacking Chad later', against the handing over to the English of equipment left on the spot which deprived Free France of resources that she particularly needed and, finally, against the right that the British had reserved for themselves of taking into their service the Special Troops of the Levant, 'recruited, trained, equipped by the French and serving under their flag'.

The conquest of Syria could not but satisfy the people in the Colonial Office who saw in it a dream come true. Hadn't they, in 1860, armed the Druse against the French? Hadn't they supported, in an underhand fashion, the 1925 revolt? The British heard with satisfaction the Druse chiefs, who had been called to Damascus, say that 'France's time is past.' Having returned home to Soueida and avoiding having the slightest relationship with Colonel Monclar, the new French delegate, these heads of families no longer addressed anyone but the British representative. Monclar alerted Catroux: the English intend to occupy the Jebel Druse alone. During a personal visit to the Syrian Prime Minister, Al-Jabri, Collet asserted that, in spite of the assertions made by Eden to de Gaulle in London, the English were plotting to place the country under their influence. At Palmyra, the visit of Glubb Pasha, the head of the Jordanian brigade, gave rise to some enthusiastic demonstrations by bedouin tribes in favor of King Abdullah of Transjordan. Clashes with the British were frequent. General Catroux sent representatives into all provinces where they were frequently in conflict with the British administration. Deprived of means and brushed aside everywhere, they could neither assert themselves nor thwart infringements on French sovereignty. The Free French, who were so few in number, did all that they could to be assertive. Barberot: 'The "13th"[44] was sent to many places to show their [French] presence and to oppose the encroachments of our English friends. In Beirut, I spent several days marching past with my section behind the drum and bugle band. In the Jebel Druse, at Homs, at Aleppo and at the Turkish frontier, the welcome was warm and friendly everywhere.' However, even though they were in their own territory, these French were a nuisance. On 2 August, Lavarack sent a report to Wilson: 'A broad scattering of Free French troops for political motives is tactically and administratively unhealthy in regions that we occupy for our own protection [...] Security decreases as the Free French take control. This reduces the security for which we invaded Syria.' In other words, the British would like to hold the Gaullists in check. On 6 August, in a letter preserved in the archives of the Foreign Office,[45] Churchill wrote to the Lord Privy Seal: 'Tell Anthony Eden to be strict with de Gaulle,

Catroux and the Free French. They must not have their hands free to harm our relations with the Arabs. Their claims must be corrected, by force if necessary. It is important that they obey. I do not see how they would be able to resist.' Several British intelligence services were waging a secret war on us, it was said, but they were so numerous that they are 'shooting themselves in the foot', it seemed, in an 'unimaginable' way. That, it was whispered in Beirut, would neutralise much of their work. In any event, no matter what they refrained from doing, the Free French were only 5,000 facing an enormous machine.

Around the region, Australian engineers were rebuilding roads, restoring bridges, and improving or setting up links with Palestine. One can read on a marble plaque affixed to the rebuilt Damour bridge, this inscription in English: 'Destroyed in June 1941, the southern arch of this bridge was rebuilt by the British Army in February 1942. Contractor: Chafyk Khoury.' Restored with English materials, the Tripoli refinery was restarted and petroleum flowed again. Never finished, the railway link between Haifa and Tripoli was commenced with considerable means. Cliffs were dynamited, trenches dug, and a big metal bridge was built over the Adonis river. The opening to traffic soon gave place to imposing ceremonies to which were invited the most important local political figures. The French seemed to be absent from the festivities and their failure for 20 years to build this track was implicitly stressed. Embossed with the insignia of the Australian Army and a symbolic badge,[46] a bronze plaque was affixed to the rocks of Nahr el-Kelb where, since the Assyrians, conquerors have engraved their exploits. One can read: 'Near this point, on 20 December 1942, the last spike on the railway from Beirut to Tripoli was laid by the Commander-in-Chief of the British Forces in the Middle East, General Sir Harold R.L.G. Alexander – followed by his post-nominals – thus completing the rail link from London to Cairo. This section was built by the Australian Railway Construction Group in 1942.' Magnificent, like the body of a star, no matter if interrupted, the line thus ran across the world, including Lebanon in the Empire.[47] One can read lower down: 'This plaque was unveiled by Sir H.R.L.G. Alexander in the presence of M. Alfred Naccache, President of the Lebanese Republic.' All that was not free of political ulterior motives. More or less slowed down during the war, political agitation resumed. The parties, the sects and the religious communities started to reawaken. The Levant again became a culture medium for trouble.

Before Auchinleck came to replace him, Wavell asked Winston Churchill for the post of Minister Resident to be created in Cairo to supervise the files and relieve the military commander of political concerns. Recommended by Major Randolph Churchill, General Wavell's spokesman, its holder will be a key political figure, Mr Oliver Lyttelton, a former President of the Board of Trade. Winston Churchill warned Wavell on 29 June that the new Minister of State in the Middle East would leave London the following day to join him. Captain Lyttelton[48] had therefore only been in his job two weeks when Catroux informed him of the refusal of General de Gaulle to ratify the Armistice convention. The question bothered the Minister. De Gaulle had prepared himself for this. He would be stiff, distant, haughty, brusque, unwavering. When, on 21 July, accompanied by Spears, he came 'enveloped in ice', according to his own phrase, 'pale with suppressed anger' according to the Englishman, it was 11:00 a.m. The heat was scorching.

Lyttelton: 'De Gaulle entered my office with great strides, surrounded by his staff, and greeted me coldly. He was white with suppressed emotion. He launched into the most violent criticism ever heard of the attitude concerning not only the secret protocol but also the whole of our action in the French territory of Syria and Lebanon.'[49] A decisive test of wills commenced. De Gaulle let fly with one of his most spectacular fits of rage but Lyttelton, who was prepared for it, did not allow himself to be flustered. Later, he described the interview as 'calm enough in tone, very explicit in content'. He wanted to discuss the mandate but refused to call into question an accord that England had signed. De Gaulle, like marble: 'This convention does not bind Free France. I have not ratified it!' He stressed that 'it was incompatible with France's political and military interests.' Either the British consider Free France as France herself or they use her as a back-up force which does not take part in the political management of the world. If that is the case 'the English attitude is incompatible with France's honour and interests.' And to support his remarks, the General took from his pocket a note which he handed to the Minister, who read it: the leader of Free France withdraws from the English command the military forces that he had put at its disposal!

Lyttelton: 'Your attitude is unjustified. We have no other goal in Syria but to win the war. The military command, responsible for public order as a last resort, must make decisions on the spot

[...] Why don't you trust us? General, I must consider that I have not received this note.' And Lyttelton tore it up! The reaction was immediate. De Gaulle, exasperated, recommenced his diatribe in a louder voice. The Englishman listened to him, then suddenly interrupted him. It was 12:30 p.m. 'General, it is the time at which I am going to dine and my office does not reopen until 4:30 p.m. It is very hot today and I suggest that we think about all that during the siesta, then we will meet again later. You will have calmed down.' All stood up and parted in anger. Phlegmatic, in charge of the situation, Lyttelton wrote: 'I considered that General de Gaulle's position was weaker than his words would have one believe, since the Free French Forces had to rely on the British Treasury for everything. De Gaulle had put on what would be called among women "a scene", but it was certainly a big one!'

De Gaulle did not allow himself to get flustered either. It was not a simple household quarrel. In threatening Britain to withdraw from the alliance, he risked a lot, but to have Churchill face the possibility of a fracture was, for him, the only way to obtain an audience. He therefore did not rest there. The next day, he sent to the British Minister a letter confirming that, on 24 July at midday, he would withdraw his forces. He remained available to settle the details of a collaboration set up on new bases.

In London, this decision provoked real emotion, remembered René Cassin. Churchill, like all the military and political circles, the Commons included, was shocked. Cassin: 'The Prime Minister sent me a member of his staff to ask me the following question: "Is de Gaulle still a general or has he become a politician?" My answer was immediate: "He is neither one nor the other: he is already a national leader." It struck the English Premier strongly by its prophetic exactitude.' As nothing was more important for the leader of Free France than to assert the authority of France over the Levant, he warned Catroux that he must now consider null and void the arrangements contained in the Saint-Jean-d'Acre armistice. Stiff and untouchable, he ordered: 'Organise immediately and carry out direct contacts with the Vichy troops with a view to their joining us [...] Take possession of weapons and equipment everywhere you find them [...] I plan to arrive in Beirut on Friday about midday. If the Vichy people, whatever their rank, continue to strut around Beirut, kindly have them arrested immediately and get rid of them.' Later, in front of the London committee, he explained his method: 'We would lose both our honour and our authority in France if we agreed to it [the Saint-Jean convention] [...] that is how I have managed to redress the situation and save the essential [...] Our greatness and our strength consist only in an uncompromising attitude as concerns the rights of France. We will need that uncompromising attitude until we reach the Rhine.'

A solution had to be found. The consequences of Franco–British dissension would be extremely grave. It would be a splendid propaganda argument for the Germans and would justify Vichy and encourage the Arab agitators. A Franco–British commission was therefore set up to advance matters. Three days later, an 'interpretive' agreement was drawn up, which was annexed to the convention of 14 July that it contradicted on numerous points.

On 22 July, the 'interpretive' agreement was concluded. The Free French authorities would be authorised to contact the troops of the Army of the Levant to 'explain their point of view to the personnel concerned', the military equipment will revert to Free France, and the Special Troops will rejoin the Free French Division and not the British Army. The Gaullists obtained the right to appoint 'zone majors' who will have authority over troops present on their territory. All French troops, even those of Dentz, will come under the authority of Free France. The arrangements for repatriation were to be under the Gaullist authorities. If the British Army ensured the strategic direction, it will not intervene in its administration. In addition, Lyttelton recognised 'the historic interests of France in the Levant, its dominant and favoured position, once the stage of independence, promised by her and guaranteed by Great Britain, had been accomplished and without it being called into question.' This point, fundamental, was thus reiterated, it should be stressed, by both sides.

Captain Lyttelton left Cairo on 6 August for Beirut in order to explain to the British military leaders the contents of the new accord. Understanding that it markedly changed the nature of the Saint-Jean-d'Acre document, they all revolted: their word of honour was pledged and they were unhappy. The atmosphere was not pleasant. 'I committed my signature on the Armistice convention!' protested Wilson indignantly. Chrystall and Lavarack stressed that Australian honour was also involved. Lyttelton gave them the reasons why they will have to obey nevertheless and apply the new convention. He described de Gaulle's intervention which, naturally, was not appreciated. The British soldiers remained reluctant with regards the Gaullists, those 'rebels'. As the servicemen were insistent, Lyttelton developed other arguments:

'The convention has been violated by the Vichy side,' he asserted. 'We do not see in what way,' exclaimed Wilson.

'I was starting to be exasperated by the apparent sympathy for the Vichy side and the complacency with which people regarded violations of the Armistice by them,' wrote Lyttelton.

Be that as it may, willingly or otherwise, the interpretive accord would be applied. With this aim, a summit conference was held on 8 August at Damascus. Along with staff members, Wilson, Spears and Catroux attended.

All the military equipment seized from the Vichy side would thus be delivered to the Free French, it being understood that once their own needs had been satisfied, they would hand back to the British Army what it asked for.[50] The Free French would carry out police duties in the assembly areas for the Army of the Levant. After the Army of the Levant had left, British units would occupy the north of Syria, and the east and west of the Anti-Lebanon Mountains: the French would remain in reserve at Beirut and Damascus and occupy, with a battalion, the majority of the large towns, Aleppo, Homs, Tripoli and Soueida.

Was peace now going to be restored between the two allies? No doubt, but trust could not be ordered. When General Catroux expressed a wish to know the order of battle of the British Army, General Wilson was rather reticent, 'given the current poor situation regarding security'. If the Englishman agreed finally to show this information to the Frenchman, it was 'exclusively to General Catroux and to another general accompanying him, and only to those two'. England did not forget Dakar [...] Finally de Gaulle had won. He had however made a 'mortal' enemy, asserted François Kersaudy, in the person of General Spears. This British soldier who, until then, had admired him, was outraged by his treatment of Lyttelton, a Minister of the Crown. He was probably also insulted by the wounding attitude that the General had adopted towards him and his wife. Having done a U-turn, Spears would henceforth work against him. He now had the means to do so: Churchill, who esteemed him greatly, appointed him the first British Minister to Syria and Lebanon. He was thus no longer a sort of *aide de camp* to General de Gaulle, but an important political person with whom de Gaulle had to deal, and he stood up to the French in the Levant. On 7 August, Oliver Lyttelton wrote to de Gaulle to repeat to him that Britain had no other goal than to win the war, but the memory of their disagreement would continue to reverberate for a long time in the political sphere, like thunder after a storm. Henceforth, France and Britain would remain on their guard, and relations between Churchill and de Gaulle, excellent until then, would continue to deteriorate, reaching almost to breaking point. René Cassin: 'It was following Syria that relations between de Gaulle and Churchill deteriorated. While the General was in Cairo, I was acting as a buffer [in London between the two]: it was I who received the General's telegrams and had the task of going to see either Eden or Major Morton[51] to explain his points of view. Inversely, I used to receive Major Morton's recriminations.'

A few weeks later, on 1 September, Churchill was outraged by an interview de Gaulle had given to George Weller, of the *Chicago Daily News*. This was the first public incident. 'Why hadn't London broken finally with Vichy?' asked the journalist of the head of Free France. Because 'England has concluded a sort of deal with Hitler for the duration of the war, in which Vichy acts as an intermediary,' answered General de Gaulle, 'Just like Germany, England exploits Vichy [...] We are witnessing in fact a mutually profitable exchange between two hostile powers which allows the government of Vichy to exist as long as it suits England and Germany.'[52]

Feeling insulted, the British Prime Minister, was beside himself: 'If the interview is authentic, it is clear that de Gaulle has lost his head. Good riddance!' De Gaulle being discredited in his eyes, he ordered all British ministers to suspend relations with the French general in order 'to let him stew in his own juice'. Until further orders, the BBC was closed to him. According to Claude Serreuilles, *aide de camp*, who accompanied him during his return to London, de Gaulle remained silent during the whole trip as far as Carlton Gardens, where he showed 'he was in a foul mood'. He brooded, blamed everyone, cursed the English, and ranted and raved about Spears in particular. According to him, their welcome to him was humiliating and unpleasant. Everyone, umbrella open, was waiting until the storm passed. De Gaulle would hardly see anyone and a gap formed around him. All work was paralysed. It was a very trying situation for his entourage to put up with. He continued to repeat: 'We will lose the war with such people, they do nothing that I have tried to recommend to them, and they want to torpedo the French in the Levant. They are scoundrels.'[53]

Churchill was also exasperated. He judged de Gaulle to be arrogant, ungrateful and anti-British. Considering him 'pretentious and even dangerous', Churchill took him for a 'crypto-fascist'. He soon spoke of 'eliminating de Gaulle politically'. The threat was not idle: Roosevelt did not care for de Gaulle either, and Free France suffered for it. Following on from Dakar, the war in Syria increased the distrust of the American president. Following indiscretions about Dakar, hadn't he already asked Churchill not to communicate any information about military operations to the Free French?[54] Roosevelt, considered Robert Murphy, had 'concluded that de Gaulle had launched a type of civil war in which he placed his personal ambitions before French and Allied interests'. The American president, he recalled, 'never departed from the distrust that he had towards de Gaulle's political clearmindedness, and this distrust was the major element in Franco-American relations until the President's death in 1945'.

Later, in a note from Churchill to Roosevelt, one can read:[55] 'De Gaulle can no longer be considered by Great Britain as a sure friend. In spite of all that he owes the English, he demonstrated hatred of the English wherever he went [...] In Syria, he caused discord between the English and the French.'

18

Brother Enemies

Following on the interpretive agreement, Catroux found himself once more in the leading position in Beirut. In order to prepare the propaganda campaign to influence soldiers of the Army of the Levant into joining the Free French forces, an important objective of the war, the officers of the Army of the Levant were immediately separated from their men. Leaving their units, awaiting the time for themselves to make their own choice, they had to go and live in hotels that had been requisitioned in Beirut. It was thought that this would make it easier to influence the men.

On 25 July, General de Gaulle arrived in Beirut. Wishing above all to not appear to be obligated to the British, but seeming to ignore his promises of independence, he delivered to those who greeted him one of those terse phrases for which he had a talent: 'The mandate continues!'[1] And he settled into the Residence. Isn't he France? Never again, however, would he use the phrase that was a bitter pill for the people.

In Beirut, de Gaulle was going to behave as a head of state. At the Residence, he gave a big reception for the civil, religious, diplomatic and military leaders. Fabre-Luce, who did not like him, reported a serious incident: 'A big reception for the diplomatic corps was announced at 4:30 p.m. The recently promoted British Minister to the Levant, General Spears, naturally expected to be entertained by his former guest: hadn't he often received him at his home in England?' Hadn't Spears invited him to spend Christmas with his family at home when in 1940 he [de Gaulle] was alone, without acquaintances and friends, and condemned to death? Alas, Spears today represented a foreign power that de Gaulle rejected. Mess jacket, decorations, long dress and jewels, the Spears got dressed and:

as they were dressed to the nines, a telephone call invited them for 4:10 p.m. precisely! Disconcerted, and to mark their astonishment, they arrived at 4:20 p.m. They were offered a glass of orangeade, then they were asked a few polite questions and, while they were expecting to move into the drawing room, an *aide de camp* escorted them back to their car. The reception took place without them. If, considered de Gaulle, Spears took part, people would think that he was at home, but Free France intended to show that it was at home.' Machiavellianism? Political act? Unforgettable boorishness in any case. Lady Spears said: 'General de Gaulle was bluffing on a grand scale. He played a devilish game almost without any cards in his hand.'

The incident remained secret. The press was unaware of it, but the rupture between the two men was final. From then on, Spears used all his means to undermine what remained of French sovereignty.

On 15 August at 10:00 a.m., in the cathedral in Beirut, seated in the front row next to General Catroux, General de Gaulle attended a solemn, but not consular, mass[2]; the Apostolic Delegate, Mgr Rémy Leprêtre, did not wish to have one. At 4:00 p.m. an unfortunate incident cast a pall over the day. In the harbour, where the liner *Champollion*, loaded with those being repatriated, was getting ready to sail, some Gaullists who were demonstrating were pushed back by the Australians, and one of these Frenchmen, who was trying to force the barricade, was shot.[3]

The Druse problem suddenly erupted. Recognising the British power, the Druse, notably the Attrache, decided to open the door to them and, on 25 July, as de Gaulle was landing in Beirut, a British brigade was installed at Soueida. The House of France, where the delegate lived, was surrounded and the delegate expelled. The Union Jack replaced the French *tricolore*! Catroux, alerted, protested immediately to Cairo. Wilson, consulted, approved the use of troops: 'The Druse are unruly', he answered, 'and the British Army itself has to look after security in this zone'. Informed of this, de Gaulle, beside himself, once more considered a rupture with London. Georges Buis, Catroux's principal private secretary: 'A meeting was held one evening. Present were de Gaulle, Captain de Courcel, his *aide de camp*, Catroux, Colonel Collet, Bob Decar and me. It was there that the decision was taken to not let the situation deteriorate at our expense. We decided to write to General Wilson. It was almost a *casus belli*. 'I have no intention of defeating the British Empire', wrote General de Gaulle, 'but if you do not withdraw your troops from Soueida and if you do not put me back in the Residence, I will be obliged to attack you'. And this was done. On his orders, Catroux sent Monclar and a whole battalion of the Legion to retake Soueida where Australian and Free French troops soon found themselves face to face, armed, ready to open fire. 'Do not come any closer', shouted the Australian brigadier, threateningly, 'It would not be the first time I have fired on the French!'[4] Before opening fire, Monclar asked Damascus for instructions by telephone: 'What must I do? I act or I wait?' 'Stay where you are', answered Catroux, who called Wilson in Cairo: 'What are you planning to do?' he asked him. 'Wait' said the Englishman, who immediately sent a threatening note to de Gaulle to demand the withdrawal of his forces. De Gaulle, as one might expect, refused to back down. A trial of strength was well and truly in the offing. De Gaulle: 'You are perfectly at liberty to settle with Catroux the question of the stationing of British and French troops in the Jebel Druse...I consider that your threatening remarks are regrettable... If I remain inclined towards a frank military cooperation, it is necessary that the sovereign rights of France in Syria and Lebanon and the dignity of the French Army remain beyond reach.' The days passed. The troops were in position facing each other. In Damascus, the French delegation became alarmed at the risk of rupture with which the leader of Free France was playing dangerously, but the British, finally, backed down. On 31 July, they hauled down their flag and withdrew from Soueida where Monclar hoisted the French *tricolore*.

London was again irritated, but de Gaulle disregarded this, and to assert the presence of France, undertook a tour of the Levant in very shaky conditions, in an old twin-engine Caudron Goéland.[5] In the Jebel Druse, where France had returned, he'd had great success. It was astonishing to see to what extent this personage, however little known, had a personal magnetism which was strengthened afterwards by all his travels in the East.

Were the French and British going to continue waging a small war under the eyes of the population? To maintain order without losing too much prestige or frittering away the means, the French and English together decided on 5 November, to place the east of Syria under a single command to look after the whole of the economic and military questions of the three eastern sectors, Jazeera, Euphrates and Palmyra, i.e. two-thirds of Syria. Put in command of this very large area, Brosset was promoted temporary colonel. Under his command, Franco–British cooperation was exemplary. The troops camped side by side around two flagpoles, the flag-raising ceremonies were carried out together, the flags being hoisted to the sound of the British bugle call in the morning and the French one in the evening. Invitations to dinner reunited officers in their respective messes, turn and turn about. On 13 November, Brosset reported to Catroux that the taxes were gathered, that a portion of the weapons had been recovered, and that the region was quiet.

The installations of the Iraq Petroleum Company's pipeline were the subject of numerous thefts and sabotage. Brosset also settled this problem. Peace returned. For lack of personnel, medical and veterinary assistance, as well as the plans for rice fields in the Hassatche region, could not unfortunately be resumed. The only major works were those by the British who, anxious about fast transport near the Turkish frontier, built the Rakka bridge over the Euphrates and repaired the Deir-ez-Zor–Aleppo and the Deir-ez-Zor–Hassatche lines. Brosset left his post on 27 April 1942.[6]

'Scarcely had I settled in Beirut', wrote de Gaulle 'than I undertook negotiations with the heads of the Nationalist Party to bring about the realization of the treaty of independence whereby Lebanon, like Syria, would recognize the favoured position of France. Naturally we were constantly and secretly thwarted by General Sir Edward Spears.'

Via inextricable political twists and turns, the conversations, started in June 1941 in Damascus upon General de Gaulle's arrival, were going to continue, either with Catroux or with his successors, but without ever ending. Negotiations never made progress. No attempt at reconciliation was ever successful. Each side stuck to its position, which was increasingly settled and less and less negotiable.

On 21 July, the [Vichy] French started to release their British, Australian, Indian and Free French prisoners of war.[7] At the end of July, they had handed back 841, but a certain number of them had left the Levant, being sent to France. The fact was not hidden at Saint-Jean-d'Acre. In the light of conditions obtaining in Europe in 1941, these prisoners were dispersed. Wishing to recover all these men as quickly as possible, the British proposed that they be sent to Gibraltar but, no one knowing where they were held, General Wilson took a drastic step: if by 7:00 p.m.

on 5 August, they were not returned, Generals Dentz, Arlabosse and Jeannekyn, as well as about 30 [Vichy] French officers would be arrested or kept in captivity until the complete surrender of all the Commonwealth prisoners. On 5 August, at 10:00 p.m., nothing having happened, General Savige, commanding the Australian troops, went to the French headquarters in Tripoli and passed on the order to General Dentz that he had received to arrest him to take him to Palestine. Savige, according to Corbeiller, understood the gravity of a disproportionate act that was inspired more by politics than rank. He carried out the order but on his return to Jerusalem he gave his resignation in a letter that he had read to the French.[8] Generals Arlabosse and Jeannekyn and 35 officers were thus arrested with Dentz and taken *manu militare* to Jerusalem. All were freed at the end of August, upon the return of the last prisoner. Moreover, the assignment to Jerusalem was not too cruel since, properly treated, they were able to go and visit the Holy City, dressed in civilian clothes.

On 2 July, well before the end of the fighting, 14 British officer prisoners, including a colonel, had been sent by aircraft to Salonika. On 11 July, 13 NCOs had also been sent to Salonika. The intention was to send them to France by train. Due to mechanical problems, one aircraft had to land on the island of Karpathos, held by the Italians. They sent 14 prisoners to Greece. The initial measures taken by the [Vichy] French Military Attaché to recover the prisoners having been unsuccessful, there was a delay until 14 August when a Potez aircraft was able to take them to Toulon. They were then sent to Beirut which was reached on 15 August.

In Tripoli, where the staff of the Army of the Levant had been installed since 15 July, inventories, operation reports and casualty lists were being drawn up, as well as letters to the families of those killed. On 5 August, the announcement of the arrest of the leaders caused consternation, and then the appearance of the Gaullists provoked exasperation. All that was, in fact, in total contradiction with the undertakings made at Saint-Jean-d'Acre. The [Vichy] French understood that they had been conned. For them, it was a betrayal. The Army of the Levant stood together.[9] In the camps, appeals for unity and calls for a sense of duty were made; past combats were honoured by awarding medals, and by increasing the number of parades and flag-raising ceremonies. The consequences of desertion in time of war were explained to the men. Everywhere, on the fronts and entrances of buildings, and on vehicles, banners and slogans appeared that the British removed as provocative: 'Long live Pétain', 'Camp Pétain', 'Pétain, the only chief'. The *francisque*[10] was sold at the entrance to camps where the appearance of Gaullist recruiters caused general outcries. Michelet: 'Those who presented themselves at the entry to camps around Tripoli were greeted with boos and their cars were stoned.' All direct contact between the Gaullists and the soldiers of the Army of the Levant was forbidden.

It was the former chief of staff of the troops in the Levant in 1940, General de Larminat, who had been chosen to lead the recruiting campaign. He knew by name practically all of Dentz's officers, but was badly received everywhere. After one lecture, a question was heard: 'Don't the Free French see that the English are the only winners? The number one enemy for the moment is England!' Larminat, who did not contradict, answered: 'Stay with us so that together we can keep for France these states under mandate which run the risk of escaping from her sovereignty.' Then a voice in the room: 'Whose fault is that?' The following incident was quoted: General de Larminat entered a room, no one stood up. A Free French officer ordered: 'On your feet!' and an anonymous voice answered: 'I do not stand up for a man condemned to death!'

The legionnaires especially were the object of constant concern. At leave times, as they left the barracks, bogus Australians would take them for a friendly drink in town and explain to them in their mother tongue where their future lay. They were given the third degree. Many let themselves be convinced. Freed on 9 August, none of the officers of the Palmyra garrison defected, but 'five NCOs, who nevertheless had conducted themselves perfectly during the campaign, had gone over to the other side.'[11]

It seemed only one airman, Martial Valin, used a less elementary approach. He explained:

> There was a lot of propaganda on the radio. Our favourite subject was the success of the Free French Number One Squadron, the name of the Free French Forces squadron in the RAF. One day I said to myself: what can that mean to the French people? The Number One Squadron didn't really care [...] They knew what it was [...] And what if they were given names that they knew, names which meant something to them, names of provinces? I chose names of occupied regions, Alsace and Lorraine, naturally.

Alsace for fighters and Lorraine for bombers [...] I went to find
General de Gaulle who gave me his agreement.

14 August 1941. Headlines on page one of the daily *L'Orient*:
'The Army of the Levant is disbanded. Its officers, NCOs and men
are placed under the command of General Catroux.' Widespread
stupefaction.

General Catroux, Commander-in-Chief, signed the following
order on 11 August 1941: The army to which you belong is
disbanded. I salute the flags, I call to mind the great feats that
it accomplished in the Middle East over the past 22 years, I
honour its dead. From this day forward and until the time of their
repatriation, its officers, NCOs and men are placed under my
command. They will obey my orders. This arrangement leaves the
full range of options given to them by the Armistice convention.
Officers, NCOs and men, you will choose without pressure but,
before deciding, you will ask yourself if your duty is not to remain
in the Levant, with me, with your comrades, in the service of
France whose flag, rights and interests I defend here. France
will inspire you as it has me. Signed at the Headquarters of Free
France in the Levant, 11 August 1941, General Commanding-in-
Chief, Catroux.

Scandalised, Verdilhac leapt up. Outraged by this betrayal of the
Saint-Jean accords, he called Chrystall, his opposite number on
the Control Commission, and gave him his views which can be
easily guessed. He was indignant that the British authorities had
'given the command of a French army to a foreign officer, that is
to say one deprived of his citizenship'.

What else could Verdilhac do other than to protest? The
vanquished have to give in. Vichy supporters or not, free or not, all
troops therefore now found themselves under the same authority.
Its leaders having been removed, the Army of the Levant had
to obey the Gaullists who, henceforth, would settle everything,
movements, convoys, embarkation, military justice, etc.

Michelet: 'In the streets of Beirut, [Vichy] French officers
were subjected to innumerable humiliations and gross insults.
In numerous cases, FFL soldiers, recognisable by their sloppy,
if not slovenly, uniform, shouted abuse at Vichy officers, calling
them "Krauts! Traitors! Renegades! Uhlans! Nazis! They are
paid in marks!" It needed a great deal of self-control to adhere

to the instructions given by General Dentz that they repeated to themselves each morning: "Do not respond to provocations. Do not respond to provocations. Do not..." In spite of that, several serious incidents happened.' The recruiting campaign turned to abuse, and sometimes even to fist fights. In the cafés, brawls occurred. In the streets, jostling occurred. Does a FFL soldier really have to salute a Vichy officer? Does a Vichy captain have to salute a Gaullist major? Sometimes it got as far as drawing weapons. Vehicles were grabbed. To try to restore a little order, outings were cancelled. The clashes were so sharp that the British ended by forbidding access to the [Vichy] French lines by Gaullists unless they were accompanied by a British officer. It was not surprising that, under such conditions, enlistments were uncommon.

The position of the Free French was therefore uncomfortable. To the hostility that their propaganda caused was added the animosity of the Australians who were irritated by the question of weapons: to whom should they go? In his report of 2 August 1941 to Wilson, Lavarack wrote: 'The French equipment reserved for the future needs of the Free French, in particular anti-tank guns, anti-aircraft guns and tanks, could replace and overcome the shortages of equipment of the troops that I command [...] This equipment could, here and now, be used for training and given to the FFL if necessary when the fighting troops are re-equipped.' Not only did the Australians lack equipment, but they were asked to hand over what they had captured on the battlefield! Their indignation bordered on revolt. Discipline became lax. Major disturbances took place. A whole company raided the military warehouses in Rayak where hundreds of gallons of whisky, held in barrels, disappeared. This *affaire,* which caused a big row, reached the ears of the Control Commission. On the order of the highest authorities, the Australians were ordered on parade in a barracks and, once they were lined up, they were asked to empty their water bottles on to the very hot ground in front of them. A strong smell of spirits filled the air, but no one breathed a word. All, moreover, was not lost: they had managed to save 'a few barrels of whisky, canned goods, machine-gun belts, a double anti-aircraft stand for light machine guns, and many other very precious things'. On 1 September, at the Tripoli cooperative store, another group carried out 'remarkably well executed looting', noted a report to the Control Commission, admiringly, 'particularly in the cellar. On two occasions, trucks came to carry away the booty [...] I must admit', went on the report, 'that Frenchmen belonging to the Free French Forces ended up joining them'. On the same day, 'the same scenes of looting occurred at the garrison NCOs' mess: break in, doors forced, removal of all the equipment [...] used for the needs of certain Australian messes'. At Homs, Australian soldiers sold to the Syrian civilians stocks of goods left in the citadel by the [Vichy] French. Trading took place at night, over the outer wall. Everything was sold. 'When we left the place', one of them said, 'there was nothing left that was not nailed to the floor'.

'In Beirut, Australian soldiers were rather joyful and happy' noted a French officer. 'About 4:00 p.m., trucks from surrounding camps brought them in, fresh and full of energy and, from 6:00 p.m., the same trucks started to pick them up, dead drunk in the gutter, to take them to aid posts where they were sobered up.' Their relations with the local population were the source of frequent incidents. Complaints poured in to the extent that, only ten days after the Armistice, General Spears sent this note to General Auchinleck in Cairo: 'The Australians are already very feared by the locals. Their behaviour, with the exception of some specialized units which are very disciplined, would be a disgrace in any army.'[12] It was said that they had taken the wedding rings of Vichy officers and had deprived the prisoners of their water bottles. 'At Mezzé aerodrome, as if to increase their contribution to the conduct of the war, they stole and destroyed essential elements from the Air France radio station, the most powerful and effective in the French territories between metropolitan France and Indochina.' Given the seriousness and the frequency of these incidents, leave to Beirut was finally cancelled, but without success it seems since on 11 October, Wilson wrote to Blamey, the Commander-in-Chief of the Australian Military Forces:

> I regret that I have to say that several cases have been reported to me recently of brutal assaults perpetrated by Australian soldiers, either against other soldiers, French or British, or against military or civilian policemen, or against civilians. I have contacted their unit commanders and I expect that exemplary punishments will be awarded. I have asked them to send the responsible ones before a court martial. Exemplary sentences of two years to be served in the Middle East can have a very deterrent effect [...] I thank you in advance for your advice in order to put a stop to all that.

The Englishman's formula did not please Blamey who was very supportive of his troops. He responded: 'It is a common type of explanation to place the responsibility for the disturbances on broad Australian shoulders. But when these accusations do not rest on any real fact, they cause an immense wrong to the good relations between the different Empire units.' And he concluded: 'I am afraid that these discipline questions are not entirely within my remit.' But Wilson did not remain passive: he sent Blamey two reports concerning serious incidents involving Australians, one, the mugging of a lieutenant-colonel by a private, and another against a nurse in Damascus. In addition, he gave figures: in the two months following the end of operations, there were 17 attacks on soldiers, four on police and 27 on civilians. Australians were involved in 15 cases, and the conclusions of 33 other enquiries were awaited. All that did not come to an end until the return of the troops to Australia that was now threatened by the Japanese advance in the Pacific where war had just broken out. Mr Menzies, the Prime Minister in Canberra, was clamouring to Churchill for the return of his troops. It was not until 15 January 1942 that the Australians started to leave the Levant for Palestine,[13] and on 30 January, started to embark for the Far East.[14]

The departure held some bitterness for troops whose conduct in battle had been beyond all praise, but who felt that they had been manipulated and involved by trickery in a questionable campaign. In addition, a campaign without glory, one of the most obvious Allied mistakes of the war, would be largely overshadowed at home as it was later in France. 'The excellent performance of the 7th Australian Division remained unknown', observed one of its officers. 'The very fine performance produced by the Australian Imperial Force, in particular by The Silent Seventh, has never been described', wrote Colonel Buckley in 1995, its former liaison officer with General Maitland Wilson, no doubt because of Churchill's wish to not give too much lustre to this fight against a former ally. No medal was struck for this campaign and more than 50 years were to elapse before members were entitled to the Africa Star.[15] While other campaigns – Libya, Papua New Guinea, the Pacific – were the subject of pilgrimages and official visits in 1991, no commemoration marked the Battle of Syria in Australia.

Impatient to see the innumerable incidents come to an end, General Wilson asked, at the end of July, the French delegates of the Armistice Commission to accelerate the repatriation process. Vichy, as soon as the accords were passed, undertook discussions with the German and Italian armistice commissions to allow free passage of ships in Greek and Italian waters. The first four liners could transport 24,000 men in the first fortnight, specified the French Admiralty. Was it too soon? Or too fast? 'At this rate', protested Colonel Kœnig, the Free French representative on the Armistice commission, 'the propaganda of the Free French Forces will not be able to work properly'. Then General Chrystall, coldly: 'I detest that propaganda. We have to get the boats to come.'[16]

Composed of half Vichy and half Gaullist officers, and in the presence of a British or Australian officer, the options commissions operated from the end of July. In the courtyard of the Hamidiye barracks in Damascus, for example, the *tirailleurs*, with full kit and weapons, were drawn up in three ranks. A big table was placed in front of them. One after the other, the men moved forward, saluted and were invited to answer individually. 'You see the two doors? Through the one on the right, you remain in Syria with de Gaulle and continue the fight. Through the left, you catch the boat and return to [French] North Africa.' The man answered and took the direction of his choice. In the 'options rooms' in Lebanon, the process was comparable. Carrying their full regulation pack, the soldiers entered a room one by one, where they found two identical tables. In front of them, as they entered, was an officer standing who asked them the regulation question, awaited the answer and, each one, according to his choice, went and signed one or the other attestation form, then left through the corresponding door. Those who became FFL were thus immediately separated from the others. For the officers, the procedure was identical. Was the process truly free? 'How clumsy were the Gaullists who, instead of trying to cajole, had only sarcasm, disdain and veiled curses on their lips!' remembered Le Corbeiller. 'How many officers and men would have said "yes" if only [the Gaullists] had known how to entice them in and if they had refrained from continuing to bully and abuse them.'[17]

Le Corbeiller: 'Legionnaires, *tirailleurs*, and *spahis* obeyed in a spirit of duty: wherever the leader is, there the soldier must go... Traumatised by the recent fighting, weeping for their comrades, the officers, NCOs and men hoped only to find once more the regular discipline of a professional army. Two thousand eight hundred prisoners liberated from Palestine did not forgive either the barbed wire, the propaganda, the watch towers, or the harassment.' Practically no airman changed his mind: their choice was already made. Testifying at Dentz's trial, Major Tézé said:[18] 'I found my Air Force friends installed on dispersal airfields in extremely difficult conditions due to the heat, dust and lack of water. All wanted to bring this fight very rapidly to an end, but none thought to shirk the orders they had been given. They had every facility, with their aircraft, to cross over to Palestine. To my knowledge, none did so.' In the Legion, the former Spanish Republicans were sensitive to antifascist arguments. However, it was at the last moment that the ones who joined the Free French made up their minds. Boissoudy: 'The 6th Foreign [Regiment] had followed the officers as a group and embarked on three ships. General Kœnig had the band come and play *Le Boudin*.[19] It was extraordinary: 1,200 legionnaires jumped into the water to reach the wharf and join the Free French Forces! One thousand two hundred is a very good figure.' In fact: out of the three battalions, the strength of two battalions changed sides: 692 according to the Armistice Commission, 1,030 according to Pierre Montagnon. With only 1,233 men, it was a regiment reduced by two-thirds which, at the end of August, landed in Marseilles. Pierre Messmer, lieutenant: 'I must say that it wasn't the officers who joined the FFL, but the legionnaires. Out of the whole Foreign Legion from Syria, there were only two officers, two captains, who joined Free France.'[20]

Numerous African *tirailleurs* chose Free France: over in Africa they were at home. Indifferent to the choices of the Europeans, many Congolese, Chadians and Senegalese joined their ethnic group – Mossis , Saras, Bayas or Wolof (*Ouolof*) – who spoke their language, danced the same way, and ate the same food as them. Moreover, would the Free French miss them? Bodman: 'The Senegalese that I had for two weeks were very mediocre, terrified of gunfire, huddling like sheep at the slightest problem, not knowing much about looking after themselves, and using the country very poorly. The European officers and NCOs in general behaved well, getting themselves killed or wounded in leading the shapeless mass of their men, who were too well fed and unfit for fighting, in a line on the broad fronts on which we were forced to fight.'

In this crowd were some outsiders. Some Vichy members wanted to continue the fight, but with the British not the Free French. Alas, it was a forbidden choice. On 2 August, Lavarack wrote to Wilson: 'An increased number of [Vichy] French would like to join the British forces because they are hostile to the Free French.' There were also, in the opposite direction, surprisingly, some people going over to Vichy. Embarked compulsorily, 120 Free French, judged undesirable by their command, were put ashore for security reasons, but some, disguised as Vichy sympathisers, returned to France secretly.

In total, according to the British control, out of approximately 37,000 men, 32,380 opted to return to France. That is 85 per cent of the officers and 90 per cent of the NCOs; 5,688 men went over to Free France, i.e. one-seventh of the total. The Vichy figures are comparable: 5,848 joining Free France – 4,070 according to Yves Gras – including 99 officers – 128 according to General de Gaulle, 72 according to Pierre Montagnon and François Brochet, a member of the Armistice Commission; 540 NCOs and men of the metropolitan troops, 692 legionnaires, 517 Lebanese and 3,593 Senegalese; 66 per cent of those who joined Free France were legionnaires or blacks. 'There were few' remarked Weygand, 'about the number of French of all kinds killed during this miserable adventure'. 'Among those who joined Free France', noted Brochet, 'many were married to Lebanese Christian women and had created families locally that they could not abandon. Others had material interests to look after.' Verdilhac said with considerable gratification: 'I proudly proclaim out loud my pride as a French officer in seeing that, in spite of the incredible situation in which it has been placed, in spite of the systematic removal of its staff, in spite of all that has been done to reduce it to the state of a disorganised flock and without leaders, the Army of the Levant, in its distress, has given a splendid example of its cohesion, of its elevated morale and of its military valour and discipline.' If the figures were disappointing for the Free French, these reinforcements were the last. After Mers el-Kebir, Dakar, Gabon and Syria, the Gaullist recruitment among the military dried up.

Before leaving the Levant, numerous officers and NCOs asked for authorisation to accompany the working parties tasked to go and remove the traces of battle. Le Corbeiller went to Kasmiyeh, where the Le Corné battalion had fought. 'Here and there', he remembered, 'a helmet, a water bottle, cut telephone wire, a broken weapon, smashed ammunition boxes, shell holes, firing pits that had fallen in [...] Here and there, the small dark piles surrounded by wild vegetation are the bodies of those who fought here two months ago. Some of these bodies, forgotten or not found, remained on the ground as they had fallen, their grimacing faces turned to the sky. We buried these poor remains

[...] How numerous were those who remained there, Gaillard-Bournazel, Lalanne, Chevigny, Pinoteau, Le Chauvelais, Bodman and all the common people, their soldiers!' Before boarding his ship, Verdilhac visited the cemeteries that he was going to have to abandon, entrusting their care to the British, the Lebanese and the Syrians. He laid flowers on the British tombs as he did on the French ones. Catroux, later, did the same: 'The remains of the dead [Free French forces] lay in the cemetery in Damascus where I gathered them together,' he wrote. 'They were not alone there. Their graves were placed side by side with those of their adversaries. All were similar and bore the same epitaph: "*Mort pour la France*" (Died for France).'[21]

On 12 August, four members of de Gaulle's tank company went to recover the Hotchkiss tanks destroyed at Nejah on 15 June.

> In the Levant, the bodies are stripped, that's the rule. Dead who have been buried are dug up, then abandoned to the wild animals. People pretend to not know, they bury just the same [...] The tanks that had been put out of action remained on the battlefield [...] Two months after the battle, there were no flies, no smell of death, but the bodies were there, Lucien Cocu in the turret, Louis Kœnig in the driver's position. The first had been hit by an armour-piercing round, the skull of the second had shattered, the jawbone torn away. They had to overcome the horror [...] On the floor of the driver's position there was an automatic pistol, with a chambered round. He had fired a bullet into his head through his mouth, concluded Perry softly. There was still some paper between his teeth, the remains of his pay book that he had not succeeded in swallowing completely. The turret was penetrated, but the engine had not been hit, nor the driver's position [...] Why hadn't Kœnig turned around? After having extracted the body and laid it on the ground, they examined it: there was a shell fragment lodged between two vertebrae [...] Paralysed, thinking that he was going to be taken prisoner, he tried to swallow the only identity document that he had on him, and then suicided.[22]

The repatriation of the 35,968 passengers, according to the report of the Control Commission – 32,380 according to the British – was carried out by eight convoys and a pickup boat[23] between 7 August and 27 September.[24] At the departure of each ship, military honours were rendered by the Australians. In order that the sailings were dignified and solemn, a note on 3 August from General de Verdilhac, drawn up with General Chrystall, specified the details:

> For each convoy, honours will be rendered at the moment when the first ship, having cast off its moorings, starts to get under way, by an honour guard of about 100 men. The band will play *La Marseillaise*. A part of the [Vichy] French troops on board will line the railings and present arms. These troops will be drawn up all along the ship's railings so that they always face the British troops during the ship's manoeuvring. With the exception of the [Vichy] French troops returning the honours, no – absolutely no passenger, civilian or military – must be on deck. No shouting, no handkerchief is to be waved, etc. by passengers who may find themselves at the windows or portholes.

On 26 September, when Verdilhac was the last man to leave the Levant, General Chrystall, President of the Armistice Commission, sent him a long, almost fraternal, letter:[25]

> My dear General, From my bedroom after our luncheon party, I write to you the last of many letters! It is to thank you most sincerely for the charming travelling clock you have so kindly given me. It is a souvenir for me to have and pass on to my children as a memory of my close association with you in such good personal relations. I value the gift extremely but more so the thought which prompted you to give it to me. I meant every word I said at our last conference today regarding the assistance I have had from you in carrying out my task, in spite of your nine hundred letters! In proposing the toast of 'France' at our luncheon I also meant every word and, as I think you have appreciated, we all look forward to the coming greatness of your beautiful country. It has been my earnest endeavour, at the Round Table and away from it, to bring all Frenchmen together. To try and infuse a spirit of forgetfulness for all that has passed and only look to the future united France, secure and free. If I may be allowed to, I wish to express my profound admiration for the skilful way you have conducted your case. Your letters, by their clarity of expression, their latent touches of humour and above all your sense of the importance of essentials as opposed to pettiness, have especially impressed me [...] I trust when you arrive in France you will have a happy re-union with

your family and that conditions in the country will not be as we hear they are. You take with you not only my personal regard and best wishes for your future happiness and as well as that of 'La France', but those from my staff down to the most junior clerk and office boy [...] Bon voyage, good luck and God bless you, your people and France. Believe me, my dear General, your sincere friend, John Chrystall.

In the same way, when General Keime was about to board his ship to travel to France, an orderly came to give him a letter from General Evetts, his former adversary. It was Evetts, at the head of the British 6th Division, who had attacked him on Jebel Mazaar: 'Dear General, I thank you very much for your very kind letter [...] I can't thank you enough for the spirit of understanding and fairness that you have shown in our dealings. In a situation which could have been difficult, common sense has, thanks to you, overcome misunderstandings. I regret greatly not being able to come and say goodbye to you myself, but I really hope to do so later. I have kept your address. Here is mine [...] I hope to be able to see you again soon and to continue a friendship that has started so happily.' The two generals never saw each other again, but until the death of one of them, they exchanged goodwill messages each year.

The correct nature of the Franco–British relations and the melancholy dignity of this final departure were sometimes disturbed by some mad men who, at the departure of the ships, abused those who were leaving. Having wanted to quieten a group who, on the docks, was hurling abuse at those leaving, an Australian officer found himself shoved aside. The atmosphere became inflamed, a brawl threatened, revolvers were drawn. The Australian fired – there were three wounded and one dead. Access to the harbour was then forbidden to the Gaullists.

There then remained only a few thousand French, including members of religious congregations who did not hide their hostility to the Gaullists – some still said public prayers in favour of Marshal Pétain. Only the promise made by General de Gaulle to never mobilise the religious communities managed to prevent their massive exodus. According to Guy Lambeau, there no longer remained in the states of the Levant 'but a frayed scrap of French sovereignty'.

The departure of all these French people who were necessary for the running of the country, the sudden exodus of that society which was settled in the cities, known by its neighbours, and sometimes for a very long time, signified the *de facto* if not the official end of the mandate, at least that of the French presence and prestige. In this territory, badly administered, an unequal struggle, which became more and more obvious, developed with the British. Devoid of substance, without weight, France's authority no longer covered more than a sham presence symbolised by a threatened flag. The Levant having become part of the sterling zone, France's position was irredeemably compromised. The fruit was ready to fall.

'The clearest result of this was to introduce a Franco-French civil war into the heart of the world conflict' noted Georges Hirtz, a member of Weygand's staff. 'The officers and men repatriated to [French] North Africa made no bones about expressing their resentment and the anger that they felt about the "abnormality" of this conflict that was purely destructive. The officers and NCOs of the 22nd and 29th Algerian Tirailleur Regiments were among the keenest to express their sickened disapproval. The antigaullism which was already deep-rooted in the Army of Africa, as in the civilian population, was only aggravated more.'[26]

A convinced collaborator with Germany, Pierre Laval succeeded Admiral Darlan[27] on 17 April 1942 as the head of the government, the latter remaining, however, the Marshal's heir apparent and head of the armed forces. Breaking with Vichy in November 1942 and making up his mind in the face of the success of the Anglo–American landings in [French] North Africa, the Admiral immediately relaunched the French Army into the battle against Germany. Thus, less than 18 months after the conflict in Syria, the former members of the Army of the Levant found themselves alongside the Allies. Dentz, then made this remark: 'If the Admiral had ordered me to make a last-ditch stand, I would have known what that meant and I would not have lost so many men, but he ordered me to undertake an all-out resistance. He made me send my fellows to their death and now I see him in [French] North Africa organising a government and negotiating with the British! I will never forgive him'

19

Vae Victis[1]

Arrested on 4 September 1944 in Grenoble and then transferred to Paris, General Dentz was put on trial in the High Court. Madame Dentz, looking haggard, was present at the trial. For a long time it was difficult, if not impossible, to think about the tragic fate of this broken man.

First in his class at Saint-Cyr, an excellent frontline fighter, first in his year at the *École de guerre* (Staff College), then *général d'armée* (British four-star general; French five-star), the fate of this Lorraine patriot, of this exceptionally gifted officer, turned tragic on 12 May 1940 when General Weygand ordered him to receive the Germans in Paris, which had been declared an open city. Next, appointed High Commissioner of France in the Levant by Marshal Pétain, he had, in a difficult local situation and subject to indecisive directions from his government, to fill extremely delicate political functions for which nothing had prepared him.

Sabotaging as much as possible the arms shipments he had been ordered to send to Iraq, urging the German aircraft that had been sent to him to disappear, warning Wavell of their departure, adopting as low a profile as possible, Dentz had done everything to minimise the consequences of Vichy's orders.

After having tried everything to avoid the conflict, but obeying his duty when his hand was forced, he defended himself with courage and initiative until his forces were exhausted. His units, except Collet's, showed exemplary discipline. Neither soft nor narrow-minded, he had confidence in his commanders, letting them carry out evolutions that he had not thought of himself. Friends or enemies, all professionals saluted his competence. Having spent more than a month among British troops, he had never been bothered, and they had rendered military honours to him when he left them. If he hesitated a few hours about soliciting

German help to spare his men's blood – those hours overwhelmed him – he had finally refused. Beaten, he tried to protect France's position: no destruction was carried out either in the cities, or in the ports, or in the industrial and economic centres of the country. He refused to destroy the pipeline and the warehouses in Tripoli. Was he a traitor?

In accordance with the note handed by the British to Free France on 19 June 1941, the former testified to the contrary:[2] 'Far from wanting to impose dishonourable conditions on General Dentz, His Majesty's Government is absolutely willing to accord all the honours of war to him, as well as to the officers and public servants who have carried out what they consider to be their duty with respect to their government. In consequence, there can be no question of condemning General Dentz or any other officer or public servant to death or any other punishment.'

On 11 July, implicating Free France, the Allies renewed this commitment: 'The Allies do not feel any resentment towards the French in Syria [...] They will not undertake any legal action against the command nor the authorities nor the troops [...] General de Gaulle has never dealt ruthlessly with any of his Army comrades who have fought against him while carrying out orders they have received. He does not intend to do so in the present circumstances.'

'Never having brought before the courts those of my Army comrades who fought against me in the execution of orders received', confirmed the General in his *Mémoires*, 'I did not have any intention of doing so in the present case'.[3] However, General de Gaulle distinguished the case of General Dentz from that of his troops:

> In his position as High Commissioner in the Levant, he had permitted, in Spring 1941, German squadrons to land on Syrian airfields as Vichy demanded, determined places where the *Wehrmacht* could possibly land and, finally, had the forces he commanded fight against Free France and the British. After an initial resistance which could pass for a 'gallant last stand' [*baroud d'honneur*] Dentz had asked on what conditions he would be accorded an armistice. These conditions, finalised by me in consultation with the English command, included the transfer of the powers of the High Commissioner of Vichy to that of Free France and, for all the military and civil servants, the possibility of joining me. I let it be known that in the case of acceptance of what we offered, no legal

proceedings would be engaged against the High Commissioner and his subordinates. But, instead of agreeing to reconciliation, General Dentz had launched into intense fighting which could only profit the enemy. The miserable fellow went as far as asking for the direct support of the German Air Force. Induced to lay down his arms after big losses had been sustained by both sides, he concluded a convention with the British which assuredly served British interests but not those of France.

Thus, a victim of his sense of duty, General Dentz found himself caught between two irreconcilable parties. Abandoned without directives by a government with ambiguous practices, left alone to face his adversaries, he ended by bringing down on to his head all the contradictions of an era of despair, resentment and vengeance. In the same way that no German after 1945 would admit to have ever been a supporter of Hitler, no one in France, at the same time, would admit to ever having approved of Marshal Pétain. All the earliest Gaullists, all resistance fighters, all were keen to prove their patriotism by following the public prosecutor in overwhelming the unfortunate Dentz. However, hadn't this magistrate, like the president of the same court, also sworn allegiance to the Marshal? This was a horrifying period when justice felt, at that time, fear and a guilty conscience, and which led to the settling of scores. Did someone have to pay for the collective guilt? It was therefore going to be him.

The prosecutor was overwhelmingly against him.[4] Dentz answered him at the end of the trial:

> I am aware of having done all in my power to safeguard my country's interests. I am aware of not having done anything against military honour. I draw this awareness from the fact that the Allies themselves rendered military honours to me and that, on my departure from Beirut, I was saluted by a company of British infantry which presented arms to me and that in Jerusalem, taking leave of he who had been briefly, alas, my adversary, General Sir Maitland Wilson, we shook hands.
>
> Gentlemen, you are going to give your verdict. This verdict puts at stake my head, my liberty and, more than that, it risks my honour. It is going to judge me with respect especially to the 1,200 officers and 30,000 men who followed me back from Syria, of whom almost all returned with me to France and who now are fighting on the battlefields in Germany and Alsace, after having

fought in Italy. Whatever sacrifice you impose on me, I accept it if I can be certain that it will serve the cause of the unity and grandeur of my country to which I have devoted by entire life.

On 20 April 1945, General Dentz was condemned to death and military degradation for 'intelligence with the enemy in order to favour his business undertakings'. An 'ignominious fate', judged Weygand.

To shoot down German aircraft would have been to break the Armistice. Not to shoot was to collaborate. There was no answer to this dilemma. 'Dentz was crucified on that cross', noted Fabre-Luce.

Pardoned on 25 October 1945 by the Head of State, his sentence was commuted to life imprisonment. Recapitulating his grievances about Dentz, General de Gaulle confirmed in his *Mémoires* that 'nothing justified any longer the immunity that I had previously been able to envisage about him. General Dentz was condemned to death but, taking into account the loyal and excellent services that he had given in other times, and sympathetic to the drama of this fallen soldier, I immediately pardoned him.'[5] A pardon that secretly was accompanied by considerable contempt. In 1947, the General confided to his brother Pierre:[6] 'Dentz was a fool. A policeman [...] I won't speak about him further: he is dead.'

Yes, but how?

On 20 April the condemned man, Henri-Fernand Dentz, 63 years of age, took off his uniform and put on the coarse woollen clothes, a coat without pockets and the trousers of those condemned to death, which button on the sides so that they can be put on over irons. The shaven skull, irons on the feet, a cap on the head, he was taken to a cell in Fresnes[7] where his torments began: the cell was damp and it was November. It was cold. He was going to become ill. On his ankles, ulcers were going to appear. Not cared for, they are going to get worse. The distress lasted 200 days.

In an appendix in a book with a small circulation,[8] can be found the note justifying his conduct that Dentz wrote after his trial:

General Dentz refused to evacuate and hand over to the Germans the aerodrome at Aleppo. He even refused the Germans any installation that could serve as the basis for the establishment of a permanent facility (unloading replacement engines, workshops, etc.) He reduced by three-quarters the quantity of weapons handed over to Iraq. There were only 15,000 rifles handed over

(Gras model 1874 rifles) instead of 50,000; 200 machine guns instead of 800; four 75mm guns instead of 24; eight 155mm mortars, and 50 trucks instead of 600. He refused to send French instructors to Iraq. The question of using the ports was pushed to one side.

One could add that, on 16 June, he refused the help of *stukas* based in Cyprus and also refused, as confirmed by Patrick Facon,[9] to attack the airfields in Palestine in order to avoid widening the conflict.

The note ends thus: 'In Spring 1941, at the height of German military power, he [General Dentz] could only measure the sum of the threats weighing on the world and leave it up to the Marshal to safeguard the country's interests. He only regrets that the explanations coming from higher up did not avoid him having to find within himself the solution to the enigma that was posed.'

On 12 November 1955, his health had declined so much that he could not be transferred to Fontevrault[10] with the other 'lifers'. He was sent instead to the infirmary at Fresnes. Walking with tiny steps, bent over, his feet shackled, his face emaciated, but the cell where he was placed was worse than the previous one. He was 'looked after' by his male nurses. Objectively, it has to be admitted, it was truly torture.

In his cell, General Dentz kept a diary:

19 November: An icy cold causes internal pain and weakness, with great tiredness. A little warmth is necessary.

22 November: They have taken away my overcoat and scarf, the regulations being made for a heated sick bay. I am writing absolutely numb in mind and body.

29 November: My heart is beating like a clock which skips beats.

3 December: I am writing absolutely frozen in a cell where the damp overcomes everything. Water trickles down the walls and I am forced to put my underwear on the bed to keep it dry.

7 December: A car had come to take me to Poissy.[11] I was not fit be transported and the prison director sent it away. It seems that there was someone who had got their knife into me.

10 December: I am frozen. The temperature was -9° C last night.

13 December: The damp is winning everywhere. The walls are running like little waterfalls in a grotto. The best time is when one goes to bed: it is warm under the covers and, for a few hours, everything is forgotten.

These were his last words. In the late afternoon, when they came to fill his mess tin, the General laid his diary on the small shelf holding his belongings. Seated on his bed, he collapsed: he was dead.

Early next morning, after a rapid absolution given in the prison morgue, a hearse took his remains to the family vault at Neuilly cemetery.[12] By a strange and final sign of the fate that had overwhelmed him, it is there that he lies today, forgotten, but in the shadow of the 'Grande Arche de la Défense'[13] (the Grand Arch of La Défense) along the axis of the Champs-Élysées.[14]

Who was infuriated by this medieval imprisonment? General Laffargue:

> A noble soldier in every sense of the word, a leader who was preoccupied about the honour of his troops and his flag, convinced to carry out his duty of obedience to the orders received from the legitimate government, he did not content himself by sticking to theoretical principles. He sought, as High Commissioner, to apply to this obedience guarantees resulting from a political and strategic examination of the situation. 'To disobey', he wrote in his diary, 'would be to bring about the rupture of the Armistice, release Germany from all restraint, expose the country to demands and invasions: occupation of the free zone, dismissal of the French Army and Air Force, loss of the whole fleet, especially the takeover of [French] North Africa'.

Dentz could thus see the big picture. An ardent patriot, a fearless soldier who was above reproach, he could not come to any other decision. General Catroux finally paid homage: 'Dentz', he wrote 'was only ever on the defensive [...] He never tried to manipulate us although, having a superiority in men and materiel [...] it would have been easy for him to take the initiative, to fall upon our rear areas and to force us back to our departure lines'.

'If nothing had come to disturb the local situation, the States of the Levant would have got by themselves until November 1942, when 30,000 excellent troops who were in garrison there would have joined Algiers and the army in Africa as a single group, as did those from Dakar. Thousands of human lives would have been spared', wrote Le Corbeiller. The final word belongs to the British admiral who, summing up all the blows against France, wrote: 'We would have done better to leave the French alone in order to devote ourselves to our real task, fighting the enemy.'

Notes

Preface: France in the Middle East

1   Brigadier-General Charles de Beaufort d'Hautpoul had seen much service in the Middle East. In 1860 he led the French expedition to Syria to protect Christians in the region. France, under Napoleon III, claimed a right to protect Christians in the Ottoman Empire.

2   General Henri Gouraud commanded the French Fourth Army in World War I. After his service in the French Mandate of Syria and Lebanon, he became Military Governor of Paris before retiring in 1937.

3   Maxime Weygand was a French five-star general, who served on the staff of Marshal Ferdinand Foch during World War I. Initially fighting the Germans in World War II, he later became a collaborator.

4   General Maurice Sarrail, during World War I, commanded all Allied forces in the Macedonian theatre. A rarity among the French officer corps, he was openly a Socialist.

5   The *Front Populaire* (Popular Front) was an alliance of left-wing groups which won the 1936 elections in France. It was headed by Léon Blum.

Chapter 1: 1939: Weygand

1   General Maurice Gustave Gamelin was Commander-in-Chief of the French armies during the early part of World War II. He is chiefly remembered for his disastrous command of the French armies in 1940. He was a convinced republican who refused to play politics in military promotions.

2   Maxime Weygand, *Mémoires*, Volume III: *Rappelé au service*, Paris, Flammarion, 1950, p.13.

3   Later Field Marshal Lord Wavell, GCB GCSI GCIE CMG MC.

4   Later Admiral of the Fleet Viscount Cunningham of Hyndhope KT GCB OM DSO and two bars.

5   Later Air Chief Marshal Sir William Mitchell KCB CBE DSO MC AFC. He was born in Sydney (Australia) and, after retirement from the RAF, became Gentleman Usher of the Black Rod in the British Parliament.

6   When in October 1940, after the disaster in France and General Weygand became the general delegate of the government in French Africa, General Wavell sent him a letter of warm congratulations. Weygand responded by

congratulating him on the series of victories that Wavell had just won over the Italians in Cyrenaica.

7   French Prime Minister and a supporter of General de Gaulle.

8   Also known as the Government Palace, it is today the headquarters of the Prime Minister of Lebanon. During the French Mandate it was the headquarters of the High Commissioner.

Chapter 2: 1940: Time of Choice

1   General Eugène Mittelhauser replaced Massiet, who had succeeded Weygand, as commander of the TOMO (*Théâtre d'opérations de la Méditerranée orientale*; theatre of operations in the Eastern Mediterranean) in May 1940. He had served as chief of staff of the Czechoslovak forces after World War I.

2   1,600,000 according to the French, 1,960,00 according to the German figures quoted by Louis-Christian Michelet, *La Flamme de la revanche*, Paris, Éditions Godefroy de Bouillon, 2002.

3   An 'armistice' is a convention, both political and military, by virtue of which the belligerents agree to suspend hostilities, but the state of war continues. 'Capitulation', on the other hand, is an exclusively military act which means unconditional surrender. It was the case with Holland. It places the capitulating entity at the total mercy of the adversary. In France, capitulation is punishable by sentence of death. In 1940, Paul Reynaud was the one to envisage it.

4   In reality it was the small poster that was posted up a month later in London.

5   French philosopher and author of several seminal books, including *The Opium of the Intellectuals*. He was a lifelong friend of Jean-Paul Sartre, with whose philosophy he disagreed. He served in the *Forces Aériennes Françaises Libres* during World War II.

6   The *chanson de geste* (literally, 'song of deeds') is a type of epic poem in Old French dealing, usually, with heroic actions.

7   Raymond Aron, *Mémoires*, Paris, R. Laffont, 2003, p.445.

8   Roger Rouy, *Etude sur une guerre inconnue*, doctoral thesis, Faculté des sciences humaines de Dijon.

9   French author and historian who wrote on *pétainisme* (the official ideology of the Vichy regime headed by Marshal Pétain) and the life of the French people under the German occupation.

10   *Valeurs actuelles*, 13 December 1992.

11   Guy Raïssac, *Un soldat dans la tourmente*, Paris, Albin Michel, 1963, p.370.

12   Not refusing to pursue resistance but not breaking with legality, General Odic, like Henri de Kérillis, André Maurois, Pierre Lazareff, Alexis Léger, Antoine de Saint-Exupéry, Jean Monnet, and many others, did not join *France Libre* (Free France). Other Frenchmen joined the British Army, such as Captains Vivier de Vaugouin MBE, Livry-Level, and Grandguillot who played a distinguished role in Libya. Some members of *France Libre*, such as Lieutenant Pépin-Lehalleur, Colonel Monclar and Captain de Lamaze, refused to condemn [Vichy] France and to fight against other Frenchmen.

13   Lieutenant-Colonel Brochet, *Mémoires et Souvenirs de guerre*, manuscript, p.121 *et seq*.

14   The Resident-General was the head of the administration in a French colony.

15 One of the chiefs of the Army of the Levant, Colonel Tony Albord, is not to be confused with his son Maurice Albord, author of *L'Armée française et les États du Levant, 1936–1946.*

16 Vichy Foreign Minister.

17 General Tony Albord, *La Guerre des dupes. Levant 1941.* Typewritten manuscript, 192 pages, Annex 1.

18 The 6th Foreign Legion Infantry Regiment (Colonel Barré) was made up of the 1st Battalion (Edart) stationed at Homs in Syria, the 2nd Battalion (Brisset) stationed at Baalbek in Lebanon and at Deir-ez-Zor in Syria, the 3rd Battalion (Taguet) stationed at Damascus, and the 4th Battalion (Boitel) stationed at Homs and Palmyra. In total, 3,500 men. The Battalion of Foreign Volunteers – 800 men – was attached to it.

19 Under the terms of the Armistice, the foreign volunteers in the service of France were taken back to France and discharged into civilian life. From then on 'the new French laws reserved an unenviable fate for many of these foreigners' (Captain Marquez, *La Légion, une légende en marche*, Paris, Éditions Atlas, p.14).

20 Prince Joachim Murat, k.i.a. in July 1944. He was a descendant of Marshal Murat, brother-in-law of Napoleon Bonaparte, who made him King of Naples. He was a noted and daring cavalry commander and embodied the ideal of a cavalryman.

21 It formed, along with stubborn elements that had remained in Cyprus, the future 1st BIM (*Brigade d'Infanterie de Marine*) (1st Marine Infantry Brigade) of the Free French Division.

22 He later became head of the FFI (*Forces Françaises de l'Intérieur*) in Finistère and died in Germany following deportation.

23 P. Dufour, *op. cit.,* p.498.

24 Commanding the unit of Colonial Infantry detached to Cyprus before the Armistice, he went over to the British with his troops, and then joined *France Libre* (Free France).

25 Grouped together under the command of Lieutenant d'Estienne d'Orves, together with about 30 sailors from the fleet in Alexandria who had chosen rebellion and had come to fight Germany, the first nucleus of the Free French squadron was formed within the RAF at Aden, but 'about 15 airmen, mainly from the Levant, refused to join the Free French Air Force' (Vital Ferry, *Croix de Lorraine et Croix du Sud,* éditions du Gerfaut, 2005, p.55). In all, about 1,100 men formed the Free French Air Force in the Middle East.

26 Short for *École Polytechnique*, which is arguably the most prestigious institute of higher education in France and one of the finest universities in the world. Most of its graduates are engineers.

27 35 km south-west of Baalbek.

28 In September, the Polish brigade – the Polish Carpathian Brigade – paraded in Palestine. As early as October, it fought in Egypt. At the beginning of 1941, it distinguished itself in Tobruk, but was roughly handled in Greece. Czechs, notably pilots, frequently arrived in Lebanon where they were greeted in a brotherly fashion by French airmen, before going on to Palestine and then to England where their success was outstanding.

29 Evacuated for medical reasons in Autumn 1940, the commander of the old *Lorraine* returned to France by train via Lebanon and Turkey. Some time

later, enduring a long and difficult journey, families of French employees of the Suez Canal took the same route.

30   Guy Simon, *op. cit.*

31   England authorised only the repatriation of reservists in autumn 1940, and, in February 1941, the liner *Providence* landed 2,000 men and repatriated others.

32   All London knew – even before setting sail, some people noisily celebrated their forthcoming victory in a restaurant. (Quentin Reynolds, *The Wounded Don't Cry*, London, Cassell, 1941, p.202.)

33   Of the *Redoutable* class; some sources give the date of her loss as 7 November.

34   They were liberated two years later, on 8 June 1943.

35   Paul Paillole, *Services Spéciaux (1935–1945)*, Paris, Robert Laffont, 1975, p.340.

Chapter 3: From One War to the Next

1   The invasion of Gabon, by Free French forces, in November 1940, resulted in the destruction of the Vichy *Bougainville*-class sloop *Bougainville* by her sister ship, *Savorgnan de Brazza*. The British sank the *Redoutable*-class submarine, *Poncelet*.

2   In 1917, Italy had claimed authority over some Ottoman territory. The Saint-John-de Maurienne Agreement had granted Italy a part of Anatolia, but she had never been able to occupy it due to the campaign led by Mustafa Kemal in 1921. It was in recognising this old claim that the *Reich* entrusted to Italy the task of overseeing the application of the Armistice agreements in the Middle East.

3   Two diplomats joined in November. The Commission remained in the Levant until the end of the fighting.

4   Michel-Christian Davet, *La Double Affaire de Syrie*, Paris, Fayard, 1967, p.25.

5   The troops in the Levant had numbered up to 80,000 men; 45,000 had been demobilised. In 1941 in the Levant, there were only 35,000 combatants, apart from the Special Forces.

6   Departures with destination Marseilles and sometimes French North Africa: 280 officers and 3,912 men on 17 October; 3,567 on 23 October; 3,659 on 31 October; the remainder in the same proportions on 9, 17, 22 November and 15 December. (M. Albord, *op. cit.*, p.106.)

7   Louis-Christian Michelet, *op. cit.*, p.56.

8   Colonial infantry.

9   Native cavalry.

10   Major Brochet, *Mémoires*, p.127.

11   There were also a battalion of Madagascan pioneers and another of Indochinese.

12   On 26 January 1941, tactlessness by the command and errors in organisation had come together to provoke a mutiny in the *Régiment de marche du Levant* (the *ad hoc* Regiment of the Levant), in barracks at Maison-Carré (Algeria). At nightfall, 800 *tirailleurs* bayonetted to death the captain on duty and several French NCOs, before spreading out through the town and firing on passers-by. They shot more than 23 people and wounded more than 100. The alert,

given by the *5ᵉ Régiment de chasseurs d'Afrique,* led to street fighting. Only the intervention by gendarmes and *gardes mobiles* allowed the mutineers to be overcome. A court martial condemned 48 soldiers to death, of whom 23 were executed. No other similar outbreak occurred subsequently.

13 The Lebanese and Syrian 'Special Forces' had 340 officers, 1,500 NCOs and 14,000 men (M. Albord, *op. cit.,* p.98).

14 *Régiment de Dragons Portés* (these were motorised or mechanised infantry, similar to the German *Panzergrenadiere*).

15 Lieutenant Prudhomme had commanded the 3rd Druse Light Cavalry Squadron.

16 Severely wounded in Belgium, Sub-Lieutenant Oddo fought in France. He joined *France Libre* and was again severely wounded in Algeria. Becoming a general officer, he was President of the *'Gueules cassées* ('Broken faces)', an organisation for ex-servicemen afflicted by serious wounds, especially of the face, and worked for a sincere reconciliation between Vichy and Free French veterans.

17 The 1st Moroccan Spahi Regiment and the 2nd Mixed Spahi Regiment, made up from the 8th Algerian Spahi Regiment and the 4th Tunisian Spahi Regiment.

18 The 63rd Tank Battalion had absorbed the 68th Tank Battalion which had been disbanded. This powerful unit of 90 R-35 tanks included four companies, comprising four sections with five tanks each (instead of three). The tanks were new.

19 The 8th Armoured Car Group inherited the 8th, 18th, and 28th Squadrons which had been present in Syria since 1919. It included four squadrons, the 1st and 2nd platoons of special Levant troops, and three Light Desert Companies. In total there were 135 armoured cars, including the independent light desert armoured cars. The equipment was worn out.

20 The 6th (Lieutenant-Colonel Amanrich) at Beirut and the 7th (Lieutenant-Colonel Le Couteulx de Caumont) at Damascus. Each comprised two groups of mixed squadrons (one of armoured cars and one of tanks). A 5th support squadron was formed of Moroccan *spahis* of the 1st Moroccan Spahi Regiment (Captain Dumont), an elite group at full strength, strongly armed. (Two platoons of riflemen with combat groups with two light machine-guns to each group as in the motorised dragoons, two machine gun platoons, an 81mm mortar platoon. This squadron received, in addition, five armoured cars specially built for it and having on each vehicle, in addition to twin-mounted 37mm cannon and a light machine gun, an 81mm mortar which could be fired from the vehicle's platform.)

21 From 1935 onward, Captain Bich motorised a battery of 155mm cannons by having them drawn by Laffly S 35 T tractors.

22 To remain within acceptable weight limits, they had to be satisfied – except for the shield of the Dodges – with 8mm thick sheet metal for parts exposed to direct fire. Under normal conditions, protection was assured for carbine fire up to 15 metres and up to 300 metres for fire from the FM 24-29 [light machine gun] and the Mas 36 rifle. Anti-tank bullets easily passed through, but they were less dangerous than with hardened steel armour from which they produced big splinters

23 In June 1941, there were only 180 finished, plus the armoured Dodges, but this equipment fulfilled its task well, since it served in 1942 with the Free French Division in Egypt. Courcel's squadron was equipped with it.

24 Former platoon commander in the 8th Armoured Car Group.

25 Later, these guns covered themselves with glory in the defence of Bir Hakeim.
26 From December 1940 to 13 July 1941, 79 Dodge 'Tanaké', 19 Dodge-White armoured cars and eight cannon trucks, i.e. 109 fighting vehicles had been produced. To this figure must be added a single squadron of recent Panhard 65 TOE (Roquemorel's squadron) and approximately 20 light desert armoured cars (*automitrailleuses légères du désert*), fast but very lightly armoured and having only automatic weapons. The total of armoured vehicles in the Levant was 95 tanks and 135 armoured cars.
27 *Infantry*: 20 battalions of legionnaires, colonial troops, and *tirailleurs*. *Cavalry*: two regiments of African Light Cavalry (*chasseurs d'Afrique*) (90 R-35 tanks, 70 armoured cars); two regiments of native cavalry (*spahis*); three companies of engineers; three transport companies; mobile Service Corps units. *Artillery*: six groups, with 75mm and 105mm cannons, totalling 56 cannons for 14 separate field artillery batteries with four guns, of which four were equipped with old 65mm mountain guns, carried on mules, dating from the colonial wars. Beside 25mm anti-tank guns of the infantry and cavalry, there were only eight 47mm cannons. The RACL (*Régiment d'artillerie coloniale du Levant*: Levant Colonial Artillery Regiment); the RAML (*Régiment d'artillerie métropolitaine du Levant*: Levant Metropolitan Artillery Regiment) which was equipped with Model 36 105mm cannons, brand new weapons with which this group arrived from France in February 1940 and which were destroyed by the Royal Navy before being brought into action. *Aviation*: 95 aircraft, of which there were 26 Morane-Saulnier MS.406 fighters, a very good quality bomber group (12 Glenn Martin 167 aircraft) plus six Bloch 200 bombers which were almost unusable, and 28 Potez 25 biplanes which were barely good enough for communications duties. *Navy*: Two destroyers – *Guépard* and *Valmy* – and three submarines – *Phoque, Caïman* and *Marsouin* – five minesweepers, the oiler *Adour* but no repair facilities or ammunition dump. A Fleet Air Arm (*Aéronavale*) squadron had six Loire scouting floatplane aircraft. *Special Troops*: 12,000 men, made up of: BDL (*Bataillon du Levant*; Levant Battalion); BCL (*Bataillon de chasseurs libanais*; Lebanese Light Cavalry); line cavalry squadrons; two special platoons of armoured cars; 3 CLD (*Compagnies légères du désert*; light desert companies) equipped with AMLD (*automitrailleuses légères du désert*; light desert armoured cars), and an artillery group.

Chapter 4: 1941: Dentz

1 The assassination by fundamentalists in July 1940 in Damascus of Doctor Chahbandar, former Foreign Minister of King Faisal, gave rise to a politically motivated trial which the French High Commissioner tried to influence. Seeking the guilty ones among the nationalists, he provoked strong emotions in Arab circles. Well before the collapse of France, this trial was, for Syria, the main event of 1940. (Cf. Salma Mardam Bey, *La Syrie et la France, 1939–1945*, Paris, L'Harmattan, 1994, p.39 *et seq.*)
2 Retired to Tunisia, Gabriel Puaux was appointed, by General de Gaulle in 1943, Resident General of France in Morocco.
3 Prefect of Police of Paris from 1927 to 1934, and accused of excessive sympathy for right-wing groups, Jean Chiappe had been transferred to

Morocco by Edouard Daladier, which had provided the pretext for the riot of 6 February 1934.

4   *Terre des hommes* is a book by Antoine de Saint-Exupéry, better known under its English title of *Sand, Wind and Stars*, published in 1939.

5   Edmond Petit, *Le dernier vol de Guillaumet*, in *Icare*, N°162.

6   Jacques Weygand, *Weygand, mon père*, Paris, Flammarion, 1970, p.328.

7   John Bellair, *From Snow to Jungle. A History of the 2/3 Australian Machine Gun Battalion*, Sydney, Allen & Unwin, 1987.

8   Appointed head of the military staff of Monsieur Chiappe, but kept on by General Dentz, Major Tézé gave him unswerving support during the darkest days of the conflict. The head of his civil staff was Monsieur Louis de Guiringaud. A graduate of the *Quai d'Orsay* competition in 1938, he became Minister for Foreign Affairs during the presidency of Monsieur Giscard d'Estaing in 1976.

Chapter 5: De Gaulle

1   On 3 June 1940, on the eve of leaving his unit to become Under-Secretary of State for National Defence and War, de Gaulle had expounded his vision for the future to a member of his staff. (Cf. H. de Wailly, *De Gaulle sous le casque*, Paris, Perrin, 1990, p.317, and H. de Wailly, *La Victoire évaporée*, Paris, Perrin, 2000, p.300.)

2   Daniel Rondeau and Roger Stéphane, *Des hommes libres*, Paris, Grasset, 1997, p.213.

3   *Nom de guerre* of Raoul-Charles Magrin-Vernerey, later lieutenant-general (*général de corps d'armée*) and hero of the Foreign Legion. He also served in Korea, dropping rank to do so as commander of the French Battalion.

4   Later Field Marshal Lord Alanbrooke KG GCB OM GCVO DSO and bar.

5   Alex Danchev and Daniel Todman, *War Diaries*, London, Weidenfeld and Nicolson, 2001, p.101.

6   Diégo Brosset became chief of staff to General Catroux in 1941, later commanding the 1st DFL in 1943. He was killed in a motor vehicle accident in 1944.

7   Geneviève Salkin, *Général Diégo Brosset*, Paris, Economica, 1999, p.261.

8   Jean-Luc Barré, *Devenir de Gaulle, 1939–1945*, Paris, Perrin, 2003, p.116.

9   Until 1942, the word was not uttered. 'Nowhere the principle or even the word appears [...] If he denies all legitimacy to the power of Vichy, he did not embarrass himself by legitimising his, or even defining it.'(Jacques Fauvet, *La IV*ᵉ *République*, Paris, Fayard, 1959, p.23.) The coins struck in London in 1942 for use in the African territories had, on the obverse, the title 'Afrique équatoriale française libre' with a cockerel and, in a shield, 'RF'. On the reverse was 'Liberté, Égalité, Fraternité' and 'Honneur, Patrie' around the Cross of Lorraine.

10 Jean-Luc Barré, *op. cit.*, p.77.

11 The station was entrusted to two men who had had no training for the job: F. Coulet, a university teacher who came from Helsinki, and R. Schmittlein, who came from Riga.

12 The astonishing thing is that this exchange took place at the very moment when France was beginning talks with the enemy. (Jacques de Folin, *Indochine 1940–1945*, Paris, Perrin, 1993, p.25.)

13 General Catroux, *Dans la bataille de Méditerranée, 1940–1944*, Paris, Julliard, 1949, p.16.

14 René Cassin, *Des hommes partis de rien*, Paris, Plon, 1975, p.174.

15 Catroux served twice in the Levant. Head of the French Military Mission to the Hejaz from 1919 to 1920, he returned there again from 1926 to 1928 as chief of the intelligence service.

16 Michel-Christian Davet, *La Double Affaire de Syrie*, Paris, Fayard, 1989, p.27.

17 Spears, *Mémoires*, in Kersaudy, 'De Gaulle et la perfide Albion', in *Historia*, Tallandier, 1998, p.130.

18 Today N'Djamena in Chad.

19 *Enseigne de vaisseau* (Sub-Lieutenant) Simon, *op. cit.*, p.130.

20 Sir Edward Spears was born in Paris and spoke perfect French; he translated some French military books into English. He served as a British liaison officer with the French Army in both world wars. A friend of Winston Churchill, he was also a British MP.

21 The conference of the Anglo-French Supreme War Council, held on 11-12 June 1940, at the Château du Muguet near Briare (Loiret). During this conference, a major disagreement arose between the French and the British about the conduct of the war.

22 Kersaudy, *op. cit.*, p.130.

23 Amiral Auphan, *Histoire élementaire de Vichy*, Paris, France-Empire, 1971, p.236

24 AN, archives de Gaulle 3AG1, dossier 263, quoted by Jean-Luc Barré, *op. cit.*, p.139.

Chapter 6: The Noose Tightens

1   Weygand, *Mémoires*. Tome III, *Rappelé au service, op. cit.*, p.470.

2   Prince Xavier de Bourbon-Parme, in *Revue des Deux Mondes*, 1 July 1954.

3   Amiral Gabriel Auphan was *chef de cabinet* of Admiral Darlan at Vichy and later became Minister of Marine.

4   Amiral Gabriel Auphan, *op. cit.*, p.231. The objectivity of this work is often questioned.

5   Marcel Déat, who was campaigning for a total collaboration with Nazi Germany, was arrested by order of Vichy on this same 13 December 1940.

6   Napoléon-François-Joseph-Charles Bonaparte, son of Emperor Napoléon 1st. He was later known as the Duke of Reichstadt and died in Vienna, aged 21, probably from tuberculosis.

7   In his book, *L'Échiquier d'Alger*, Paris, Laffont, 1966, Claude Paillat gives a gripping description of this meeting.

8   Antoine de Saint-Exupéry was a very successful commercial pilot prior to World War II, notably in South America and Africa. He was killed in action in July 1944 while flying a Lockheed P-38 Lightning aircraft. He was also a famous author of, for example, '*Le Petit Prince*', winning many prizes.

9   Antoine de Saint-Exupéry, *Écrits de guerre 1939–1944*, Paris, Gallimard, 1982 (posthumous).

10 Jean Ferniot, *Je recommencerais bien*, Paris, Grasset, 1991.

11 Géo London, *Le procès du général Dentz*, p.193.

12 Posted to Pekin, Teheran and Constantinople, Hentig had served in Holland and in America before becoming involved with the Orient. Placed at the head of Section VII of the Wilhelmstrasse, which covers an immense area going from Turkey to India, he had had a career full of ups and downs caused by his emotional instability. (R. Rouy, *Étude sur une guerre inconnue*, doctoral thesis, Dijon.)

13 A Sunni landowner, who was Prime Minister of Lebanon twice. He was assassinated in 1951.

14 The Najjadeh Party (in Arabic 'The rescuers') was a Lebanese nationalist party that was officially secular but had a mainly Sunni Muslim membership.

15 Glubb Pasha, *The Story of the Arab Legion*, London, Hodder & Stoughton, 1948.

16 It was then that the British Admiralty agreed to the free passage of the liner *Providence* which brought 200 officers and repatriated the Gaullists.

17 Arthur Bryant, *The Turn of the Tide, 1939–1945*, autobiographical notes of Field Marshal Alan Brooke, London, Weidenfeld and Nicolson, 2001, p.201.

18 The Italian losses were: battleship: *Vittorio Veneto* (severely damaged); heavy cruisers: *Fiume, Zara, Pola* (sunk); destroyers: *Vittorio Alfieri, Giosue Carducci* (sunk).

19 Under the orders of General Wilson, essentially the 6th and 7th Australian Divisions and the Polish division of General Kopanski.

20 The immense consequences of this campaign will be understood later; by slowing the attack on Russia by more than a month, the Italians pushed the Germans into the mud and snow of Russia from which they never extracted themselves. The defence by the Greeks and the Belgrade uprising, along with the courage of the Australians and the Poles, directly prepared for the final victory.

21 Mussolini had wanted to pass through Tunisia but the French ports were protected by the Armistice. 'The French' wrote the English historian Playfair, 'acted to avoid having to give concessions that were useful [to the Axis]. It was a great piece of luck for the British.'

22 Troops from Sudan under the command of General Sir William Platt, Commander-in-Chief East Africa Command, and those of Lieutenant-General Alan Cunningham, East Africa Force, from Kenya.

23 A cavalry brigade group.

24 Gavin Long, *Greece, Crete and Syria*, Canberra, Australian War Memorial, 1953, p.321.

25 Marie-Pierre Kœnig later commanded the French troops at Bir Hakeim. He later served as Free French delegate at Allied Supreme Headquarters. After the war, he served as Minister of Defence on two occasions. He was promoted posthumously to the dignity of Marshal of France.

26 Along with Catroux and Muselier, General Legentilhomme was one of three general officers who rallied to Free France. Former commander-in-chief at Djibouti, General Legentilhomme tried in vain to get French Somaliland to join Free France. He was condemned to death *in absentia* on 10 July 1940. Colonel de Larminat received the same sentence on 25 September, as did General Catroux on 10 April 1941, by a court martial sitting at Gannat (Allier) for 'crimes and intrigue against the unity and safety of the country'.

27 Daniel Rondeau et Roger Stéphane, *op. cit.*, p.172.

28 Charles de Gaulle, *Mémoires de guerre. Tome I: L'Appel, 1940–1942*, Paris, Plon, 1954.

Chapter 7: Rachid Ali

1   It had 235 members in 1935. NSDAP = *Nazionalsozialistische Deutsche Arbeiter Partei*/National Socialist German Workers Party, usually abbreviated to the 'Nazi Party' in English.

2   Michel-Christian Davet, *op. cit.*, p.42.

3   A military intelligence organisation which, under the leadership of Admiral Canaris, confronted the SS and SD in Nazi Germany.

4   On the action of the Axis in Muslim countries, cf. Paul Paillole, *op. cit.*, p.340 *et seq.*

5   Glubb Pasha's Arab Legion, in Amman, had only a single desertion.

6   At this time, petroleum from Kuwait and Saudi Arabia was not yet exploited. The only petroleum in the Middle East was that in Iraq and Iran. Iran was a neutral country, and only Iraq was controlled by the British.

7   *Ober Kommando der Wehrmacht*, Supreme Command of the Armed Forces; in reality Hitler's staff.

8   'Middle East'.

9   This arrangement had already been used during the Spanish Civil War.

10   To read more about this period, see Yves Buffetaut, *De l'Irak à la Syrie*, Paris, Histoire et Collections, 2003.

11   Outdated in Europe, the Iraqi materiel was still effective in the Middle East. Its 14 Crossley armoured cars were of the same generation as the French Whites and British Rolls-Royces. Mainly equipped by Great Britain, Iraq also had Italian weapons bought in 1937 (Savoia trimotor bombers, Breda 65 fighters, light tanks). Its Air Force had 63 aircraft, including 27 Hawker biplane fighters provided by Great Britain in 1934. Supported by 12 Caproni CR42 biplane fighters of the *Squadriglia Irachena* (*161° Grupo Autonomo Caccia Terrestre*), which rarely met with success, they were opposed by ancient British biplanes: Westland Wapitis, Hawker Demons and Gloster Gladiators of 94 Sqn RAF. Quickly driven from the sky, the Iraqi Air Force took part in the last combats between biplanes in aviation history. German aid played no part.

12   Later Field Marshal Sir Claude Auchinleck GCB GCIE CSI DSO OBE. Auchinleck was a regular soldier of the British Indian Army, initially serving with the 62nd Punjabis. He was Commander-in-Chief of the Indian Army in 1941.

13   21st Brigade, 10th Indian Division.

14   In Davet, *op. cit.*, p.68.

15   Comparable to American Task Forces and German *Kampfgruppe*, these were units in the British Army constituted for a single mission which were baptised with the first syllable of the name of their objective or their commander. Thus one has '*Habforce*' to clear the forces investing Habbaniya, '*Kingcol*' under the orders of Brigadier Kingstone, and '*Gentforce*' under the orders of General Legentilhomme.

16   '*Habforce*', under the command of Maj-Gen J.G.W. Clark, comprised six mechanised squadrons of the 4th Independent Cavalry Brigade (Brigadier Kingstone; itself composed of three regiments: Household Cavalry, Royal Wiltshire Yeomanry, and Warwickshire Yeomanry); one infantry battalion (1/Essex Regiment); one motorised battalion of the Transjordan Frontier Force (TJFF) (350 men); one artillery regiment (60th Field Regiment, RA); one anti-tank battery; an engineer detachment. A detached part (*flying*

column) of *Habforce* was *Kingcol* (Brigadier J.J.Kingstone) composed of the Household Cavalry, a battery of the 60th Field Regiment, two companies of the Essex Regiment on Bren carriers, an anti-tank battery and an engineer section. It was joined from Egypt by No.2 Armoured Car Company of the RAF Regiment and 200 men of the TJFF. On all these operations, *vide* Yves Buffetaut, *op. cit.*, p.14.

17 Maj-Gen John George Walter Clark, CB MC and Bar.

18 Géo London, *op. cit.*

19 SHAT, 4 H 278, telegram 344, quoted by M. Albord, *op. cit.*, p.120.

20 Géo London, *op. cit.*, p.200.

21 F. Kersaudy, *op. cit.*, p.128.

22 Jacques Soustelle was a close friend of de Gaulle's, who served as head of the Free French intelligence service in London during World War II. An anthropologist, he wrote a number of books on Mexico and was a member of the *Académie française,*

23 Jacques Soustelle, *Envers et contre tout*, Paris, Laffont, 1947, p.243.

24 Charles de Gaulle, *Mémoires de guerre*, Volume 1: *L'Appel, 1940–1942, op. cit.*, p.392.

25 Catroux, *op. cit.*

26 Sir Winston Churchill, *Messages*, Vol.III, p.290.

27 In spite of the language difficulties, the Poles – who numbered almost 100,000 – were totally integrated into the British forces. In 1941, their contribution was already considerable, notably in the skies over England and in Greece, and General Maczek's 1st Polish Armoured Division was already training in Scotland.

28 Charles de Gaulle, *Mémoires de guerre*, Vol.I: *L'Appel, 1940–1942, op. cit.*, p.396.

Chapter 8: Darlan/*Die Pariser Protokolle*

1 In his *Mémoires* and his work *A l'épreuve du temps. Souvenirs*, Paris, Julliard, 1989, Vol.II, pp.108–9, Jacques Benoist-Méchin, does not show approximately the same dates.

2 The President of the Council was Marshal Pétain. The Vice-President of the Council, Admiral Darlan became on that day, Minister of the Interior, Foreign Minister, Minister of the Navy and Minister for Information. General Huntziger became Minister of War, General Bergeret was Secretary of State for Air and Admiral Platon was Secretary of State for Colonies.

3 Between the wars, the technical outcome of the Washington Naval Conference, initiated by England, was very unfavourable to France, the attacks on Mers el-Kebir and Dakar, and the destruction of the submarine *Poncelet* at Gabon were sufficient to explain his distrust of Great Britain. Naturally, to this can be added the old French traditional maritime culture, but overall, and contrary to legend, it was in no way preponderant.

4 Sir Alexander Cadogan OM GCMG KCB PC, Permanent Under-Secretary for Foreign Affairs 1938–1946.

5 Several books have dealt with the negotiations in Paris. The definitive work by Hervé Coutau-Bégarie and Claude Huan, *Darlan*, Paris, Fayard, 1989, was used here. Also, the *Mémoires* of Benoist-Méchin are essential reading.

6 Hervé Coutau-Bégarie and Claude Huan, *op. cit.*, p.389.

7 Telegram 2914 from Huntziger to Dentz of 4 May, A.N. 3 W 188, quoted by Hervé Coutau-Bégarie & Claude Huan, *op. cit.*, p.396.

8 In his book, *Un combat sans merci, l'affaire Pétain-de Gaulle*, Paris, Albin Michel, 1966, Guy Raïssac prints, on p.314, the account written by Abetz.

9 Otto von Hentig, who returned from the Levant, became after the war, *Chargé d'affaires* of the Federal German Republic in Jakarta.

10 Otto von Hentig, *Mein Leben, eine Dienstreise*, Göttingen, Vandenhoek und Rupprecht, 1963, p.339 *et seq.* Quoted by Jeanne de Schouteete in 'Les préliminaires de la campagne du Levant d'après les témoignages allemands', in *Revue des Deux Mondes*, September 1973.

11 Guy Raïssac, *op. cit.*, gives the full text of this telegram in Annexe XXI.

12 Since January 1941, the secret service had continued to warn Vichy about the threat of a German attack in Russia. Since May 'the mass of intercepts and decrypts reveal the imminent timing of the offensive'. (P. Paillole, *op. cit.*, p.337.)

13 Alphonse-Pierre Juin, later commander of the French Expeditionary Corps in Italy. He was made Marshal of France and a member of the *Académie française*.

14 Georges Hirtz, *Weygand, années 1940–1965*, Gardanne, Imprimerie Esmanjaud, 2003.

15 Weygand, *Mémoires*. Vol.III: *Rappelé au service*, *op. cit.*, p.420.

16 General Jean-Marie Bergeret was initially an army officer who later joined the air force. He remained loyal to the Vichy regime and was later Minister for Air. Following disputes with Laval, he resigned and later became Inspector of Air Defences. He later joined General Henri Giraud in North Africa.

17 The German pressure to obtain the transport of equipment to Tunisia in support of the *Afrika Korps* would nevertheless become increasingly pressing. From 24 to 26 June, the question was asked without receiving an answer, and negotiations continued. The Germans suggested further discussions about the protocols on 3 July, but the French negotiator, Captain Marzin of the French Navy, dragged things out under various technical and diplomatic pretexts. On 7 July, Darlan and Marzin met Abetz and Vogl, but attitudes had changed. On that date the drama in Syria had erupted, France refused German military help, and war started in Russia. On 11 July, at Vichy, Weygand noted: 'He [Darlan] took an enormous step, he has less confidence in the Germans, he feels his responsibilities better as regards the Empire, there is no longer any question, in spite of renewed German requests, of giving access to Dakar or Bizerta without prior consolidation and the written guarantees requested. Leusse cannot get over his transformation.' Following the meeting of General Juin and Goering in Berlin on 20 December, Vichy, would in the end, deliver only trucks.

Chapter 9: Stirring Up a Hornet's Nest

1 *Sonderkommando Jung* was composed of 3 *Staffeln* (flights): 4/KG4 (bombers) (7 Heinkel 111), 4/ZG76 twin-engined fighters (14 Messerschmitt 110), 1/KGrzb106 transport (Junkers 52 trimotors); a *Kette* of three four-engined Junkers 90 aircraft, and an anti-aircraft battery of 20mm guns. There were also attached 12 Italian biplane fighters (Caproni

CR 42 of *Squadriglia Irachena, 161° Grupo Autonomo Caccia Terrestre*), accompanied by 3 trimotor Savoia transport aircraft. (Cf. Vincent Grécict, 'Les Allemands au Proche Orient et la révolte irakienne' in *39–45 Magazine*, N° 80; Paul Gaujac, *L'Armée de la victoire*, Paris, Lavauzelle, 1984, p.16; Christian Erhengardt and Christopher Shores, *L'Aviation de Vichy au combat. La campagne de Syrie*, Paris, Lavauzelle, 1987, p.24).

2   Rudolf Rahn, *Rubeloses Leben* ('A busy life'), Düsseldorf, Diedrichverlag, 1949, p.149 *et seq.*, article quoted by Jeanette de Schoutheete, in *Revue des Deux Mondes*. Written without documents in a prisoner-of-war camp, this report contains many errors.

3   Error: Guérard was Darlan's emissary. It was Mulhausen *alias* Malaucène, who edited *La Gerbe*. Rahn is often wrong. He spoke of a Junkers when, in fact, it was a Heinkel, but technical details regarding armaments – type or calibre, models of ships or aircraft and tonnages – are frequently wrong in witness statements and always subject to caution. Historians in Europe often held technical details in contempt.

4   From 9 May to 6 June, during the four weeks that the German traffic lasted, not a single aircraft bearing the German swastika or the Iraqi triangle was attacked by the RAF in the skies above the Mediterranean.

5   The aircraft was shot down by Iraqi guns as it landed and Blomberg was killed.

6   Rudolf Rahn, *op. cit.*, p.149 *et seq.*

7   Two vehicles driven by chauffeurs from the French Administration. Renouard and Malaucène did not leave them at El Ourdou, on the Turkish frontier, until 12 July, just before the Armistice. (Report by H. Seyrig, in Jeanne de Schoutheete, *Revue des Deux Mondes*, article quoted.)

8   Quoted by Maurice Albord, *op. cit.*, p.145.

9   Wilhelmstrasse is a street in Berlin which, at the time, housed the Reich Chancellery and the German Foreign Office.

10 Géo London, *op. cit.*, p.208.

11 Michel-Christian Davet, *op. cit.*, p.102.

12 In following days, Sub-Lieutenant Labat 'deserted the rebellion' to return to the regular Air Force. Cf. C.J. Ehrengardt and C.F. Shores, *op. cit.*, p.30.

13 All these dates are questionable. If the witness statements concerning the facts match up more or less, they are often several days apart. The dates given are those that fit best.

14 Sub-Lieutenant Simon, *op. cit.*, p.84.

15 Free French Air Force (*Forces aériennes françaises libres*). Cf. *Icare*, N° 128. Pilots of the French Squadron refused to fight against their comrades in the Levant and did not take part in the war in the Middle East.

16 Cf. René Génin, Compagnon de la Libération, *Itinéraire d'un méhariste*, Paris, Éditions Sépia, 2004, p.368.

17 It should be remembered that in 1939, a mission composed of RAF officers had come to examine the possibility of using Syrian airfields in order to bomb Baku. Wavell's intelligence was thus precise, extensive and up-to-date.

18 Maurice Albord, *op. cit.*, p.145.

19 J. Le Corbeiller, *La Guerre de Syrie, juin–juillet 1941*, Paris, éditions de Fuseau, 1967, p.48.

20 The Fourth Bureau dealt mainly with transport of various types, and posts and telegraphs.

21 Letter to General Le Groignec in *Guerre en Syrie,* p.35, note 7.
22 Major-General I.S.O Playfair, *History of the Second World War,* United Kingdom Military Series, ed. J.R.M. Butler, 1954–1960.
23 Larminat had already complained in 1939 that 'We had to declare unfit for service three-quarters of the vehicles of a transport group.'
24 Michel-Christian Davet, *op. cit.,* p.108.
25 Géo London, *op. cit.,* p.213.
26 There is no indication that these arms were recovered later by the Free French Division when it seized French weapons in the Middle East.
27 J. Le Corbeiller, *op. cit.,* p.50.
28 Géo London, *op. cit.,* p.193, and J. Le Corbeiller, *op. cit.,* p.IV.
29 J. Le Corbeiller, *op. cit.,* p.36.

Chapter 10: War Clouds Gather

1 Quoted by Hervé Coutau-Bégarie and Claude Huan, *op. cit.*
2 The liner *Normandie* was totally destroyed by fire on 9 February 1942 when it was undergoing conversion to a troop transport.
3 An agreement between Weygand and Murphy [the US Consul], which was accepted by Great Britain, authorised the delivery of supplies, particularly foodstuffs, to Morocco. Note also: General Marshall, the US Chief of Staff, Mr MacCloy, Under-Secretary of State, then Mr James Dunn, of the State Department, received, on 20 May at Fort Knox, an emissary from Vichy, Prince Poniatowski who, according to Major Paul Paillole, 'refuted, with conviction and good humour, the lies often peddled by the French [in London] regarding the behaviour of our unhappy country'. (P. Paillole, *op. cit.,* p.299).
4 Général Catroux, *op. cit.*
5 Anne Collet, *The Road to Beyrouth,* Beirut, Les Lettres françaises, 1943. Translated into French under the title *Collet des Tcherkesses.*
6 Made KCMG in the King's Birthday Honours List, June 1941.
7 J. Le Corbeiller, *op. cit.,* p.9.
8 Général Saint-Hillier, *Historia Magazine,* N°278. The SHAT (*Service historique de l'Armée de Terre*) (4 P 5) said 450 men.
9 J. Le Corbeiller, *op. cit.,* p.52.
10 Rachid Ali later went to Berlin to organise an Arab army which never saw daylight. Leaving for Australia following the fall of the Third Reich, he made his way to Saudi Arabia. Amnestied in 1958, he resurfaced in the political world. The Grand Mufti wandered across Europe and, after all sorts of incredible episodes, pursued his struggle against England and Israel.
11 Général Lafargue, *Le Général Dentz,* Paris, Éditions Les Îles d'or, 1954, p.66.
12 Rudolf Rahn, *op. cit.*
13 10,000 well-armed Greek soldiers, elements of the 6th Australian Division and the 2nd New Zealand Brigade.
14 Later Lieutenant-General Lord Freyberg VC GCMG KCB KBE DSO and three bars. In World War I, he served initially with the Royal Naval Division, later transferring to the British Army. He ended the War, as one of the youngest generals in the British Army and one of its most highly decorated soldiers. In World War II, Freyberg commanded the 2nd New

Zealand Expeditionary Force. He later became the 7th Governor-General of New Zealand.

15 Tobruk was not relieved until 5 December 1941.

16 Later General Sir Richard O'Connor KT GCB GBE DSO and bar, MC commanded the Western Desert Force that, in the early days of World War II, almost drove the Italians from North Africa. This provoked the entry into North Africa of the German *Afrika Korps*. He was captured on 7 April 1941.

17 Later Lieutenant-General Sir Philip Neame VC KBE CB DSO. He was captured at the same time as Richard O'Connor. He won a gold medal at the 1924 Paris Olympics, being the only person to win both the VC and an Olympic gold medal.

18 General Wilhelm Ritter von Thoma, was captured by the British in North Africa on 4 November 1942.

19 B.H. Liddell Hart, *Les généraux allemands parlent*, Paris, Stock, 1948, p.178.

20 Gavin Long, *op. cit.*, note 4, p.321.

21 In January 1941, the General declared to General Odic: 'France must enter the war alongside Germany to prove the guilt of Vichy.'

22 Claude Guy, *En écoutant de Gaulle. Journal 1946–1949*, Paris, Grasset, 1996, p.304.

Chapter 11: War Approaches

1 Alfred Fabre-Luce, *Deuil au Levant*, Paris, Arthème Fayard, 1950, p.151.

2 Sir Winston Churchill, *The Second World War*, Vol.II, *op. cit.*, p.611.

3 Later General Lord Ismay, KG GCB CH DSO.

4 Churchill was a descendant of the Duke of Marlborough, but he had renounced his title in order to pursue a political career in the Commons.

5 Quoted by Colonel Buckley in his preface to Jim McAllister and Syd Trigellis-Smith, *Largely a Gamble, Australians in Syria, June–July 1941*, Sydney, HQ Training Command Australian Army, 1995.

6 *War Diaries, 1939–1945*, edited by Alex Danchev and Daniel Todman, London, Weidenfeld and Nicolson, 2001, p.101.

7 Later the Right Honourable Viscount Chandos KG DSO MC PC. Prior to World War II, Lyttelton had business conections with Germany. He entered Parliament in 1940 and became President of the Board of Trade, He later became Minister of State in the Middle East 1941–2.

8 Later Field Marshal Lord Wilson GCB GBE DSO.

9 Having become commander-in-chief of the Allied armies in the Mediterranean in 1944, General Wilson had under his command, at the time of the landing in Provence, the majority of his former adversaries in Syria, the officers of the former Dentz army.

10 Operation order N° 1 of 5 June 1941, paragraph 32. Quoted by Tony Albord, *op. cit.*, p.86.

11 The composition of the AIF (about 14,500 men): 6th Aust. Div. (not engaged in Syria), 16th Brigade (Brig. 'Tubby' Allen); 17th Brigade (Brig. Stanley Savige); 19th Brigade (Brig. Horace Robertson) 7th Aust. Div. (Maj-Gen. John Lavarack, then General Allen); 18th Brigade (Brig. George Wootten); 21st Brigade (Brig. A.R. Baxter-Cox). The 7th and 9th Aust. Divisions fought

in Libya, but the latter was not engaged in Syria. Each infantry division theoretically had more than 3,000 vehicles (but this total was far from being achieved), a machine-gun battalion and an anti-tank unit. Each brigade had three battalions (36 officers and 812 men), commanded by a lieutenant-colonel. Each battalion had a headquarter company and three companies commanded by a captain, each with three sections of riflemen armed with .303 Lee-Enfield rifles, commanded by a lieutenant and having a Bren LMG, a 2-inch mortar, and a Boyes anti-tank rifle. The headquarter company had an administrative section, with six fighting sections: a mortar section, a Bren-gun carrier section (with Carden-Lloyd universal carriers armed with a Bren LMG), a transport section, an engineer section and an anti-aircraft section.

12   Poorly armoured, the Vickers Mark VI tanks of 6 Aust. Div. Cav. Regt. had only a large and a small machine gun, whereas the big Marmon Herrington and AEC (Associated Equipment Company) armoured cars of 9 Aust. Div. Cav. Regt. were fitted with a 75mm cannon and a 7.62mm machine gun.

13   Christopher Buckley, *Five Ventures*, London, HMSO, 1954, p.49.

14   Ignorance regarding aircraft types caused frequent confusion among troops who had not had appropriate instruction. The French Dewoitine D.520, with its tricolour roundels, was often confused with the British Hurricane.

15   Having obtained, from the Jewish Agency in Palestine, details of the preparations taken by Beirut, Professor Nicholas Hammond, who in 1941 worked for the British Special Operations Executive, drew up a very exhaustive report on this subject. Later, when he was attached to the staff of General Lavarack, he was dismayed to learn that this report had never been passed on to him. (Glyn Harper, *Journal of the Oral History Association of Australia*, N° 15, 1993.)

16   Later Field Marshal Sir Thomas Blamey GBE KCB DSO ED, Australia's first field marshal. In 1954, Prime Minister Menzies made Prince Philip, Duke of Edinburgh an Australian field marshal. Currently there is a campaign to have General Sir John Monash promoted posthumously to the rank of field marshal.

17   These troops were destined for Europe but, being in transit in Egypt at the time of the Allied collapse in France, they stayed there.

18   Later Lieutenant-General Sir John Lavarack KCMG KCVO KBE CB DSO, later Governor of Queensland 1946–57.

19   Hill 95 is quite close to Gaza Ridge where, on 31 October 1917, the Australian Light Horse of General Chauvel had driven the Turks from the field in in a legendary charge (also known as Beersheba).

20   Soldiers of C Company, 2/3rd Battalion captured on 26 June 1942 near Sidon.

21   Later Lieutenant-General Sir Stanley Savige KBE CB DSO MC ED. He was also one of the founders of Legacy, the Australian military widows' and orphans' benevolent society.

22   New Zealand soldiers wear a hat with a pointed crown similar to those worn by Boy Scouts.

23   Pierre Quillet, *Le Chemin le plus long*, Paris, Maisonneuve et Larose, 1997, p.319.

24   *Les Carnets du lieutenant-colonel Brunet de Sairigné*, Paris, Nouvelles Éditions latines, 1990, p.76.

25   George H. Johnston, *Australia at War*, Sydney, Angus and Robertson, 1942.

26   General Maurice-Paul Sarrail commanded the French forces which suppressed the Great Druze Revolt of 1925–27, during which his artillery fired on Damascus.

27   Ken Clift, *War Dance*, Kingsgrove, 2/3rd Bn. Association and P.M. Fowler, 1980, p.188.

28   Roald Dahl, *Boy* and *Going Solo*, London, Penguin, 2008, p.371.

29   Jim McAllister and Syd Tregellis-Smith, *op. cit.*, p.1.

30   Davet, *op. cit*, p.115.

31   On 8 June, there were no more than six wrecked German aircraft. In his report Henry Seyrig confirmed that 'the Allies found three hundred German airmen's uniforms at Aleppo-Nérab airport.'

32   A.N., 3W 168. Quoted by Hervé Couteau-Bégarie and Claude Huan, *Darlan*, Paris, Arthème Fayard, 1989, p.792.

Chapter 12: The Free French at Kastina

1   The *BFO* grouped together the 3rd Marine Infantry Battalion (*3ᵉ Bataillon d'Infanterie de Marine*), a battalion of the Foreign Legion (of the 13th Demi-Brigade), a transport company, an artillery section, an engineer section, a medical corps section, and a supply detachment. At the disposal of General Wavell, the brigade had successfully fought the Italians.

2   Free French Division (*DFL*) (General Legentilhomme), Chief of staff: Lieutenant-Colonel Kœnig, 1st HQ Company (Captain Bellan). Colonel Monclar, commanding 1st Division Infantry; 1st Brigade (Colonel Cazaud): *1st Marine Infantry Battalion* (Major Delange): 1st Company (Captain de Boissoudy); 2nd Company (Captain Rougé); 3rd Company (Lieutenant Brousset); 4th Company (Lieutenant Guéna); Support Company (Captain Langlois). *2nd Marine Infantry Battalion* (Major de Roux); 5th Company (Captain Amiel); 6th Company (Captain Hautefeuille); 7th Company (Lieutenant Fériaud); Support Company (Captain Duché de Bricourt), 1st Foreign Legion Battalion (Major Amilakhvari); 1st Company (Captain Saint-Hillier); 2nd Company (Captain de Bollardière); 3rd Company (Captain Moul); 4th Company (Captain de Lamaze).
    2nd Brigade (Lieutenant-Colonel Génin): *3rd Marine Infantry Battalion* (Major Garbay); 1st Company (Captain Allegrini); 2nd Company (Captain Magny); 3rd Company (Lieutenant Euphrasie-Clotilde). *4th Marine Infantry Battalion* (Major Bouillon); 1st Company (Lieutenant Revault d'Allonnes); 2nd Company (Captain Son); 3rd Company (Captain Defosse); Support Company (Captain Brisbarre); 1st Marine Infantry Brigade (*1ʳᵉ Brigade d'Infanterie de Marine*) (Major de Chevigné); 1st Company (Captain Folliot); 2nd Company (Captain Girod); 3rd Company (Captain Savey). 1st Marine Battalion (*1ᵉʳ Bataillon de fusiliers marins*) (Capitaine de corvette Detroyat); 1st Tank Company (13 H-39 tanks) (Captain Volvey); 1st Spahi Squadron (Captain Jourdier); 1st Artillery Battalion (Captain Jacquet); 2nd Battalion (no weapons) (Captain Chavanac). One section of sappers/mine clearance team (Lieutenant Desmaison). One transport company (Captain Renard). 101st Automobile Company (Lieutenant Dulau); Medical Corps (Surgeon-Captain Delavenne); Mobile operating theatre (Surgeon-Major Vernier); Hadfield-Spears Hospital (Surgeon-Major Fruchaud). [Paul Gaujac, *op. cit.*, p.13.]

3　　10,000 Spanish Republicans enlisted in the Foreign Legion in 1939.

4　　Pierre Quillet, *op. cit.*, p.225.

5　　Prince Dimitri Amilakhvari was a Georgian nobleman who moved to France and graduated from Saint-Cyr. He became a lieutenant-colonel in the French Foreign Legion (*Légion Étrangère*) and distinguished himself particularly at Bir Hakeim. He was killed in action at El Alamein.

6　　*Enseigne de vaisseau* Simon, *op. cit.*, p.65.

7　　Three Potez 63, four Morane 406, two Caudron Simon, two Potez 29, one Bloch 81, one Loire 130 seaplane (Vital Ferry, *op. cit.*, p.254). The best known of those who went to Egypt was Captain Tulasne, future commander of the Normandie-Niémen fighter group, which distinguished itself in Russia. Major Jean Tulasne was killed in action in Russia on 17 July 1943.

8　　Essential and permanent, the role of aviation in the war in Syria will only be mentioned here. You are referred to the remarkable work of Christian Ehrengardt and Christopher F. Shores, *L'Aviation de Vichy au combat.* Tome II: *La Campagne de Syrie*, Paris, Lavauzelle, 1987. For the Navy, read: *En Syrie, combats sans espoir. Guerre navale en Syrie, 1941*, Paris, Éditions de la Couronne littéraire, du Capitaine de vaisseau Pierre Guiot, former commander of the *Valmy*. The land operations are described in full detail from the French side by Roger Rouy, in his doctoral thesis, *Étude sur une guerre inconnue* (SHAA and Faculté des sciences humaines of Dijon) and from the British side by Gavin Long in his book, *Greece, Crete and Syria*.

9　　Pierre Quillet, *op. cit.*, p.227.

10　Forty-one years later, the Israelis adopted the same natural invasion routes.

11　A landing by Royal Marine Commandos planned for Latakia did not take place.

12　The 5th Indian Brigade of Brigadier Lloyd: three infantry battalions (King's Royal Rifle Corps, 3/1 Punjab Regiment, 4/6 Rajputs); four artillery batteries; 12 English Mark VI tanks, which were lightly armoured; and a British squadron of 12 armoured cars.

13　The British Admiral E.L.S. King flew his flag in *Phoebe*. He had about 20 ships: *Ajax, Kandahar, Kimberley, Janus, Jackal* and *Coventry.*. The landing ship *Glengyle* was protected by *Isis* and *Hotspur*. Later the Australian ships *Stuart, Nizam* and *Perth* arrived, as did *Leander* (New Zealand) and *Naiad, Kingston, Jaguar, Havock* and *Hasty* (British).

14　Christopher Buckley, *op. cit.*, p.135.

15　Labouna, Alma Chaab, Hanita in front of Nakoura; Yaroun, Aïn Ebel, Bennt-Jbaïl, Aitaroune, El Malikiya to the east in the mountains. (Jim McAllister and Syd Trigellis-Smith, *op. cit.*, p.19).

16　Eleven battalions of infantry, eight artillery batteries, 24 squadrons of cavalry, four motorised squadrons, and a mobile armoured unit.

17　Including three 105/L/36 cannon, the most modern in the Levant.

18　François Lehideux, *De Renault à Pétain, Mémoires*, Paris, Pygmalion, 2001, p.296.

19　Alan Moorehead was born and educated in Melbourne and graduated BA from Melbourne University. He went to the UK in 1937, and became an acclaimed war correspondent for the London *Daily Express*.

20　The American magazine *Time*, 15 June 1941.

Chapter 13: 8 June: The Offensive

1 Général Catroux, *op. cit.,* p.141
2 SHAT 4P5.
3 SHAT 4P5. The text published in the newspaper *La France* on 9 June 1941, differs slightly in its terms, but its meaning is identical, without omitting anything.
4 Salma Mardam Bey, *op. cit.*, p.64.
5 Charles de Gaulle, *Mémoires*, Vol.1: *L'Appel 1940–1942*, p.416.
6 A. H. Hourani, *Syria and Lebanon* (1946) quoted by Gavin Long, *op. cit.*, p.323.
7 Maréchal Pétain, *Paroles aux Français*, Paris, Déterna Éditions, 2010, pp.118–19.
8 SHAT 4 P5
9 Operations report of the 8th Algerian Spahis.
10 Hillary St. George Saunders, *The Green Beret*, London, Michael Joseph, 1949, p.70; preface by Lord Mountbatten. The 11th (Scottish) Commando was named the 'Scottish Commando' as most of its members were drawn from Scottish regiments.
11 Later Major, 2/4th Field Regiment, AIF.
12 Gavin Long, *op. cit.*, p.364, note 5.
13 Son of an Admiral of the Fleet, this 24-year-old Scot was killed soon afterwards in Cyrenaica in a famous, but unsuccessful, attempt to capture General Rommel. He was awarded a posthumous VC.
14 2/14th Battalion and 2/6th Field Company.
15 Besides the *Palestine Volunteer Force*, created in December 1940, 800 Palestinian Arabs and Jews formed four infantry companies attached to the Royal East Kent Regiment (The Buffs). In July 1942, more than 10,000 Palestinian Jews were serving in the British Army. (Guilhem Touratier, 'Un Palestinien au service de Sa Majesté', *Militaria*, N° 240, p.44.)
16 A Jewish paramilitary organisation – the word means 'the defence' in Hebrew – which apart from defending Jewish settlements also carried out attacks on British military establishments
17 Davet, *op. cit.*, p.122.
18 René Cassin, *op. cit.,* p.354. Nevertheless, at the beginning of May 1941, Salvo Seidenberg, a Palestinian Jew, contacted the French Liaison Office – at 479 Jaffa Road, Jerusalem – to enlist but the latter not following up, he joined the British Army.
19 Having become chief of staff of *Tsahal* in 1953, General Moshe Dayan commanded the Israeli Army with great success, notably in the Six Days War in 1967. His face, with a patch over the left eye, is known worldwide.
20 The Australian cruiser HMAS *Perth* was part of this force. Remember that the cruiser HMAS *Australia* had taken part in the bombardment of Dakar in September 1940.
21 Thirty kilometres, as the crow flies over particularly rugged terrain.
22 Colonel J.P. Buckley OBE ED, preface to *Largely a Gamble, Australians in Syria* by Jim McAllister and Syd Trigellis-Smith, *op. cit.*, p.II.
23 *Soûr*, in Arabic. *Soûr* gave its name to Syria: Sourya.
24 Gavin Long, *op. cit.*, p.352.
25 Very spread out, the town seems to have been moved today.

26 Arriving from France with important aviation reinforcements, 14 twin-engine Glenn Martin bombers, much more modern, did not arrive in Syria until 14 June. The 12 Glenn Martin aircraft that were present in Syria, of N° 1 Squadron of the 39th Bombardment Group (*GB/1/39*), were not involved in operations on the coast that day.

27 Pierre Le Gloan, with 18 victories, was the 4th leading French ace of World War II. He was killed in action on 11 September 1943.

28 Robert Surcouf (1773–1827), a French privateer and slave trader.

29 The nickname of the *Marine nationale*, the French Navy.

30 A J-class destroyer, she was commissioned in August 1939 and, after service in the North Sea, she served at the Battle of Calabria (1940) and the Battle of Matapan (1941). She was sunk off Anzio on 23 January 1944.

31 The two ships sortied on 14th to support troops ashore but the arrival of the British made them withdraw. On the 15th, a night action lasting ten minutes did not produce a result. See: Capitaine de vaisseau Guiot, *En Syrie, combats sans espoir, op. cit.*

32 An Algerian battalion, 1st Battalion 29th Algerian Tirailleur Regiment, a group of *spahi* horsed squadrons from Nabatiye, two artillery batteries borrowed from the position at Damour, a 155mm battery (new guns of a recent model). Behind these forward elements were an ammunition column, two companies of the Legion (13th Company under the command of Captain Babonneau and 14th Company under the command of Captain Laimay from Damascus; the 15th being at Palmyra), a squadron of tanks and a squadron of armoured cars (Major Lehr).

33 According to the statement of an Australian recorded by a French escapee, the ruse had been suggested by a deserter. Beirut never believed this version of the facts and never justified it, the disproportion between the forces being sufficient in its view to explain the fall of the strong point (Le Corbeiller, *op. cit.*, p.75). At Sidon after the war, Australian bodies were buried as well those of 30 *tirailleurs* found on the battlefield. The locals confirmed that the caves sheltered many more bones.

34 Saint-Cyr 1935; 6th Company (Captain Rafalli) of the 2nd Battalion, 22nd Regiment of Algerian Tirailleurs.

35 A Saint-Cyr graduate aged 37, Babonneau was a person well liked in the Legion. Tall, powerfully built, enthusiastic and warm, he was fleeing an overwhelming series of family problems. Seriously roughed up by the Australians, then taken to Palestine, he joined the FFL (*Forces Françaises Libres*; Free French forces) after the Armistice, on the urging of his classmate Amilakhvari, bringing with him 80 legionnaires. At Bir Hakeim, Major Babonneau commanded the 2nd Battalion of the 13th Demi-Brigade of the Foreign Legion.

36 The attackers had big losses. They said that they had captured 45 legionnaires, two mortars, five machine guns and two anti-tank guns, which were undamaged and plentifully supplied with ammunition (Gavin Long, *op. cit.*, p.377) A prisoner in Palestine, then repatriated to Algeria, Warrant Officer Pierre Forgerit took part in the liberation of Corsica where he was again wounded. He then took part in the landing in Provence and was killed, on 9 October 1944, serving with de Lattre's army in Upper Savoy (*Haute-Savoie*).

37 H. du Moulin de Labarthète, *Le Temps des illusions*, Genève, Constant Bourquin, 1946, p.226.

38 Charles de Gaulle, *Discours et Messages*, Paris, Plon, 1970, pp.94–5.
39 5th Battalion of the 24th Mixed Colonial Infantry Regiment (*Régiment Mixte d'Infanterie Coloniale*).
40 Two squadrons the 6th African Chasseur Regiment (*Régiment de Chasseurs d'Afrique*)
41 Artillery: 2/4th Field Regiment; Infantry: 2/16th Battalion, a unit which had not yet been engaged. Two companies followed in open order.
42 Christian-Jacques Ehrengardt and Christopher Shores, *op. cit.*, p.51 *et seq.*
43 Sqn Ldr Peter Turnbull DFC, 3 Sqn, RAAF was the leading British ace of the Syrian campaign with at least five kills officially recognised in Syria, making nine in the Middle East; he was awarded the DFC on 10 October 1941. He was credited with a 'probable' Fiat CR.42 at Bardia, and a 'damaged' Fiat G.50 while flying a biplane Gloster Gladiator, before converting to Hawker Hurricanes. He destroyed four Messerschmitt Bf.110 in a single sortie over Maraua on 3 April 1941. He destroyed a French Martin 167 on 15 June 1941, two more Martins less than two weeks later, and two French Dewoitine D.520 fighters on 10 July 1941. He returned to Australia and was posted to 75 Sqn in New Guinea, where he destroyed three Japanese aircraft. He was killed in action on 27 August 1942. (Ehrengardt and Shores, *op. cit.*, p.101, and AWM).
44 The D.520 was shot down six kilometres south of Sidon, between the road and the coast. The remains of the pilot were found, after the campaign, buried beside the wreckage of his aircraft. The majority of the aircraft which took part in the attack were also hit. By 12 June, GC III/6 had carried out 34 sorties but after that date did not have more than 12 serviceable aircraft.
45 McAllister and Trigellis-Smith, *op. cit.*, p.227.
46 Hervé Couteau-Bégarie et Claude Huan, *op. cit.*, p.429.
47 Géo London, *op. cit.*, p.218.
48 Sources: At the request of General Dentz, top secret message N° 91 of 12 June, repeated on 14 and 15 June, *Archives nationales*, file of trial of General Dentz, 3 W 365; and on the answer of the Admiral, message 2619 of 16 June, with the original in Darlan's handwriting, same file, *in* Hervé Couteau-Bégarie and Claude Huan, *op. cit.*, p.429.
49 Communications sent by courier pigeon.
50 The evacuation of wounded on mules on the Turkish mountain slopes during the fighting on Gallipoli in 1915 is part of the Australian military tradition. At the Australian War Memorial in Canberra there is a life-size bronze sculpture to their memory.
51 Potassium permanganate ('Condy's crystals').
52 2nd Battalion 29th Algerian Tirailleur Regiment (Major Dilleman), 1st Battalion 22nd Algerian Tirailleur Regiment (Major Sirot), 1st Lebanese Chasseur Battalion (Major Oziol) and three batteries of the Colonial Artillery Regiment of the Levant: one battery of 75mm guns, one of 65mm guns and one of 105mm mountain guns.
53 François Garbit, *Dernières Lettres d'Afrique et du Levant (1940–1941)*, Paris, éditions Sépia, 1999, p.75.
54 The Australian unit was probably Captain T.R.W. Cotton's company of the 2/33rd Battalion (of Baxter's 25th Brigade). Opposing it was the 1st Company of the 1st Battalion of the 17th Senegalese Tirailleur Regiment.
55 1st and 2nd Companies of the 1st Battalion of the 22nd Algerian Tirailleur Regiment.

56 Lavarack was an artilleryman, commissioned a lieutenant in the Royal Australian Artillery in 1905.

57 The 3rd Battalion of the 6th Foreign Legion Regiment from Damascus.

58 Commanding respectively 2nd Battalion and 1st Battalion of the 22nd Algerian Tirailleur Regiment.

59 Later Lieutenant-General Sir Frank Berryman KCVO CB CBE DSO. A regular soldier, Berryman was an artillery officer who excelled at staff duties, holding many important positions, including Deputy Chief of the General Staff under the Commander-in-Chief, General Blamey. He was knighted for his services as the Director-General of the Royal Visit of 1954.

60 Three battalions, 22 guns, the Royal Scots Greys and 6th Division Cavalry Regiment.

61 Merdjayoun was held by a battalion of Australian Pioneers and four British squadrons.

62 The 2/33rd Battalion, 6th Cavalry Regiment., 2/5th Pioneer Regiment, the Royal Scots Greys and an artillery battery. Each unit had anti-tank guns.

63 Gavin Long, *op. cit.*, p.388.

64 Colonel Amanrich commanded the 6th African Chasseur Regiment. The force comprised two companies of the 3rd Battalion of the 6th Foreign Legion Regiment (the 11th Company having been sent to Jezzine to reinforce the 1st Battalion of the 6th Foreign Legion Regiment), the Marion group of squadrons of the 6th African Chasseur Regiment: three Circassian squadrons and a squadron of R-35 tanks.

65 Later Lieutenant-General Sir John Evetts CB CBE MC. After his command of the 6th British Division in Syria, he became Assistant Chief of the Imperial General Staff. After the war, he was involved in the setting up of the Woomera rocket range north of Adelaide.

66 The Australians and a composite regiment formed from the Royal Scots Greys and the Staffordshire Yeomanry.

67 1st and 2nd Battalions of the 22nd Algerian Tirailleur Regiment, 3rd Battalion of the 6th Foreign Legion Regiment and the 2nd Battalion of the 16th Tunisian Tirailleur Regiment.

68 The Indian 4/6 Rajput Regiment and 3/1 Punjab Regiment and the British 2/ King's Own Regiment.

69 Five kilometres to the west of Deraa.

70 The order was the following: '5th Brigade. Operation Order N°1, 17-C. No fire to be opened before 5:00 a.m. on D-Day. All opposition that cannot be overcome by persuasion will be settled with a bayonet.'

71 Tony Albord, *op. cit.*, p.95.

72 According to Yves Gras (*op. cit.*, p.64), the Indians recovered a 47mm cannon, two 75mm cannon, and three armoured cars – Lambert's – which were passed over to the Free French division.

73 The 2nd Battalion of the 17th Senegalese Tirailleur Regiment under the command of Major Boyer.

74 They were Carden-Lloyd carriers, called Bren carriers from the name of the light machine gun with which they were equipped.

75 Pierre Quillet, *op. cit.*, p.248.

76 Or Benet Yacoub – 'the well of the daughters of Jacob' – an outpost held by the 1st Battalion, 17th Senegalese Tirailleur Regiment, which withdrew.

77 2/9th Field Regiment AIF.

78 Lieutenant-Colonel Milliet was second-in-command of the 17th Senegalese Tirailleur Regiment.

79 Nineteenth-century composer and librettist.

80 French Army slang for members of the Army Service Corps.

81 The BIM (*Brigade d'Infanterie de Marine*; Marine Infantry Brigade); 1st Battalion (Lieutenant-Colonel Génin) and 4th Battalion (Major Bouillon).

82 A company of the 16th Tunisian Tirailleur Regiment and the Special Railway Sapper Company.

83 Freitag, *op. cit.*, p.123.

84 Colonel Bouvier, *Compte rendu de renseignements*, Soueida, 10 June 1941. Interrogation of Legionnaire Joseph Vidal, escaped to Palestine in September 1940, attached to the BIM.

85 Collet's group: one squadron of Circassians on horseback, two squadrons of Circassians in trucks, one squadron of *spahis* in trucks.

86 Eighteen kilometres north-west of Sheikh Meskine, held by Senegalese of the 17th Senegalese Tirailleur Regiment.

87 Yves Gras, *op. cit.*, p.67.

88 T/Major Alexander Hore-Ruthven, Rifle Brigade, died of wounds in Libya in 1942. He was the son of Brigadier-General Sir Alexander Hore-Ruthven VC GCMG DSO&bar, later Earl Gowrie, 10th and longest serving Governor-General of Australia.

89 Armoured vehicles from the 7th African Chasseur Regiment in Damascus and sections of the 2nd Battalion, 6th Foreign Legion Regiment.

90 The originals were handed to the staff in Damascus.

91 *Gentforce* units: <u>Free French</u>: three infantry battalions, 12 tanks, 300 cavalry, practically no artillery. <u>British units</u>: 5th Indian Brigade (Brigadier Lloyd, two infantry battalions), the Australian artillery regiment attached to him (a group of two batteries of four 25pdr guns each, and two batteries of 40mm Bofors guns).

92 Deraa was where the Hadfield-Spears Ambulance Unit was situated.

93 Gavin Long, *op. cit.*, p.391.

94 5th Battalion, 1st Moroccan Tirailleur Regiment (Major Rabineau, Captain Perdrix, Lieutenant Engel; the last two were killed).

95 1st Marine Battalion (Major Delange, Captain de Boissoudy and Captain Rougé).

96 Or TJFF. Ordered to safeguard the frontier, this regular unit of the Transjordanian Army was commanded by British officers. It was a different unit to Glubb Pasha's Arab Legion, a desert police unit, about a thousand men strong.

97 Pierre Quillet, *op. cit.*, p.260.

Chapter 14: The Battle for Damascus

1 Army Intelligence.

2 Keime Archives.

3 Mobilised in 1939 in the 2nd Colonial Infantry Regiment, M. Sichel, aged 21, Parisian, left Brest on 18 June 1940, on board a cargo ship for England; J. Henry, aged 19, Parisian, boarded a sailing ship at Roscoff; L. Ancel, aged 20, from Douarnenez, left for England on a fishing boat; mobilised in the 5th

Infantry Regiment, withdrawn to the Landes; P. Lavoi, aged 26, from Belfort, embarked at Saint-Jean-de-Luz for England. Members of the support section of the tank company commanded by Volvey, all joined the Free French Forces during the summer of 1940.

4   Respectively, a company of the 3rd Battalion 29th Algerian Tirailleur Regiment and the 12th Company of the 17th Senegalese Tirailleur Regiment.

5   Galène, who was immediately sent to hospital in Damascus.

6   Villoutreys afterwards spoke unkindly of the treatment he received in hospital at Damascus, before being sent to prison in Aleppo, then by plane to France to face a court martial. He was sent back to Syria after the Armistice of Saint-Jean-d'Acre.

Chapter 15: Kuneitra: The Counter-attack

1   A squadron and a half of R-35 tanks of the 7th African Chasseur Regiment (Captain de Gastines) – minus the vehicles given to Simon and two platoons of tanks left at Damascus at the disposal of General de Verdilhac – a staff (Major Rolin), four platoons of Panhard 35 TOE armoured cars (Captain Grandpierre), a company of motorised Senegalese (3rd Battalion, 17th Senegalese Tirailleur Regiment, Captain Quarez), the 12th motorised squadron (Major Gaillard-Bournazel), the 14th Circassian horsed squadron (Captain de La Chauvelais) and four 47mm guns.

2   Second-in-command of the 17th Senegalese Tirailleur Regiment.

3   Staff (Captain Gandy), a platoon of five R-35 tanks of the 7th African Chasseur Regiment (Lieutenant Dunand), the 1st Armoured Car Squadron (Captain Ricard) with two platoons of five Dodge-White armoured cars (Sub-Lieutenants Michelet and Weil), a motorised platoon of the 1st Moroccan Spahi Regiment (Captain Dumont and Lieutenant de Cannecaude), a support group with a machine gun platoon, a 81mm mortar platoon and a 25mm anti-tank gun (Captain Dumont). Coming from Soueida, a section of Tunisian *tirailleurs* (16th Tunisian Tirailleur Regiment) joined the group at Ezraa, with two 75mm guns and two 25mm anti-tank guns.

4   80 carbines, seven light machine guns, three machine guns, and one 60mm mortar for 80 men.

5   Letter dated 26 April 1942 from Captain Quarez to General Keime.

6   Originally part of the French Army Cavalry School at Saumur, the *Cadre noir* is now an equestrian display team, some of whose members have been Olympic or world champions. It is now part of the Ministry of Health and Sports.

7   Joachim Murat, made Marshal of France and King of Naples by his brother-in-law, Napoleon Bonaparte, was a noted cavalry commander.

8   C. N. Parkinson, *Always a Fusilier* (1949), quoted by Gavin Long, *op. cit.*, p.402.

9   The senior NCO plays a key role in the British Army. We are dealing here with a particularly glorious traditional unit.

10   The two men saw each other again and maintained excellent relations afterwards.

11   A machine-gun company, two light armoured vehicles belonging to the Palestine Police and two anti-tank guns.

12   Later Brigadier A.S. Blackburn VC CMG CBE.

13   The 2/Queens Royal Regiment.

14   It was this route that was taken by the Indian brigade three days earlier in their progress towards Damascus.

15   At 5:30 a.m., three Dewoitine D.520 aircraft of No.3 Squadron, 6th Fighter Group (*GC.III/6*) were accompanying a Potez 631 of No.2 Squadron, 39th Reconnaissance Group (*GR.II/39*) over Deraa. At 8:30 a.m., a double patrol from *GC.III/6* led by Sub-Lieutenant Le Gloan, took off to patrol in the Ezaa-Soueida sector. At 9:45 a.m. they sighted six Gloster Gladiator biplane fighters. C. Ehrengardt and Christopher Shores give the story of the fight, *op. cit.*, p.58.

16   The 16th Tunisian Tirailleur Regiment of Captain Lequesne.

17   Middle Eastern headdress, made from a square of, usually, cotton material, to protect from the sun and cold. It is often red-and-white checks.

18   Six twin-engine Glenn Martin bombers of Squadron 6B carried out the bombing. Two were shot down by Tomahawk fighters: N° 111 crashed near Deraa and N° 118 fell in flames, killing its four crewmen. (Ehrengardt and Shores, *op. cit,* p.60).

19   Two companies of the 3rd Marine Battalion in reserve at Sannamein and a Royal Artillery battery, withdrawn from the Kiswe front, joined the 3rd Company of the Marine Infantry Brigade taking part in the defence of Deraa.

20   Inevitably subject to firing on fixed lines, which was effective even at night.

21   It was on the radio, in Brittany, two months later, that Colonel Génin's family learned of his death while listening to a speech by General de Gaulle at Brazzaville, relayed by the BBC: 'Catroux, d'Argenlieu, Legentilhomme, Sautot, Bonvin, Kackin, Génin have saved parts of the Empire from the control of the enemy and the collaborators. Kackin and Génin have died for France, but the others are at their post.' A legend, that all his comrades – Kœnig, Messmer – absolutely refute, would have it that Génin had got himself killed on purpose to escape the dishonour of having taken part in a fratricidal combat. Walking along the road was in fact suicidal, but would he have done so if his intention was to die? Colonel Génin was posthumously made a *Compagnon de la Libération* (Companion of the Order of the Liberation).

22   Later General Sir John Hackett, GCB CBE DSO and Bar MC. Hackett was born in Perth (WA) and educated at Geelong Grammar School and Oxford University. He was a member, though his mother, of the prominent Drake-Brockman family.

23   Viven-Bessières rifle grenade.

24   Lieutenant de Rostolan protested vigorously against the Free French, although Captain Lequesne, who commanded the Tunisians, joined the Free French. In 1944 he commanded the 22nd BMNA (*Bataillon de Marche Nord Africain/* North African March Battalion) during the fighting along the Garigliano near Naples, in Italy.

25   Gavin Long, *op. cit.*, p.407.

26   Gavin Long, *op. cit.*, p.391.

27   Davet, *op. cit.*, p.139.

28   The 16th British Infantry Brigade (two battalions, Brigadier Lomax), the 6th Infantry Division (three brigades, Major-General Evetts) and the 10th Indian Infantry Division (three brigades, Major-General Slim) came from Egypt; the 25th Australian Brigade (Brigadier Plant) came from Crete and the

17th Australian Brigade (Brigadier Savige) joined the 21st Australian Brigade (Brigadier Stevens) within the 7th Australian Infantry Division (Major-General Allen); *Habforce* (one reinforced brigade, Major-General Clark) came from Iraq.

29 Major-General Arthur Samuel Allen CB CBE DSO VD commanded the 16th Brigade of the 6th Australian Division in North Africa at Bardia and Tobruk, as well as serving in Greece, He took command of the 7th Australian Division in Syria/Lebanon.

30 *Active Service, with Australia in the Middle East,* Canberra, Australian War Memorial, 1941, p.63.

31 Equipped with rifles and light machine guns, the 70 men of the 'Kelly Gang' rode horses recovered from the Vichy French cavalry, notably at Rachaya. They found the French saddles particularly uncomfortable but, 'under intense fire on three occasions, they were astonished to find that the horses, well trained by the French, were not at all frightened by the shelling'. The unit, which was in existence for only about four weeks, gave valuable service between Bmerik and Kafr Hamam.

32 Chouf Force: 1st Battalion of 6th Foreign Legion Infantry Regiment; 2nd and 3rd Battalions of 17th Senegalese Tirailleur Regiment; several squadrons of the 4th Tunisian Spahis (Major Bodman); five artillery batteries.

33 Gavin Long, *op. cit.*, p.407.

34 *Op. cit.*, p.412.

35 2/31st Bn; *L.G.* 24 October 1941. Gordon later joined the Australian Regular Army, retiring as a WO2.

36 The problem of the wounded grew in such a manner that the free passage of the hospital ship *Canada* was authorised by the belligerent nations. 'Its status did not permit any other transport than that of its mission. Not even a letter was authorised'. The big ship, painted white, set sail from Toulon on 16 June (Marc Saibène, *La Marine marchande française 1940–1942,* Nantes, Marines éditions, 1998. p.153.)

37 J. Le Corbeiller, *op. cit.*, p.113

38 An agricultural belt surrounding Damascus to the south and east.

39 A region with fields which are bordered by earthen banks with hedges or trees on them. The vegetation is often very thick and may be impassable for armoured vehicles.

40 Roger Barberot, *A bras le cœur*, Paris, Robert Laffont, 1972.

41 Under the command of Major Delange, the 1st Marine Battalion then had a staff and four companies (Boissoudy, Rougé, Brousset, Guéna) plus a support company (Langlois).

42 From the 29th Algerian Tirailleur Regiment and the 1st Moroccan Tirailleur Regiment.

43 Under the command of Major Pacaud of the 17th Senegalese Tirailleur Regiment, this small formation comprised the 1st Battalion, 29th Algerian Tirailleur Regiment (Major Blanc), Captain de Carmejane's Circassians, 60 legionnaires under the command of Captain Hourtané, some *spahis* of the 1st Moroccan Spahi Rgiment, and elements of the 7th African Chasseur Regiment from Damascus.

44 Report of Lieutenant-Colonel de Chaléon, of the Damascus staff.

45 Circassian squadron of Lieutenant Le Masson and, at the end of the afternoon, Captain Rémy's squadron of Moroccan *spahis*.

46 Pierre Quillet, *op. cit.*, pp.283 and 289.
47 Letter of Captain Chaumeil to General Keime, Rabat, 13 May 1942.
48 He died two days later.
49 Colonel Le Couteulx de Caumont was the former commander of the armoured cars (3rd RAM/*Régiment d'automitrailleuses*) in Colonel de Gaulle's 4th DCR (*Division Cuirassée de Réserve*/Reserve Armoured Division) in 1940 He again showed his ability at the head of an armoured formation in Tunisia in 1943. He was appointed Military Governor of Rome by General Juin in 1944.
50 Le Corbeiller, *op. cit.*, p.113.
51 On 13 June, the High Commissioner required the director of the *Banque de Syrie et du Grand Liban* to hand over to him the gold in order to send it to France. The *Gendarmerie* took charge of it on the morning of 14 June. Two and a half tonnes of gold, partly in ingots and partly in pounds sterling, i.e. 119 million francs, were sent to France where they were deposited in the *Banque de France* at Clermont-Ferrand. When the Unoccupied Zone was invaded, the treasure remained hidden and its documentation was concealed under the padding of a leather armchair. The gold was handed over to the paymaster general of the Puy-de-Dôme in December 1944. (Cf. Davet, *op. cit.*, p.150.)
52 Le Corbeiller, *op. cit.*, p.115.
53 The official march of the French Foreign Legion, the title (lit. 'The Black Pudding') refers to the blanket roll that used to carried on top of the legionnaires' pack.
54 A few scattered people drawn from a depot, the 6th Foreign Legion Regiment being engaged at Jezzine and Palmyra.
55 *L'Épopée de la '13'*, p.154.
56 Later, General.
57 The motto of the French Foreign Legion: 'The Legion is our Fatherland.'
58 Interview by Daniel Rondeau and Roger Stéphane, and *op. cit.*, p.183 *et seq.*
59 Report by Lieutenant-Colonel Dobree of the Indian Brigade.
60 Later Lieutenant-General Sir Sydney Rowell, KBE CB and Chief of the General Staff.
61 Gavin Long, *op. cit.*, pp.417, 420.
62 C Company and part of A Company of the 2/3rd MG Battalion.
63 Later Brigadier, CBE DSO.
64 Yves Gras, *op. cit.*, p.82.
65 The 13ᵉ DBLE (*13ᵉ Demi-Brigade de la Légion Étrangère*/13th Half-Brigade of the Foreign Legion).
66 Later Prime Minister of France and a member of the *Académie française*.
67 With one leg amputated, the future General de Boissoudy, who had played a key role in the winning over of Brazzaville in 1940, became a Companion, and then member of the Council, of the Order of the Liberation in 1942. From 1943 to 1945, he was the representative of the Free French Division to the Consultative Assembly in Algiers.
68 Nasty proceedings for complicity in murder were brought against General de Verdilhac on 7 October 1942 in the Beirut court by General Catroux for having ordered the execution of a spy disguised as a bedouin during the fighting on 10 June 1941, but the Paris Court of Appeal declared the charge inadmissible on 8 June 1948.
69 Army Intelligence.

70   From the 1st Battalion, 17th Senegalese Tirailleur Regiment.

71   The support company later pushed on as far as Homs where the whole 1st Marine Battalion assembled in the Military School, but the battalion, as such, had no further combats.

72   Pierre Quillet, *op. cit.*, p.287.

73   Open-air market places.

74   Lit. 'in the interior of the country' or 'in the middle of nowhere'.

75   According to General Prudhomme, then a sub-lieutenant, General Keime knew the exact time of Legentilhomme's entry into the city. He could have shelled it, but abstained from doing so.

76   General Henri Gouraud, commanded the 4th French Army in World War I and the French Army of the Levant, 1919–23.

77   Oriental-style usher.

78   Operations.

79   The code name for Germany's invasion of Soviet Russia during World War II.

80   After the war, it became the French Embassy.

81   Under the command of Major-General J.G.W. Clark, basically the 4th Cavalry Brigade in trucks (the Household Cavalry, the North Somerset Yeomanry, and the Royal Wiltshire Yeomanry) (Brigadier J.J. Kingstone); 1st Battalion, Essex Regiment; two batteries of artillery (237 Battery RA less two troops and one troop 239 Battery RA); nine armoured vehicles of the 2nd Armoured Car Company RAF Regiment; and 350 men of Glubb Pasha's Arab Legion.

82   Twin-engined LeO 451 (Lioré et Olivier) bombers of GB (*Groupe de bombardement*) I/25, I/31 and I/12 (Ehrengardt and Shores, *op. cit.*, p.78; Captain Menu's citation, p.79.)

83   During the fighting at Palmyra, Squadron 4F of the *Aéronavale* (French Fleet Air Arm) fought alongside the *Armée de l'air* (French Air Force). Six of its aircraft were shot down.

84   *Groupe de chasse II/3* (2nd Squadron, 3rd Fighter Group).

85   *Escadrille d'observation* (Observation squadron), equipped with Potez 25 biplanes

86   Twin-seat, single-engine, biplane multipurpose aircraft from the 1920s.

87   Gilbert Poincelet, *Dans le ciel de Syrie*, Paris, Séquana, 1941. In 1987, these figures were revised downward by Ehrengardt and Shores, but the Vichy French effort remained very great.

88   *Groupe de reconnaissance II/39.* 2nd Squadron 39th Reconnaissance Group.

89   It was the Curtiss P-40, a development of the Curtiss 75 which mainly equipped the French fighter force in 1940.

90   *1re Compagnie légère du désert* (1st Light Desert Company).

91   On 30 April 1863, a small group of the Legion, consisting of three officers and 62 men, under the command of Captain Jean Danjou, was besieged by 2,000 Mexican infantry and cavalry at Camerone (Mexico). All but five were killed, including Captain Danjou, whose wooden hand (to replace one lost in Algeria) is paraded at each anniversary of the battle, the greatest symbol of the French Foreign Legion.

92   Gavin Long, *op. cit.*, p.479.

93   *Gringoire* was a weekly newspaper, which had high-quality articles, an excellent literary section and satirical cartoons. Initially centre-right, it became more definitely right-wing and nationalistic.

94   *Les Croix de bois* ('The Wooden Crosses') was published in 1931 and is his masterpiece. It depicts, in a very realistic way, trench life and warfare during World War I, in which Dorgelès served as a volunteer. It was made into a very successful film.

95   Desert scarf worn around the neck and across mouth.

96   Six officers, 87 German and Russian legionnaires, 48 Air Force men and 24 bedouin of the Light Desert Company (Gavin Long, *op. cit.*, p.477).

97   The 10th Indian Division (17th, 20th and 21st Brigades) was commanded by Major-General, later Sir, William Slim GBE KCB DSO MC, a future field marshal and Commander-in-Chief Allied Land Forces SE Asia, future Chief of the Imperial General Staff, and finally Governor-General of Australia. It was the 2/4th Gurkhas (21st Brigade) which appeared before Mayadine. The 13th Lancers and 4/13th Frontier Force Rifles (21st Brigade) appeared before Abu Kemal.

98   Forty kilometres south-east of Deir-ez-Zor.

99   Essentially a battalion of Syrian infantry and a Light Desert Company, with some artillery.

100   *Capitaine de vaisseau* (= captain) in September, Admiral Marzin commanded the battleship *Richelieu* at Dakar at the time of the Anglo-Gaullist attack.

101   The 'French Legion of Ex-Servicemen' was an organisation set up by Vichy in which all the ex-service organisations were grouped under the one banner.

102   Its crews called it the 'Stringbag'.

103   During the negotiations, Benoist-Méchin suggested the following exchange: the Turks would hand back to the French the 100 Renault-35 tanks which had been delivered to them as mutual assistance in 1939, equipment for which they had not yet paid and, in exchange, the debt would be remitted. The Germans would deliver another 100 armoured vehicles. The Turks refused, agreeing to the passage of the convoys only in exchange for the permanent cession of Aleppo and Al-Jezirah. Vichy refused, preferring to see these territories go eventually to de Gaulle than to the Turks.

104   Ehrenhardt and Shores, *op. cit.*, p.146 and p.151.

105   Among others, ten 75mm guns and 12 25mm antiaircraft guns (M. Saibène, *op. cit.*, p.152).

106   The negotiations opened to discuss their repatriation did not end for a month. Repatriation was only possible after the Armistice, with the agreement of the British. General de Verdilhac, on 25 July, handed a note on this subject to General Chrystall, co-president of the Armistice Commission, asking him to authorise the distribution, from the stocks of clothing, of supplies needed to clothe these survivors, 221 of them having lost everything.

107   The three destroyers were scuttled on 27 November 1942. At the end of June, off Khalde beach, five kilometres south of Beirut, while it was carrying out surface manoeuvres during an exercise, the French submarine *Souffleur* was sighted and sunk by the British submarine *Parthian*. The sailors could not understand how their comrades could have allowed themselves to be surprised. On the other hand, the oiler *Adour* had been torpedoed.

108   Some enlistees escaped and succeeded, after a long journey, in crossing Turkey and joining the 1st Free French Division. On 15 July, the war being over, a group of cavalry squadrons, having left by train for Salonika, was stopped at Zagreb and sent back by the Germans without regard for the circumstances.

Chapter 16: Negotiate?

1   The Algerian *tirailleurs* of the 2nd Marine Battalion under the command of Major de Roux, three tanks, a single French cannon, and a British battery of four guns.

2   A company of the 16th Tunisians, two tank platoons, two Circassian squadrons, one squadron of *spahis*, a battery of 75mm guns and the five armoured cars of Michelet's platoon.

3   Gavin Long, *op. cit.*, p.468.

4   The Free French Division then represented no more than seven per cent of the whole.

5   Australian 17th Brigade: 2/3rd and 2/5th Infantry Battalions and 2/2nd Pioneer Battalion, which were far from being at full strength.

6   2nd Battalion of the reconstituted 21st Algerian Tirailleur Regiment (Captain de Lanlay) and the 2nd Battalion of the 6th Foreign Legion Regiment (Major Brisset).

7   The position, covering Beit ed Dine from two to six kilometres away, covered Hill 877, Aïn Bal, Mazraatesh Chouf, Gharife, Baïqoun.

8   2/5th Fd Regt. Later, Sir Roden Cutler VC AK KCMG KCVO CBE, and, Australian High Commissioner to New Zealand and Governor of New South Wales.

9   Gordon's VC was gazetted *L.G.* 24 October 1941; Cutler's appeared in *London Gazette*, 28 November 1941.

10 Two Victoria Crosses were awarded during the very short Syrian campaign, which was exceptional.

11 'The Song of the Departure' is a French revolutionary and war song dating from the end of the eighteenth century.

12 In Le Corbeiller, *op. cit.*

13 Made by Renault, these were one of the world's first modern tanks. They weighed 6.5 tonnes, with a two-man crew.

14 Learning that France was asking for the cessation of hostilities, Ribbentrop, Minister of Foreign Affairs of the *Reich*, transmitted this request to Vichy: 'Avoid concessions favouring the Gaullists...especially avoid recognition of the Gaullists as military and political agencies.' Berlin joined Vichy in this wish.

15 SHA Air, order 3715/3.

16 Fourteen officer prisoners had already been sent to Salonika by air on 2 July.

17 The submarines reached Bizerta. The small ships and service vessels – tugs, tankers, minesweepers and lighters – left Beirut for Alexandretta where they were decommissioned, then sold, on 8 November 1943, to Turkey. Among them was the sloop *Elan*, which had reached Beirut on 26 December 1944. (SHM, *Le Théâtre méditerranéen*, Tome III). All the naval aircraft with sufficient range reached France or French North Africa. Turkey having refused landing rights on its territory for short range aircraft, 16 Morane-Saulnier MS.406 aircraft of *Groupe de chasse* 1/7 remained in Syria and were handed over to the British on 30 July 1941 at Rayak. To register their disapproval, the pilots burned two, but these machines no longer had any operational value. They were finally handed over to the Free French. (J. Le Groignec, *op. cit.*, p.48, note 21).

18 Foreign Office 371/27298, 3.7.41, quoted by Salma Mardam Bey, *op. cit.*, p.60.

19 In the French text, the expression used is 'le ver est dans le fruit' (*lit.* 'the worm is in the fruit').
20 Gavin Long, *op. cit.*, p.512. (a fuller version).
21 Marc Saibène, *op. cit.*, p.152.
22 Dimas, 16 km to the west of Damascus, is at the entrance to Barada gorge.
23 Later Major-General, CB CBE DSO MC, commanding 26th Indian Division.
24 *Brigade d'Infanterie de Marine* (Marine Infantry Brigade).
25 2/3rd Battalion, later Major-General, AO MC RFD ED.
26 Gavin Long, *op. cit.*, p.435.

Chapter 17: Armistice at Saint-Jean-d'Acre

1 Admiral Sir Sidney Smith commanded the British ships which, in 1799, defended Saint-Jean-d'Acre against Napoleon Bonaparte.
2 The British delegation included Air Commodore Brown for the RAF, and the Australians, Generals Lavarack and Allen, Brigadiers Bridgeford, Rowell, and Stevens in field dress, without decorations.
3 General Wavell, Commander-in-Chief in the Middle East, had in theory been replaced on 1 July by General Auchinleck, whose place he was to take as Commander-in-Chief, India, but given the difficulties in communications, Wavell kept control of operations until the signing of the Armistice.
4 René Cassin, *op. cit.*, p.356.
5 Davet, *op. cit.*, p.166.
6 Davet, *op. cit.*, gives the shorthand account of the debate, p.171 *et seq.*
7 Major-General John I. Chrystall CBE MC. His parent regiment was the 13/18th Hussars and he had commanded the Transjordan Frontier Force 1936–40.
8 Marie-Pierre Kœnig, later commanded the Free French troops at Bir Hakeim, which held out against five Axis divisions commanded by Rommel, for 16 days (26 May–11 June 1942). He was posthumously raised to the dignity of Marshal of France.
9 It will be soon, since in only 16 months' time, the two parties will find themselves shoulder to shoulder in Tunisia in the struggle against the Axis, and during the landing in Provence, former soldiers of Dentz's army will find themselves under the command of General Wilson.
10 At the siege of Saint-Jean-d'Acre in 1799, the city was defended by the combined forces of the British fleet under the command of Admiral Sir Sidney Smith and the troops of Djezzar Pasha, advised by an émigré French artillery officer, Louis de Phélippeaux. A former fellow pupil of Bonaparte at Brienne, then at the *École militaire* de Paris (Military School in Paris), Louis de Phélippeaux had, like the Free French Forces, chosen to ally himself with the British to fight against his government. To see two Franco–French conflicts take place at Saint-Jean-d'Acre was already astonishing, but another coincidence is even more surprising: the great-grandmother of Phélippeaux was born Verdillac (without the '*h*' but this doesn't signify anything. Genealogical source: Gildas de Massé, g.demasse@free.fr)
11 Modern day Martyrs' Square.
12 An extremely popular song among Commonwealth troops in France in 1918.
13 At its head, an element of the 6th Australian Division, the 2/16th Battalion, and staff.

14 Pierre Quillet, *op. cit.*, p.314.

15 The British confirmed that a detachment of the Cheshire Yeomanry also rendered military honours.

16 George H. Johnston, *Australia at War*, Sydney, Angus & Robertson, 1942, p.246.

17 Lieutenant-Commander Hugh Hodgkinson, *Before the Tide Turned*, London, Harrap, 1944.

18 *Sydney Morning Herald*, 14 June 1941.

19 AIF: Australian Imperial Forces. Colonel Buckley, preface to *Largely a Gamble*, *op. cit.*

20 Lieutenant-Colonel J.D. Rogers, AIF, report on the campaign.

21 Christopher Buckley, *Five Ventures*, *op. cit.*, p.135.

22 A Viceroy's Commissioned Officer of the British Indian Army, equivalent to a 2nd Lieutenant.

23 *Active Service*, Canberra, Australian War Memorial, 1941, p.65.

24 Gavin Long, *op. cit*, pp.524–5. It was also the opinion of Admiral Émile Muselier, who led the Free French Naval Forces during World War II, who said: 'If the Free French had not taken part, the fighting would have been much easier for the British.'

25 Gavin Long, *op. cit.*, pp.527–8.

26 Gavin Long, *op. cit.*, p.525.

27 The branch of the staff responsible for organisation, personnel and equipment.

28 Christopher Buckley, *op. cit.*, p.137.

29 Gavin Long, *op. cit.*, p.526.

30 Gavin Long, *op. cit.*, p.525.

31 Arthur Bryant, *The Turn of the Tide, 1939-1943*, p.270. At the end of 1941, of the 16 divisions in the Middle East, six were in Libya, two in Ethiopia, two in Palestine and Syria, and four in Iraq and Persia to protect the wells of the Anglo–Iranian Oil Company.

32 Formed in response to Article 21 of the Saint-Jean-d'Acre accords, the Control Commission functioned from 16 July to 27 September 1941. Besides General de Verdilhac, the [Vichy] French delegation included Admiral Gouton and General Beucler. The British delegation included Lieutenant-Colonel Sir Ranulph Fiennes and Colonel Kœnig for the Free French, who was replaced later by Major de Kersauson. A certain number of sub-commissions were in operation to settle technical problems, armaments, fuel, railways, ports, banks and currency, etc.

33 He had been made Acting Major General while co-president of the Commission. He later relinquished his acting rank and reverted to that of Brigadier (= *général de brigade* in French).

34 *Rapport du général de division de Verdilhac*, Arles, 19 February 1942, Chapter II, p.2 *et seq.*

35 *Ibid.*, p.15.

36 Davet, *op. cit.*, p.182.

37 Colonel Keime, *Cavaliers du Levant*, illustrated, 1942.

38 Davet, *op. cit.*, p.182.

39 Ken Clift, *War Dance: The story of the 2/3 Australian Infantry Battalion, 16th Brigade, 6th Division*, *op. cit.*, p.192.

40 Ken Clift (1916-2009) won one of the first Australian DCM of World War II when, as a signaller in the 6th Division, AIF, he captured an Italian gun battery at Tobruk.

41 Photograph published in 1942 in *Pour maintenir l'Empire, Syrie, Liban* (To Preserve the Empire, Syria, Lebanon), a brochure published by the Vichy Secretary General for Information and Propaganda.

42 In 1945, France would find her rights restored in Indochina and Madagascar that were also occupied by the British.

43 René Cassin, *op. cit.*, p.357.

44 It is the familiar name of a popular unit, the 13th Demi-Brigade of the Foreign Legion/*la 13ème Demi-Brigade de la Légion Étrangère,* much as the Americans called the 8th USAAF the 'Mighty 8th'.

45 FO 371/27308, 6 August 1941.

46 The legendary dog of Nahr el-Kelb sitting on a boomerang!

47 These works were part of the military organisational plan involving the Turkish frontier which could thus be serviced by fast transports. Important defence works were developed at the same time on two east–west lines, one to the north, facing the frontier, the other to the south, near Merdjayoun – the Eden line – where large excavations were carried out and a big subterranean hospital was dug.

48 It was a custom, current at the time in Britain, to give reserve officers their former rank. Lyttelton had served in the Grenadier Guards during World War I, winning the DSO and MC.

49 Quoted by Davet, *op. cit.*, p.186.

50 The Free French Division thus recovered enough weapons to equip two mixed brigades and an armoured group. Too out of date to be used in Libya, the Renault R-35 and Hotchkiss H-39 tanks were left in the Levant, but the Dodge-White armoured cars and the Tanaké armoured trucks will be used by the Free French in Cyrenaica, and the low-slung 75mm guns on Laffly metal wheels will have their hour of glory at Bir Hakeim. One of them is today displayed at the *Musée de l'Armée* (Army Museum) at the *Invalides* in Paris, and another in the French military cemetery in Tobruk.

51 Major Sir Desmond Morton KCB CMG MC, Winston Churchill's Personal Assistant during World War II.

52 *Chicago Daily News*, 27 August 1941, in François Kersaudy, *op. cit.*, p.87.

53 Quoted by Jean-Luc Barré, *op. cit.*, p.158.

54 The Allies in fact kept the French systematically apart from the major strategic decisions, even those concerning French territories. This can be verified all through the war, in Madagascar, North Africa and Normandy.

55 *Washington Post*, 2 July 1943.

Chapter 18: Brother Enemies

1 A. Fabre-Luce, *Deuil au Levant*, Paris, Arthème Fayard, 1950, p.179.

2 A 'consular' mass is a special ceremony at which the representative of France was supposed to be present. On 28 July, in Algiers, General Weygand had a requiem mass celebrated for the soldiers killed in Syria. When he came out of the cathedral, the crowd cheered him. (P. Ordioni, *Tout commence à Alger*, p.208.)

3 Report of Major de Bodman, commanding the 6th Spahis, Biskra, 15 April 1942.

4 Davet, *op. cit.*, p.189.

5   The Caudron C.440 Goéland was a small twin-engine utility aircraft, developed in the 1930s, usually seating six passengers, with luggage compartments and an on-board toilet.

6   In 1944, Colonel Brosset commanded the 1st Free French Division as part of the French Expeditionary Corps in Italy, then as part of de Lattre's 1st French Army during the campaign in Alsace. He was unfortunately killed in a jeep accident. All who met him, even in the Army of the Levant, agreed in praising the rare qualities of this exemplary leader.

7   786 British, including seven senior and 38 junior officers; 16 Australians, including one officer; 342 Indians, including seven officers; one Iraqi; 16 Palestinians and Transjordanians (Summary of 13 July 1941; South Syria Command, Intelligence Section). Plus about ten Free French soldiers.

8   Le Corbeiller, *op. cit.*, pp.155–7.

9   During the campaign, desertions to the enemy were rare: about 50 Frenchmen, the 3rd Light Desert Company and some Senegalese.

10   The *Ordre de la Francisque* was a decoration awarded by the Vichy regime. The badge was based on an old Gallic double-headed axe, in French red-white-blue. The badge came to be used on official documents as a symbol of the Vichy regime, the *État français* ('French State').

11   Report of Captain Passet, former commander of the 1st Light Desert Company, at Palmyra to General Keime, Miliana, 11 June 1942.

12   Gavin Long, *op. cit.*, p.545.

13   64,151 men: 18,465 from the 6th Division, 18,620 from the 7th Division and 17,866 from the 9th Division (not engaged in Syria), and 9,200 from staffs, administrations and liaison teams.

14   General Lavarack left by plane on 21 January 1942.

15   Entitlement is based on one day's operational service in Syria between 8 June 1941 and 11 July 1941.

16   Davet, *op. cit.* p.182.

17   Le Corbeiller, *op. cit.*, p.160.

18   Géo London, *op. cit.*, p.235.

19   The regimental march.

20   The 6th Foreign Legion Regiment was soon disbanded, but an enduring animosity followed its former members. Among them we find the names of Pierre Segretain, commanding the 1st Foreign Parachute Battalion in Indochina, who was killed in 1950 on *Route Coloniale* 4; Hubert Liesenfelt, who commanded the 2nd Foreign Parachute Battalion in Diên Biên Phu; Pierre Jeanpierre, deported to Mauthausen, who fell at the head of the 1st Foreign Parachute Regiment at Guelma (Algeria) in 1958 – a graduating class at Saint-Cyr bears his name; Jacques Pépin-Lehalleur, who later occupied major posts in the military hierarchy.

21   Wherever they came from, the bodies of French soldiers killed in Syria since 1920 are today buried in a single military cemetery situated in the desert 40 km from Damascus. In Lebanon, there are military cemeteries in Beirut, Tripoli and Rayak. Those from Merdjayoun, Jezzine and Sidon were moved to Beirut. The British Empire dead are buried at Sidon and Tripoli. This list is not exhaustive.

22   Pierre Quillet, *op. cit.*

23   For stragglers.

24   Fifteen liners took part in the repatriation programme, the hospital ships *Canada* and *Sphinx*, operating from Haifa. 1st Convoy (Convoy Z, 7 August, 4,777 passengers): liners *Champollon*, *Mariette-Pacha*, *Explorateur-Grandidier*.

2nd Convoy (Convoy A, 16 August, 5,094 passengers): *Providence, Florida, Maréchal-Lyautey.* 3rd Convoy (Convoy B, 22 August, 4.952 passengers): *Marrakech, Sinaia, Croix.* 4th Convoy (Convoy C, 29 August, 4,044 passengers): *Massilia, Colombie, André-Lebon.* 5th Convoy (Convoy D, 1 September, 5,216 passengers): *Djenné* and *Katoubia.* 6th Convoy (Convoy E, 4 September, 3,156 passengers). 7th Convoy (Convoy A1, 7 September, 4,472 passengers). 8th Convoy (Convoy B1, 12 September, 2,842 passengers). The *Colombie*, a 'sweeper ship', left Beirut on 27 September with General de Verdilhac and 1,415 passengers, and reached Marseilles on 4 October. (These figures, taken from the Verdilhac Report and from the book by Marc Saibène, *op. cit.*, p.160, do not completely correspond. I have taken Verdilhac's figures.)

25 Author's archives.
26 Georges Hirtz, *Weygand*, p.82.
27 Darlan was assassinated on 24 December 1942 by a young French monarchist, Fernand Bonnier de la Chapelle.

Chapter 19: *Vae Victis*

1   'Woe to the conquered (ones).'
2   Charles de Gaulle, *Mémoires de guerre,* Tome I: *L'Appel*, documents, p.375 de l'Édition Pocket, 1999.
3   Charles de Gaulle, Mémoires de guerre, Tome II: *Le Salut, op. cit.*
4   Géo London, *op. cit.*
5   Charles de Gaulle, *Mémoires de guerre*, Tome II: *Le Salut, op. cit.*
6   Claude Guy, *op. cit.*, 13 April 1947, p.304.
7   The second largest prison in France, located in the town of the same name, about 12 km south of Paris.
8   Prince Xavier de Bourbon, *Les Accords secrets franco-anglais de décembre 1940*, Paris, Plon, 1949.
9   Patrick Facon, 'Les Gardiens de l'Empire', in *L'Aviation*, Paris, éditions Larivière, 1999.
10 In the Loire, formerly an abbey, it served as a prison from 1804 to 1963. It now belongs to the Ministry of Culture. The official spelling is *Fontevraud.*
11 An industrial area 24 km to the west of Paris.
12 Chanoine Jean Popot, *J'étais aumônier à Fresnes*, Paris, Perrin, 1965, pp.73–4.
13 A cube-shaped building in the La Défense business district in the west of Paris that was inaugurated in 1989, to celebrate the bicentenary of the French Revolution.
14 There is an *Axe historique* (Historic Axis) the *Arc de Triomphe*, along the Champs-Élysées, to the *Grande Arche de la Défense.*

Bibliography

Albord, Maurice, *L'Armée française et les États du Levant 1936–1946*, Paris, CNRS, 2000.

Andréa, Général, *La Révolte druze*, Paris, Payot, 1937.

Aron, Robert, *Histoire de Vichy*, Paris, Arthème Fayard, 1959.

Auphan, Amiral Paul, *Histoire élémentaire de Vichy*, Paris, France–Empire, 1971.

Auriol, Vincent, *Journal du Septennat 1947–1954*, Tome I: 1947, Paris, Armand Colin, 1970.

Ballarini, Philippe, *L'Armée de l'Air de l'armistice*, at www.aérostories.free.fr/dossiers/AA/Vichy/4. Le Levant (accessed 20 September 2015).

Barberot, Roger, *A bras le cœur*, Paris, Robert Laffont, 1972.

Barré, Jean–Luc, *Devenir de Gaulle, 1939–1943*, Paris, Perrin, 2003.

Benoist-Méchin, Jacques, *De la défaite au désastre*, Paris, Albin Michel, 1985.

——*A l'épreuve du temps. Souvenirs*. Tome II: 1940–1947, Paris, Julliard, 1989.

Bourbon, Prince Xavier de, *Les Accords secrets franco–anglais de décembre 1940*, Paris, Plon, 1949.

Bourget, P.A. *De Beyrouth à Bordeaux*, Paris, Berger-Levrault, 1946.

Brunet de Sairigné, *Les Carnets du lieutenant-colonel B. de S.*, Paris, Nouvelles Éditions latines, 1990.

Buffetaut, Yves, *De l'Irak à la Syrie 1941*, Paris, Histoire et Collections, 2003.

Buis, Georges, *Les Fanfares perdues*, Paris, Le Seuil, 1975.

Cassin, René, *Les hommes partis de rien*, Paris, Plon, 1975.

Catroux, Général Georges, *Dans la bataille de la Méditerranée, 1940–1944*, Paris, Julliard, 1949.

Chaneterac, Arnaud de, *L'Assassinat de Darlan*, Paris, Perrin, 1995.

Corm, Georges, *Le Proche-Orient éclaté, 1956–2003*, Paris, Gallimard, 'Folio Histoire' N°93, 2003.

Couteau-Bégarie, Hervé and Claude Huan, *Darlan*, Paris, Arthème Fayard, 1989.

Crémieux Brilhac, J.-L., *La France libre*, Paris, Gallimard, 1996.

Darlan, Alain, *L'amiral Darlan parle*, Paris, Amiot Dumont, 1952.

Davet, Michel Christian, *La Double Affaire de Syrie*, Paris, Arthème Fayard, 1967.

de Gaulle, Charles, *Mémoires de guerre*. Tome I: *L'Appel, 1940–1942*, Paris, Plon, 1954.

——*Mémoires de guerre*. Tome II: *Le Salut*, Paris, Plon, 1954.

——*Lettres, Notes et Carnets, 1941–1943*, Paris, Plon, 1959.

——*Discours et messages*. Tome I: *1940–1946*, Paris, Plon, 1970.

Destremau, Bernard, *Weygand*, Paris, Perrin, 1991.

Du Moulin de Labarthète, Henri, *Le Temps des illusions*, Genève, Constant Bourquin, 1946.

Ehrengardt, Christian-Jacques and Christopher Shores, *L'Aviation de Vichy au combat. La campagne de Syrie*, Paris, Lavauzelle, 1987.

Fabre-Luce, Alfred, *Deuil au Levant*, Paris, Arthème Fayard, 1950.

Fauvet, Jacques, *La IVe République*, Paris, Fayard, 1959.

Feller, Jean, *Le Dossier de l'armée française. La guerre de 50 ans, 1914–1962*, Paris, Perrin, 1966; preface by Robert Aron.

Ferry, Vital, *Croix de Lorraine et Croix du Sud*, Paris, éditions du Gerfaut, 2005.

Freitag, Captain Joseph, 'Syrie 1941', in *Histoires Vécues*, éditions FFI, 1977.

Gamelin, Général Maurice, *Servir*, Paris, Plon, 1946.

Garbit, François, *Dernières Lettres d'Afrique et du Levant (1940–1941)*, Paris, éditions Sépia, 1999.

Gaujac, Paul, *L'Armée de la victoire, Le réarmement*, Chapter II, 'L'Affaire du Levant', Paris, Lavauzelle, 1984.

Génin, René, *Itinéraire d'un méhariste*, Paris, éditions Sépia, 2004.

Girard, Louis-Dominique, *Montoire, Verdun diplomatique*, Paris, André Bonne, 1948.

Giraud, Henri-Christian, *De Gaulle et les communistes*, Paris, Albin Michel, 1988.

Gras, General Yves, *La 1reD.F.L. – les Français Libres au combat*, Paris, Presses de la Cité, 1983.

Guiot, Capitaine de vaisseau Pierre, *Combats sans espoir, Guerre navale en Syrie, 1941*, Paris, éditions La Couronne Littéraire, 1941.

Guy, Claude, *En écoutant de Gaulle. Journal 1946–1949*, Paris, Grasset, 1996.

Kammerer, Albert, *La Vérité sur l'armistice*, Paris, Médicis, 1945.

Keime, Général Amédée, *Cavaliers du Levant*, 1942.

Laffargue, André, *Le Général Dentz*, Paris, éditions Les Îles d'or, 1954.

Langer, William, *Le jeu américain à Vichy*, Paris, Plon, 1948.

Larminat, Edgard de, *Chroniques irrévérencieuses*, Paris, Plon, 1962.

Le Corbeiller, J. *La Guerre de Syrie, juin–juillet 1941*, Paris, éditions de Fuseau, 1967.

Le Groignec, Général Jacques, *Entre ciel et terre*, Paris, Nouvelles Éditions latines, 1988.

Lehideux, François, *De Renault à Pétain, Mémoires*, Paris, Pygmalion, 2001.

Liddell Hart, Captain Basil, *Les généraux allemands parlent*, Paris, Stock, 1948.

London, Géo, *Le procés du général Dentz*, Lyon, Roger Bonnefon, 1945.

Mardam Bey, Salma, *La Syrie et la France, 1939–1945*, Paris, L'Harmattan, 1994.

Melton, George, *Darlan*, Paris, Pygmalion, 2002.

Mengin, Robert, *De Gaulle à Londres vu par un Français libre*, Paris, La Table ronde, 1965.

Michelet, Louis-Christian, *La Flamme de la revanche*, Paris, Godefroy de Bouillon, 2002.

——— *La Revanche de l'armée d'Afrique*, Paris, Godefroy de Bouillon, 2003.

Montagnon, Pierre, *La France coloniale*, Paris, Pygmalion, Gérard Watelet, 1990.

——— *Histoire de la Légion*, Paris, Pygmalion, 1999.

Nachin, Lucien, *Charles de Gaulle, général de France*, Paris, Colbert, 1944.

Paillat, Claude, *L'Echiquier d'Alger*, Paris, Robert Laffont, 1966.

Poincelet, Gilbert, *Dans le ciel de Syrie*, Paris, Séquana, 1941.

Quillet, Pierre, *Le chemin le plus long*, Paris, Maisonneuve et Larose, 1997.

Raïssac, Guy, *Un combat sans merci, l'affaire Pétain-de Gaulle*, Paris, Albin Michel, 1966.

Ramspacher, Emile, *Chars et blindés français,* Chapitre 2: 'Combats de Syrie', Paris, Lavauzelle, 1979.

Rondeau, Daniel and Stéphane Roger, *Des hommes libres,* Paris, Grasset, 1997.

Rucker, Laurent, *Staline et les juifs,* Paris, PUF, 2001.

Saibène, Marc, Jean-Yves Brouard and Guy Mercier, *La Marine marchande française, 1940–1942,* Nantes, Marines édition, 1998.

Salkin, Geneviève, *Général Diégo Brosset,* Paris, Economica, 1999.

Shipley White, Dorothy, *Les Origines de la discorde: de Gaulle, la France libre et les Alliés,* Paris, éditions de Trévise, 1967.

Soustelle, Jacques, *De Londres à Alger, 1940–1942,* Paris, Robert Laffont, 1947.

Vernoux, Général M., *Wiesbaden, 1940–1944,* Parois, Berger-Levrault, 1954.

Weygand, Général Maxime, *Mémoires.* Tome III: *Rappelé au service,* Paris, Flammarion, 1950.

——*En lisant les Mémoires de guerre du général de Gaulle,* Paris, Flammarion, 1955.

Weygand, Jacques et Stéphane, Roger, *Des hommes libres. Weygand, mon père,* Paris, Flammarion, 1970.

Works that are cited only once are not listed in this bibliography, but are referenced in the endnotes.

Other Publications

'Batailles et blindés. L'épopée du Royal Cambouis', two instalments by Yannis Kadari, 2003.

d'Estaing, René Giscard, 'Weygand administrateur', in *Revue Hebdomadaire,* 7 May 1932.

de Lannoy, François, 'Hitler et les nationalismes arabes', in *39–45, Histoire Magazine,* N° 80, 'Hitler et l'islam'.

de Larminat, Edgard, 'La Syrie', in *Revue de la France libre,* N° 40.

de Schoutheete, Jeanne, 'Les préliminaires de la campagne du Levant d'après les témoignages allemands (1940–1941)', in *Revue des Deux Mondes,* septembre 1943.

En ce temps-là de Gaulle, N° 18.

Facon, Patrick, 'Les gardiens de l'empire' (L'aviation de Pétain)', in *Fana de l'aviation,* N° spécial, 1999.

Gréciet, Vincent, 'Les Allemands au Proche-Orient et la révolte irakienne', in *39–45, Histoire Magazine,* N°80, 'Hitler et l'islam.'

Kersaudy, François, 'De Gaulle et la perfide Albion', in *Les Dossiers d'Historia,* 'De Gaulle', Tallandier, 1938.

'La Deuxième Guerre mondiale', in *Historia,* under the direction of Général Beaufre, Tallandier, 1982.

Masson, Philippe, 'Des Français contre des Français', in *Les Années 40,* Tallandier, N°33.

Militaria Hors-Série, N° 50. Histoire et Collections, Paris, 2003.

Mordal, Jacques, 'De Weygand à Dentz', in *Historia,* '2ᵉ Guerre mondiale', N° 20, Tallandier, 1966.

——'Les opérations aéronavales en Syrie', in *Historia,* '2ᵉ Guerre mondiale', N° 20, Tallandier, 1966.

Promé, Jean-Louis, 'Les combats fratricides de l'Été 1941', in *Fana de l'aviation* , éd. Larivière, Nᵒˢ 358, 359, 360, 361.

Revue des Troupes du Levant, juillet 1938 – janvier 1939, Atelier des TFL, Beyrouth.

Saint-Hillier, Général Bernard, 'La campagne de Syrie', in *Historia*, '2ᵉ Guerre mondiale'. Nᵒ 20, Tallandier, 1966.

Sicard, Jacques, 'L'armée du Levant', in *Militaria*, Nᵒˢ 40, 45, 59, 60, 68, 69, *la DFDL*, Nᵒ 107.

'Syrie, Vichy ordonne de résister le plus longtemps possible', in *En ce temps-là de Gaulle*, Nᵒ 26 (anonymous).

'Vichy livre la Syrie à Hitler' in *En ce temps-là de Gaulle*, Nᵒ 19 (anonymous).

Weygand, Jacques, 'Weygand en Orient', in *Historia*, '2ᵉ Guerre mondiale', Nᵒ 20, Tallandier, 1966.

Unpublished Studies and Private Archives

Albord, Général Tony et L. Dilleman, 'La Guerre des dupes. Levant 1941' (192 typed pages).

Cabiro, E., *1940–1941,* 'La France déboussolée' (171 typed pages).

Houzel, Roger, 'Une année parmi d'autres 1939–1940' (105 typed pages)

Keime, Général Amédée, 'De la cavalerie à l'arme blindée' (194 typed pages) including 'Au Levant, le temps des illusions et des déceptions, septembre 1939 – juin 1940 – mars 1941' (29 pages).

Keime Archives.

Rouy, Roger, 'Étude sur une guerre inconnue›, doctoral thesis, Faculté des sciences humaines de Dijon.

Stoop, Noémie de, 'Le Baron Pierre de Bodman, 1897–1994', master's dissertation, Paris IV, 2000–2001.

Verdilhac, Général de, 'Rapport au sujet des négociations de Saint-Jean-d'Acre et de l'action de la commission de contrôle', Arles, 19 February 1942 (120 typed pages plus 151 supporting documents).

Verdilhac Archives.

British Sources

Alanbrooke, Field Marshal Lord, *War Diaries, 1939–1945*, (edited by Alex Danchev and Daniel Todman), London, Weidenfeld and Nicolson, 2001.

Bellair, John, *From Snow to Jungle, History of the 2/3 Australian Machine Gun Battalion*, Sydney, Allen and Unwin, 1987.

Buckley, Christopher, *Five Ventures*, [Chapter 3: 'Syria, Unwanted campaign'], London, Her Majesty's Stationery Office, 1954.

Churchill, Winston, *La Lutte sans relâche, Discours de guerre*, London, Heinemann et Zsolnay, 1943 (in French).

———*Mémoires sur la Deuxième Guerre mondiale* Tome III: *La Grande Alliance*, Paris, Plon, 1950 (in French).

Clift, Ken, *War Dance, A Story of the 2/3 Australian Infantry Battalion*, Kingsgrove, 2/3 Bn Association, 1980.

Curie, Eve, *Journey among Warriors*, London, William Heinemann, 1944.

Eastgate, Ross, 'An Australian as UN Military Observer in the Middle East, 1977–1978' (manuscript, 270 pages).
Johnston, George H. *Australia at War*, Sydney, Angus and Robertson, 1942.
Long, Gavin, *Greece, Crete and Syria*, Canberra, Australian War Memorial, 1953.
McAllister, Jim and Syd Trigellis-Smith, *Largely a Gamble: Australians in Syria June–July 1941*, Headquarters Training Command Australian Army, 1955.
Military History and Information Section (AIF Middle East), *Active Service*, Canberra, Australian War Memorial, 1941.
Moorehead, Alan, *Mediterranean Front*, London, Hamish Hamilton, 1941.
Murphy, Robert, *Diplomat among Warriors*, New York, Doubleday, 1964.
Pasha, Glubb, *A Soldier with the Arabs*, London, Hodder and Stoughton, 1958.
Rock, George, *History of the American Field Service, 1920–1955*, (Chapter 2: 'June 1940–November 1941') New York, The Platen Press, 1956.
Saunders, Hilary St George, *The Green Beret*, London, Michael Joseph, 1947.
Slessor, Kenneth, *War Diaries* (edited Clement Semmler), Brisbane, University of Queensland Press, 1985.
Strategicus, *From Tobruk to Smolensk*, London, The Right Book Club, 1942.

Press

Aeroplane Monthly, February 2000, *The Fireflies of Rhodes. Italian Nightfighters over the Aegean.*
Daily Telegraph, 1941.
Sunday Telegraph New Review, June–July 1941.
The Sydney Morning Herald, 1941.
Time Magazine, 1941.

Filmography

Des hommes libres, Roger Stéphane.
Filmed interviews with 70 former members of 'France Libre'. Directed by Daniel Rondeau and Alain Ferrari, *France 3*, 1960.
Five Bloody Weeks, Syria 1941, Lieutenant-Colonel Don Keyes, 1997. Production: Headquarters Training Command, Australian Army and the Australian Broadcasting Corporation.

Index